The Ottoman Turks

The second courtyard of the Topkapı Palace. The chamber of the Imperial Council is directly to the right of the tower, with the harem stretching behind to the right. The domed gate (The Gate of Felicity) on the center-right leads to the throne room of the sultan. Janissaries and officials are gathered for an official reception of a European ambassador. (Antoine Ignace Melling, *Voyage Pittoresque de Constantinople et des rives du Bosphore d'après les dessins de M. Melling*, Paris, 1819.)

The Ottoman Turks

An Introductory History to 1923

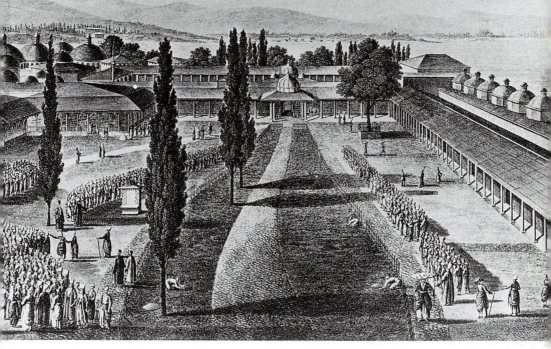

Justin McCarthy

Longman
LONDON AND NEW YORK

Pearson Education Limited
Edinburgh Gate
Harlow, Essex CM20 2JE
England
and Associated Companies throughout the world

Visit us on the World Wide Web at:
www.pearsoned.co.uk

First published 1997

ISBN 0 582 25656 9 CSD
ISBN 0 582 25655 0 PPR

British Library Cataloguing in Publication Data

A catalogue record for this book is available from the British Library

Library of Congress Cataloging-in-Publication Data

McCarthy, Justin.
  The Ottoman Turks: an introductory history to 1923 / Justin McCarthy.
    p.   cm.
  Includes bibliographical references (p.   ) and index.
  ISBN 0–582–25656–9 (CSD).– ISBN 0–582–25655–0 (PPR)
    1. Turkey – History – Ottoman Empire, 1288–1918.   2. Turkey – Social
life and customs.   I. Title.
DR486.M33   1996
956.1'015–dc20   96-16824
                                                                      CIP

10 9
08 07 06 05

Set by 8 in 10/12pt Sabon
Produced by Pearson Education Asia Pte Ltd
Printed in Malaysia, VVP

Contents

Contents

Contents

List of Illustrations

List of Illustrations

Acknowledgements

I wish to thank the funding agencies and individuals whose training, advice, and financial assistance of past projects ultimately allowed me to write this book. I am especially grateful to those who helped me specifically with *The Ottoman Turks* – Justin McCarthy Sr., Bruce Adams, Colin Heywood, Heath Lowry, David Morgan, William Ochsenwald, Lee Shai Weissbach, Rita Hettinger, Debbie Jordan, and the research committees of the Graduate School and College of Arts and Sciences of the University of Louisville. I am indebted to H.E. Nüzhet Kandemir, Aykut Sezgin, and Mustafa Siyahhan of the Turkish Embassy in Washington, D.C. for their indispensable assistance in obtaining illustrations. The help of librarians and archivists at the University of Louisville, the Library of Congress, the School of Oriental and African Studies, The British Library, and the Topkapı Sarayı Müzesi was essential to the project. As always, my greatest thanks go to my wife, Beth, and my children for their support and understanding and the flowers, coffee, and brownies they brought up to my study to sustain me.

The publishers would like to thank the following for granting permission to reproduce illustrative material: Robert Harding Picture Library for the illustration on page 34 and The Illustrated London News Group for the illustrations on pages 194, 284, 328, 348 and 370.

To Anne Maureen

Chapter 1

Prologue: Origins of the Turks, to 1281

Prologue: Origins of the Turks, to 1281

In the beginning of their recorded history Turks were nomads. Their original home was in Central Asia, in the vast grassland region that spreads north of Afghanistan and the Himalaya Mountains, west and northwest of China. By any normal standards of human comfort, Central Asia was a good place to leave. Its lands ranged from desert to forested mountains, but the general environment was bleak – high plains that were only slightly more attractive than desert for human habitation. Temperatures in winter could fall below $-34\,°C$ $(-30\,°F)$ and in summer rise to over $49\,°C$ $(120\,°F)$. Average temperatures over most of the region were below freezing in January, well over $27\,°C$ $(80\,°F)$ in August. Spring was short, winter long, with snow covering the ground at an average depth of two and a half feet (75 cm) for almost half the year. Geographers classify some of the land as tundra, some as steppe.

The steppe grasses of their homeland best supported livestock and the Turks were primarily hunters and herdsmen. Because sheep devoured the grass in any one area fairly quickly, the Turks were forced to move from one pasturage to another in order to feed the flocks upon which they depended. Large groups would have quickly over-grazed the land and small groups could not defend themselves, so the earliest Turkish political units were tribes. Although the size of each tribe varied according to its environment and the success of its leadership, none could have been considered large or important.

Had the Turks remained solely in their tribes, they would have had little effect on world history, but they did not. When necessary the Turkish tribes proved able to cooperate. Out of mutual necessity they joined together for defence or conquest under strong leaders to form armies and ultimately empires. Accepting the overlordship of a strong leader (called *han* or *khan*) meant that tribal feuds were diminished and the tribes could be organized for major conquests. The tribes remained as separate units, but they cooperated with one another. When united, the Turkish tribesmen were a formidable force. Turkish nomads were raised in harsh surroundings,

3

Handwritten marginalia:
- early turks were nomads
- Original home: central Asia.
- earliest Political units were tribes
- tribes banded together out of mutual nessesity for defence or conquest
- ✱ tribes came together under a han or khan defusing much tribal feuding.
- [tribes remained seperate as units but help eachother

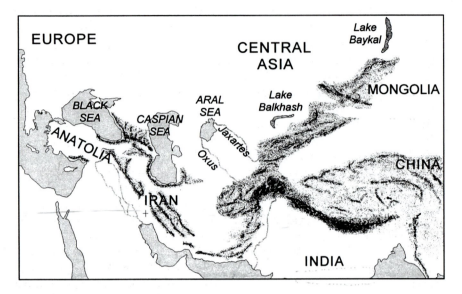

Central Asia and the Middle East.

taught from childhood the necessity of discipline and the use of weapons. Armed with bows and riding small steppe horses, they formed a swift light cavalry that could defeat more traditional standing armies with 'hit and run' tactics. Battling against the Chinese and others, the Turks very early created nomad 'empires' in central Asia and beyond.

The best known of these early confederations were the Huns, who threatened China from the third century B.C. As the Romans were defeating Hannibal and the Carthaginians in the Second Punic War, Turks were first invading China. Divided into different hordes and under different leaders, the Huns attacked both China and Iran in ensuing centuries. Under their leader Attila, known best in Europe for being persuaded (or bribed) by Pope Leo I to spare Rome in 452, Huns reached as far as Italy and France in the fifth century. Attila's empire extended through what today is southern Russia and the southern Ukraine, Romania, and much of Central Europe. In the sixth and seventh centuries a great Turkish empire, the Türküt, ruled from the Aral Sea to the borders of the Chinese empire and into Mongolia. In the eighth and ninth centuries the Uygur Turks ruled an empire south of Lake Baykal, superseded by other Turkish groups in the ensuing centuries throughout Central Asia.

The Turks were among the major waves of invaders who first attacked, then settled in the Middle East. There was a constant tension between the inhabitants of settled areas and the nomadic peoples of the steppes and deserts that surrounded the Middle East. Nomadic tribes were often peaceful trading partners of settled peoples. But in large numbers they

Handwritten margin notes:
Early turks used hit and run tactics.

3 Empires
1. Huns
2. the Turküt
3. Uygur turks

were a threat to both rulers and farmers. If vast armies of nomads entered the Middle East from Central Asia, they could be expected to turn farm land into grass land to support their flocks, to the considerable detriment of those who had farmed the land. Nomad raids would disrupt trade, damage farming, and generally harm the tax base upon which rulers depended. Nomads themselves did not pay taxes. Therefore, Middle Eastern rulers defended their borders against nomads. Nevertheless, nomad groups periodically succeeded in overwhelming the defences. After a period of upheaval, nomads settled down and their rulers became the new guardians of the Middle East against the next group of nomads.

The Arab Muslims who conquered the Sassanian Persian Empire in the seventh century extended their dominion into the borderlands of Central Asia, across the River Oxus into the region called Transoxania, the area between the Oxus (today the Amu Darya) and the Jaxartes (today the Syr Darya) rivers. There they came into contact with the Turks.

Under the Prophet Muhammad (c. 570–632) and his immediate successors, Arabia had been unified under the rule of Islam. The religious and political descendants of Muhammad had then taken lands from North Africa to the borders of Central Asia. During the rule of the Umayyad Caliphs (661–750), Arab armies had conquered Transoxania. The Abbasid Caliphate, which succeeded the Umayyad Caliphate in 750, cemented Islamic rule from western India to the Atlantic Ocean in a vast empire. No other state of the time could compare to it. Charlemagne (ruled 771–814) and the Abbasid Caliph Harun al-Rashid (ruled 786–809) of Arabian Nights fame both ruled at the same time, but the area of Charlemagne's empire would have fitted many times over into Harun's Caliphate. Moreover, the Frankish standards of learning and commerce were considerably lower than those of the Abbasid Caliphate. The bastion of the Abbasid Caliphal Empire in the east was in Khurasan (northeastern Iran) and Transoxania. In the eighth to ninth centuries, Islam became the majority religion in Iran and Transoxania, which was a cultural and economic extension of the Iranian world. Transoxania became a centre of Muslim religion, administration, and culture. Samarkand and Bukhara, the great cities of the region, became major economic centres, profiting from their position on the main routes of East-West trade. All the trappings of Muslim culture were to be found in them – great mosques, schools, charitable institutions, and the organs of Middle Eastern government. The traditions of Islam and pre-Islamic Persia mixed there, creating a high civilization at a time when the empire of Charlemagne had disintegrated, vikings raided, and much of Europe had descended into near-anarchy.

The Turks of Central Asia came into contact with the civilization of Transoxania through trade and warfare. Although nominally a province of the Abbasid Caliphate, the region was in fact ruled by a dynasty of Persian Muslims, the Samanids, from 875–999. The Samanid rulers expanded their rule and raided into Central Asia, across the River Jaxartes, coming into close contact with the Turks. Other Turks contacted the Samanid dominions through merchant enterprises or as slaves, captured and taken back to the Middle East. The contact also went the other way, into Central Asia. Muslim merchants from Transoxania and beyond traded in Central Asia itself. Nomadic Turks could see that the Middle East had many things they did not, especially riches. But it was Muslim missionaries who had the greatest effect on the Turks.

The Turks and Islam

The life of the Turks was greatly affected by communication with the Arab Muslims and with Persians who had converted to Islam. The Turks were not complete strangers to monotheistic religion, since a significant number had converted to Nestorian Christianity, which had been spread throughout Central Asia by missionaries. Turks had also become Buddhists. Judaism had been the official religion of one large group of Turks, the Khazars. However, the greatest number of Turks followed what has been described as a 'shamanistic' religion. The Turks, led by holy men, or shamans, worshipped or propitiated elemental forces of nature, believing that spirits lived among them in the earth and the skies. The spirits could be dangerous and needed to be appeased. Animals such as the wolf or bear were taken as totems. Nevertheless, over all the gods or natural forces was the one supreme God, Tanrı, who lived in the highest heavens. When they died, those who were moral went to a heaven, thought to be in the sky. Those who were evil went to a hell, under the earth. From early times, the Turks also were concerned with what can be called mystical religion, a desire for personal contact with the Divine that included ecstatic religious practice. They also showed reverence for holy men, alive and dead, who were felt to be close to God.

The basic understanding of one most powerful God and some experience with Christianity may have predisposed the Turks to accept Islam easily. Although it was much more sophisticated than the nomads' religion, Islam also held that there existed one supreme being, a heaven, and a hell. It accepted the presence of a sort of spirit, the jinn (or genies), who coexisted with man. Islam did not accept the propitiation of spirits or many of the other Turkish religious habits, but there were enough similarities in basic belief to make Islamic monotheism attractive to the Turks.

Islam and the central Asian Turks

Islam was a religion concerned with rules that governed the lives of its adherents, as well as with salvation, prayer, and spiritual growth. The

6

normal path to salvation was through membership in the Islamic community and obedience to its rules. The Holy Law of Islam, the *Sharī'ah,* which was drawn from the Muslim Holy Book, the Quran, and the sayings (*Hadīth*) and practices (*Sunnah*) of the Prophet Muhammad, was to govern all human endeavour. Islamic scholars and judges applied the Holy Law to all aspects of life. Islam can thus be called a religion of laws. Despite the attractive power of monotheism and Law, it is easy to see that the restrictions of Islam might have made conversion to Islam difficult for nomads of the steppe. The nomads had their own laws, their own traditions of authority, shamanistic beliefs, and a proclivity for mystical religion – all of which might have come into conflict with orthodox Islam. However, Islam showed a practical tolerance for the beliefs of new converts, expecting the descendants of the converts to become gradually more orthodox as generations passed. Moreover, the Muslim missionaries who converted the Turks were themselves not always orthodox. Conversion of the heathen in an uncomfortable and dangerous region such as Central Asia appealed more to heterodox zealots than to the theologically conservative. The missionaries often accepted more ecstatic religious experiences and practices than did the more Law-minded orthodox Muslims.

The new converts were allowed latitude in their religious beliefs, keeping much of their reverence for their saintly ancestors as well as certain shamanistic practices. It is doubtful if they were much bothered by questions of theology. The full panoply of Islamic Law only gradually applied to them. In particular, many Turks kept their mystical orientation. Turkish Muslims showed a desire to extend religion beyond the realm of Islamic legalities into mystical communion with God. Mysticism remained a basic part of Turkish religion, and in time this mystical orientation was even recognized by the Islamic religious establishment as being a legitimate, if always somewhat suspect, part of true religion.

Islam proved to be an opening for the Turks into the Middle East. Because it was a religion that stressed the community of believers over ethnic or linguistic differences, Islam accepted the Turks as brothers upon their conversion. They advanced from a position of outsiders into one of religious brotherhood. Their entry into the Middle East and integration into Middle Eastern Islamic culture and society was thus facilitated.

Turks had already come into contact with the Middle East though trade. The ancient Silk Road between the Middle East and China passed through Turkish lands. Turks were especially integrated into the economy of the borderland province of Muslim Transoxania, trading in the great cities of Samarkand and Bukhara. One trade proved to be especially important in bringing Turks into the Middle East, the slave trade. Muslim rulers bought or captured Turkish warriors and made them slave-soldiers in the Abbasid Caliphate, the great Muslim empire that began in 750, and in other Muslim states. Converts to Islam, these Turks

7

often rose to high position, sometimes even usurping the power of the Caliph. Nevertheless, their numbers were relatively small. The great mass of Turks in Central Asia were outsiders to the Middle East until they embraced Islam.

Once the Turks became Muslims, Middle Eastern rulers were more readily able to use them as they might use any other group of Muslim troops, as mercenaries. By the tenth century the Islamic Empire was breaking into small units, each accepting the rule of the Caliph in theory, but actually independent. In eastern Iran, Muslim rulers and governors hired confederations of Turkish tribes to fight on their behalf. Once the Turks realized they held the balance of power they took charge themselves. One of these groups, the Ghaznavids, took Afghanistan, part of eastern Iran, and much of India. Another, the Seljuks, moved to the west.

The Seljuks

In the tenth century a large group of Turks known as the Oğuz inhabited the region of Central Asia north of Lake Balkhash. One clan of the Oğuz, the Seljuks (named after a prominent ancestor, Seljuk), moved south in the eleventh century toward the border of the Middle East in Transoxania, to the River Jaxartes. There they fought as vassals and mercenary soldiers for various other Turkish rulers. By 1040 they had defeated the Ghaznavid Turks to the south and took northeastern Iran for themselves. The Seljuk Turks, under their leader Tuğrul, then moved to the west, conquering all of Iran by 1054.

Contrary to what might be expected of conquerors from outside the Caliphal Empire, the Seljuks seem to have been welcomed by the Islamic establishment of the Empire. They were seen as the best hope for a revival of the Caliphal Empire of old, a centralized orthodox Islamic empire, ruling from Baghdad. More importantly to the Islamic establishment, the Seljuks were champions of Sunni Islam against its enemies.

After the death of the Prophet Muhammad and the rule of his first four successors as Caliphs, the Islamic world had begun what was to be a long tradition of dynastic rule. In both the Umayyad and Abbasid Caliphates, the Caliph was more than an emperor. He was also the guarantor of Islamic Law and the concept of political rule accepted by most Muslims. The majority community, the Sunni Muslims, was made up of those who, with slight variations, agreed on the structure of the Holy Law and accepted each other as orthodox. The leaders of the *Sunni* can be styled the religious establishment. The Caliph supported orthodoxy and the orthodox establishment supported the Caliphate. The members of the orthodox establishment were powerful, often rich, and concerned to uphold their traditions, their beliefs, and their livelihoods. They included officers of state, landholders,

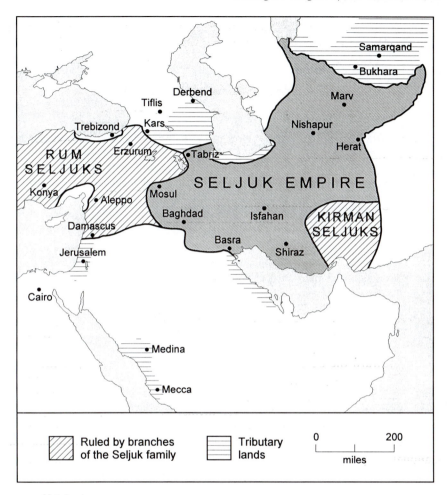

The Seljuk Empire in 1092.

merchants, and, especially, the learned theologians/jurists of Sunni Islam, the ʾulamā (in Turkish, *ulema*). Opposed to the Islamic establishment were the *Shia* Muslims. The Shia accepted much of the same law as did the Sunni, but they regarded Ali, the cousin of the Prophet Muhammad, and his descendants as *imam*s or rightly guided leaders who should have ruled over all Islam, a theological position not shared by the Sunni majority. Because Islam was a religion that intended to govern all aspects of life, the Sunni-Shia split was political and legal, as well as religious. Shia Muslims intended to introduce not only a somewhat different set of beliefs into the Islamic world, but also a new group of rulers and a new group of Islamic religious leaders. They were thus a threat to all aspects of the life of the establishment.

Sunni and Shia Difference

9

At the time of the Seljuk irruption into the Middle East, the Caliphate and the orthodox establishment were in disarray. The central authority of the Abbasid Caliphs had been deteriorating for some time. Eastern Iran and Egypt had been taken by autonomous rulers in the latter half of the ninth century. While the local rulers declared themselves to be governors ruling in the Caliph's name, in fact they were independent. From the standpoint of the traditional rulers and theologians, the tenth century had been a much worse disaster than the ninth. One group of Shia rulers, the Fatimids, had taken control of Egypt in 969. Eventually they had conquered all of southern Syria and even held the allegiance of the Holy Cities of Mecca and Medina. The Fatimids were both a theological and political danger to the Abbasid establishment, appealing to the disaffected and dispossessed throughout the Islamic world. Another group of Shia, the Buyids, although more tolerant of Sunni beliefs than the Fatimids, were nevertheless a mortal danger to the establishment, because they had seized control of Baghdad itself. They had taken Baghdad in 945, put their own candidate in as Caliph, and taken control of the administration of the Empire. The Caliph, although theoretically the commander of all the Abbasid Empire, was in fact a prisoner of the Buyids. The Empire was in considerable political uproar, with the Buyids fighting losing wars in the east, and the region controlled by Baghdad ever shrinking. Even though a Sunni Caliph still theoretically reigned in Baghdad, the Abbasid Caliphate had in fact dissolved.

The Seljuks appeared as champions of Sunni Islam. They welcomed this status. How much of their support of Sunni orthodoxy was sincere belief and how much political expediency is unknown. The beliefs of the Turks in Central Asia at the time could not have been styled 'orthodox'. The first Seljuks, not far removed from the same environment as their nomadic followers, probably shared the religious beliefs of the nomadic Turks – Islam with more than a modicum of mystic and old shamanistic additions. However, espousing the cause of orthodoxy undoubtedly gave the Seljuks support of many who might otherwise have naturally opposed the advent of rude nomads from the steppes. In order to rid themselves of the Shia Buyids, the Caliph and his Sunni subjects welcomed the intervention of the Seljuk Turks. Tuğrul entered Baghdad, the Caliph's capital, in 1055. The Seljuks were hailed as the saviours of the Sunni Caliphate.

Seljuk rule

Upon entering Baghdad in triumph, Tuğrul was hailed as the 'king of kings'. He and his descendants took the title *sultan* ('holder of power'), signifying that they were the secular power of the Caliphate, relegating the Caliph to a vague spiritual power and small real influence over politics. The Seljuks then set about the considerable task of moulding a settled empire out of nomadic Turkish power.

The great Seljuk sultans

1038–1063	Tuğrul	1094–1105	Berkyaruk
1063–1072	Alp Arslan	1105	Malikshah II
1072–1092	Malikshah	1105–1118	Muhammad
1092–1094	Mahmud	1118–1157	Sanjar

Although the Seljuk rulers and their followers are usually referred to as the Seljuk Turks, in reality there was no such thing as a 'Seljuk people' or 'Seljuk nation'. The concept of nation or people would have been alien to the Turks who arrived from Central Asia. Except for a small number of royal retainers, the highest political loyalty of all the Turks was to their individual tribe. As occasions warranted, they might attach themselves to a tribal confederation and follow the leadership of a *han*, such as the Seljuk sultan, but the *han* was only followed as long as his interests and the tribe's interests coincided. Insofar as the Turks were gradually assimilating orthodox Islam, they might feel a loyalty to the sultan as leader of the forces of Islam, but tribal loyalties were primary.

Opposed to tribal loyalties was the legacy of Middle Eastern rule, a tradition that the Seljuk rulers were anxious to emulate. At the time of the Turkish conquest, a great tradition of government had evolved for centuries in Iran, Iraq, and Syria. The system drew from both old Persian practices of government and from Islamic tradition. The state was theoretically an ordered government, with bureaucrats, standing armies, and tax-collectors. The ruler was removed from his people; his was a different order of existence. None of these was familiar, or desirable, to the nomads upon whom Seljuk power was based. However, the Seljuks realized that settled rule, the advancement of the empire, and their own authority ultimately rested on the creation of a relatively peaceful land, ruled by an established government. They proceeded largely to adopt the system of government that they had found.

The greatest Seljuk sultans, Alp Arslan (1063–72) and Malikshah (1072–92), put the government in the hands of their principal *vezir* (minister of state), Nizam al-Mulk. Nizam al-Mulk was a Persian who was schooled in the old system of Middle Eastern Islamic government. He organized the Seljuk state along the lines of the traditional Persian and Arab empires, with some success. A governing bureaucracy was created and an attempt made to settle the nomadic Turks down as landlords who ruled local areas and sent taxes to the central government, or at least used the sums they collected to support fighting men who would be available at the sultan's command. Seljuk sultans began to rule as had the Caliphs of old, not as nomadic chieftains, but as glorious emperors, surrounded by wealth and pageantry. Nevertheless, despite the labours of Nizam ul-Mulk, the Seljuk state still depended on the military forces of the nomads. Moreover, old Turkish traditions from Central Asia made it difficult to retain a stable empire. Turks had traditionally divided governing among members of the ruling family. Younger sons and cousins of the han were allowed authority over armies and were given vast regions to command. Under the Seljuks, family members were sent out as governors of provinces. Once away from central authority, they often showed a propensity to revolt. This was especially true when the Great Sultan died. Members of his family expected to divide his possessions, which included the empire, according to the old Central Asian tradition of inheritance. They also expected to fight among themselves to gain the territories ruled by their relatives. The succeeding sultan was too often left to fight his relatives to regain the power of his predecessor.

The military basis of Seljuk rule was also its greatest difficulty. Turkish nomads were fine fighters, but poor tax-payers. As Seljuk successes increased, more and more Turks were attracted from Central Asia. They were a disruptive element to the farmers and city merchants who were the financial support of any state. As the Seljuks set themselves up as traditional Muslim rulers of the Middle East, they needed a settled society and economy. Ideally, the Seljuks wished to use the nomads for their fighting abilities, but not to have them living in the Seljuk back yard. One solution was to move the nomads to the borders of the Seljuk Empire. Nomad raids would then damage the lands of the Seljuks' enemies, not the Seljuk lands.

Further conquests and disintegration of the Seljuk Empire

The empire of the Seljuks, known as the Great Seljuk Empire to distinguish it from smaller regions ruled by members of the Seljuk family or tributaries, was short-lived. Like the Abbasid Empire before it, its capital was in Baghdad. Indeed, legally it was simply an extension of the Abbasid Caliphate. The Seljuks always acknowledged the theoretical leadership of the Caliph as Leader of Islam.

The Seljuks extended their rule to the west by accepting the overlordship of regions overrun by Turkish nomads. Azerbaijan, the western part of the region south of the Caucasus Mountains, came to them in this way in 1054. In the same way, eastern Anatolia (today, eastern Turkey) began to be occupied by the nomads. When the Byzantine Emperor attempted to move against them, Alp Arslan, the nephew and successor of Tuğrul, defeated him at Manzikert (1071), opening Anatolia to nomad incursion (see Chapter 2). The Seljuk destruction of Byzantine power at Manzikert had rid them of any threat to the north and west, and the Seljuks proceeded to the conquest of Syria. An independent Turkish lord, Atsız, took Jerusalem in 1071 and Damascus in 1076, driving out Fatimid garrisons. Atsız put himself under the protection of Malikshah, Alp Arslan's son and successor, and the Seljuks claimed Syria and most of Palestine. The Holy Cities, Mecca and Medina, accepted Seljuk rule. Outside of Egypt, the Fatimids were left with only a small sliver of the coast of Palestine. Malikshah also defeated enemies of the Seljuks, the Turkish Karakhanids of Transoxania, and forced them to accept his overlordship.

Ultimately, the inherent instability of the Seljuk system proved to be the downfall of the Seljuk Empire. The custom of dividing rule among members of the Seljuk household eventually divided the empire. Instead of cementing control through generations of stable rule, each Seljuk ruler had to fight for his throne. Even the greatest of the sultans were insecure in their rule. Sultan Alp Arslan was forced to defeat a rebellious nephew and a rebellious uncle. Sultan Malikshah was forced to put down revolts by a brother and an uncle. Even when they did not revolt against the Great Sultan, members of the Seljuk family still fought against one another to expand the fiefs they held. Such conflict proved to be too much for the state.

After Malikshah's death in 1092, the Seljuk Empire began to disintegrate. The Turks who had moved into Anatolia formed into a separate empire, the Rum Seljuks, at first nominally vassals of the Great Seljuks, then independent. Seljuk princes set up kingdoms in Damascus and Aleppo. These Seljuk governors in Syria and Anatolia might acknowledge the overlordship of the Great Seljuk sultan, but they did all they could to be independent of central rule. They often rose in full revolt. European soldiers of the First Crusade appeared in Syria in 1097 and defeated the independent Turkish lords who had sprung up there after Malikshah died. Palestine had been briefly reconquered by the Fatimids (1098), but it too was soon lost to the Crusaders (Jerusalem was conquered in 1099). The core of the Great Seljuk Empire, Iraq and Iran, was first divided in two, an eastern and a western empire, then into smaller independent states. The Seljuk sultans of the twelfth century ruled over ever smaller areas, in a time of almost universal strife and near-chaos.

Another cause of the dissolution of the empire was the Seljuk failure to control the nomads who were the basis of their power. Sultans found it necessary to expend force and treasure on disciplining nomads who ravaged tax-paying territories. Most importantly, the Seljuk sultans never managed to become the sort of indispensable rulers who held the loyalty of their nomad followers. The nomads still followed them only because it was in the nomads' interest, not out of any loyalty to a state or a ruler. When the conquests ended, the allegiance of the nomads tended to disappear. The last Great Seljuk sultan, Sanjar, attempted to reconstitute Seljuk rule in eastern Iran, but was captured by Turkish nomads, held prisoner for three years, and only freed a year before his death in 1157.

The significance of the Great Seljuks

Though surely important in itself, the primary significance of the Seljuk Empire in a book on the Ottoman Turks must be the legacy they left for the

13

Physical features of the Middle East and Southeast Empire.

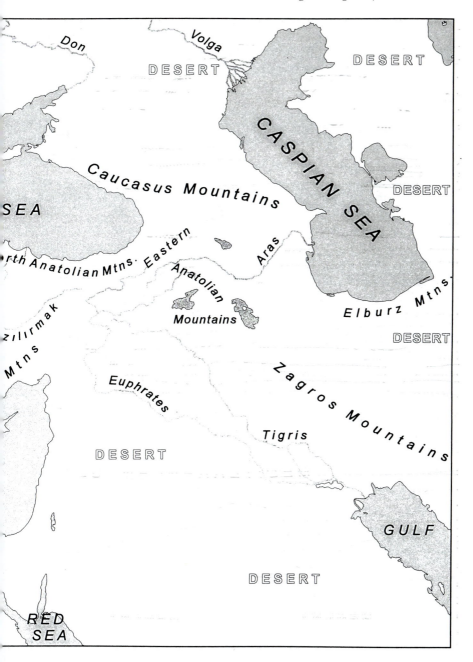

Seljuk
effects

on

the

Ottoman
Empire.

Turkish states that followed. First among their bequests is the transfer of Turks to Anatolia. Had Alp Arslan not defeated the Byzantine emperor at Manzikert, Asia Minor might never have become Turkey. But the Seljuks also began to develop the system that the Turks of Anatolia would use to create a great empire that lasted for 600 years. The administrative and religious structures created by the Seljuks facilitated the integration of Turks into the Middle East.

Systems of government originated or developed by the Great Seljuks were to provide a basis for later Turkish rule. Among these were the *ikta* system of supporting the state, the slave army, and the acceptance and revision of traditional Middle Eastern methods of bureaucratic governance.

The *ikta* (in Arabic, *iqtâ*) system of the Great Seljuks was developed and regularized from earlier practice in Iran. It involved the award of lands, and sometimes whole provinces, to military leaders. Unlike the medieval European feudal system, *ikta* grants were not either legally owned by their recipients nor necessarily heritable by their descendants. They remained as lands owned by the sultan, but were used to support the army. The sultan could and did change the holders when it suited the purposes of the state. The system was a fairly effective attempt to alter the traditional Turkish nomads' relation with the land, which was to either to ravage it or to use it for pasture. Now villagers paid their surplus to the *ikta* holder, who used it to support his military followers. It was a reasonable way to preserve farm production and to make sure the state benefited from it. The Seljuks did not have the state machinery to collect taxes in the usual way, and the *ikta* was thus a way for the state to exploit its potential revenues and to impede the less desirable activities of its soldiers. The system did not save the Seljuks from their own nomads, but it was to allow their successors to do so.

To provide the rulers with personal power, the Seljuks adopted the Middle Eastern tradition of the slave army. Sultans and high administrators such as Nizam al-Mulk, who had a large slave army under his command, took bought or captured soldiers into their personal service. These became an armed force that was dependent on the sultan, one he could, at least in theory, use to discipline recalcitrant Turkish nomads. In utilizing the slave army, the Seljuk sultans made a step toward rule that was independent of their nomad followers. The slaves were the followers of the sultan, loyal to him, not followers of tribal leaders who were attached to the han as long as it benefited them. It was one sign of the transition of the sultanate into an empire on the traditional Middle Eastern model.

Another sign of the beginnings of a Turkish sense of Empire was the bureaucracy created by Nizam al-Mulk. The Seljuks developed the administrative trappings of a settled state, with bureaucrats, officials, and even a secret police to watch over the others. If the Turks were to evolve from nomads to settled subjects, the apparatus of a regular state was essential.

Through financial and political support, the Seljuks had a great and positive effect on Islam. Their intervention came at a critical time for Sunni orthodoxy. Under the Fatimids, Shia Islam had experienced a great resurgence. Its scholars, gathered at the al-Azhar theology centre in Cairo, formulated and regulated the Shia beliefs of their Ismaili sect, sending out missionaries to spread their creed and Fatimid propaganda. By its nature, which stressed the consensus of religious thinkers who laboured all over the Muslim world, Sunni Islam was diffuse, with no central body to organize either its theology or its defence against the Shia attack.

Some attempt to remedy the situation had begun when the Seljuks appeared in Iran and Iraq. Schools, called *madrasas* (*medreses* in Turkish), had appeared where Sunni teachers came together to teach students law and theology. Under the guidance of Nizam al-Mulk, the Seljuks adopted and greatly expanded the *madrasa* system. Nizam al-Mulk himself founded the greatest of the *madrasas*, that of Baghdad, in 1067. The *madrasas* were colleges of learned teachers and students, with mosques for prayer, living accommodation, kitchens, etc. The learned were paid salaries to do their research and writing and teach their students. Many students were given scholarships to study. Once their learning was sufficient to satisfy their teachers, the students became religious judges and scholars who perpetuated the system. (Although there were no large lecture classes, teaching assistants, or student unions, the system resembles that of modern universities.) The skills the students learned were also put to use in the government, where graduates found employment as scribes and record keepers.

The madrasa system gave a structure to Islam, supporting the learned who were the backbone of the religion and insuring that judges and scholars were properly trained. Because various schools (*madhhabs*, codified differences of legal interpretation, each acceptable as orthodox) of Islamic law were represented, the *madrasas* fostered understanding and the exchange of theological ideas. The system proved so effective that it spread throughout the Islamic world, long outlasting the Seljuks.

The Seljuks also influenced the theology of Islam. It seems odd that rulers of what was basically a nomad kingdom, themselves only lately removed from their tents and flocks, should have a major effect on theology, but the Seljuks left a great theological legacy. They did this by supporting the theologians who integrated mysticism and Sunni orthodoxy, thus reinvigorating Islam and making orthodoxy more acceptable to the Turks. The greatest of these was al-Ghazāli, a teacher in the great *madrasa* in Baghdad. Feeling the need of more than the strictures of orthodox Islamic Law, Ghazāli left his teaching position to develop his own spirituality. Through study and contemplation he became a mystic (a *sufi*) as well as a theologian, writing theology that justified the mystical concept of personal communion with God with the Quran and the Law. Without the theology of Ghazāli and his disciples, the mysticism of the Turks might not have found a place in the orthodox community. With their work, the Turks could retain their mystical beliefs and take their place as Sunni Muslims. Sunni Islam was broadened. It gained a new dimension of mysticism and ecstatic religion that had great appeal to the Muslims. Ghazāli's synthesis of mysticism and orthodoxy has lasted as a strength of Islam to our day.

The fact that the Seljuks proved that the Turks could create a great Islamic Empire was a significant achievement in itself. In their time, much of Europe would have welcomed the order they gave to the Middle East, if only for a brief period: England was enduring raids by vikings, then Normans (1066), the kings of France were struggling for a very limited supremacy with the dukes of Normandy, and feudalism was triumphant. By creating their empire, the Great Seljuks not only brought stability, but changed the status of the Turks forever. After the Great Seljuks took power, Turks could no longer be viewed as essentially nomads who might raid, remain for a while, then disappear because they had created no real state. Turks had created, or were intelligent enough to borrow, a state system, a standing army, and a court that supported great artists, poets, and theologians. Turks had become *rulers* as the Middle East understood rule. The tradition of Turkish rule was to continue for almost a millennium.

Anatolia

The Byzantine Empire

Before the coming of the Turks, Anatolia (Asia Minor) was a part of the Byzantine Empire. The Byzantines claimed governmental descent from the Romans, and had kept a continuous tradition of rule from the Eastern Roman Empire, but the Byzantine Empire was culturally Greek. Greek was the language of state, art, and high society. In 1054, the Greek and Latin churches had broken ties in a schism that was to prove permanent. The schism symbolized a cultural and political as well as religious division between the East and the West. The West was to be Latin, the East Greek. By 1000 the many different cultures of western, northern, and central Anatolia largely had become Hellenized. In eastern Anatolia, Christian groups considered heretics by the Byzantine Greek Orthodox Christians held sway. The largest of these groups, the Armenians, had sometimes been independent, sometimes allied with the Byzantines, and sometimes under Byzantine control.

The Byzantines had managed to retain intact some of the Roman Empire's conquests in the East. Under Basil II (976–1025), they ruled an empire that stretched from western Iran to the border of the Germanic

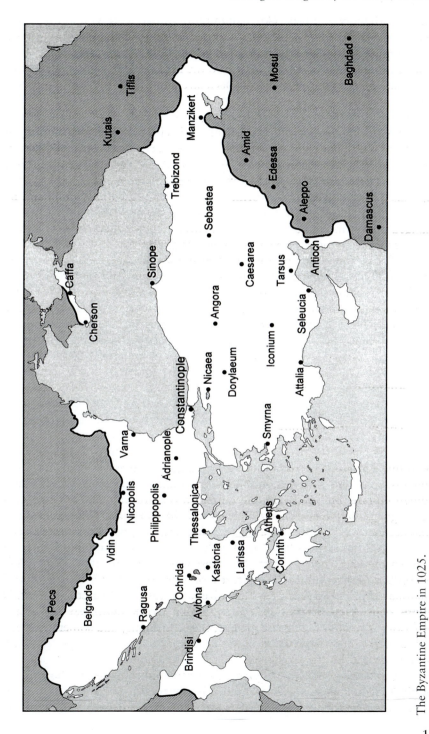

The Byzantine Empire in 1025.

Empire of Henry II (1002–24). The Byzantines had lost Syria and Egypt to the Arab Muslims in the seventh century, but had held Anatolia. Indeed, Anatolia had become the military mainstay of the Empire, providing hardy troops upon whom the defence of the Byzantine Empire depended. Byzantine power in southern and eastern Anatolia had for centuries rested on a strong defence of Anatolia against their Muslim neighbours. Arab armies had been able to penetrate into Anatolia, even as far as the gates of Constantinople, but had never been able to hold the territory. By the year 1000 the Byzantines had evolved a system of defence that relied on forti-fiications. The border forts, as well as local lords and their troops, were supported by the villages in their region. In time of war, the forts made it difficult for attacking armies to pass through into the Byzantine heartland. Armies were forced either to stop for long sieges, and thus allow time for the Byzantines in Constantinople to organize a counter-attack, or to pass by the forts. If they left the forts intact, the defenders would be able to sortie forth later, destroying the communications and baggage trains upon which the invading armies depended.

The Byzantine fort system, while very effective against traditional armies, was no match for the Turkish nomads. The nomads were depen-dent neither on communications nor baggage trains. They operated in small groups and lived off the spoils of their conquests. By the time troops could be organized to fight them they had moved on to new attacks. In this way the nomads destroyed the support of the fort system. By the second half of the eleventh century the farms that had supported the Byzantine system of defence had been devastated. Food for Byzantine frontier soldiers and taxes for their lords were cut to the point where the Empire was in grave danger.

In Constantinople, the Byzantine Emperor Romanus Diogenes mobi-lized his army to defeat the nomad threat. After extensive preparation the army moved east. The Seljuk sultan Alp Arslan also prepared his army, unwilling to allow the Byzantine Emperor to overcome the nomads. Had the nomads been defeated, their expansion into Anatolia might have ended, forcing them back into Iran. Moreover, defeating the Byzantines would open a new area for Seljuk imperial expansion. In August of 1071, the two armies met at Manzikert (Malazgirt) in eastern Anatolia. The Turks triumphed, destroying the Byzantine army and opening all of Anatolia for conquest. Within a few years the nomads had raided across Anatolia, almost to the city of Constantinople.

Turkish nomads continued to stream into Anatolia after the victory at Manzikert. Sultan Alp Arslan died in 1072, the year after his victory, and was succeeded by his young son, Malikshah. Malikshah's reign was spent in consolidating the Great Seljuk power by putting down revolts and attempting to subordinate his nomad army to the demands of a settled state. Anatolia was not a main concern. However, a young member of the

Seljuk family, Süleyman, and his followers came to Anatolia and organized the Rum Seljuk Empire.

The Rum Seljuks

The empire founded by Süleyman is known as the Rum Seljuk Empire, to distinguish it from the Great Seljuk Empire. 'Rum' was the Turkish form of the name Rome, so the Rum Seljuks were the Seljuks who ruled what had been part of the Roman (i.e., the Byzantine) Empire. The Rum Seljuks made their capital first at İznik, later at Konya in Central Anatolia.

The Rum Seljuks shared many of the problems that ultimately destroyed the Great Seljuk Empire. Soon after the battle of Manzikert, Turkish forces in Anatolia were already dividing into independent sources of power. Turkish leaders, usually called *bey* (prince or chief), attracted nomads to their standards. One group, the Danışmends, controlled north central Anatolia, another made its capital at İzmir, created a navy, and took islands of the Aegean as part of their principality. Along with other 'states', many of them short-lived, these principalities accepted the overlordship of the Rum Seljuk sultan and provided soldiers for the Seljuk wars, but it cannot be said that their territories were actually governed by the Rum Seljuks. They did, however, accept the need of an Anatolian sultan as a unifying focus for battles against the Turks' enemies. There were many enemies: the Great Seljuks desired to assert their control over what they viewed as breakaway provinces in Anatolia, and so menaced Rum Seljuk independence; the Byzantine Empire threatened to regain its lost Anatolian territories, and a new threat appeared when Crusaders from Europe passed through Anatolia on their way to the Holy Land and set up crusader states in southern Anatolia. The Rum Seljuk sultan Kılıç Arslan (1092–1107) lost one great battle to the Europeans of the First Crusade at Eskişehir (1097), but won great battles against them at Malatya, Amasya, and Ereğli (1100). In addition, there was always a tension between the independent *beys* and the sultans, who constantly attempted to assert their control. Kılıç Arslan, once he had defeated the Crusaders, defeated the Danışmends and other Turkish *beys*, accepted the submission of others, and for a time the Rum Seljuks ruled in fact over Seljuk Anatolia.

The assertion of central control was brief. The next century and a half was to be a period of confused rule and nearly incessant internal conflict.

Kılıç Arslan was killed in battle with forces of the Great Seljuks in 1107. After his death, his sons fought over the throne and the Turkish *beys* reasserted their independence. Taking advantage of the Turks' disarray, the Byzantines reconquered the coasts of northern, western and southern Anatolia. The Turks of Anatolia became isolated from other regions of the Middle East; Islam fought the Third Crusade (1189–92) without assistance

The Rum Seljuk sultans

1077–1086	Süleymanşah	1246–1254	*Period of Three*
1086–1092	interregnum		*Sultans*
1092–1107	Kılıç Arslan I		Keykâvus II
1107–1116	Melikşah		Kılıç Arslan IV
	(Şahinşah)		Keykubad II
1116–1155	Mesut I	1254–1262	*Period of Two*
1155–1192	Kılıç Arslan II		*Sultans*
1192–1196	Keyhüsrev I		Keykâvus II
1196–1204	Süleymanşah II		Kılıç Arslan IV
1204–1205	Kılıç Arslan III	1262–1266	Kılıç Arslan IV
1205–1211	Keyhüsrev I	1266–1284	Keyhüsrev III
1211–1220	Keykâvus I	1284–1297	Mesut II
1220–1237	Keykubad I	1298–1302	Keykubad II
1237–1246	Keyhüsrev II	1302–?	Mesut III

from those Turks, its most warlike champions. From 1107 to 1155, the wars in Anatolia were almost incessant, as Seljuk sultans, Byzantines, Crusaders, and Turkish *bey*s fought for power. Sultan Kılıç Arslan II (1155–92) reasserted the Rum Seljuks' power, permanently ending Byzantine power in Anatolia at the battle of Myriokephalon (1176) and reconquering much of the territory that had been taken by the Byzantines. He then, following traditional Turkish practice, divided actual rule among his sons, of whom he had eleven. These did fight to extend Seljuk rule against what remained of the Anatolian Byzantine possessions, but also fought among themselves both before and after their father's death.

The fifty years after the death of Kılıç Arslan II saw much fighting between brothers for the Rum Seljuk throne. Keyhüsrev, Kılıç Arslan's chosen successor, was forced to battle his brothers and was even briefly dispossessed of the sultanate by one of them. His son, Keykâvus, also only held the throne by defeating his brothers. Nevertheless, it was during these years that the Seljuks gained their most extensive territory since the first days of the dynasty. This expansion was largely at the expense of the Byzantines, extending the Empire's borders on both the Black and the Mediterranean Seas and opening it to international trade. Keykâvus's successor, Keykubad, brought the Turkish beys of eastern Anatolia under firm Rum Seljuk control and extended the Empire in the East and on the Mediterranean. Armenian and Georgian kings became his vassals.

Often considered the greatest of the Rum Seljuk monarchs, Keykubad was much concerned with trade as well as conquest. He entered into pacts with his neighbours to facilitate commerce, particularly at the Black Sea ports. Under him, the Rum Seljuk sultans began to approximate the regal

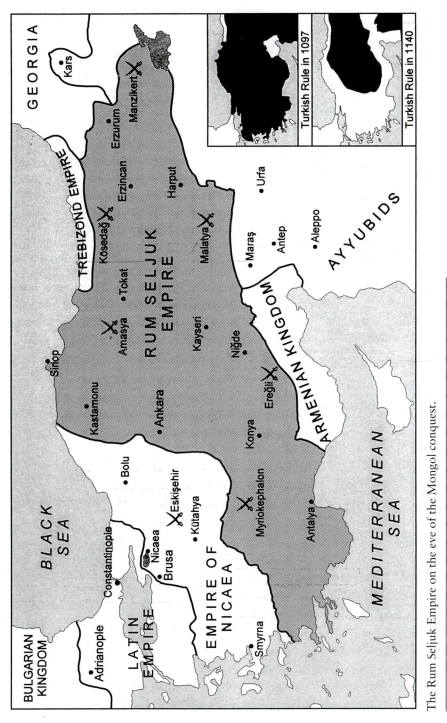

The Rum Seljuk Empire on the eve of the Mongol conquest.

splendour of traditional Middle Eastern emperors, dispensing charity, building mosques and *medrese*s, and favouring scholars and artists.

The practical end of Rum Seljuk rule in Anatolia came with their defeat by the Mongols. The devastation wrought by the Mongols in Eastern Europe from 1241 onwards is often known in the West, but the Mongol effect on the Middle East was, if anything, worse. The Mongols under Jenghiz Khan had first invaded the Middle East in 1220, spreading the worst destruction ever known in northeastern Iran. Transoxania was largely destroyed. Neither it nor eastern Iran would ever again rise to its former eminence. After a digression in Europe, invading Russia, Poland, and Hungary from 1237 to 1241, the Mongols returned to the Middle East. In 1258, Baghdad fell to Jenghiz Khan's grandson, Hülegü, who founded the Ilkhanid dynasty that ruled over Iran until 1335. Compared to the Iranian world, Anatolia was relatively luckily. A Mongol army defeated the Rum Seljuk sultan, Keyhüsrev II in 1243 at Kösedağ, near Sivas. As part of this campaign, eastern Anatolian cities were destroyed. The Rum Seljuk sultan accepted Mongol suzereignty. From that point, the power of the Rum Seljuks dwindled until it disappeared. Mongols and Turkish advisers both interfered with Seljuk rule and succession. Sultans ascended to the throne when they were small boys, incapable of ruling. At one point three young sultans, aged 11, 9, and 7, reigned at once. For a time, Mongol rule superseded Turkish rule in Anatolia.

The Rum Seljuk Empire is listed in the chronologies of Islamic kingdoms as having lasted for 230 years, from 1077 to perhaps 1307 or 1308. (The exact final date is unknown, because the Empire disappeared with a whimper. When it ended it was so weak that no one noticed.) This chronology of the Rum Seljuks is deceptive, because it gives the idea of a long-lasting, centralized empire such as the Ottoman and Roman Empires. In fact, the Rum Seljuks were only such an empire for brief periods, such as the reign of Keykubad I. The Rum Seljuk sultans laid claim to Anatolia and even, for a time, to part of Syria, but in fact usually personally ruled only smaller territories. Real power in local areas was sometimes in the hands of local *beys*, sometimes in the hands of quasi-independent governors, such as the many sons of Kılıç Arslan II. For much of its history, the Rum Seljuk state was an image of an empire, rather than a reality. Nevertheless, it did often serve to keep anarchy at bay, began the transformation of nomads into settled inhabitants of Anatolia, and transferred the Great Seljuk traditions of society and rule to Anatolia.

Rum Seljuk society and rule

The Rum Seljuks never were able to create in Anatolia the type of centralized government that is ordinarily expected from an empire. Part of the reason was the nature of the Turkish forces that came to Anatolia. After

Manzikert, the Turks who conquered Anatolia most often acted in small bands and tribes. They were the nomads who came west from the Great Seljuk Empire. When the Mongols began their conquests more Turkish nomads went to Anatolia, rather than come under direct Mongol rule. Their motives were a combination of religion and self-interest. Known as *gazis* (in Arabic, *ghāzī*, or fighters for Islam), they conquered to extend the power of their religion. They fought to extend the *rule* of Islam rather than to convert the inhabitants of Anatolia to Islam. (Despite some lapses, the Turks kept to the rules of Islam that stipulated that Christians and Jews were to be allowed to keep their religion, as long as they accepted the rule of an Islamic state.) The *gazis* also fought for booty. To the *gazis*, as to all steppe nomads, fighting was simply what they did in life. It had never been different. The chance to fight in the Middle East was accompanied by new justification – the *ghazāh*, a holy war – and better chances for booty, but the *gazis* were fighting the old fight in new lands.

The *gazis* were not easily controlled by anyone. They often rejected central authority and acted as they saw fit. No government, including the Rum Seljuks, found it easy to command their obedience. At the same time, they were fine fighting men, and Turkish military successes in Anatolia depended on them. The Rum Seljuks never developed the sort of large, independent standing army that would have allowed them to keep the nomads in check. They were dependent on the force of the Turkish nomads. Probably more than any other factor, it was this that kept them from developing a truly settled state. They simply had no reliable source of state power, and centralized power is the one requirement of a centralized empire.

Like that of the Great Seljuks, the history of the Rum Seljuks illustrated the two great shortcomings of Turkish rule – division of authority and dependence on nomad soldiers. Whatever the abilities of its leaders, a state could not survive if it constantly underwent a cycle of division and bloody reunification. As long as brothers divided the empire then battled until one emerged triumphant, the state would be in disarray. Periods of relative state power under a great sultan would be followed by chaos at his death. Power that might have been used against external enemies would instead be expended internally and uselessly. Almost complete dependence on nomad soldiers made the Seljuk sultans, in effect, only the greatest of the Turkish *beys*. Like the *beys*, they had to appeal to the nomads by promising them benefits, especially by appearing as the leaders who would bring them more conquests, more booty. Yet it could never be in the interest of the state or the sultan to battle constantly. Periods of calm consolidation were needed by any state. With a standing army that could keep the nomads in check, a sultan could have ensured that the nomads fought for the interests of the state, not against them, but the Rum Seljuks had no such army.

Considered from the perspective of the great empire that was to follow them, the Ottoman Empire, the Rum Seljuks were most important for the traditions they carried on. The Rum Seljuks were an image of Turkish legit-imacy in Anatolia, carrying the Great Seljuk ideas of government into the new territory and passing them on to those who followed. When they could, the Rum Seljuks acted more or less as traditional Islamic rulers, sponsoring great art and architecture, for example, and acting as patrons of religious men, poets, and artists. They ruled from an imperial capital, with the trappings of imperial rule. They also acted as an organizing principle for the Turks of Anatolia, titular rulers behind whom all groups could unite in time of need. The existence of the Rum Seljuks helped keep Anatolia from descending into an anarchy of fighting nomadic tribes. Their greatest contribution was the transfer to Anatolia of the systems developed by the Great Seljuks and the Middle Eastern dynasties before them.

The conveyance of Middle Eastern traditions to Anatolia is illustrated by Rum Seljuk government. It should be remembered that forms of govern-ment do not necessarily indicate practice; the existence of Ethics Committees in Congresses and Parliaments throughout modern history adequately demonstrates this. Nevertheless, the Rum Seljuks did carry the idea of structured Islamic government to the new land. At the apex of the system was the sultan, from whom all power theoretically flowed. A *vezir* headed the administration, as in other Islamic states. Under him laboured a chancellory which directed communications and financial officers who kept fiscal records.

The systems of land tenure developed under the Great Seljuks were carried on in Anatolia by the Rum Seljuks. Conditions were too confused through most of Rum Seljuk history for any system to take firm hold, but the Seljuks did keep the old systems alive. Primary among these was the *ikta*. Ideally, any state would prefer to pay its officials, soldiers, and bureaucrats from the central treasury, ensuring control over them. Tax collection on that scale was impossible for the Rum Seljuks, who had neither enough bureau-crats to keep the records nor the force to ensure collection. They needed a system that was decentralized. In Anatolia, the *ikta* was a system of allotting crown lands. The sultan's government awarded grants, usually of land, to retainers for their support. Administrators of state were granted land to sup-port themselves, their men, and the business they carried on for the state. Some soldiers, not a great number, were also given land that was to support themselves and their men. The land was not owned by the recipient, but was a method of paying salaries and expenses. In a state with little bureaucracy and a small treasury, the *ikta* was an efficient method of operation. The Ottomans were later to develop it into a major instrument of state finance.

Islam

Turkish Muslims introduced the traditions of Islam into Anatolia. For the most part, the Islam of the Turks was the basic Turkish admixture of beliefs, including some that predated the Turks' conversion to Islam, that can be called neither Sunni nor Shia Islam. However, the Seljuk family carried the high tradition of Islam into the new territories. Unlike most of the nomad chiefs of Anatolia, the Rum Seljuks at least aspired to the status of orthodox sultans who guarded and maintained all the structures of Sunni Islam. These included the system of Islamic theology and law. Turkish nomads might have made little use of Muslim judges, but the Seljuks supported Islamic courts and some learned jurists in their cities. The *vakıf* (a 'pious foundation', Arabic, *waqf*), through which the rich and pious ceded income-producing property and businesses for good purposes, such as supporting mosques or providing hospitals, was brought as an institution to Anatolia. Traditional Islamic taxes, such as the head tax levied on non-Muslims, were instituted. These were essential to the creation of an Islamic society.

While carrying on the orthodox tradition, the Rum Seljuks also favoured the mystical traditions of Islam. Numerous holy men and leaders of mystical orders were attracted to their court. The greatest of these was the mystic, poet, and philosopher Jelal al-Din (Celalüddin) Rumi, whom the great mystical order of Mevlevi dervishes (mystics following his path) consider their founder. The coexistence of orthodoxy and mysticism was another tradition transferred to Anatolia from Great Seljuk practice. It religiously defined the Turks.

Co-existence trans ferred by Rum Seljuks.

Cities and commerce

The Rum Seljuks bequeathed to those who followed them a considerable Anatolian urban network. During the final centuries of Byzantine rule the urban system in Anatolia had gradually deteriorated. Cities declined further in the first decades of Turkish invasion, which disrupted the trade upon which cities depended. In the twelfth century, both Rum Seljuk sultans and Turkish *beys* began to realize that towns and commerce were a source of power and income. They fostered the growth of what today would be called urban infrastructure. Government buildings, residences of sultans and governors, and great mosques were built as focal points in cities. Most importantly, because security was a problem in Anatolia, the Seljuks built city fortifications or caused them to be built by local lords. As they had in both the Byzantine and Islamic worlds, cities and towns functioned as centres of politics and religion. Islamic institutions were based in the towns. Though the majority of town dwellers remained Christian, the Rum Seljuks transformed the governing systems of Anatolian cities to an Islamic system. Islamic judges and market inspectors provided the legal structure of urban activities. It was usual for governors and independent *beys* both to live in towns, even if the latter depended on nomad horsemen who scorned the urban life.

The largest Rum Seljuk city was probably Konya, the capital. Although not as great a trading centre as others, its political status guaranteed it a certain pre-eminence. The main trading city was Sivas in central Anatolia.

Sivas was on or near main north–south and east–west trading routes. Although trade was greatly decreased by the upheaval that accompanied the Turkish incursion, Seljuk coastal cities such as Samsun and Sinop on the Black Sea and Antalya on the Mediterranean still carried on considerable trade, transported in Italian boats. Many towns lay on transit lines to Byzantium, and Seljuk produce, raw materials from mines, and some finished goods such as carpets passed to Constantinople and beyond. The Byzantines may have been the enemy, but business was business. The cities and towns themselves had been inherited from the Byzantines, as the names of major Seljuk cities indicate: Ankara/Ancyra, Antalya/Attalia, Kayseri/Caesarea, Konya/Iconium, Sivas/Sebastea. Most of the main cities had retained their Christian populations. These served as middle men, for example, for Turkish herdsmen who sold wool and skins that would be exported to the Byzantines and/or Italy.

The cities did not remain as they had been under Byzantine rule. As Turkish and other Islamic merchants began to live and do business in them, distinctly Middle Eastern markets began to arise. Civic buildings reflected the religion and culture of the rulers, whether Rum Seljuk sultans or lesser *beys*. Like other Islamic leaders throughout history, the Rum Seljuks proclaimed their position through their architecture. The urban orientation of the Rum Seljuks is seen in the religious and civic monuments they built, especially in the major cities of Konya, Kayseri, and Sivas. Impressive mosques and *medreses* were built as the symbols of the Islamic nature of cities and states. Throughout the Rum Seljuk era, the majority of the urban population of Anatolia was Christian, but the cities had began to develop a Muslim character through the construction of Islamic buildings and the settlement of Turks in them.

The Rum Seljuks and lesser Turkish lords fostered trade by protecting it. Great caravansarays were built along trade routes. These fortified inns, built one day's journey apart, offered overnight shelter and safety to men and animals. Large permanent markets were constructed and supported by the Rum Seljuks, as well. They understood the necessary place of trade in a successful state. The need to foster trade was even greater in Anatolia, where nomad incursions and wars had partly ruined the traditional economy.

Creating a Turkish homeland in Anatolia

Weak though they often were, the Rum Seljuks provided an organizing structure for Anatolian society after the Turkish incursion. It cannot be said that they, any more than the Great Seljuks, were successful at turning the Turkism nomads into ordinary subjects of a settled empire. But by carrying the traditions of Middle Eastern rule to the new land they did leave a structure that could guide those who would come later, when the Turks finally did settle down. They presided over a transitional time, when Anatolia was becoming Turkey and the nomads from Central Asia were beginning to change and adapt to their surroundings. The Rum Seljuk success in retaining a continuity with the Islamic past should not be underrated. They did not create a great empire along the lines of the Abbasids or even the Great Seljuks, but they did carry the traditions of Islamic empire into Anatolia. There the traditions waited for those who would weave them into their own imperial structure – the Ottomans.

By providing even a small amount of security, the Seljuks fostered change among the Turkish nomads who had conquered Anatolia. The gradual transition of the Turks from nomads to farmers was perhaps the greatest social change in Turkish history, surely the greatest change before the twentieth century. The nomads themselves proved to be able to adapt to new situations. As nomadism became less successful, most Turks turned to farming. Others became 'two-pasture nomads'. The latter were partly agricultural, sowing crops in spring, leaving the crops under the care of watchmen, taking their flocks off to high summer pastures, then returning in the autumn to harvest the crops. Where nomads settled, even if only for half the year, Turkish villages sprang up. Turks also slowly became integrated into the economic life of Anatolia. They bred new types of camels, able to stand up to the Anatolian winter, for example, and started businesses in long distance haulage. Taking advantage of the abundance of fleece from their flocks, some nomads even became craftsmen, especially rug makers. Melding Central Asian styles and techniques with Greek and Armenian traditions of carpet-making, Turks created large carpet-making 'industries' in cities such as Aksaray and Sivas. Other settled and semi-nomadic Turks produced cotton, wheat, and rice for export to Italy. The Turks were slowly settling down. The process took centuries, but it was irreversible.

In the two hundred years that passed between Manzikert and the appearance of the Ottomans the ethnic identity of Anatolia radically changed. No one knows how many Turks came into Anatolia in successive waves of migration. The numbers must have been sizeable, judging by their ability to conquer and rule over the people already there. Seen another way, there must have been enough Turks to maintain the Turkish identity. A thin veneer of military conquerors would probably have ultimately been submerged in the culture of the overwhelming majority. This happened to the Mongols in China, the Arabs in Iran, and many other conquerors, and would surely have been the fate of a small contingent of Turks. On the other hand, the Turks must have been a minority through most, if not all, of the Rum Seljuk period. But the proportion of Turks in the population was constantly increasing. Mortality and emigration decreased the Christian population. Women of the conquered bore the children of the conquerors, and these were raised as Turks. Moreover, as it became obvious that the Turks were in Anatolia to stay, many of the original inhabitants became Turks.

Conversion must have been an important factor in making Anatolia Turkish. 'Conversion' is the proper word, because the most important part of the process was conversion to Islam. The Turkish conquerors and rulers of Anatolia were Muslims who accepted the Islamic rules against forced conversion. They also accepted the Islamic tradition of wholly accepting new members into their community if the newcomers accepted Islam. As practised by the Turkish nomads, Islam was an easy religion to accept. The religion of the nomads took in many customs that would never have been accepted in Mecca. Many a local Christian saint found his way into the ranks of the departed holy men to whom the Turks prayed. Some local Christian religious customs simply became local Muslim religious customs. (In truth, many of the customs and saints would have been equally foreign to Muslim or Christian theologians.) Conversion had distinct benefits – especially fewer taxes, an opportunity to join the Turks in their lucrative conquests, and access to the sources of power. To become a part of the dominant social, economic, and political group, one needed only to accept the dominant religion. Conversion to the language and habits of the Turks would follow, probably in the next generation. The identifying characteristics of a Turk were Islam and language, so the converts became Turks.

The conversion of Anatolian Greeks and others into Turks was surely accelerated by the breakdown of their traditional societies. Many Christian communities, especially those in the interior, were isolated after the Muslim conquest. Greeks in Central Anatolia had been part of a society that was based on Byzantine government and, especially, on the Greek Orthodox Church. The Church, which can be called the essential element of the culture, had been based in Constantinople. Upon the arrival of the Turks, priests fled, monasteries were closed, and bishops were no longer sent out from the capital. It is not at all strange that Greeks living under such conditions, without the religious culture that had unified their ancestors, would gradually be assimilated into the culture of their conquerors. Any Christian desire to hold their ground and wait for a Christian resurgence must have been considerably dampened by continuing Turkish occupation. After the first hundred years of Turkish occupation had passed, it must have been evident that the Greek Emperor was not going to return.

The numbers of nomads who took up farming or the proportion of Christians who converted to Islam in Rum Seljuk times is unknown. Large nomad and Christian communities lasted long after the Rum Seljuk era had passed. However, Anatolia was gradually becoming a land of settled Turks.

Mongol rule in Anatolia

As Seljuk rule declined then disappeared, the Turks of Anatolia fell to fighting among themselves. The Mongol Ilkhans, ruling at a distance, from Iran, proved unable to rule effectively. They never developed an effective administrative machinery to rule Anatolia themselves. Government degenerated into autonomous principalities which often fought each other and frequently courted the Mongols to take sides in their disputes. While unable to rule effectively themselves, the Mongols were able to keep anyone else from doing so. In 1291, the Ilkhan monarch Gaykhatu entered central Anatolia to cement his rule among his rebellious subjects. His troops ravaged widely and left chaos behind them. Indeed chaos was the principal result of Mongol rule. Their armies smashed those *beys* who tried to develop too much power or independence, thus preventing the creation of a strong Anatolian state. The Mongol state in Iran was at the same time declining. Mongol governors in Anatolia both attempted to become independent and took part in dynastic struggles with the Ilkhans in Iran.

Although not necessarily recognized at the time, the Mongols had a long term effect on the Middle East that was to elevate the place of Anatolia in the world of Islam. From the first days of the Abbasid Caliphate in the eighth century through the reign of the Great Seljuks Islam had turned its face to the East. Before the appearance of the Mongols, Iraq had been recognized as the political and cultural centre of Islam for five centuries. The cities of northeastern Iran (Khurasan) and Transoxania – Merv, Nishapur, Herat, Samarkand, and others – were among the most prosperous in the Middle East, centres of culture and learning as well as politics and economy. Jengiz Khan and his successors did much to destroy the preeminence of both Iraq and the East. Great eastern cities such as Herat and Nishapur were utterly destroyed, their people massacred. Irrigation canals, which had provided food to large populations for centuries, were destroyed. Regions that had been economically vital for millennia were reduced to destitution. In Iraq, the attentions of the Mongols were perhaps not as damaging as they had been in the East, but were sufficient to ruin the economy for generations. Baghdad suffered perhaps 200,000 deaths when Hülegü conquered it in 1258. As in the East, irrigation works were destroyed, acts that destroyed the agricultural economy. The effects of the Mongol invasion on commerce are little known, but it is hard to believe many caravans transversed Iran, Iraq, and Transoxania while the Mongol armies were at work. The damage of the initial invasions was exacerbated when Mongol rulers, the Ilkhans of Iran, remained behind in the Middle East and proved to be particularly bad rulers.

One effect of the Mongol devastation of the East was to raise the relative position of the West in the Islamic world. Muslim theologians and poets found the courts of Egypt or Anatolia more congenial than the ruined cities of Transoxania. Turkish soldiers from Iran and Transoxania rode into Anatolia, escaping the Mongols and increasing the Turkish population of Asia Minor. Whether for nomads, mystic holy men, merchants, or Islamic scholars, the West was the place where reputations, followers, and fortunes were to be made. Egypt and Anatolia vied for prestige and authority, but the 'power and glory' of the West were ultimately sealed by the creation of the Ottoman Empire. The centre of Islam was to be in the West.

Although the last Ilkhanid ruler died in 1335, effective Mongol rule in parts of Anatolia had ended some time before. Mongol garrisons were stationed in major Anatolian towns, but their rule did not extend far beyond central Anatolia. Western Anatolia had become a region for the *gazis*, who migrated there both to escape direct Mongol rule and because the West was the scene of renewed war against the Christians. In western and, later, in central Anatolia, the *gazis* were left without even the appearance of a central government to hold them in check. They responded by creating their own *gazi* states, including states in western Anatolia, where they prospered by attacking the Byzantine Empire. At first, the various states accepted the overlordship of the Mongol *khan*. They later became independent. When Mongol power ended, other Turkish states asserted their independence in central and eastern Anatolia. One of the smallest of the new Turkish states was the small western Anatolian principality ruled by Osman, a leader of *gazis*. He and his descendants were to found the Ottoman Empire.

Chapter 2

The First Ottomans, 1281–1446

Overleaf

The garden of the mosque built in Bursa by Murat II in 1425. Forced to be a warrior sultan, Murat had no desire for war. He ordered that his tomb be placed in this garden. The tomb had no roof: he commanded that it 'be left open to the rain and to the sky'. (© Robert Harding Picture Library.)

The First Ottomans, 1281–1446

The Ottoman family entered history as nomad chiefs. Although their court historians later created elaborate genealogies tracing their lineage back to the Prophet Muhammad and other notable figures in history, the Ottoman ruler, in fact, was only one of a great many leaders of Turkish tribes who ranged over Anatolia. Their ancestors were the rude but mighty horsemen of Central Asia. They themselves were nomad chieftains.

Nomad chiefs drew their power from achievement, not inheritance or breeding, and proved their abilities through their own survival. Competence, particularly competence in warfare and politics, was demanded of a nomad leader. A chief without ability was deposed. Even if an incompetent chief were kept on, perhaps because his family was powerful, his authority would evaporate. The fighting men who were the basis of his power would simply ride off to another leader. Correspondingly, a particularly able chief would attract more and more followers, even whole tribes, as had the Seljuk family.

A considerable empire might be built by a nomad chief. The Seljuks had done so, as had Jenghiz Khan and his children. Numerous other states in Central Asia and eastern Iran had been based on the support of Turkish and Mongol nomads. However, such states did not often last long. The Seljuks are rightly thought to have been a successful empire, yet the Seljuk Empire was divided less than fifty years after it took Baghdad. Within little more than a hundred years of taking Baghdad their empire had virtually disappeared, only smaller successor states such as the Rum Seljuks remaining. Part of the problem was the nomadic custom of dividing inheritance among surviving members of the deceased's family. This works considerably better for a family business or the deceased's stocks and bonds than it did for a great empire. When sons each inherited a share of an empire they were soon at war with each other; the result was either one weakened empire or a number of smaller states. The military basis of nomadic states also made them inherently unstable. Nomads often benefited from governmental instability, which allowed them freedom of action, but empires naturally wanted to stabilize their political situation. They wanted to see more settled agriculturalists, paying taxes, and more merchants trading, again paying taxes. Nomads could and often did upset such plans – raiding farms and merchant caravans or turning agricultural land into pasturage for their sheep. There was an inherent flaw in the Seljuk system of government, and it eventually destroyed the Seljuk Empire. The nomads wanted a strong sultan to lead them in battle, but there was a point at which they would rebel against the sultan rather than obey orders, especially orders to settle down and leave the farmers alone. The sultan needed the nomads to fight for him, but wanted them to change their ways. Thus the sultans were always trying to balance the needs of state against the danger of nomad rebellion or nomad desertion to another leader, a precarious political juggling act. Eventually, the sultan dropped the ball.

The astonishing achievement of the Ottomans was breaking the cycle of birth, short life, then dissolution that characterized the earlier nomadic empires. Unlike the Seljuks, the Mongols and many others, the Ottomans were able to create a stable, long-lived Middle Eastern empire out of a nomadic state.

Turkish Anatolia

The society of Anatolia was unsettled as the Ottomans began their rise to power. Any central government that might claim rule over all of Turkish Anatolia was weak or nonexistent. The Rum Seljuks, defeated by the Mongols in 1243, had virtually disappeared as a power. Mongol overlords were content to collect tribute, and they too soon lost control. By the end of the reign of Osman, the first Ottoman sultan, he and the other Turkish leaders of Anatolia were in reality independent lords.

The Turkish states of Anatolia are often called principalities (*beylik* in Turkish), too small to be called kingdoms, but independent nevertheless. Most of the Turkish principalities were formed during the latter part of the thirteenth century, when Rum Seljuk and Mongol power in Anatolia were both on the wane. The strongest of the Turkish states was Karaman, which stretched over central and southern Anatolia. Because they had taken as their own the Rum Seljuk capital of Konya and because of their power, they claimed to be the successors of the Rum Seljuks. Other principalities, such as the Ottomans, grew by annexing previously Christian regions. One of the most interesting of the nomad states was Aydın, which developed a powerful fleet (not a normal accomplishment for a state founded by Turkish nomads, the most land-locked of soldiers). Aydın captured Greek islands and even raided into the Greek Peninsula. Other principalities appeared in central Anatolia after Mongol power over the region disappeared in the fourteenth century. None of the Turkish states was a major power in the world, and their multiplicity divided the military force of the Turks.

The main Turkish principalities.

The governments of the principalities were somewhere between what is usually meant by a 'state' (i.e., a capital, a treasury, bureaucrats, police, etc.) and a confederation of nomads. The Turkish leaders of the principalities were not at first part of the great tradition of Arab and Persian statecraft that had been adopted by the Seljuks, but as the years passed they attempted to emulate Seljuk models, building great mosques and attempting to set up organized governments. In their attempts at organizing states the leaders always had to consider the nature of their strength. Although regular armies were being formed, the principalities depended militarily on nomad horsemen. The nomads strengthened the armies, but made it difficult to organize a settled state. Indeed, the greatest Turkish states of eastern Anatolia (the Ak Koyunlu and Kara Koyunlu) were primarily nomad confederations along the central Asian model. Other *beyliks*, such as Karaman, were further along the path to settled, more centralized states.

The first Ottomans

The royal myth of the House of Osman held that one Süleyman led the Kayı tribe of Turkish nomads, who had more or less settled in northeastern

Iran until the Mongols appeared. He and the tribe then fled west. Süleyman drowned in the River Euphrates, but one of his sons, Ertuğrul, took part of the tribe into Anatolia. There, in the last half of the thirteenth century, he fought as a vassal of the Seljuks of Rum. As a reward for his services he was given the small territory of Söğüt in western Anatolia. When he died (c. 1280) his place was taken by his son, Osman.

The chances of the story being literally true are not good, but the essential elements are probably fairly accurate. Turkish nomads did flee to the west in great numbers when the Mongols advanced. Entire tribes entered Anatolia and were either granted or took small territories which they ruled. At first, the territories provided grassland for flocks, booty from farmers (it cannot really be called taxes at that stage), and a base from which to carry out raids. Osman's land must have been such a small state. When necessary Ertuğrul and Osman paid tribute to the Rum Seljuks or to the Mongols who succeeded them. When they were powerful or their overlords were weak they paid nothing to anyone.

The greatness of the Ottomans was that they rose above their nomad inheritance. They incorporated their nomadic inheritance into a new system of government that combined the great traditions of Middle Eastern Empires and the vitality of Turkish nomad life. Although they were initially the smallest and weakest of the principalities, they had two factors that allowed them to rise – geography and brilliant leadership.

The position of the Ottoman state was especially fortunate. Other principalities abutted the borders of the Byzantine Empire. Germiyan, Saruhan, Aydın, and Karası all advanced at Byzantine expense. However, the Ottomans were the Turks who were astride the path to Europe. Nomad soldiers streamed to the leaders who could promise them the 'best wars', wars against settled Christian kingdoms that would provide the most booty. After their initial successes, the other principalities could only war against the other Turkish states that were on their borders. There was little glory or booty in fighting brother Turks. The Ottomans, on the borders of Christendom, were able to become the foremost among the *gazis* who were fighting to expand the rule of Islam. Men rode from all over Anatolia and even Central Asia to put themselves under Ottoman command and fight for religion and booty.

The most important factor in Ottoman success was the ability of the early sultans. As soldiers, they were able to marshal nomadic Turkish warriors to defeat the power of settled kingdoms and more regular armies. This implied more than tactical abilities. The sultans knew how to take advice and learned from their enemies. Christian advisors were a prominent feature of the Ottoman court and army. One of them, Evrenos Bey, a convert to Islam, led the Ottoman armies in their conquest of Macedonia

and Thrace in Europe. The sultans were also able politicians, playing their
enemies off against each other, securing one front with treaties while they
conquered on another, and marrying the daughters of Turkish princes or
Christian kings for political gain. A different type of political awareness
allowed them to keep the nomad tribes together under their command – a
great feat, given the independent nature of nomads. The sultans were able
to function both as kings in Europe and Turkish nomad lords in Anatolia,
and keep all sides off balance and in fear of their power.

The Ottoman leaders were also able to exploit the nature of Turkish
society in Anatolia. With little centralized control, Anatolia was held together
by popular culture, popular religion, and the economic life of the people. The
Turks were essentially the same people, no matter the principality in which
they lived. Their religious and social patterns were an amalgam of those they
had brought from Central Asia and those they found in the Middle East. In
centuries of living in Anatolia they had forged these into a new ethnic identity
as Anatolian Turks. When civil order broke down it was that ethnic identity
that provided a structure for society. The Turks of Anatolia organized into
mystical religious groups, following religious traditions and religious organizations that transcended political borders. The mystical brotherhoods crossed
Anatolia, and many extended much further throughout the world of Islam. A
traveller would find lodging and fellowship with his brothers in a lodge of his
mystical brotherhood. News would pass through the fellowships' connections
all over Anatolia. The support of the mystical fraternities was thus very
important to anyone claiming authority over the Turks. Associated with the
religious fraternities were popular urban defence fellowships (*ahi*s), which
provided protection for the city populations when the governments could
not. Craft guilds and merchants were also linked to the mystic orders. Mystic
leaders were the spiritual advisors of the guilds and *ahi* fellowships, and
members of the guilds and fellowships were also members of the religious
fraternities. It was through these interconnected groups that the people of
Anatolia held together.

The Ottoman sultans and their followers were, according to tradition,
members of the mystical fraternities with close ties to their networks among
the Turks. They were also tied to the craft guilds. (Long after they had
become leaders of an empire, the sultans were still trained in a craft, such as
bow-making or leatherwork, retaining their traditions.) Ottoman sultans
may have been leaders of *ahi* groups. They surely provided support and
assistance to the *ahi*s and mystics. The benefits to the Ottomans are obvious. A network of spies and financial support were natural corollaries of
close bonds with the religious fraternities, the *ahi*s, and the guilds.

The picture of the earlier Ottoman sultans that emerges from history and
legend is of men who deeply understood their society. They did manipulate
Anatolian society to their advantage, but they could not have functioned so
well if they had not been part of it. In no sense were they removed and

39

aloof as rulers. If they understood the *gazi*s, *ahi*s, and mystical religious brotherhoods, it was because they were *gazi*s and *ahi*s and they practised mystical Islam. As the empire developed they were to break out of that mould and alter their position, becoming much more like traditional Middle Eastern rulers, removed from their subjects. This, too, was managed so that their power and the scope of their empire increased.

Much energy can be spent on the antique argument between those who espouse the 'great man' theory of history and those who prefer environmental explanations for change. Currently, the environmental explanations seem to be winning, with good reason, but it is hard to deny that the personal abilities of the first ten Ottoman sultans were extraordinary. It is also true that the Ottoman family appeared just as the political environment in Anatolia and the Balkans was ready for them.

The Balkan Christian states

The Ottomans were first to create their empire through conquest of Christian empires and kingdoms in Anatolia and the Balkans.

The pre-eminent state in the Balkans and Anatolia had for centuries been the Byzantine Empire. Descendent of the Roman Empire in the East, the Byzantine Empire was a centralized state that had spread its culture and religion, Greek Orthodoxy, throughout the region. Although beset by internal conflicts and changes in ruling dynasties throughout its history, the Empire had built upon the riches afforded by its privileged position on East-West trade routes to create the richest and most powerful of the European medieval states. Before the battle of Manzikert, the Byzantine Empire had stretched from the River Aras in the East to the River Danube in the Balkans. Beginning in 1071, it was dealt blows by the Turks and the Western Christians that ultimately destroyed it, but the fact that its destruction took almost 400 years is a tribute to its vitality even in decline.

At first, the forces of Western Christendom aided the Byzantines, even though their assistance was not intended. The knights and soldiers of the First Crusade helped the Byzantines drive back the Turks from western Anatolia and south coastal Anatolia in the early twelfth century. In 1204, though, the Crusaders turned on Byzantium. Led by Venetian intrigues, the Fourth Crusade captured Constantinople and installed a Latin Empire (1204–61). Latin rulers reigned in eastern and southern Greece, Thrace, northwestern Anatolia, and in Constantinople itself. Venice held the Byzantine islands in the Aegean and the Mediterranean. The remnants of Byzantium held out in the Empire of Nicaea, sandwiched between the Rum Seljuk dominions and the Latin Empire. As the Byzantines struggled to retake their capital, Balkan Christians took advantage of the situation to create their own kingdoms in what had been the Byzantine Empire. The Bulgarian Empire, which had grown even before 1204, expanded its holdings to stretch in 1241 from the Danube in the north almost to the Aegean in the south and from west of Belgrade to the Black Sea. In the fourteenth century, the Serbian kingdom expanded into much of what had been the Bulgarian Empire, including most of today's Serbia, Montenegro, Albania, and northern Greece.

In 1261, the Byzantines managed to reconquer Constantinople and re-establish the Byzantine Empire. However, the weakened Empire was never able to regain its old position. The Byzantines retook the southern Balkans and northern Greece, but Serbia forced them from the western Balkans at the end of the thirteenth century. Serbian expansion, under Emperor Stephan Dushan (1331–55) continued into the fourteenth century, just as the Turks were taking what remained of Byzantine Anatolia. At this point, the Byzantines began to battle among themselves for what remained. Two families, the Palaeologus and the Cantacuzenus, each claimed the imperial throne. Neglecting the greater threat, emperors and would-be emperors even allied themselves with the Turks to attack their Byzantine enemies. Even though chance and the fortified walls of Constantinople kept a rump of the Empire alive until 1453, the fate of the Byzantines was set irrevocably a century before.

In the middle of the fourteenth century, there was no one great Christian power in southeastern Europe. The Bulgarian Empire had been defeated by the Serbs in 1330 and remained enfeebled. The Serbian Empire itself disintegrated after the death of its great champion, Stephan Dushan in 1355. In the West, Croatia, Bosnia, and Hungary vied for power and conquest. To the north, Romania was divided into two principalities, Moldavia and Wallachia. The third section of Romania, Transylvania, was part of the Hungarian Empire. Hungary, Moldavia, and Transylvania were all internally weakened by conflicts between rulers and the nobility. As the Christians fought among themselves, there was no unified power to oppose the appearance of the Ottoman Turks in Europe.

Opposition to the Ottomans in other Christian states

The Christian powers of Europe viewed the coming of the Ottomans with alarm. For centuries the rule of Islam had stopped at the borders of Anatolia. Now eastern European Christendom was falling to the Muslim Turks. The Byzantine Empire soon became little more than Constantinople and its hinterland. The question was where the Turks would stop. By the beginning of the fifteenth century, the distance from the Ottomans' first land in Söğüt to their new European borders was greater than the distance from the Ottoman border to Paris, and this was the type of fact that made the Europeans stop and think.

Europe outside the Balkans was undergoing its own troubles. The Black Death had wreaked havoc throughout Europe in the middle of the

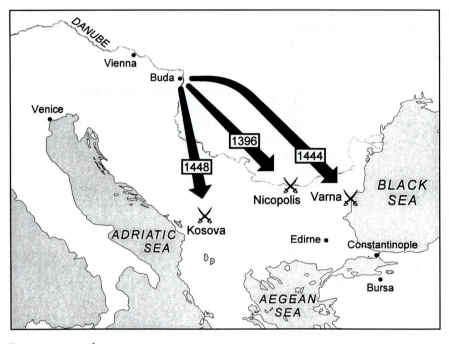

European crusades.

---

fourteenth century. Italian city states had broken free of German attempts to unify Italy within the Holy Roman Empire. Germany itself went through civil war and by the middle of the century the Holy Roman Empire had devolved into a federation of independent states (the Golden Bull of 1356). Poland was battling against the expansion of the Teutonic knights, contending with Lithuania and Hungary, and experiencing internal conflicts between nobles and king. England and France were fighting the Hundred Years' War (1338–1453). The Papacy, which had reached the height of its power in the thirteenth century (Innocent III, Pope 1198–1216, Boniface VIII, Pope 1294–1303), declined precipitously in the fourteenth. From 1303 to 1378, the Popes resided in Avignon, the so-called Babylonian Captivity. In 1378, the Great Schism began, with competing Popes at both Avignon and Rome. Thus neither the Pope nor the Holy Roman Emperor possessed the power to organize a mighty force to oppose the Turks.

The disarray in Europe did not mean that Turkish successes went unnoticed. As might be expected, the main voice calling for a crusade against the Turks was the Pope. Christian knights and soldiers were still willing to fight for their faith and, more realistically, the booty to be found in war. But the circumstances were very different from what they had been when Christian Crusaders took the Holy Land four hundred years earlier. Under the Ottomans, the forces of Islam that faced the Crusaders were far more united than they had been in the time of the first Crusades. Christians were less united and less committed to the fight. France now refused to cooperate in wars that might strengthen its enemies, especially its enemies in Germany. No western European kings were personally willing to fight the Crusade. There were exceptions to the Christian policy of temporizing with the Ottomans. Hungary stood against them, leading three Crusades against the Ottomans. Poland was an important contributor to Crusades. However, it would have taken a much more concerted approach to finally defeat the power of the Turks. A divided and contentious Europe was unable to do anything in concert.

Christian Europe was to send three Crusades to defeat the Ottomans. All attracted soldiers from Europe, especially Germany and Poland. Each resulted in disaster. The European defeats in the Crusades were to be the end of significant offensive actions against the Ottomans in the Balkans for more than two centuries. Europe went on the defensive, abandoning the Balkans and what remained of the Byzantine Empire to the Ottomans. Christendom's defensive lines were drawn in Hungary, Croatia, the Mediterranean, and Poland, and even those lines were pushed back by Ottoman attack.

The conquests of the first Ottoman sultans

Osman translated his geographic advantages into successes against the Byzantines. Under his leadership, the Turkish horsemen proved able to conquer territory to the south, north, and west of Söğüt. They could not so easily take the Byzantine cities of the region. Nomadic cavalry was at a disadvantage when it came to attacking city walls, which were impervious to even the best cavalrymen. The Ottomans could only lay siege to cities such as Brusa (today's Bursa), Nicomedia (İzmit), and Nicaea (İznik). Nevertheless, the Ottomans needed a city. Without one they would appear to be distinctly inferior to the other Turkish principalities, and organizing a state and economy beyond the rudimentary nomadic system would have been impossible. With cities in their control, the Ottomans could build mosques, sponsor craft-guilds, and draw Muslim scholars to their patronage. In other words, they could begin to act as traditional Muslim rulers.

The break came just after Osman's death. His son, Orhan, finally accepted the surrender of the city of Bursa in 1326, a number of years after the Ottoman siege had begun. Nicomedia, Nicaea and Scutari (Üsküdar) soon fell as well, leaving Orhan, Osman's successor, in command of all northwestern Anatolia. Ottoman territory could now be seen from the walls of Constantinople.

With Bursa as their capital and their prestige increased, the Ottomans faced a choice. They could try to expand their control over the other

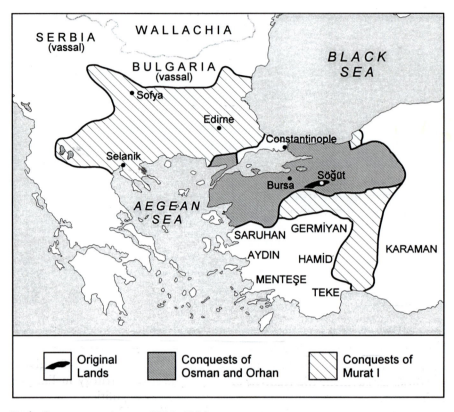

Early Ottoman conquests, 1281–1389.

Turkish states on their borders or attack into Europe. They did take over the Karası principality to the south, but Europe was a more lucrative field of operations. At first, the appeal of Europe must have been the booty to be gained there. Except for a few raids from principalities such as Aydın that possessed naval power, Byzantine Europe had escaped Turkish raids. It was a far more fertile source of booty than Anatolia. Moreover, Turkish *gazis* were attracted to the fight to expand the rule of Islam as well as to the booty. The Ottomans therefore adopted a policy of more or less peaceful acquisition of territory in Anatolia and of war in Europe.

It might be thought that the Christian kingdoms of the Balkans would unite against the Ottoman threat, but this was not the case. The various Balkan states often claimed the same territories. They were as jealous of each other as they were of the Ottomans. Therefore, in each campaign against the Turks Christian rulers considered what would be the best short-term gain for themselves. Self-interest often dictated that a Christian prince stay neutral or even fight alongside the Turks against another Christian ruler. Perhaps the best example of Christian assistance to Ottoman con-

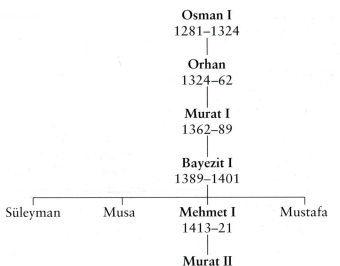

Osman I
1281–1324

Orhan
1324–62

Murat I
1362–89

Bayezit I
1389–1401

Süleyman   Musa   **Mehmet I**   Mustafa
1413–21

Murat II
1421–44 and 1446–51

quest came from the Byzantines. At the time of Sultan Orhan the Byzantine Empire still ruled a sizeable portion of Thrace and some of northwestern Anatolia. Two families fought for the Empire, the Palaeologus and the Cantacuzenus. The Cantacuzenus pretender to the throne actually hired the Ottomans to fight for him in the 1340s, giving the Turks as payment the right to plunder Byzantine territory in Europe. Orhan's troops continued to intervene in Byzantine politics, crossing to Europe to assist the Cantacuzenus side, until in 1354 the Ottomans remained in Europe. Orhan's son and general, Süleyman, held Gallipoli, on the northern coast of the Dardanelles. From there the Ottoman occupation of the Balkans began.

From their foothold in Gallipoli the Ottomans raided into Thrace, flooding the region with Turkish nomads under their command. Orhan's first son, Süleyman, died in 1357. By 1359, the sultan had passed control of the Ottoman forces to his son, Murat, who succeeded to the throne in 1361 or 1362 (date unknown). Murat I briefly turned his attention to Anatolia, defeating a threat from the Karaman principality and extending Ottoman power eastward. He then turned to Europe, where some of his forces had been expanding the empire even while the sultan was in Anatolia. In 1361, his forces took the major city of Adrianople (in Turkish, Edirne), which was to become the second Ottoman capital, signifying the Ottoman intention to concentrate on European conquest. A Serbian army, which intended to expel the Ottomans from the south Balkans, was defeated in 1371. The Ottomans had cemented their hold over Thrace, southern Bulgaria, and most of Macedonia, and the Bulgarian ruler and the Byzantine Emperor were forced to accept vassalage to the Ottomans.

The Ottomans in the Balkans applied different methods of conquest from those the Turks had used earlier in Anatolia. In Anatolia, the land had been conquered outright and ruled by Turks. Migration of Turks and conversion provided the manpower at first for a dominating Turkish presence, then for a majority. It was not so in the Balkans. After the Turks had settled in Anatolia there were simply not enough Turks to colonize the Balkans, an area of denser settlement with many more people to displace. Turkish nomads did move into Europe, at first to fight, then to settle, eventually to become local Balkan Turkish forces. Murat and future sultans settled Turks to defend sensitive regions and to 'water down' potentially rebellious districts. The political rule of the Turks in Europe thus began to be cemented demographically. However, there were never enough Turks to make the Balkans into another Turkey. Therefore, the Ottomans adopted a programme of conciliation and vassalage, rather than outright conquest. Defeated kings were allowed, at least at first, to keep their lands, but as tribute-paying vassals who contributed troops for Ottoman wars. The Ottomans were thus provided with troops and funds and the Balkan kings kept their thrones. Self-interest being an even more important thing with kings than with the rest of humanity, those who had at least some autonomy as vassals would be less likely to chance all in a rebellion. Later, when the vassals had been gradually weakened and Ottoman force firmly established, the sultans could institute direct control.

In Anatolia Murat extended his rule through marriage, accepting land from the Germiyan principality as the bride price for his son Bayezit's marriage to the daughter of the ruler. He also purchased land, although the 'sale' must have been motivated by fear of the consequences of refusal. These gains brought the Ottoman state to the borders of Karaman and subsequent war with Karaman. But while Murat was in Anatolia defeating Karaman in 1386, Balkan princes took advantage of his absence.

The Serbs had accepted Ottoman overlordship in 1386, and Serbian vassal soldiers had assisted Murat in his defeat of Karaman, but they and other Europeans almost immediately renounced their vassalage. The Serbian prince Lazar defeated an Ottoman army in 1388 and Murat was compelled to return from Anatolia by forced march. His forces, which included Christian lords and their men, met the Serbs and their allies at Kosova in 1389. Although Murat died in the battle, his forces triumphed. His son Bayezit ruled over all of the Balkans.

Bayezit I and the transformation of the Empire

Bayezit, the son of Murat I, took the throne after his father's death at the first battle of Kosova in 1389. He was an innovator who attempted to change the political direction of the Ottoman Empire. Under Murat and Bayezit, the Ottoman state began to resemble past great empires of the

Middle East and Balkans. The sultans aspired to fit the ideal of both the traditional Islamic and Byzantine states – an empire with one leader who exerted strong control through an army and bureaucracy that were primarily loyal to the state. By radically altering the Ottoman state system, the sultans placed themselves in opposition to the Turkish nomadic heritage. Traditional Turkish government was essentially practical – individuals and tribes followed leaders as long as it was advantageous for them to do so. Personal loyalty to the *han* was probably not even considered outside his own tribe or immediate followers. The *han* was the leader because his followers gained from his leadership, or because he was powerful enough to punish those who did not follow his standard. The traditional Emperors and Caliphs of the Middle East and Emperors of the Romans and the Byzantines held very different positions. The offices of Caliph or Emperor had lives of their own. The offices carried a dignity to which leaders aspired and to which populations gave respect, even if some of their incumbents were less than proficient rulers. The office was as important as the man, perhaps more important. Murat began the transition of the Ottoman state from the *gazi* state, led by a *han*, to the type of state known in the Balkans and the Middle East for centuries – a centralized, bureaucratized empire led by an all-powerful emperor.

The creation of a state bureaucracy was essential for one of the main functions of a state, the collection of taxes. Then as now, a ruler found nothing so appealing as a successful system of tax collection, and this demanded bureaucrats, records, and a way to make the people pay. Building on innovations begun by his father, Bayezit accelerated change in the Ottoman system. In redefining the Ottoman state he drew on two traditions – the Middle Eastern tradition that had been developed under the Great Seljuks and the Byzantine traditions of the Balkans. In his relatively short reign, Bayezit began to create a truly centralized state. In the regions of the Balkans which were under direct Ottoman administration, Bayezit regularized administration, creating new provinces (*sancak*s). In Anatolia, Bayezit organized old Ottoman lands and new conquests into a new administrative unit. He added to the small financial bureaucracy he had inherited from his father and began to regularize the collection of taxes.

The new methods of governing were antithetical to the nomad tradition, none so much as the efficient collection of taxes. Friction between the new and the old methods was heightened by the incursion of non-Turkish elements into the operation of the government. The nomadic and semi-settled Turks were obviously untrained in running a bureaucracy. Murat and, especially, Bayezit therefore engaged those who, though they might be Christians, knew the older governmental systems of the conquered lands and who could train new bureaucrats loyal to the sultan. Christian advisors were appointed and the sultan's personal slaves were trained as administrators. His personal slaves were put

47

in charge of much of the bureaucracy.

The resentment of the Turkish establishment increased as its power decreased. Bayezit was creating an empire whose strong central authority, including centralized records and tax-collecting, would deny the nomadic freedoms that had been an essential part of Turkish life from the beginning. The entire meaning of government was changing. It was moving far from the traditions of the Central Asian conquerors.

To put the sultan's plans into operation, a new army was needed. Previously, the Ottoman state had been an extension of nomadic power. The conquests and rule of the sultans depended on the abilities and good will of the Turkish nomadic horsemen and their leaders. This was not enough for the large state the Ottomans now ruled. The history of the Rum Seljuks told what happened to an empire that continued to depend on the traditional Turkish system. A fine system for conquest, it was also a system that eventually turned on its masters. If the Ottomans were to remain in control, they needed an independent source of power that could balance traditional Turkish forces. Traditional Turkish forces did not find this desirable. Murat had begun the creation of a slave army and administrator corps that was to become a hallmark of the Ottoman system. Taking men rather than treasure as his share of the spoils of war with the Balkan states, Murat had created an army from prisoners of war. The new soldiers were trained in Ottoman ways and melded into units that were dependent solely on the sultan and part of no old Turkish organization. Bayezit augmented the slave army with children taken from Christian villages, raised by the state as Muslims and trained to become Ottoman soldiers. From their ranks the brightest were further trained in administrative methods and made officials of the Empire. The intention was to place power in the hands of men who had no family, tribe, or region to which they were loyal. Completely dependent on the sultan for survival and advancement, and knowing that others were envious of their power, they would perforce be loyal to the sultan. The slave soldiers and administrators, the *kapı kulları*, to be described in the next chapter, became a force that bolstered the sultan's personal power.

Bayezit built up and increasingly relied on the new military units, until he led perhaps 7,000 slave soldiers. In addition, he commanded soldiers from vassals in the Balkans, Christian troops led by their own commanders. Bayezit's intention to be less a *gazi han* and more an emperor was evident in his treatment of conquered Christians in Europe. His methods were pragmatic tools to develop the strength of the sultan and the state, not especially to advance the interests of Turkish Muslims (although it can surely be argued that creating a strong state would be in the long run more in every Turk's interest than was the alternative, as seen in the deficiencies of the Great Seljuk and Rum Seljuk Empires). He saw that outright conquest, the Ottoman tradition, was not always as beneficial to an empire as was a system of divide and rule. Therefore, in Europe, Bayezit adopted a policy of both warfare and conciliation. The system of vassalage rather than direct conquest, begun by Murat, was utilized to maximize Ottoman military power. The Serbian kingdom remained, despite the defeat at Kosova, on the condition that it paid tribute and sent Serbian troops to fight alongside the Ottomans. Other Europeans were attacked unless they too accepted vassalage. Ottoman troops raided in force against the remaining European Christian states. As a result, Bosnia and Wallachia both became Ottoman vassals and other countries were thrown on the defensive. Bayezit received levies of soldiers that he was to use in the conquest of Anatolia, use in battles against Turkish states in which he could not trust his Turkish soldiers to fight against their fellows.

The change from an army made up solely of Muslim Turkish nomads was radical indeed. The sultan now had an independent source of power. Its numbers and power were far less than those of the traditional Turkish forces, but those forces were disunited. The sultan's personal slave army force was stronger than any smaller groups of Turkish soldiers who might revolt, and thus they kept the Turkish forces from potential rebellion. Of course, the fact that Bayezit remained a successful conqueror whose victories rewarded his troops made it all the more likely that they would remain under his command.

In the new empire the Turks themselves were changing. Some remained as military nomads, increasingly utilized as raiders on the Ottoman borders. Others settled in the new territories. Nomadic chiefs were settled on government-granted lands where they and their men were supported by the peasants of their region. Their leaders, usually called the Turkish notables, were naturally displeased with the ascendancy of non-Turkish elements in the state. Nonetheless, they were dependent on the sultan for their holdings. They too were becoming part of a state apparatus that kept records of their grants of land, watched over their activities, and called them to war when needed.

Bayezit's conquests

After the battle of Kosova, the European opponents of the Ottomans were for a while quiet. Much of Europe was occupied with its own business. As stated above, the Papacy and other Europeans who might have contributed to a great Crusade were embroiled in their own conflicts. You cannot fight abroad while you are fighting at home. Even when central and eastern European Christians did form a new Crusade in 1396 (see below), many nations could not or would not send troops. With Europe secure, Bayezit was able to turn to conquests in Anatolia.

The Turkish principalities, from whose numbers the Ottomans themselves had sprung, were a thorny problem for Ottoman strategy. They were to be feared, because another family of Turkish leaders might arise in Anatolia to supplant the Ottomans. Conquering the Turkish principalities was obviously in the Ottoman interest, but it was a difficult project. The Ottomans had benefited from their status as *gazis*, warriors dedicated to the expansion of the rule of Islam. Turks who rallied to them fought on the side of religion and self-interest, defeating non-Muslims who had riches to plunder. Could the sultan count on those same troops to attack brother Turkish Muslims with far less to plunder? Probably not. Instead, Bayezit relied on his European vassals to defeat the Anatolian Turks, just as he had relied on his Turkish troops to defeat the Europeans. Serbian, Byzantine, and other European vassal armies were used by Bayezit in campaigns in 1390–91 and 1393–94 against the principalities. Along with the slave army, the European Christians provided an independent strength that made it difficult for the sultan's Turkish armies to refuse their orders. The principalities were forced to accept Ottoman sovereignty, but remained rebellious.

Bayezit's use of Christian troops was a stroke of military genius. The Christian vassals might have proved untrustworthy in a Balkan war, but in Anatolia, far from their own lands, they were necessarily loyal to the sultan. His defeat would have been theirs, as well. At the same time, Bayezit could leave heavy garrisons of Turkish soldiers in Europe, taking with him to the Anatolian wars only the most loyal of his Turkish army.

The Turks call Bayezit I Yıldırım Bayezit, 'Bayezit the Lighting Bolt,' because he was able to move so quickly from battles in Asia to battles in Europe. In 1390–91, Bayezit seized all of western Anatolia. He faced the Ottomans' bitterest enemy in Anatolia, the principality of Karaman, the most powerful of the traditional *beyliks*, and forced the *bey* to sue for peace. He was kept from further conquest in Asia by events in Europe. Taking advantage of his absence in Anatolia, the Byzantines had renounced their vassalage to the Ottomans and the Wallachians, supported by the Hungarians, had moved south of the River Danube into Bulgaria, an Ottoman vassal. Bayezit retook and annexed his Bulgarian lands in 1393, took Salonica from the Byzantines in 1394, then put Constantinople under siege. He led the army into Wallachia and southern Hungary, which he ravaged in 1394. At the same time, Ottoman forces were fighting in Anatolia against the forces of the *bey* of Sivas and other principalities.

European Crusaders, who hoped to reverse the Ottoman triumphs, gathered in Hungary. In 1396 they moved down the Danube, taking and destroying forts on the Ottoman northern border and laying siege to the Ottoman fortress city of Nicopolis. Sultan Bayezit returned by forced march from battles in Anatolia to defeat the Europeans. The slaughter of Christian fighting men in that battle was enough to deter European intervention for almost fifty years, allowing the Ottoman Empire in Europe to survive after an abrupt change of fortune.

In 1397, Bayezit turned once again to Anatolia, defeating and annexing Karaman. He then advanced through western and central Anatolia and occupied the remaining principalities. For a brief time, most of Anatolia was Ottoman. Bayezit had created an empire that joined the old Rum Seljuk holdings to most of what the Byzantines had held in Europe. Constantinople, the Byzantine capital, held out alone, surrounded by Ottoman holdings, and it seemed as if it too would fall quickly. However, Bayezit had triumphed by turning his back on many of the traditions that had made the Ottoman state. In particular, he had attacked and annexed the Muslim Turkish states of Anatolia, rather than directing all his power against non-Muslims. Previous sultans had taken Anatolian lands, but they had done so with a combination of marriages, threats, even purchase, seldom outright conquest. Bayezit's bold step was to be his downfall.

Bayezit's conquests brought his rule far to the East, to lands claimed by the great conqueror Tamerlane. (His name was actually Timur, meaning 'iron', but the European corruption 'Tamerlane' has long since passed into general usage in the West.) Timur's career had begun in Transoxania, in the principality of Samarkand, where he first overthrew his prince, then attracted nomad support through the traditional method of showing himself to be a great general and successful conqueror. By 1389, he had taken all of Iran, the southern Caucasus region, and Iraq. He had even defeated the Mongols of the Golden Horde who ruled over Russia. The lands he subdued were melded into an empire, but in reality were a great ravaged region where absolute terror held sway. Parts of the Middle East never recovered from his devastation. His ruthlessness makes it unlikely that he can truly be called a good Muslim, but he was willing to make Bayezit's conquest of brother Muslims a case for 'righteous' indignation, forgetting his own far worse depredations against Muslims. When the Turkish beys who had lost their lands to Bayezit fled to him and asked for assistance, he saw a cause that would allow him to expand his empire and defeat the Ottomans, who by expanding east had become a threat to him. He invaded eastern Anatolia in 1400, then advanced into central Anatolia in 1402. The armies of Tamerlane and Bayezit met outside Ankara (July 28, 1402), and the Ottomans were defeated. In the battle, at least some of his Turkish nomad forces turned against Bayezit. Bayezit was defeated and taken prisoner. He later died in captivity.

Interregnum and reconstitution of the Empire

The Ottoman Empire survived Bayezit's defeat largely through the failures of its enemies. Tamerlane had no desire to continue his conquests into Ottoman Europe – his sights were aimed at China. Instead he merely redivided Anatolia roughly along the old lines, rebuilding the Turkish principalities.

The Ottomans had been one of the old principalities, so he allowed them to remain in northwestern Anatolia. Their lands in Europe were untouched. The Europeans were also unintentionally kind to the Ottomans. Although they launched Crusades both before and after the Ottoman debacle, they stayed away while the Ottoman Empire was in distress. Hungary, the only local Christian state that had the power to organize resistance, fought battles elsewhere and squabbled internally. Thus were the Ottomans left to regroup.

The greatest enemies to Ottoman recovery were those who fought among themselves to become sultan. From 1402 to 1413 four of Bayezit's sons – İsa, Mehmet, Musa, and Süleyman – vied to take power. During that period, known as the interregnum, Ottoman armies fought each other for control. Alliances were made between brothers, then broken, and the brothers defeated each other one by one, until only Mehmet remained, sultan Mehmet I.

The reigns of Mehmet I and his son, Murat II, exemplified the 'growing pains' that came with turning a nomadic state into a great settled empire. Bayezit I had begun one model of the Ottoman state – integrating Balkan traditions into the Ottoman system, reliance on Christian advisors, acceptance of vassal Christian states, and favouring the slave army. Against this model stood the traditional model – a *gazi* state, drawing its power from Turkish settled and nomad soldiers and excluding Balkan Christian influences, a state much like the Rum Seljuk Empire. When Mehmet I finally took power from his brothers both models existed within the empire. Because Europe, along with the new capital Edirne, had remained to the Ottomans, Bayezit's governmental innovations in Europe had survived as well. At the same time, Anatolia had reverted to the old ways – there the Ottomans were only one of many *beyliks*, and Ottoman support in Anatolia was based on traditional Turkish forces. Mehmet knew that destroying the *beyliks* might bring another disaster. Tamerlane, who died in 1405, had passed his 'protection' of Anatolia into the hands of his son and successor, Shah-Rukh, who might intervene as had his father.

Mehmet had no choice but to appease the *beys* in Anatolia and the traditional Turkish elements in his own following. Indeed, it was due to the support of the latter that he had become sultan. Although sides changed often in the fighting of the interregnum, Mehmet had generally not enjoyed the support of the *kapı kulları*, which had gone to his brothers. Therefore, when he became sultan he favoured the Turkish notables.

In addition to practical causes, there were what might be called philosophical reasons behind Mehmet's swing away from the policies of Bayezit. Mehmet's supporters felt that Bayezit had been too much in the hands of Christian advisors. These advisors, they believed, had naturally directed him toward Anatolian, rather than European, conquests, because they preferred that Muslims suffer. Moreover, they believed that Bayezit had entrusted too much military power to the slave soldiers, who had also been

Christians before becoming Ottoman soldiers. It was felt that this desertion of the old Ottoman way of dependence on Turkish cavalry and Turkish advisors had led to the downfall of the Empire.

Mehmet directed his Empire back to the *gazi* tradition: Christian advisors were put out. The slave army and *kapı kulları* officials were deprived of much of their power, although not abolished. Power in Mehmet's government was in the hands of descendents of the Turks who had followed Osman. Ottoman policy, as seen in retrospect, began to develop toward annexing the Balkan states, rather than leaving them as vassals and using their armies as units. Vassalage was probably a system that had out-lived its usefulness; even Bayezit seems to have been about to end it when he died. However, the power of the *kapı kulları* was eclipsed for only a short time. The idea of a force that was tied only to the sultan, a force of absolute reliability, was too irresistible to be long set aside. Even in Mehmet's time the *kapı kulları* were never completely abandoned. His son Murat began to build them up once again.

Those in power

True to its traditions, the Ottoman Empire considered itself to be a military state. Those who were in charge of the state, the so-called ruling class, were called by the Ottomans themselves simply 'the military' (*askeri*). Their primary occupations were the defence and expansion of the Empire and Islam and administration of the state. This was an Ottoman innovation on the tradi-tional Middle Eastern system of government. Under Nizam al-Mulk, for example, the Great Seljuk government had deliberately kept the administra-tion separate from the military, the better to watch over it, and the bureau-crats had mainly been members of the religious hierarchy, the *ulema*. In the Ottoman Empire, many of the government leaders and bureaucrats were still members of the *ulema*, but even they were 'military'. Çandarlı Hayrettin (see below), for example, was a religious leader and judge who led armies into battle, organized military units, and became chief minister in charge of the bureaucracy of Murat I.

By the period of the interregnum, the forces that would vie for power in the Ottoman Empire during the next decades were already in place. Although the degree of centralization of the Empire was not yet settled, the position of the sultan was unassailable. Nomads, Turkish notables, and slaves of the sultan might prefer different candidates for the sultanate, or even support rebels who tried to overthrow and replace a sultan, but all agreed that there needed to be a sultan.

Kapı kulları, *the slaves of the sultan*

The association of Turks and military slavery reaches back to the Abbasid Caliphate, when it was the Turks who were the military slaves. Purchased or captured near Transoxania, the slaves were organized into military units. They eventually reached tens of thousands of armed slaves in the Caliph's service. Other Islamic monarchs and governors also enrolled slaves in their armies.

In the West, particularly in America, slavery is usually thought of as a lack of power as well as a lack of freedom. Slaves in the southern United States were poor and had little control of anything, and were surely kept from gaining power that might threaten their masters. In the Middle East, military slaves often gained great power and riches, but lack of freedom was still the defining quality of slavery. A slave might rise to high status, live in a palace, even have personal control over many slaves himself, but his position, his belongings, and even his life were all legally the property of his master. Unlike the property of a free man, what a slave held might be taken from him at any time. Islamic law, though much less harsh than laws of slavery in other cultures, denied most basic rights to slaves. Kings and lords always had ways to remove the property and lives of free men, but Islamic monarchs had to exercise these often illegal 'rights' circumspectly or face the wrath of the populace and the religious leaders. Not so with slaves, who theoretically were completely in the hands of the rulers.

Middle Eastern monarchs gravitated to military slave systems because they mistrusted the other sources of their power. Troops from the provinces might be more loyal to their local lords than to the Caliph or sultan. Nomad troops kept their allegiance to their tribal chiefs. Administrators might build up personal followings and property at the ruler's expense. Slaves had no local loyalties, because they were separated from their homelands. Their property might be legally seized by their masters at any time. Because of the legal dependence of slaves, the theory was that slaves would be loyal to their masters. In fact, the slaves usually became loyal to their commanders, themselves slaves or freedmen. Often the slaves took over real power in the state, sometimes establishing their own dynasties, as occurred in Egypt in the ninth century and again in the twelfth century, when the military slaves revolted and took control.

Middle Eastern military slaves often held high positions in government. This was particularly true among the Turks. Turkish rulers might themselves have been descended from military slaves, and Turkish rulers kept armies of Turkish slaves. These slaves were generals and advisors, as well as lowly soldiers. The Great Seljuks had a particularly successful system of military slavery. Slaves often led Seljuk armies. The Seljuk's slaves also remained loyal to their masters when free Turkish nomads rebelled. High positions of state were given to slaves, including service as official tutors for the children of the sultans. This position gave them great influence at court.

The tradition of military and administrative slaves passed to the Ottomans from the Great Seljuks through the Rum Seljuks. The first two Ottoman sultans made use of slaves as commanders and soldiers, but the Ottoman state slave system formally began under Murat I. Tradition and law gave the sultan one-fifth of all booty taken by his troops. Murat took much of his one-fifth in the form of soldiers captured in battle. These were organized into 'new troops' (in Turkish, *yeni çeri*) or janissaries. Another method of recruiting imperial slaves was to take into the Ottoman palace sons of rulers and lords from conquered or vassal lands. Along with the most qualified of the captured soldiers, these were trained for government and placed in high positions. Bayezit I developed this system most fully, sending slaves out as governors and commanders in the provinces and granting them lands to support themselves. Murat II expanded the system. However, appointments in the central administration, later including the treasury and grand vezirate, remained in the hands of freeborn Turks. It was only in the reign of Mehmet II that this changed and imperial slaves began to occupy key positions in the central government.

The efficacy of the slave system for the Ottomans caused them to expand it beyond the numbers obtainable from captives. A system of child-levy or child-tax (*devşirme*, 'collection') was developed, probably begun in the reign of Bayezit I and conclusively established in the reign of Murat II. Children, usually Christians, were taken by the Ottomans, converted to Islam, taught Turkish language and customs, and trained as soldiers and later administrators. These *devşirme* soon became the prime source for members of the sultan's slave army and slave administrators. (In later chapters, the term *devşirme* is used to describe the class of slave soldiers and administrators. The system is described in more detail in Chapter 4.) Together, the slaves of the sultan were called *kapı kulları*, 'slaves of the gate'. In common with Oriental monarchies, the Ottomans held that the gate leading to the throne was a symbol for the sultanate.

Native-born Turks: the Turkish notables and the Çandarlı family

By the end of the fourteenth century, the transformation of the Turks from nomads to a settled population was already well under way. The descendents of the central Asian nomads had been in Anatolia for centuries; naturally many of them had become settled, taking up farming and trade. Those Anatolian, and later Balkan, natives who had become Turks through adoption of Islam and Turkish culture simply remained as farmers or town dwellers and never were nomads. From settlement and conversion, Anatolia had become Turkish. Now the sultans began to transform Turkish demography and military power further by settling the Turkish nomad soldiers, using a concept similar to the *ikta* of the Great Seljuks. Leaders of Turkish nomad soldiers and descendents of old tribal chieftains were given grants of land called *timar*s (to be described in detail in Chapter Four). *Timar*s were tax-free grants of land, the proceeds of which supported Turkish leaders and their men until the sultan needed them for battle. The sultans particularly picked for Turkish settlement regions where the population was likely to resist Ottoman rule. One can theorize that the nomads themselves saw that the business of nomad raiding was less and less likely to be a long-term career. As the Ottoman Empire began to reach geographical limits in Europe and come up against strong enemies there, as will be seen below, the old forms of nomad expansion became less possible. The nomads were undoubtedly also changed by extended contact with settled society. Perhaps the lure of a warm house and a fire on a winter's night was a factor in the acceptance of this new way of life. Whatever the reason, the sultans were successful in settling the nomads.

The remaining true nomads were increasingly pushed to the borders of the empire, where they raided against the Ottomans' enemies. Both geographically and politically, the nomads were marginalized. They were never again of great importance in the Ottoman state. By sedentarizing the nomads the Ottomans finally overcame the curse of the Seljuks – they were able to keep the power of the Turks in the army, but end the nomad depredations that always threatened civilized society and, more important to the government, tax-collection.

Those who led the settled Turkish soldiers, the Turkish notables, held authority in the state. Their power passed from their position as nomad leaders to that of 'generals' of settled troops, but they retained it. One family, the Çandarlı, came to personify their authority.

The Çandarlı family were members of the religious hierarchy, the *ulema*. It was natural for the Ottomans to take their first administrators from among the Muslim religious scholars, if for no other reason than that these were the men who were educated. Moreover, the *ulema* were also those who best knew the Holy Law and were allowed by Islam to apply its provisions to the affairs of men. A Muslim state was constrained to act within the provisions of the Holy Law, and a Muslim ruler of necessity kept on his staff learned scholars who could find the explications of the law that were most favourable to the ruler's wishes. Çandarlı Hayrettin was a *kadi*, a religious judge, when Murat I put him in charge of both the administration and the army, a position that was later to be called Grand Vezir. He was as much a general as an administrator, as was the case with most Ottoman leaders. After his father's death, Hayrettin's son, Ali, served as Grand Vezir for Murat I, then for Bayezit I.

It was reasonable for high religious leaders to ally themselves with the Turkish notables and to represent their interests at court. Both groups were made up of freeborn Muslims, and the high *ulema* were also warriors who held *timars* from the sultan. There was intermarriage between the two groups, and the Çandarlı themselves were Turks and related to the notables. While politics in the Ottoman court were never simple, and alliances between various groups and individuals were made and broken, the Çandarlı generally espoused the cause of the notables against that of the royal slaves and Christian vassals. They were forced to accept Bayezit as sultan because his supporters had assassinated the only other viable claimant to the throne, Bayezit's brother Yakup. Çandarlı Ali and his followers urged Bayezit not to attack Anatolia, but to concentrate on conquest in Europe. Confident after his victories, he did not need to follow their advice.

During the interregnum, Çandarlı support went from one claimant to another, choosing the prince who would best support the cause of the Turkish notables and stand against Bayezit's innovations. Çandarlı Ali died in the service of Prince Süleyman. His brother İbrahim first supported Süleyman, but turned against him when Süleyman became increasingly close to the *kapı kulları*. The same scenario was acted out with Prince Musa. Çandarlı İbrahim became his Grand Vezir, but plotted against him when he too began to depend more on the *kapı kulları*. İbrahim finally supported Mehmet, who triumphed and made İbrahim his second Grand Vezir (from 1421 until İbrahim died in 1429). İbrahim's advice to Mehmet was a counsel of caution. He advocated a pacific policy toward Anatolia and cementing Ottoman rule in Europe. It was no coincidencece that this was to the advantage of the Turkish notables' holdings in Europe and the opening of new lands for their occupation.

As members of the *ulema* the Çandarlı may have felt a religious impulse to stand against what might have been viewed as the 'Christianization' of the Ottoman administration. The ascendancy of Christian advisors and once-Christian slave soldiers under Bayezit cannot have appealed to their religious sentiments. The Çandarlı and the notables also turned firmly against the nomad tradition of preference for a weak central authority. The Turkish notables began to favour a strong Ottoman state once it became obvious that a strong state was to their advantage. An empire advancing into Europe would provide more lands for the notables to claim as *timars*, thus increasing their power. Strength was also necessary to preserve what they already had. As long as the Çandarlı and the notables were in charge of the central administration they could direct the state toward their own interests.

Conflict and cooperation

As will be seen below, the struggle for political power in the Ottoman central administration was eventually won by the *kapı kulları*. The Janissary Corps became the best standing army in Europe and *devşirme* administrators took over the management of the state machinery. European observers of the Ottoman Empire often categorized the dichotomy between the Turkish notables and the *kapı kulları* as a contest between Turks and those who were born Christians. In fact, this distinction is neither very helpful nor completely accurate. The *devşirme*, who became the dominant then virtually the only members of the *kapı kulları*, were just as much Turks as were the other Turks of the Balkans and Anatolia. Their parents may have been local Christians, but so were the ancestors of many of the others. Conversion, as described above, had made it impossible to trace the Turks' lineage solely to Central Asia. As with the other Turks, the language of the *devşirme* was Turkish, as were their customs. Contemporaries spoke of the dedication of the *devşirme* to Islam. In short, they were Turks.

The conflicts between the Turkish notables and the *kapı kulları* can easily be overstated. It is true that the two groups generally had differing interests. It is also true that conflicts among the Ottoman leaders were often personal, not 'class' conflicts. Leaders were very capable of making alliances with members of antagonistic groups for personal benefit, and groups came together in defence of their most common interest, the continuance of the Empire. Individuals frequently sided with those who could help them or who they believed could help the Empire, despite underlying antagonisms. Çandarlı İbrahim, for instance, was friendly with the Byzantines, to mutual advantage. Through his office as Grand Vezir, Çandarlı Halil exercised considerable influence on the Janissary Corps, the primary armed force of the *kapı kulları*. The best example of cooperation in the Empire's interest will be seen below when common interest brought the leaders together in supporting Murat II's return to power to face a crusading army.

Mehmet I and Murat II

Mehmet's armies returned the Empire's borders roughly to their position immediately after Bayezit's victory at Nicopolis. Some of the European vassals had regained independence or taken territory during the interregnum. Now the Ottomans reclaimed land and renewed vassalage. Raids into Wallachia forced that kingdom to accept Ottoman sovereignty. The Ottoman position in Albania was restored, although this was mainly a matter of occupying key fortresses, not ruling the country. The Ottomans raided Hungary, as well, but more to forestall Hungarian conquests than to take new territory. In Asia, the Ottomans regained most of western Anatolia. Mehmet brought the Ottoman possessions in Anatolia roughly to where they had been before Bayezit launched his fatal and final conquests there. Mehmet's reign was too occupied with survival and renewal to attempt much centralization. In Europe, the vassal system remained largely intact, because it had taken wars just to retain the status quo. However, in Anatolia Mehmet did manage to bring previous vassal principalities under direct Ottoman administration.

In long-term implications for the Empire, the most important activity of Mehmet I's reign was the defeat of rebels who represented the old nomad tradition. One of these rebels was a heterodox religious leader, Şeyh Bedreddin. By standing for the mystical religious impulses of the Turks and against the concept of a settled, centralized empire, Şeyh Bedreddin greatly appealed to nomads in Anatolia and to nomads who served the Ottomans as raiders on their European borders. As Bedreddin's followers revolted in Anatolia and the Balkans, another rebel appeared in Europe. This rebel claimed to be Bayezit's son Mustafa, who had been captured with his father by Tamerlane, taken to Tamerlane's capital in Samarkand, and later released. Although the warmth of the reception given him in Ottoman Anatolia and Europe make it likely that he was indeed Mustafa, son of Bayezit, his claim was not accepted by the sultan's followers, who called him Düzme Mustafa ('the False Mustafa'). Düzme Mustafa's following was considerable. While Mehmet's forces fought elsewhere, Mustafa was even able to occupy the Ottoman capital of Edirne, where he was declared sultan in 1419. Mehmet was faced with two simultaneous revolts. Both were defeated, with great difficulty, and Bedreddin was executed. Nevertheless, the revolts showed that there were powerful forces that stood against the new Ottoman system. Although his rebellion was defeated, Düzme Mustafa escaped capture, fleeing to safety in Constantinople, where the Byzantine emperor gave him refuge. He reappeared to plague Mehmet's successor.

The reign of Murat II

Having restored much of the Ottoman Empire, Mehmet I died in 1421. His son, Murat II, was faced with a continuation of the Düzme Mustafa revolt as soon as he took the throne. The Byzantines, who could only profit from Ottoman confusion, released Mustafa, who once again began his revolt successfully and took Edirne easily. The battle between Mustafa and Murat was also a battle between the nomads and the Turkish notables. The latter were committed to a centralized state, because such a state best represented their own interests. The nomads wanted a state dedicated almost exclusively to war, because this would bring them booty. Murat went to Anatolia to raise soldiers. Not satisfied with control of Ottoman Europe, Mustafa followed Murat to Anatolia, where Mustafa was defeated. He fled to Edirne, where he was perhaps killed by Murat's forces in 1422 (the historical record is confused on the subject of his death). This was the last gasp of nomad power in the Ottoman Empire.

The reign of Sultan Murat II was essentially one of consolidation, not conquest. His military achievements were victories against those who would dismember the state. In Anatolia, he managed to defeat enemies and make small territorial gains. Most important of his successes was the reduction of Karaman to vassalage. The continuing threat from Tamerlane's son, Shah-Rukh, kept Murat from seizing Karaman altogether. In Europe, Murat experienced more difficulties.

The major Ottoman enemies in Europe were Hungary and Venice. In the early fifteenth century, Venice had a significant maritime empire. Its commercial might outstripped that of its rival, Genoa. Venetian land holdings included Adriatic islands and land outposts on the Adriatic, the island of Cyprus, and regions of southern Greece, but it was its navy that made Venice a formidable opponent. Venice's wealth and seaborne mobility made it a power in the region. Ultimately its possessions and trade monopolies would be threatened by any land power that could conquer Venetian colonies and deny it trade rights. Therefore, the Venetians were Ottoman enemies. They had defeated the fledging navy of Mehmet I in a brief and disastrous battle in 1416 and began an extended war against the Ottomans in 1425. Hungary was an expansionist land power, much like the Ottomans. It held part of Romania, Transylvania, and wished to take what remained. It also envisaged expansion through Croatia to the Adriatic. Both were regions coveted by the Ottomans as well. Therefore, the Hungarians were Ottoman enemies. Also, whether or not they foresaw the possibility at the time, both Venice and Hungary were geographically close enough to the Ottomans to be conquered themselves someday.

At first, the Ottomans were triumphant against the Venetians and Hungarians. Serbia had renounced vassalage to the Ottomans in favour of Hungary, but Murat invaded Serbia in 1428 and restored it to Ottoman suzereignty. A Venetian-sponsored revolt in Macedonia was defeated and, when Venetian possessions in Greece were threatened, Venice made peace in 1431. All looked well, but the Ottoman Empire was about to be nearly overpowered by its enemies.

In 1432, the new ruler of Wallachia, Vlad Drakul, backed by the Hungarians, declared independence from the Ottomans, and allied himself with the Hungarians against the Ottomans. Murat was occupied with threats in Anatolia. Murat's Anatolian lands were still nominally held in vassalage from Shah-Rukh, who ruled in Iran and seemed likely to reassert his actual control of Anatolia. In 1435, Shah-Rukh indeed invaded Anatolia. Murat was forced to be ready for him, although they never went to war, and Murat did what he could to avoid war by leaving Karaman independent. Nevertheless, the Ottomans' attention was necessarily taken from Europe. In Europe, the Hungarians began to test Ottoman strength. In alliance with the Serbs, the Hungarian Jànos Hunyadi inflicted major defeats on the Ottomans in 1442, killing tens of thousands of Ottoman soldiers at the battles of

Hermanstadt and Vazağ (Jalomitcha). Aided by Crusaders from Europe, Hunyadi conquered as far as western Bulgaria in 1443. Although historians have often attempted to justify Murat, it is hard not to describe his next actions as capitulation to his enemies. He signed a treaty with Hunyadi in 1444 that enlarged Serbia and much reduced its terms of vassalage. Wallachia became a Hungarian vassal. Murat further agreed to remove the main Ottoman army to Anatolia, making it much harder to defend Ottoman Europe from what he must have known would be fresh attacks by Hungarians, Serbs, and Wallachians. Murat then abdicated his throne, naming his son Mehmet to succeed him. Mehmet was then twelve years old.

Only a man so thoroughly sick of war and rule that he did not care what occurred after him, or one who was so sure he had failed that anything would be better than him, could have left the empire in such peril. Mehmet was undoubtedly a genius, and was well liked by many in the upper class of rulers, particularly the *devşirme*, but he was still only a twelve-year-old boy, and it is impossible to think of him as either knowing enough of politics or of generalship to save the empire. Murat probably expected his own trusted advisors to actually govern. Nevertheless, an effective sultan was needed, if only as a rallying point for soldiers' loyalty. There is some evidence that Murat suffered what would today be called depression, and mental illness may indeed explain his actions.

The result of Murat's abdication was disaster. Internal conflict flared between the Grand Vezir, Çandarlı Halil, who favoured Murat's peaceful programme, and Mehmet's teachers and advisors, who favoured conquest. Hunyadi's successes against the Turks had convinced many in Europe that the Muslim threat to Christendom could be ended. The Pope preached a Crusade. Crusaders from Poland and Germany gathered in Hungary in summer of 1444.

The Ottoman leadership must have been in a state of near-panic as the Crusaders gathered. After all, Hunyadi and his allies had defeated the Ottomans even without the added force of the Crusader knights. All sides of the ruling class, even the *devşirme* who had supported Mehmet, saw that an experienced hand was needed. They approached Murat and he agreed to lead the Ottoman army against the Crusade.

Murat still needed to reach the Crusaders. He was in Bursa and most of the Ottoman army was in western Anatolia. In order to gain favour and trade concessions and because Venice was on the other side, the Genoese were willing to help the Ottomans. They provided boats to ferry the Ottoman army across from Anatolia to Europe. In September, the Crusaders and Hungarians invaded Ottoman territory and moved east toward the Black Sea. Murat moved north. They met at Varna (November 10, 1444). Rallied by the old sultan, the Turks won. The king of Hungary was killed, Crusaders died in great numbers, and Hunyadi barely escaped.

Murat still hoped to retire, but the Çandarlı and Turkish notables finally convinced him that he was indispensable to the Empire. He resumed his sultanate in 1446 and ruled until he died in 1451. Murat seems to have warmed to, or at least resigned himself to the military duties of a sultan. The remainder of his sultanate was spent consolidating the victory at Varna by bringing the Balkans back into subjugation. Hunyadi organized another crusade in 1448. It too was defeated, at the second battle of Kosova (October 17–19, 1448). Sultan Mehmet had been sent back to his tutors for more training in statecraft. He finally succeeded to the throne when his father died in 1451.

The policies of Murat II

Murat II continued his father's policy of cementing Ottoman power but attempted to balance power within the government. He renewed Bayezit's system of slave soldiers, first taking conquered soldiers into his slave army, then training them to become cavalry, infantry, and artillery corps. Added to the captured soldiers were troops from the *devşirme* child-levy, reconstituted by Murat. Murat armed the new corps with gunpowder weapons, making them a formidable force. His concept was one of balance. A strong slave army balanced the power of a strong traditional army. The leaders of each would fear the other, leaving the sultan to play one off against the other and retain his personal authority. The balance between the two forces was an instrument in increasing central control.

Murat II may be considered as a peaceful man who was forced to make war. He was personally more concerned with the internal workings of his empire and his court. Under him, the Ottoman court increasingly began to resemble the great courts of past Middle Eastern rulers. Edirne increased greatly in size and economic power. The city took on the aspect of an Islamic capital, despite a large Christian population, and Murat built a great *medrese* and other distinctly Islamic buildings. Murat was concerned with the economic infrastructure of the Empire, building bridges, for example. He and his officials were patrons of men of art and letters. In religious matters, he favoured mystical Islam. Murat built a large *tekke* (lodge) in Edirne for the sufis (dervishes) who followed the path of Jelal al-Din Rumi (the Mevlevi dervishes) and contributed to the support of dervishes throughout the Empire. Mystical leaders (*şeyhs*) came to Edirne from Persia, Transoxania, and Iraq.

While he did not greatly enlarge the empire, Murat II did increase direct Ottoman power over it, bringing some territories in Anatolia under direct control. Bulgaria and most of mainland Greece were also put under central authority. Murat's victories in the two Crusades of Varna and Kosova so weakened the independent power of the remaining Balkan states that within fifty years they too would succumb to direct Ottoman control.

The Ottoman Empire was more and more becoming the sort of centralized empire that had long existed under the Byzantines. At Murat's death most of the empire was under the complete authority of the sultan, with Ottoman tax-collectors, civil servants, and judges, all directed from the Ottoman capital.

Murat II left a unified empire to his son. Unlike most of his predecessors, Mehmet II was able to begin his reign in peace, with an orderly administrative system and a functioning treasury. This fact alone showed that the Ottoman Empire had fundamentally changed since the days of Osman and his nomad followers. Despite ongoing antagonisms, the various forces that made up Ottoman power had combined to create a unified state. Unlike many of the subjects of the Great Seljuk or Rum Seljuk sultans, these Turks were now reasonably united in dedication to preservation of the state. Nothing shows the maturity of the empire as much as the deposition of young sultan Mehmet II. Such situations were not unknown in past Turkish states – a weak sultan, in this case weak only because of youth, but weak nonetheless, and strong advisors and governors. In the past, what could have been expected from such a situation? Either the sultan's advisors would have taken power themselves, ruling through him, or the strong men would have rebelled, perhaps dividing the state into smaller principalities that each of them could rule independently. Yet this is not what happened to the Ottomans. Beset by problems too great for the young sultan to cope with, the leaders of the empire did not rebel or keep Mehmet on the throne but under their control. Instead they called on the old sultan, because he could save the day. In due course, they then accepted the accession of an older, more experienced Mehmet II to the throne. Self-interest? Of course, but self-interest of a high order – the realization that it was in their best interest to save the Empire.

The Ottoman Classical Age, 1446–1566

The Ottoman Classical Age, 1446–1566

The era that spanned the reigns from sultans Mehmet II to Süleyman I is styled the 'apogee' or the 'Classical Age' of the Ottoman Empire. It was during this period of more than a century that the Ottoman Empire became the most powerful state on the earth, stretching from the Atlantic shore of North Africa to the borders of Iran, Austria, Poland, and Russia. For centuries following, the Turks themselves looked on the reigns of Mehmet II, Selim I, and Süleyman the Magnificent as the exemplars of proper rule.

The reign of sultan Mehmet II

To the Turks, sultan Mehmet II is known as Fatih ('the Conqueror'). Because of his conquests and the grandeur of his court, Süleyman is usually described as the greatest of the sultans, but Mehmet II has at least as great a claim on that title. Under him, the Ottoman state became a great centralized and unified empire that rivalled the empires of antiquity in size and power.

The fall of Constantinople

Immediately upon assuming the throne, Mehmet began to plan the conquest of Constantinople. His predecessors had previously laid siege to the city. Indeed, Bayezit might have taken it had not problems with Tamerlane intervened. Mehmet II was most resolute. He had inherited an empire that was strong and unified. Despite opposition, to be seen below, Mehmet was able to bring all of the Empire's power to bear on Constantinople. The city was such a prize that none in the Ottoman ranks could publicly oppose the undertaking.

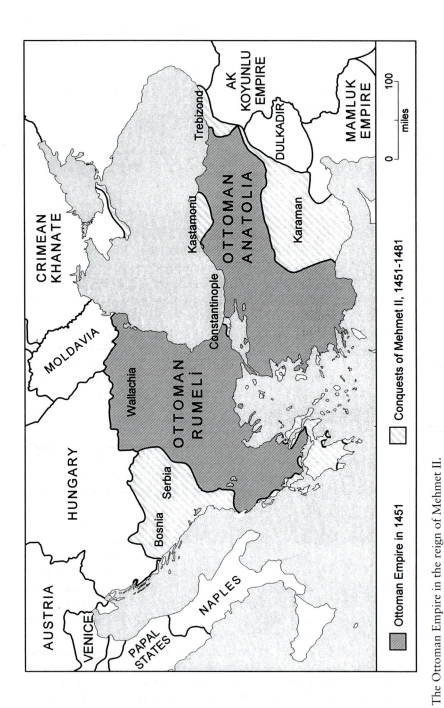

The Ottoman Empire in the reign of Mehmet II.

OTTOMAN ANATOLIA

OTTOMAN RUMELİ

CRIMEAN KHANATE

AK KOYUNLU EMPIRE

MAMLUK EMPIRE

DULKADIR

Karaman

Kastamonu

Trebizond

Constantinople

Wallachia

MOLDAVIA

HUNGARY

AUSTRIA

VENICE

PAPAL STATES

NAPLES

Bosnia

Serbia

0   100
miles

Ottoman Empire in 1451

Conquests of Mehmet II, 1451–1481

The strategic importance of Constantinople for the Turks is obvious. As maps demonstrate, Constantinople sat between Ottoman Europe and Ottoman Anatolia. It commanded the best transport routes between the two. By sea, the city also might impede internal communications and transport, for the sea routes between the eastern Balkans and western Anatolia passed the walls of Constantinople, as did the routes between the rest of Ottoman Europe and northern Anatolia. In the fifteenth century, when the Byzantines were too weak to interfere with the Ottomans, this presented little problem, but the potential difficulties were immense. Constantinople was always a potential rallying ground for anti-Ottoman forces – a potential armed camp, which could be reinforced by sea, in the middle of the Ottoman Empire.

Constantinople was an economic prize. Although it had fallen on hard times, it was still one of the best-situated ports in the world. Much of the trade between Asia and the Mediterranean naturally passed from the Black Sea or the Aegean Sea to Constantinople, then onwards. Land trade from Iran and further afield also came to the city. In the fifteenth century, as always, the real profits were made by the middlemen in trade, and Constantinople was the middleman city *par excellence*. If it were once again a part of a great empire, its profits would be immense.

Harder to analyse, but very real, were the psychological benefits, the prestige, of conquering Constantinople. Muslims had tried and failed to conquer it since soon after the death of the Prophet Muhammad (sieges of 674–78 and 717–18), so its conqueror would truly be a hero who had brought the armies of Islam to previously unattainable heights. Furthermore, the Byzantine Empire was the direct descendent of the Roman Empire. Its rulers styled themselves by right as 'Caesar', and Constantinople was recognized in both the East and the West as the 'new Rome'. Any rulers who desired to be great emperors – the new Caesars – in what had been the Eastern Roman Empire would need Constantinople. The Ottoman sultans aspired to that position. They were, by many standards, upstart rulers, descended neither from the Roman emperors nor the Islamic Caliphs. The prestige they gained from taking 'new Rome' would go far in establishing them as great emperors and as the primary champions of Islam.

Mehmet was aided considerably by the absence of any real threat to his plans. The Europeans were still occupied with other things: the last gasp of the Hundred Years' War, the Wars of the Roses, the culmination of the *reconquista* in Spain and Cosimo de Medici building his family's fortunes in Italy. Germany and Russia were too internally divided at the time to aid anyone. Serbia and Hungary, the former barely surviving as a state, were in no position to march through the Ottoman Balkans to aid Constantinople. In the East, the campaigns of Murat II had removed any immediate threat that might have drawn Mehmet's forces from Constantinople's walls. The only countries that could have offered practical assistance to the Byzantines were the Italian naval powers – Venice and Genoa. But Venice had recently signed a new trade treaty with the Ottomans and had not done well in its war with the Ottomans in 1425–31. Genoese merchants in Galata, the suburb of Constantinople in which European traders lived, had declared their neutrality, but were in fact under Ottoman control. They were coming to an accommodation with those who were to be their new masters. Only a few Italian ships tried successfully to run the Ottoman blockade of the city. Perhaps the Renaissance was too seductive for the Italians to leave home for long. Constantinople was on its own.

The Ottoman army began the siege of Constantinople in spring of 1453. In addition to the usual provisioning of the army, special plans had been made prior to the siege. A fleet had been built to blockade the city by sea and a castle, Rumeli Hisar (the 'European Castle') built on the Bosphorus to keep provisions from reaching the city by sailing down the Bosphorus from the Black Sea. Special siege cannons were built. In all, the Ottoman force was overwhelming. The wonder is that Constantinople held out for months, until May of 1453. The population had sunk so low that large parts of the city were deserted, help from Europe was negligible, and the defenders fought against one of the greatest armies on earth. Part of the reason for the stubborn Byzantine defence was the strong walls of the city, part the determination of the people. Nevertheless, on May 29, 1453, Constantinople fell to the Ottomans. The last Byzantine Emperor, Constantine XI, died in the fighting. The great church built by the Emperor Justinian, Haghia Sophia, became a mosque.

After his troops had pillaged what remained in the city, Mehmet set upon a policy of conciliation and rebuilding. Following Islamic law, Mehmet allowed the continuation of the Greek Orthodox Church, under the authority of a new Patriarch of Constantinople. The city was rebuilt by workmen brought from around the Ottoman Empire. Populations of Christians and Muslims were transported to live in and rebuild the new Ottoman capital.

Mehmet built two palaces in the newly conquered city. The first was built immediately after the conquest, in the centre of the city, but its position was considered too exposed and its size too limited. In 1465, his artisans began construction of a new palace on the point of land where the Sea of Marmara turned into the Golden Horn. At first prosaically called the New Palace, it later took on the name Topkapı ('cannon gate'), and was to remain the seat of the Ottoman sultans until near the end of the Empire. Separated from the city by high walls, on a hill overlooking the sea, the Topkapı Palace became a city unto itself, with thousands of inhabitants. There the sultan began to rule as an emperor removed from the ordinary life of the city.

Mehmet and officials of his state fulfilled their duties as Muslims by building mosques, schools, and other charitable institutions in Istanbul. All

Muslims who had the means were expected to contribute to the poor and to the upkeep of the fabric of society. The Ottoman concept of government did not extend to much that the modern world considers to be the province of the state. As will be seen in the next chapter, most matters of civil and criminal and civil justice, education, and welfare were left to religious communities. In practice, this meant that wealthy members of the Christian, Jewish, and Muslim communities built dining halls for the poor, hospitals, etc. They also provided public welfare necessities, such as drinking water fountains and baths. Mehmet II was a Muslim, so charity was expected of him, all the more because he had much to give. His ancestors had provided all manner of public buildings, soup kitchens, mosques, prayer halls, and other buildings and services for the public good, particularly in the old capitals of Bursa and Edirne. Now Mehmet put his own charitable donations to use in rebuilding the city. For example, his main contribution to the religious and charitable life of Istanbul was the erection of buildings that served both society and Faith. The grandest of these was the Mosque of the Conqueror, built in 1462–70. Next to the converted church of Haghia Sophia (in Turkish, Ayasofya), it was the grandest mosque in the city, rising on a hill and flanked by numerous outbuildings. Unlike Ayasofya, Mehmet's mosque was a distinctly Islamic structure, built to fit the needs of the Muslim community. The outbuildings housed schools for training Islamic scholars and judges, dormitories for students, an elementary school, libraries, kitchens to feed both the students and the poor, and a hospital for the poor.

Mehmet ordered his government's officials and other rich men to follow his charitable example. Each was expected to emulate his master, even if on a smaller scale. All over the formerly Byzantine city, distinctly Muslim buildings and institutions sprang up. Each new large mosque, with its attendant soup kitchens or schools, became a focus for settlement and shops, including the shops built by Mehmet and his followers, where the rent was dedicated to the support of the mosques and charitable institutions. Neighbourhoods grew up around the new institutions.

The charitable impulse was politically constructive. As a proper Islamic monarch, Mehmet II would undoubtedly have contributed heavily to Islamic charities even if he had not taken Constantinople, but the conquest of the city provided the opportunity for practical benefit as well as divine blessing. Faced with a devastated city that he wished once again to be a grand capital, Mehmet turned virtue to practical purpose. The grand mosques might stimulate prayer among the believers, the learned might benefit from the new schools, and the poor obviously gained from the free food and health care provided in Mehmet's grand new buildings. However, the buildings and charitable institutions also drew in skilled workers to build the mosques, shopkeepers to man the businesses created to support the charities, and probably even the occasional beggar who realized that

71

benefits were better in Istanbul. The city grew and developed a new Islamic focus. The mosques, schools, libraries, hospitals, and palaces built by Mehmet and his vezirs gave an Islamic character to the city. By the end of Mehmet's reign, the city had regained its past grandeur, but it was now an Islamic grandeur – it had become the greatest city of Islam.

Political power

Mehmet II had not forgotten his brief first reign as sultan, before the return of his father to the throne. In the interest of peaceful succession to the throne, he had at first retained in office those who had caused him to relinquish the throne in 1446. Çandarlı Halil, who had orchestrated Mehmet's downfall, remained Grand Vezir. Halil and the Turkish notables opposed Mehmet's plans for the conquest of Constantinople. However, because Mehmet was the only possible adult claimant to the throne, they could only hinder, not stop, his plans. Mehmet personally took advice from the *kapı kulları*, the *devşirme*, who supported his plans, and bided his time.

Immediately after the conquest of Constantinople, drawing on the power and prestige he had gained from his conquest, Mehmet removed Halil from office, seized the Çandarlı properties, and imprisoned leading members of the Çandarlı family. The Turkish notables and old guard could do nothing to stop him. Mehmet's prestige had made him impervious to attack. No one could threaten the position of the Conqueror who by his victory had become the leading ruler in the Islamic world. Confiscations of land from the Turkish notables and wholesale diminution of their position followed. The government positions of many of the Turkish notables were taken by the officials of the *devşirme*, led by a new Grand Vezir, Mahmud Paşa, drawn from their ranks. Mehmet relied on those who had supported him, the *devşirme*, and remembered that the Turkish notables had not been in his camp. He felt that the *devşirme* had been trained to personal loyalty to the sultan, so he could trust them to carry out his wishes. The centre of power in the Ottoman administration had shifted once again.

The fall of Constantinople and position of the Ottoman sultan as first ruler in the Islamic world brought changes to the Ottoman internal balance of power. For a time there was little to fear from the predominance of one group in the government. Mehmet's personal prestige as the Conqueror meant that his will could not be challenged. Internally, he kept any one leader or one group of the *devşirme* from claiming too much power by giving powerful posts to a number of *devşirme* leaders so that they would compete among themselves. The Turkish notables remained, although their power was lessened. Nevertheless, the *devşirme* as a group were in the ascendancy.

Mehmet ruled through Grand Vezirs, the chief administrative officers of the Empire. After Çandarlı Halil's fall from power, all but one of the grand vezirs were from the *devşirme*. The Grand Vezir was in charge of the administration and the armed forces, but the sultan personally commanded the Janissaries. The chief financial officer of the Empire, the *defterdar*, though supervised by the Grand Vezir, also reported directly to the sultan. Mehmet thus kept personal control of the most important forces of government – military power and finance. Lesser officials were generally drawn from the ranks of the *devşirme*. This included governors and provincial officials who carried central authority into regions where local Turkish notables would otherwise have been in control. Administrative practice was written into administrative laws (*kanun*s) and codified into collections of imperial law (*kanunname*).

As was to be seen in the reigns of later sultans, there was an inherent danger in relying on only one power base. A ruler with two or more military groups at his command could play off one against the other and keep his own power by encouraging rivalries amongst his followers. Mehmet's personal strength, and that of his descendants Selim I and Süleyman, however, was so great that he could give power to one group, the *devşirme*, and still retain control.

Mehmet II kept control of the *devşirme* and the *devşirme* fighting force, the Janissaries, through his personal position and a good political sense. As the most powerful leader in the Islamic world, the conqueror of Constantinople, and a great general, Mehmet's personal position was unassailable. No one laughed when he called himself Caesar. Opposing Mehmet meant opposing the Sword of Islam, a daunting prospect. It helped that as soon as Mehmet became sultan he had his younger brother, the other possible claimant to the throne, strangled. Thus his position helped him to keep potential opponents in check. In addition, Mehmet kept the loyalty of his followers by treating them well when they obeyed and harshly when they did not. On his accession he ruthlessly put down a Janissary revolt, then greatly increased the pay of loyal Janissaries. He organized the Janissary Corps into a 'rapid reaction' force that was more powerful than the forces behind any rebel who might oppose the sultan. Janissaries were given control of key fortresses and Janissary forces stationed in main cities. Since revolt was obviously doomed from the start it did not occur. Mehmet was so successful in securing his personal power that there was no real internal opposition after the first years of his reign.

Mehmet II and his Christian subjects

The heart of Greek Orthodoxy fell into Muslim hands upon Mehmet II's conquest of Constantinople. Mehmet seized churches, the visible sign of the Christianity of the city, and converted them into mosques. He did not, however, act against the Church as such. Islamic law commanded respect for the religious rights of Christians. There were also practical reasons for toleration. Christians were a majority of the population of his empire. A tolerant policy was likely to result in civil peace and resignation to Ottoman rule. The machinery of the Greek Church also afforded a method of administrative control of his Christian subjects. Even though authority in the Greek Orthodox Church had always been more decentralized than in the Western Church, in Byzantine times the Church had been led from Constantinople. Ecclesiastical operations had been severely dislocated by the Turkish conquests. Mehmet's policy was to return authority to the centre, to give the Patriarch of Constantinople heightened authority over the Church, and to use the Church as a means to exercise his own power.

Mehmet began his policy of toleration by showing favour to the church. The rules of Islam that enjoined freedom of worship were strictly adhered to. The Greek clergy were exempted from taxes and left in charge of Church administration. In fact, church authorities were given greater powers than they were ever allowed under the Byzantine emperors. By imperial order, the Patriarch was made head of the Orthodox community in the Empire. The Church was given the right to levy taxes on Christians to support itself and its endeavours, which included schools, welfare, and civic activities, as well as churches. Greek courts were given authority over matters of personal law, such as marriage and inheritance, and eventually took over civil cases between Christian litigants. A system developed in which Orthodox Christians were dependent on Church authority in matters both civil and religious.

Mehmet began the new ecclesiastical system by naming a respected scholar, Gennadius, as Patriarch. In order to centralize the power of the Church the sultan brought the Ottoman Slavs into the Greek Orthodox fold. Serbs and Bulgarians had both declared their churches to be independent when Byzantine power declined. Now Mehmet abolished the separate Serbian patriarchate. (The patriarchate of the Bulgarians had already ceased to function in 1394.) He envisaged one church structure for all the Christians of the Empire, largely independent, but under the ultimate control of the sultan. The Patriarch was made an official of the state and he and his officials acted as arms of the Ottoman government. It was a system that suited both the sultan and the churchmen.

After the fall of Constantinople

From 1453 until his death in 1481 Mehmet intensified the drive to centralize rule over the Empire. In order to avert any return of Byzantine power, Mehmet set upon the eradication of the last vestiges of Byzantine rule in Europe and Anatolia: the independent Byzantine state of the Morea in southern Greece was occupied by 1460, as was the Byzantine Empire of Trebizond (Trabzon) in 1461.

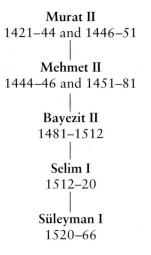

Murat II
1421–44 and 1446–51

Mehmet II
1444–46 and 1451–81

Bayezit II
1481–1512

Selim I
1512–20

Süleyman I
1520–66

After the fall of Constantinople Mehmet cemented Ottoman control over the Balkans. By 1459 he had ended Serbian autonomy and put Serbia under direct Ottoman rule. Bosnia was occupied and incorporated into the Empire in 1463. Unable conclusively to defeat the Hungarians, Mehmet nevertheless kept them at bay and neutralized their threat to the Ottoman territories.

From the standpoint of future events, among the most significant of Mehmet's actions were a series of diplomatic and military conflicts between the Ottomans and the principality of Moldavia from 1460 to 1476. Mehmet was unable to completely defeat the forces of Stephen the Great of Moldavia, although Stephen was neutralized as a threat to the Ottoman domains. The lasting significance of the Ottoman campaigns in the north Black Sea region lay in the relations the Ottomans forged with the Crimean Tatars. The Tatars, Turkish-speaking descendants of the conquerors of what today is southern Ukraine and southwest Russia, could not stand on their own against Poland, Moldavia, and Muscovy. The Ottomans, in turn, needed the Tatars for their north Black Sea ports (see below) and for military support against their common enemies to the north. In 1475, the Tatars accepted Ottoman sovereignty. They remained most valuable Ottoman vassals until 1774, providing some of the best fighting men in the Ottoman army and standing for centuries against increasing Russian encroachment.

Mehmet II met his greatest challenge in a war with Venice that lasted from 1463 to 1479. Fearful that Ottoman conquests would threaten their hold on trade and perhaps Venice itself, the Venetians attacked the Ottomans in the Morea in 1463, seizing territory recently conquered by the Ottomans. While the Ottomans were able to retake the Morea in 1467, the sea power and the diplomacy of the Venetians remained a great threat.

Only by creating his own powerful fleet was Mehmet able to protect the Dardanelles and the sea path to Istanbul from the Venetian navy. In 1472, the Venetians entered into a treaty with Uzun Hasan, the leader of the Ak Koyunlu Turks, who ruled eastern Anatolia and Iran, promising to provide the Ak Koyunlu with weapons and support. Mehmet had defeated the Karaman principality in 1468, finally ending the independence of an old Ottoman enemy, but forces loyal to the Karaman *bey* remained in the Taurus mountains. They joined with Uzun Hasan in a grand attack westward in 1472, destroying Ottoman cities and reaching as far as Akşehir in western Anatolia. Mehmet responded with the entire Ottoman army, chased the Ak Koyunlu army into eastern Anatolia, and defeated Uzun Hasan in 1473. By 1474, Ottoman forces had liquidated the last resistance of the Karaman forces. Mehmet then turned his attention to Venice, which could not stand alone. When Ottoman raiders reached the outskirts of their city in 1478, Venice sued for peace. Venice gave up cities on the Adriatic, islands in the Aegean, and a tribute of 10,000 ducats a year, but was allowed to trade in the Ottoman Empire.

To repay the Pope for his support of the Venetians and, perhaps, because he saw the conquest of Rome as final proof of Ottoman status as a world empire, Mehmet sent his army against Rome. Ottoman forces took the city of Otranto in southern Italy in 1480, advanced northward, and would likely have taken Rome. The Pope certainly anticipated Ottoman success; he prepared to flee to France. However, the Ottoman invaders returned home after learning of Mehmet's death in 1481.

The sultan and the finances of the Empire

Mehmet II was not afraid to make enemies. He carried out a ruthless policy of taking the finances of the Empire into his own hands. Many were hurt by his policies. Their complaints, just and unjust, could be ignored by a powerful sultan. At different times during his reign Mehmet withdrew all coinage and exchanged old coins for new at five-sixths of their old value. Merchants and the thrifty suffered. Those who hoarded old coins were hunted out and their silver confiscated. Monopolies in essential goods such as salt were sold to individuals at great profit to the state but higher prices to consumers. Customs duties were raised throughout the Empire. Tariff exemptions which had been granted to Europeans were discontinued.

The most contentious financial exactions of Mehmet's administration were aimed at those who had held high position in the Empire. In the time of previous sultans, conquered lands had been seized by Turks, particularly by the Turkish notables. The legal status of these lands was questionable. Some had been granted by the sultans as *timar* lands, theoretically the property of the state, but converted to private ownership by those with enough power to claim them. Mehmet claimed that all conquered lands were the property of the sultan. The legal situation was complicated by the fact that much of the land had been converted to *vakıf* (Arabic, *waqf*), pious foundations. These foundations were a system sanctified by Islamic Law in which owners could set aside income-producing properties for good purposes, such as the support of mosques or hospitals, paying no taxes. They were beneficial to the donor, because the grantor could name his family as salaried administrators of the grant in perpetuity, providing support for the grantor's family forever. Many *vakıf*s were also in the hands of the *ulema*, the Islamic religious leaders, who were paid the administrators' salaries. Their schools and mosques were supported by the grants.

Drawing on his personal power, Mehmet ignored the complaints of both the notables and the *ulema*. His officials examined deeds, denied claims, and seized lands, regardless of whether they had been given over to charitable purposes. Undoubtedly, many of the lands taken by the sultan belonged to Mehmet's enemies, whatever the validity of their deeds. Most of the seizures were given over to the sultan's supporters as *timars*. Old Turkish families and religious leaders were harmed, and they were powerful enemies.

While Mehmet's policies hurt many, they did aid the finances of the state. Conquests were a tremendous drain on the treasury. Land that supported soldiers was more important to the state than land that supported charitable purposes, especially since much of the proceeds of the property went to the support of its administrators. In addition, the increase in customs dues and seizure of properties did target much that had previously been unfair or illegal. Why, for example, should the Genoese pay no customs dues while others, including Ottoman subjects, paid? It can surely be argued that charging higher customs duties and reducing the value of savings by exchanging coins paid for more soldiers to patrol the roads, made commerce safer, and ultimately was better for merchants and the society. Modern economists might have preferred a balanced overall increase in taxation to Mehmet's policies, which selectively hurt certain groups, but Mehmet II was not a modern economist.

Mehmet II left behind him a much altered and centralized Ottoman Empire. The Empire had almost complete control up to what might be called the natural borders of the Balkans – the River Danube and the River Sava (the north of Bosnia). South of that border only a few pockets of non-Ottoman land remained. Within the Ottoman Balkans the vassal system was effectively destroyed. Albania and Serbia were Ottoman provinces. Hungary and the Romanian principalities of Wallachia and Moldavia were neutralized. In Anatolia, the last independent Turkish principalities, including Karaman, were absorbed, bringing the Ottoman Empire to approximately the borders held by Bayezit I before Tamerlane's incursion. Of greatest importance, Byzantine Constantinople had ceased to exist as a wedge between Ottoman Europe and Asia and a focus for European crusades.

Mehmet seemed to realize in the final years of his rule that power had shifted too much into the hands of the *devşirme*. His last Grand Vezir, appointed in 1477, was a Turk from the central Anatolian city of Konya, Karamani Mehmet Paşa. Mehmet Paşa's appointment indicates a swing in royal favour toward the Turkish notables. Other non-*devşirme*, members of the ulema, also were made vezirs and members of the imperial council, the *divan*. Those who had most suffered through Mehmet's confiscations now appeared to be coming back into power. They began to support a policy of renewed conquests in Europe, knowing that the new lands would pass into their hands as *timars*. However, the bureaucratic apparatus of the state remained in the hands of the *devşirme*. If he had lived longer, Mehmet might have created a more balanced administration, but he died in 1481 at the age of forty-nine.

The reign of sultan Bayezit II

On Mehmet's death the rivalry between the *devşirme* and the Turkish notables again broke out. The Janissaries almost immediately murdered Grand Vezir Karamani Mehmet Paşa in Istanbul. One of Mehmet's sons, Bayezit, had the favour of the *devşirme*, the other, Cem, was the candidate of the Turkish notables. Because they were a standing army, the Janissaries could mobilize support for their candidate immediately, while bringing together armed support from the Turkish notables naturally took more time. The *devşirme*, moreover, were still in control of most offices in the central administration. Cem seemed likely to follow the policies of his father's last decade – paying for conquest through financial exactions. Bayezit, on the other hand, promised the return of property that had been seized by Mehmet and an end to Mehmet's policy of forcibly exchanging new coins for old: in other words, 'no new taxes'. Such a policy attracted even members of the aristocracy and the ulema, groups who had begun to be favoured in the final decade of Mehmet's rule. Bayezit was able to claim the throne, but Cem organized revolts. Defeated by Bayezit's army in 1481, Cem returned in 1482. His second attempt was also a failure. Cem spent the rest of his life in exile. He at first escaped to the Knights of Rhodes, a Catholic military order of soldiers and pirates, to whom Bayezit paid 45,000 gold pieces a year to keep Cem quiet, They imprisoned Cem in France, then later gave him over to the Pope.

Internal politics preoccupied Bayezit's reign. He was so in the hands of the *devşirme* that much of his early reign was spent in finding ways to assert his independence. The *devşirme* had put him in power, while the Turkish notables had largely supported the claim of Cem. If the sultan was to assert his own authority, he would have to redraw the balance between the two. He encouraged this through court intrigue, arranging the deposition of his first two Grand Vezirs, and by cultivating his former enemies, increasing the size of forces of the notables. The *ulema* were cajoled with new properties and religious buildings, as well as by increased support of Sunni religious institutions. However, Bayezit was never entirely successful. The *devşirme* remained a dominant political force throughout his reign.

Bayezit was a different sort of man from the sultans who preceded or followed him. He was deeply religious, a reluctant warrior, personally preferring peace to conquest. The two main campaigns of his reign were against Moldavia and the Mamluks (see below) who ruled in Syria and Egypt. Fighting against Moldavia in 1484 and against the kingdom of Poland in 1496–98, Bayezit managed to conquer the Black Sea coastal section of Moldavia and territories to the north, thus bringing the Empire's border past the mouths of the Danube. He also forced Moldavia into renewed vassalage to the Ottomans. This was a small but very significant conquest. Ottoman territory now reached to the border of its vassal, the Crimean Khanate. The Christian kingdoms of Central Europe were cut off from the Black Sea. Its trade thus passed completely into Ottoman hands.

Bayezit battled against the Mamluks inconclusively for six years (1485–91), with no resulting changes in borders. With the exception of the conquests in the northern Black Sea region, Bayezit managed only to keep what he inherited. He was hampered by the spectre of Cem, who proved to be a useful tool in the hands of the Europeans. Though defeated, Cem remained popular. The Turkish notables resented the triumph of the *devşirme* and many would have rallied to a renewed threat to unseat Bayezit. Because Cem was in the hands of the Europeans, there was also the danger that a new revolt would be accompanied by a Crusade. The Europeans thus used Cem as a tool to enforce Ottoman peace on their western border; internal Ottoman disunity kept the Catholic lands of Venice and Hungary safe from Ottoman attack.

It is not coincidence that Bayezit only began to intervene in the West after Cem's death in 1495. When he did fight the Catholic powers the results were inconclusive. In a war with Venice from 1499 to 1503, the Ottomans only managed to take Lepanto and some Venetian fortresses in the Morea. However, the Ottomans did develop a new and powerful fleet in the eastern Mediterranean.

The relative lack of military expansion under Bayezit was not all bad for the Ottomans. They had passed through a long period of almost constant wars. After generations of conquest, there was a need to 'settle down', to consolidate gains and to develop systems of rule. Time and attention were needed for the economic development of the Empire. Farmers could not grow their crops or merchants trade their goods if they were constantly called off to war. So Bayezit's reign can be said to have provided a needed breathing space for the Ottoman Empire. Trade especially benefited. Peace and security in Anatolia meant that goods such as silk from Iran reached Istanbul in greatly increased quantities, with accompanying increases in customs revenues and employment. An imperial construction policy and a steady expansion of trade both enlarged the main cities of the Empire and confirmed the place of Istanbul as the economic centre of the Middle East and Balkans.

Bayezit's conservatism proved to be good for business. The policies of Mehmet II, despite their successes, had left the sort of distrust among merchants and land holders that is never good for the economy. If investments are insecure, people prefer to hide their money under the bed rather than invest it productively, and under Mehmet's policies of confiscation investments were very insecure. Bayezit rolled back Mehmet's changes. Lands that had been seized from individuals and pious foundations were returned. Changes in customs dues and taxation were rescinded. While this must have hurt revenues, it did create an environment of stability in which all knew that they could rely on the continuance of traditional laws and practices. This allowed planning and some certainty that a profit could be made. All indications are that the treasury ultimately benefited.

Bayezit II generally gave his empire peace, improved and regularized the state's tax system, and reduced inflation – the sort of good government that is seldom celebrated by historians, who love a good war as much as the next person, but was essential for the continuation of the Empire. He left the Empire in fine financial shape, ready for renewed expansion.

The reign of sultan Selim I

As sultan Bayezit grew older, he became more reclusive and less inclined to be involved in affairs of state. As will be seen below, the Empire was beginning to feel pressure from the Safavid rulers in Iran, and many felt an energetic sultan was needed. Of Bayezit's three surviving sons, one certainly fitted the bill – Selim. Selim does not appear to have been especially likeable. Turks have labelled him 'Selim the Grim', a great soldier, but not a particularly nice fellow. The Janissary Corps supported him for the succession even before Bayezit had died. Selim, with their backing, overthrew his father in 1512, took the throne, and subsequently killed his brothers. Later, to keep *his* sons from treating him as he had treated his father and to ensure an orderly succession to the throne, Selim killed all his sons but one, Süleyman. Selim was a great sultan, one who saved the Empire from external threats and added vastly to its territory, which shows that political greatness is not necessarily accompanied by a kindly attitude toward humanity.

Like his father, Selim was indebted to one group of the Ottoman ruling class for his success. In his case, the Janissary Corps, the military backbone of the *devşirme*, had been behind him. Selim paid his debt by increasing Janissary salaries and Janissary numbers. Despite that, he was not a man to be controlled by anyone. By putting leaders loyal to him in charge of the Janissaries he made the newly strengthened Janissary Corps into an instrument of his own power.

Selim was the antithesis of his father, Bayezit. He preferred to spend his time on campaign, away from Istanbul. He was an intelligent and ruthless general, and that was what was needed by the Empire. An ideological and political threat against the Ottomans was mounting in the East from another Turkish dynasty, the Safavid rulers of Iran. It is hard to believe that Bayezit or any equally mild sultan could have faced the threat successfully.

The Safavids

In a sense, the Ottomans were confronting their own history when they fought the Safavids. The Ottomans had evolved considerably from the Turkish nomad state of Ertuğrul and Osman. Two hundred years after their beginnings in Söğüt, the Ottomans had become a settled empire in the grand tradition. Like the Romans, the Byzantines or the great Arab Caliphs, they ruled a settled empire from a great capital, Istanbul, successor of Constantinople, itself successor to Rome. The sultans resided in palaces, not tents. While the sultans still went out personally on military campaigns, more and more of a sultan's occupation was political business in the capital. A vast bureaucracy ran the empire. Turkish nomads still served in the Ottoman army, but they were raiders and auxiliary troops. The settled troops of the Turkish notables and the Janissaries were now the foundation of the army.

The Ottoman conflict with the Safavids was played out in eastern Anatolia and northwestern Iran. Since the days of the Great Seljuks, this region had been home to nomads, both Turks and Kurds. The Turkish nomads had never been assimilated to settled empires. The mountainous terrain, as well as the sentiments of its population, made centralized control difficult. The states that exercised some control over them in many ways resembled the nomadic confederations of Central Asia. Their names indicated their pastoral nomadic heritage – the Kara Koyunlu ('Black Sheep') and Ak Koyunlu ('White Sheep') Empires. The Kara Koyunlu, a dynasty of Shia Turks, ruled over southeastern Anatolia, northern Iraq, and southwestern Iran in the fifteenth century. The Sunni Ak Koyunlu Turks succeeded them in 1466. In the reign of Mehmet II, the Ak Koyunlu became a considerable threat to Ottoman Anatolia. However, when Mehmet II defeated the Ak Koyunlu leader Uzun Hasan in 1473 the Ak Koyunlu threat diminished. It was replaced by a greater threat.

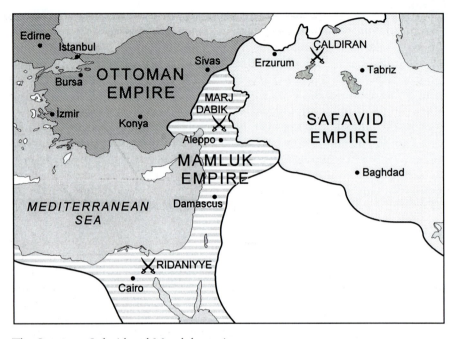

The Ottoman, Safavid and Mamluk empires.

The Safavid rulers resembled what the Ottomans had been. They were leaders of Turkish nomads and were closely tied into the religious and social life of the Turks of eastern Anatolia and Iran. Their power began with religion. The Safavid family were *shaykh*s (in Turkish, *şeyh*s, literally 'elders' – respected leaders) of a widespread mystical religious fraternity that had spread all over eastern Anatolia and western Iran. The beliefs spread by the Safavids were a mixture of heterodox religion and revolution against accepted order, both of which had great appeal to the Turkish nomads of the East. Partly because of personal belief and partly because the establishment adhered to Sunni Islam, the Safavids began to espouse a Shia version of Islam, which also attracted new followers.

In the fifteenth century the Safavids successfully transferred their religious prestige into secular power. The Safavid ruler, Shah İsmail, defeated the Ak Koyunlu in 1501–3. By 1510 he had conquered Iran, eastern Anatolia and Azerbaijan (northwestern Iran and the southeastern Caucasus). He ruthlessly set upon a policy of making Shii Islam the state religion, punishing disobedience to his religious rules with death. The state he created was dependent military on his Turkish nomad troops, known as the *kızılbaş* ('redheads' for the distinctive red headgear worn by Ismail's followers).

For the Ottomans, the Safavids were more than a threatening empire on their borders. The Safavid combination of state and mystical religion

82

had immense appeal to many of the sultan's Turkish subjects, whose personal religious beliefs were often very close to those of the Safavids. Moreover, the Janissary Corps also found the Safavid religious ideas attractive. The Janissaries were members of a mystic order, the Bektaşis, whose heterodox beliefs mirrored many of the Safavid beliefs. The Safavids had sent missionaries throughout Anatolia to spread their message, finding many adherents. The Ottoman sultan was thus presented with an internal and external threat.

Where his father Bayezit might have temporized, Selim responded with cold calculation and ferocity to the Safavid threat. His forces hunted down Safavid supporters in Anatolia, killing thousands. The Safavids themselves were met militarily. In Spring of 1514 Selim's army moved east.

A strong analogy can be made to Selim's march and the Byzantine march east that resulted in the battle of Manzikert. The settled empire, ruling from Istanbul/Constantinople, was threatened by nomads and an empire (the Great Seljuks or the Safavids) which controlled Iran and Iraq. Both Selim and the Byzantine Romanus Diogenes had mobilized their main armies to meet the threat. As Selim marched through Anatolia he encountered problems with supply and disaffection of his troops. In a bold stroke he sent the potentially least loyal half of his forces home, curing his supply problems by having fewer to feed and ridding himself of those most likely to side with Safavids. He also spread what might seem a strange sort of propaganda. Selim accused the *kızılbaş* tribes of cowardice, because they were afraid to face the Ottoman forces. Shah İsmail knew that the Ottoman army was formidable and would have preferred to retreat until the Ottoman supplies and will to fight were exhausted, but the *kızılbaş* forced him to stand and fight. The two forces met at Çaldıran on August 23, 1514, where the Ottomans gained a bloody victory. There the analogy to Manzikert ended.

Selim moved on from Çaldıran to take Tabriz, the Safavid capital, but was forced to abandon it because of limited supplies for the Ottoman troops. He remained in the East that winter, but supply problems and the unreliability of his troops' religious sentiments forced him to return to Istanbul. İsmail learned the lessons of Çaldıran. Henceforth he adopted a 'scorched earth' policy that denied the Ottomans the food they needed to campaign. For two centuries the Safavids were to continue the policy, destroying crops, poisoning wells, and leaving Ottoman armies with a devastated land in front of them. It was an effective defensive tactic, keeping the Ottomans from the heartland of Iran. (Selim's successor, Süleyman would make only small inroads in eastern Anatolia.) Offensively, the Safavids abandoned any plans to carry their rule into the Ottoman lands. Selim's march to the East had removed the main Safavid threat, although they were to remain a potent enemy to the Ottomans for many decades.

The Mamluks and Ottoman conquest of the Arab world

The other great power in the Middle East, in addition to the Ottoman and Safavid Empires, was the Mamluk Empire. The Mamluk state, which controlled Egypt, Syria, and western Arabia, seems so odd to Western minds that it is difficult to describe in a believable fashion. It was an empire run by slaves.

Military slaves (in Arabic, *mamlūk*, meaning 'owned') were common in the Middle East. Some were prisoners of war, who were by centuries-old tradition the property of their conqueror. Some were children bought in slave markets and raised as soldiers. Rulers kept soldiers as their personal slaves, feeling that they could rely on them as they could on no others, because their own slaves were completely dependent on them, at least in theory. If the ruler's fortunes rose, those of the slaves rose as well. If the ruler's power fell, the slaves would suffer with him. Therefore, the slaves were assumed to be loyal. This was the theory behind the Ottoman slave corps, such as the Janissaries, as well as the Mamluks in Egypt. Difficulties arose when the slaves revolted against their masters. This had happened in Egypt in the thirteenth century. Egyptian slave soldiers had overthrown the last member of the dynasty of Saladin, the great opponent of the Crusaders, and had taken control of Egypt.

Rather than declaring their freedom and making themselves a new ruling class in Egypt, the Mamluks remained as slaves. However, they became slaves of their own 'family' of slaves, called a Mamluk household. Each household bought new slaves continuously, trained them in martial arts and loyalty to their household, and brought them into their 'family'. Households chose their own leaders, with the strongest Mamluk taking charge through force or politics. The household had the power of life and death over its members, and obedience was demanded. The households were separated from the populace to the point of speaking among themselves a different language, Mamluk Kıpçak, from the language of the Kıpçak Turks who were the original slaves. As self-sufficient units, they were removed from ordinary society, and pains were taken to retain their separate identity. Even the sons of Mamluks could not usually become Mamluks themselves, although they might take places in the army or administration.

It would be a mistake to think of Mamluk slaves as comparable to slaves in the New World. Only in theoretical lack of individual freedom were they the same. Mamluks had power and wealth, both of which were denied to slaves in the Americas.

As might be expected, the Mamluk system did not necessarily endear itself to the people of Egypt or of Syria, once Syria too was conquered by them in the 1260s. In their first century, Mamluk rule was buoyed by relative peace and the geographical position of the Mamluk Empire. Situated on main routes between East and West, the Mamluk treasury and populace profited from trade. Stable conditions ended in the fourteenth century when Egypt suffered from both famine and the Black Death. The invasion of Syria by Tamerlane in 1400 irreparably damaged its economy, and the costs of defence against Tamerlane bankrupted both state and people. From 1400 on the state was perpetually threatened on its northern borders, and the populace suffered from special taxes and confiscations to meet the threats. The fifteenth-century Mamluk system of government contributed to general disorder. Each Mamluk sultan was supported by his own mamluks. When he died, after a power struggle, the new sultan rid himself of the old retainers and substituted his own mamluks. There was no stability in the state. The Mamluk system was not designed to develop loyalty among the populace. By the nature of the state, the local population was excluded from governing. Revenues of the state were primarily exploited for the benefit of the Mamluks. Mamluk rule has not gone down in history as a benevolent system of government.

Selim I was an accomplished strategist. With two enemies in the East, the Safavids and the Mongols, Selim had to choose his battles wisely. When he went east for the campaign of 1516 it was not known if he would attack the Safavids once again or move south against the Mamluks. Of the two, the Mamluks were surely the softer opponent. Poor leadership and their system of government had ensured that many in Syria and Egypt would gladly side with the Ottomans against the Mamluks. By not making his intentions known, Selim caused the Safavids to fall back into defensive positions, from which they could not mount a major offensive. Knowing the Safavids would not be able to overrun Ottoman Anatolia if he moved south, Selim invaded Syria. The Ottoman and Mamluk armies met at Marj Dabik on August 24, 1516, where the Ottomans won easily. They were welcomed by the people of Syria. The Mamluks in Egypt were beaten that winter (the battle of Ridaniyye, January 22, 1517) and Syria and Egypt were incorporated into the Ottoman Empire.

Politics and economy

Selim I did not spend much of his reign in Istanbul. He was more comfortable in a campaign tent than in the imperial palace. Consequently, his was not a reign known for its administrative initiatives. He relied on the *devşirme* and particularly the Janissary Corps as the central instruments of his power. The Janissaries were paid a large fee when he took the throne (called the 'accession gift', a bribe that became customary when a new sultan took the throne). The Janissaries were given new barracks and their numbers were increased. The sultan's slaves were put in charge of military units whenever possible.

In economic matters, Selim was something of an interventionist. At the beginning of his reign he tried to use trade as a weapon, ordering that

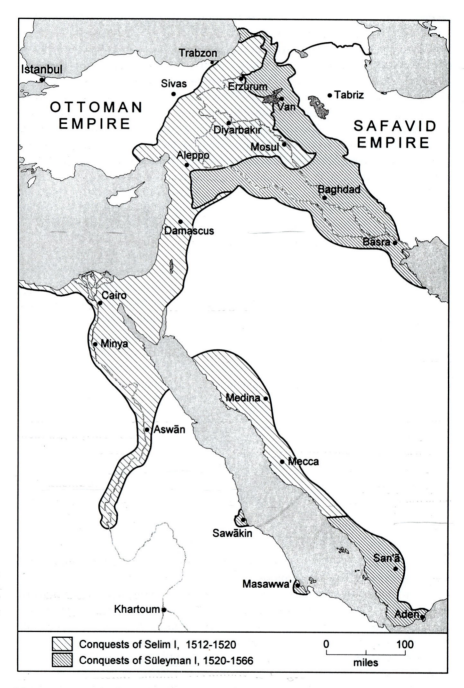

The conquests of Selim and Süleyman.

trade with his enemy Safavid Iran be ended. This proved to be not only unpopular but impossible, and the attempt to end trade with Iran was abandoned by Selim's son, Süleyman. The most important economic event of Selim's reign was the conquest of Syria and Egypt. This put the Ottomans in position to claim the taxes on all the major routes of the Asia to Europe transit trade: Mehmet II's conquest had made the Ottomans masters of the Istanbul entrepôt. Egypt and the Red Sea trade were now completely Ottoman. The Safavids still controlled Iraq, but trade could only pass to Europe through Ottoman Syrian ports. Despite political conflicts between Mamluks and Ottomans, Egypt and Syria had long carried on a thriving internal Middle Eastern trade in textiles, fruits, metals and lumber with Anatolia and Istanbul. Now this trade was all in Ottoman hands.

Selim died young, only slightly more than forty years of age, in 1520. He had reigned for only eight years, but had left the Empire in a more powerful and secure position than had any of his predecessors. The state coffers were full from the revenues of the newly conquered lands. The threat from the Safavids had been minimalized and the Mamluks destroyed. No power could truly threaten the Ottoman state. Selim's son Süleyman inherited a vast, rich, and secure empire.

The reign of Süleyman the Magnificent 1520–1566

Sultan Süleyman I is usually called Süleyman the Magnificent in the West. Europeans so named him because of the splendour of his court, a grandeur that was not matched in European kingdoms. Turks, more concerned with his practical side, call the sultan *Kanuni* ('the Lawgiver'), because one of Süleyman's greatest services to the Ottoman Empire was the codification of its laws. Most legal matters were the province of the Muslim religious law, or the laws of the various non-Muslim groups of the Empire, but there was considerable scope for the sultan's law, especially administrative law – matters of taxation, land tenure, and like. Süleyman transformed the state into an organization of rules and set procedures, a feat as important in the long run as his military conquests.

But there were military conquests. Like Selim, Süleyman was a warrior. He, himself, and the generals he chose were able to marshal together the resources of a vast empire for war. This involved considerable change from the military system of the early Empire. The Ottoman military had evolved into a regular army with cannon corps, quartermaster corps, etc. It was a complicated mixture of regulars, volunteers, raiding horsemen, infantry, 'feudal' troops who lived on their own lands, tribesmen, vassals, and others, all of whom had to be fed and organized in wartime. The days of a sultan grabbing his horse's reigns and calling the Turkish equivalent of 'Follow me!' were long gone. Süleyman's genius as an organizer of state thus also made him a great general, given the needs of the state in his time.

The Habsburgs and Ottoman conquests in the West

In Europe, Süleyman was faced with a formidable obstruction in the way of Ottoman conquest, the Habsburg family. The Habsburgs were originally the ruling family of Austria, elected emperors of the diverse Holy Roman Empire from 1438 to 1806. The Holy Roman Empire was a collection of actually independent states over whom the emperor had but limited power, but the Habsburgs nevertheless managed to dominate European politics in the sixteenth century. The emperor Maximilian (ruled 1493–1519) acquired the Netherlands and lands in Germany through marriage. Maximilian's son Philip married the heir of Ferdinand and Isabella of Spain. Their son, Charles, consequently inherited Spain and Spanish possessions in Italy and the Americas, Austria, the Netherlands, German lands, and Italian and Mediterranean possessions. Charles reigned as the Holy Roman Emperor Charles V from 1519 to 1556. He was unquestionably the most powerful ruler in Christian Europe, and only the geographic diversity of his possessions kept him from complete domination.

The Habsburgs were not a threat to the existence of the Ottoman Empire – such widespread power could not easily be concentrated to invade the Ottoman Empire in force. The Habsburgs also had to face enemies other than the Ottomans. France was their implacable enemy and conflicts with German Protestants sapped the Habsburgs' strength in the Holy Roman Empire. The Habsburgs, however, could mount a strong defence against Ottoman incursions in Europe. In addition to land-based power on the Ottoman northwest borders, they possessed a strong navy which opposed the Ottomans in the Mediterranean and economic power derived from the silver extracted from the mines of the New World.

The main Habsburg conflict with the Ottomans came in Hungary. Hungary had long been the dominant Christian country in southeastern Europe. Sometimes as Ottoman vassals, sometimes as opponents of the Ottomans, the Hungarian kings had managed to keep their independence. This changed when Süleyman invaded Hungary in 1526, defeated the Hungarian king (the battle of Mohacs, August 29, 1526) and exacted tribute and recognition of his overlordship from the Hungarians. The brother of Charles V, Ferdinand, the Habsburg governor in Austria and himself a claimant to the Hungarian throne, invaded Hungary in 1527, declaring himself king. Süleyman returned in 1529 and put his own vassal, John Zapolya, back in charge, then went on to Vienna and laid siege to the Austrian capital. The siege failed and the Ottomans retreated, but they left their own vassal in charge of most of Hungary, with the Habsburg

Austrians ruling only the northern and western borderlands of Hungary. Ferdinand returned and occupied the country again in 1540, to be driven out by Süleyman in 1541. Other wars followed. The upshot of this confusing set of conquests was little exchange of land beyond the first Ottoman invasion. Hungary was made a regular province of the Ottoman Empire in 1541, ending its independence, so Süleyman had successfully expanded the Empire in Europe. However, the Habsburgs were obviously to be pushed no farther. In the century after their failure at Vienna the Ottomans were to make small territorial gains at the expense of Austria, but their expansion in Europe was effectively over.

Süleyman's forces also came up against the Habsburgs on the Mediterranean. At the beginning of Süleyman's reign, Ottoman naval power was not sufficient to press any attacks against the Christian sea powers. The bulk of Muslim sea power was in the hands of pirates, well organized naval forces who mainly operated from North African ports, raiding Spanish and Italian coasts and attacking shipping. Charles V responded to this threat by organizing a great fleet under the leadership of admiral Andrea Dorea. The Muslim pirates, in turn, were forced to unite under the Ottoman flag. Süleyman named the pirate leader Hayrettin (called Barbarossa by the Europeans) Grand Admiral (*kapudan paşa*) in 1533. The Ottoman and pirate fleets were consolidated under his command. North African coastal regions, in particular Algiers, became tributaries of the Ottoman Empire.

Over the next thirty years the battle for the Mediterranean went back and forth. The seaport of Tunis was captured and recaptured by both the Ottoman and Habsburg forces. The Ottomans captured islands in the Aegean, but failed to take the great Christian sea base of the island of Malta. The sea power of Venice, allied with the Habsburgs on the Mediterranean, was dealt a terminal blow, but the Christians lost no large territories. In the end, as in Central Europe, the Ottomans found that they could not advance far on the sea. There, too, they had reached the effective limits of their expansion.

On their southern sea borders the Ottomans also fought inconclusively with the Christian powers. With the conquest of Egypt and Iraq (see below) the Ottomans had gained control of the traditional routes of the trade between Europe and Asia. However, control of the Middle Eastern ports on the Gulf and the Red Sea were no longer enough to ensure economic control of the East–West trade. In 1497, the Portuguese captain Vasco de Gama sailed around the Cape of Good Hope, reached India, and returned. Portuguese sea trade with the East began in 1500. In order to secure their trade supremacy, the Portuguese began a campaign to destroy Muslim trade. Vasco de Gama. Francisco de Almeida, and Alfonso de Albuquerque destroyed Muslim fleets, seized sea ports as military stations, and hindered all Muslim trading. Süleyman realized the danger to the

Middle Eastern economy that was the necessary result of the Portuguese advent in the southern seas. He sent a fleet from Egypt in 1538 which, while it was able to conquer coastal Yemen from its Arab rulers, did nothing against the Portuguese. In 1552, another Ottoman fleet was completely routed in the Gulf, ending Muslim control over the Gulf trade route. The Portuguese retained bases on the Gulf and restricted naval traffic. The Ottomans were able to keep control of the Red Sea route, but European trade with the East grew and Muslim trade stagnated. Ottoman trade with India did not decrease; indeed it sometimes increased, but the *proportion* of the transit trade between Europe and the Orient that passed through the Middle East began to decrease dramatically. Henceforth Europeans were to reap the new riches of a greatly increased eastern trade.

Conquests in the East

The success of Ottoman land armies in the East stood in contrast to the failure of the Ottoman navies there. Süleyman had good reason to campaign in the East. The Safavids were a perennial threat, due to their appeal to the heterodox and semi-nomadic inhabitants of eastern Anatolia. Defeating them decisively would allow Ottoman attention to be focused elsewhere. Perhaps more important, Safavid possession of central and southern Iraq stood in the way of economic benefit. The great sea route from India and the Orient passed through the Middle East by two routes – up the Red Sea, then through Egypt to the Mediterranean and onto Italian boats or through the Gulf to Basra, then up the Euphrates, overland to Aleppo and coastal Syria, and onto other Italian boats. By conquering Egypt the Ottomans had gained control of the Red Sea route, but the Safavids controlled the other. The benefits of a monopoly to the Ottomans are obvious. Moreover, by controlling the entire route of the Gulf–Iraq–Syria trade the Ottomans could control security for caravans and thus increase trade. The taxes to be collected were significant. Although the Portuguese might reap some of the benefits of increased trade, the trade of the East with southern Europe through the Middle East was still an important economic factor.

The Ottomans also had religious motivation and a religious excuse for campaigning in the East. The Safavids had adopted the form of Shia Islam known as Twelver or Imami Shiism (which held that there had been 12 *imam*s, or rightly-guided leaders, descendents of Ali, the cousin of Muhammad and the first imam). They had ruthlessly suppressed Sunni Islam, the faith of the Ottomans, throughout their dominions, exiling or killing Sunni religious leaders and seizing Sunni religious establishments. As part of their campaign to make Shiism dominant in their Empire, the Safavids had despoiled Sunni sacred shrines in Iraq, which they controlled. A campaign against the Safavids could thus be considered a Holy War (*jihad*), because the Sunni Ottomans could no more officially tolerate Shia beliefs than the Safavids allowed Sunni ones.

Süleyman prepared for war with the Safavids after making peace with Austria in 1533, freeing his western borders from possible attack. Rather than wait until the campaign season the next year, Süleyman daringly (if he had not won, the words imprudently or rashly would have been more appropriate) set out in the autumn, less than two months before snowfall made the roads in the East impenetrable. As the Ottoman army moved east, the Safavid Shah, Tahmasp, anticipated an Ottoman attack on the main Safavid lands in Persia. He prepared by retreating from the border and destroying lands through which the Ottomans would pass – the proven 'scorched earth' policy. But Süleyman instead attacked south, over the mountains into central Iraq. By the end of 1533 his army had routed the Safavids and taken Baghdad. Basra later passed into Ottoman hands and all of Iraq became Ottoman.

The conquest of Iraq put virtually all of the Arab Middle East under Ottoman control. Selim I's authority had been recognized in Mecca and Medina, the traditional cornerstone of a Muslim dynasty's prestige. Damascus, the seat of the Umayyad Caliphs, was Ottoman, and now Baghdad, the capital of the Abbasid Caliphs, was Ottoman as well. The integration of most of the Arab world into the Ottoman Empire would last for nearly 400 years.

Süleyman's later campaigns against the Safavids foundered on the determination of the Safavids to avoid battle. Unable to fight, the Ottomans were unable to conquer, because territory occupied by the Ottomans could always be retaken by the intact Safavid army once winter's approach or lack of supplies caused the Ottomans to retreat. In eastern Anatolia, only a small region around the city of Van was actually taken and held by the Ottomans. In the end, both sides accepted political realities – the Ottomans would never completely defeat the Safavids and the Safavids would not regain the land lost to the Ottomans. The treaty of Amasya, signed on May 29, 1555, cemented peace for another two decades and set what became the permanent border between Anatolia and Iran.

Political power in Süleyman's Empire

Süleyman's reign saw the complete triumph of the *devşirme*. The Turkish notables retired from political life at the centre, although many retained considerable power in the provinces. It became an accepted principle that those who ran the Empire would be the slaves of the sultan. With no natural enemies to unite them, the *devşirme* began to splinter into competing factions. Political power increasingly resided in two areas – the 'political parties' of the *devşirme* and the harem. The former were parties based on personal loyalty and formed by *devşirme* leaders in furtherance of their political aims. The harem, especially the women of the sultan, possessed power because of their closeness to the centre of power, the sultan. The harem women allied themselves with *devşirme* parties to control the Empire. Süleyman's wife, Hürrem Sultan, and his daughter, Mihrimâr, held especially great political influence. Hürrem managed to convince Süleyman to kill the great Grand Vezir İbrahim Paşa in 1536 and influenced the selection and deposition of vezirs until her death.

Süleyman was much in love with Hürrem (called Roxelana in the West) and gave her great trust, but Hürrem was a schemer, very much involved in political intrigues in the court and more than willing to take advantage of her place in the sultan's heart. She was particularly concerned to have one of her two sons, Bayezit or Selim, succeed Süleyman on the throne, rather than Süleyman's more able son, Mustafa, Süleyman's son by another mother. Mother love allied itself with politics, because Hürrem's power would thus hold beyond Süleyman's death, exercised through her son. In collusion with Hürrem, the Grand Vezir Rüstem Paşa convinced Süleyman that Mustafa was plotting against him. Mustafa was killed in 1553. Hürrem herself died before Süleyman, but the less able of her two sons, Selim, eventually took the throne. The pattern of a new sultan being chosen through court intrigue, and of that choice by no means being the best, was to continue for centuries.

Süleyman's most lasting contribution to the Ottoman state system lay in the codification of laws. Building on the law code of Mehmet II, Süleyman's vezirs and *ulema* law experts wrote or recorded a great body of law that included the workings of the state and more. The codes emphasized the power of the sultan and government over people and property. Laws covered rights and obligations of both rulers and ruled – how officials were named and their rights and obligations; how the bureaucracy was to function; taxes and how they were paid; the rights of the sultan to confiscate property, etc. To the eyes of conservative Muslim jurists the Ottoman codes must have appeared at best presumptuous. Sunni Muslim jurisprudence held that, in essence, all law came from God and was only applied by men. Ottoman law asserted the absolute right of the sultan to make laws of administration and state. Süleyman's law codes included many regulations that traditionally were matters of the religious law and gave the sultan and his deputies authority over matters decided by the *ulema* in other Muslim societies. For example, penalties for many civil crimes were set by the Ottoman codes. The Ottoman *ulema*, chosen and paid by the government, found religious justification for it all. This bending of religious law allowed the Ottoman sultans latitude in their rule and their judgements that may have served the state better than would more strict adherence to tradition. It demonstrated a continuing adaptation to circumstance and liberal interpretation of tradition that was one of the hallmarks of the first Ottoman centuries. At the same time, the laws codified an absolute system of central rule that would later be open to abuse.

The last years of Süleyman's rule undid some of the benefits of his reign. To support an extravagant court and the costs of campaigns, Süleyman's government began to raise taxes and debase the coinage, spreading inflation throughout the Empire. As later governments have discovered, this was not an effective road to prosperity. Good money was driven out by bad. When tax-paying merchants and labourers were ruined by the economy, the government resorted to confiscations of property to raise new income for the state, ruining still more and making further exactions necessary. The Empire was strong enough to stand such folly for some time. The bill came due later, after Süleyman's time, when deterioration of both the state and the economy accelerated.

Süleyman the Magnificent is one of those few rulers whose reign has passed into the mythology of rule. Later generations of Ottoman subjects, who lived when the power of the Empire was in decline, looked back at the time of Süleyman as a golden age. Many thought that if only the Empire could return to the values held by the Turks of Süleyman's time, all would be well. Westerners have followed in the adulation, often calling him the greatest of sultans. As a rule, such judgements should always be questioned, but, as no one knows what are the criteria for the award of the title 'greatest of sultans', it is perhaps better to avoid the issue altogether.

What can be defined is the title given Süleyman by the Turks, 'Lawgiver', because his sponsorship of the Ottoman law codes was an exceptional contribution to the Ottoman state. The title 'the Magnificent' is also apt. Süleyman's empire was magnificent in size and power. In terms of their ability to make enemies tremble, Süleyman's army and state were unquestionably magnificent. Süleyman was also magnificent in his charity, the sort of charity described above for Mehmet II, charity which built glorious edifices as well as providing for the poor. In Istanbul and all over the Empire, Süleyman and his courtiers sponsored grand charitable works that did much good while they awed subjects and foreigners alike. Chief among them was the great Süleymaniye complex in Istanbul. Designed and built by one of the greatest architects of any age, Sinan, the complex was founded around the great Süleymaniye mosque, which is perhaps one of the two most beautiful grand mosques in the world, the other being Sinan's mosque in Edirne. The complex's *medrese*s became a centre of learning in the Islamic world, rivalling the Azhar in Cairo, and the college of the highest judges and jurists in the Empire. Everything in the complex, from soup kitchen for the poor to library for the learned, was built on a grand scale, glorifying the image of the sultan, its patron. Yet its purposes were admirable – the advancement of religion and learning and the care of the poor and the sick. Like the complex built earlier by Mehmet II, it contained a hospital (and a medical college), an elementary school, a soup kitchen, a bath, and many residences. Other imperial donations built mosques, soup kitchens, caravansarays, and schools all over the empire.

On balance, Süleyman's reign must be considered a success. Despite the problems of his later years, he expanded the Empire in both Europe and the Middle East, defeated its enemies or at least held its enemies at bay, and sealed Ottoman control over regions as diverse as Hungary and Iraq. His law codes created an organization that was to last for centuries. His public works made Istanbul a wonder of the world. After Süleyman's reign, the preponderance of the *devşirme* and political intrigues in the government would be a major detriment to the state, but Süleyman himself was in no danger of losing his authority. His rule remained magnificent, even when he grew old and increasingly retired from administration and military campaigns. He left the Empire larger and better organized than he had found it.

The achievement of the first ten sultans

At Süleyman's death in 1566 the Ottoman Empire had already lasted for more than 200 years. Through all but a short part of that time, the Empire had been one centrally-ruled state, an empire in reality as well as name. This made the Ottomans almost unique among the Islamic empires. The Umayyad Caliphal dynasty had lasted less than a hundred years, the Great Seljuks only slightly more than a hundred. Both the Abbasid Caliphs and the Rum Seljuks reigned for more than two hundred years, but cannot be said to have ruled for that length of time. Short-lived dynasties littered Islamic history. Yet the Ottomans in 1566 had ruled for two hundred years in full power and were to continue for centuries thereafter. How did they do it?

The causes of success

One reason for Ottoman success has to be slow development of the Empire. Unlike their predecessors the Great Seljuks, the Ottomans developed their empire over a long period, starting small and growing large. This gave them time to assimilate the peoples they had conquered and to alter their governing methods to meet the needs of an expanded state. Indeed, whole sultanates, those of Murat II and Bayezit II can be said to have been largely given over to consolidation. Another reason was the fact that the Ottomans had no need to invent their basic system of government anew. Pragmatic and eclectic, the Ottomans developed a new governmental system by borrowing both from contemporaries and from the past. Luck was also a factor. Much of the success of the Ottomans was not based on planning or hard work; it was just luck, but luck recognized and properly acted upon by wise rulers.

Military success

Early Ottoman conquests can be said to have arisen from the nature of Turkish nomad society. The *gazi* tradition expected war with infidels. Since they had first ridden out of Central Asia the Turks had lived by overrunning the lands of those who stood in their way. The first Ottoman conquests were a continuation of that tradition. Nomads fought as a way of life, and the Ottomans were nomad chiefs. Their luck was to be placed on the border of a decaying Byzantine state, ripe for conquest. It was also their luck to arrive at a time when no large Islamic empire ruled. The conquests of their small state were retained by the conquerors, not given over to a Caliph or Great Sultan. What they took, they kept.

Ottoman military genius lay in taking advantage of good fortune and adapting to changing circumstances. The high quality of the generalship of the Ottomans is obvious from their successes. However, the greatest achievement of the Ottomans as military men lay in the administration of change. The sultans led a nomad army as long as it furthered their ambitions, then converted to a standing army that partly replaced the nomads, then to a combination of a standing army, the Janissaries, and a 'militia', the forces of the Turkish notables. An army that had begun as an unruly confederation of nomad tribes became a disciplined force centred on regular soldiers armed with gunpowder weapons. An army that under sultan Osman had for decades been unable to capture cities, because nomads' horses could not jump city walls, became an army whose artillery forced a breech in even the great walls of Constantinople. Sultans whose nomadic ancestors had never seen the sea became masters of the eastern Mediterranean. How many other states or military forces in history managed change so successively?

Surprisingly, given their success, the Ottoman conquests cannot be said to have been thoroughly planned. Mehmet II and, perhaps, Süleyman had long-range plans, but most Ottoman conquests followed from need or opportunity. Some conquests were essential: Constantinople had to be conquered because its existence meant that it would always be a focus for Christian opposition, and because Constantinople stood on the line of communication between Ottoman Europe and Asia. No empire could long tolerate an enemy placed in the middle of its possessions. The Safavids had to be defeated because they were a threat to the Ottoman East and, through their appeal to the Turkish nomads, a threat to the entire Empire. Some conquests were opportunistic: contenders for the Byzantine throne who hired the Ottomans to defeat their enemies presented too good an opportunity to overlook. The Mamluks were too weak for the Ottomans to neglect the chance to gain the riches of Egypt and the status of Protectors of the Holy Places of Mecca and Medina. These were conquests from circumstance or necessity, which is not to denigrate the abilities of those who could do what had to be done.

The empire of Süleyman with modern states.

Conquest had a inherent dynamic. Conquests fed on themselves. When the Ottomans took a new region of Europe they naturally came up against a new set of enemies. Usually the latter coveted the lands the Ottomans had taken. Therefore, they in turn had to be defeated. This went on until the enemies, especially the Habsburgs in Austria and on the Mediterranean, were simply too powerful and the battles too distant from

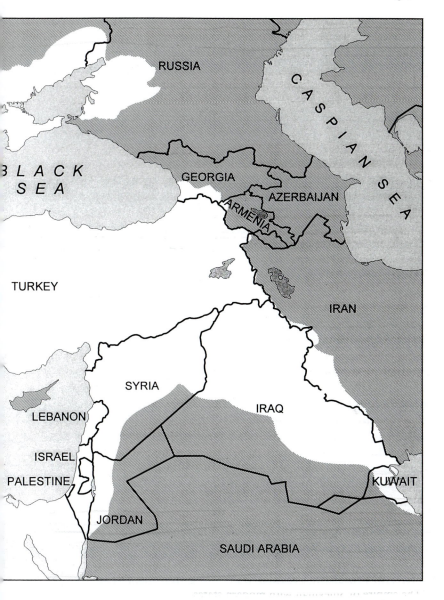

the Ottoman heartland for new conquests to be possible or, even if possible, profitable. The dynamic of imperial conquest was not unique to the Ottomans. One can look to the Romans or to the British in India for comparisons. Great empires grew to their natural limits or until they met opponents, such as German tribes for the Romans or Afghan tribes for the British, who could not be conquered.

There was also an economic demand for conquest. Plunder was an important source of income to the early Ottoman state and its soldiers. Indeed, the first Ottomans and their followers can be said to have lived on booty. Later Ottoman soldiers drew their support from the lands they had conquered. As the Empire expanded and the army and government grew to match, there was always need for new lands to be awarded to followers and need of new revenues to pay the salaries of the Janissaries and others.

Finally, the Ottomans were like other men of their time. Conquest was the rule in both Middle Eastern and European states. Stephan Dushan of Serbia, Shah Ismail of Persia, Ivan the Great of Russia, or the Habsburg Charles V all took what they could. Their conquests only stopped when they came up against too strong an opponent to defeat. The Ottomans took more than others because they were better at conquest. They kept their conquests because they were efficient rulers.

Administrative success

Having read of the problems of Ottoman rule, 'administrative success' may not seem a proper description of Ottoman rule. Brother fought brother for the throne. Civil wars recurred. Turkish notables contested with the *devşirme*. Tamerlane almost destroyed the Empire. Yet the many problems actually illustrate the success of the Ottomans. Through civil war, military defeat, political conflict, and even the deposition of sultans, the Ottoman system of rule survived. Whatever the troubles of individual rulers, the system remained to serve whoever was sultan. The state went on, and would continue to do so for three and a half centuries after the death of Süleyman. With such a record, someone must have been doing something right.

The Ottomans owed much to the Great Seljuks and Rum Seljuks. Both had tried to create a state that synthesized the vigour of Turkish nomads and the administrative culture of the great tradition of Persian-Islamic statecraft. Both had failed, but had left a legacy for their successors. The Seljuk system became the basis of the Ottoman system. Future sultans were trained in the tradition of Nizam al-Mulk. Unlike the Seljuks, the Ottomans were not forced to create a system of government. The Turkish-Islamic-Persian system of the Seljuks was already there, awaiting refinement. The Ottomans did refine it, particularly by incorporating governmental traditions of the Balkans and the Byzantine Empire. That was one basis of the administrative greatness of the Ottomans – eclecticism. The sultans and their retainers were not great innovators. They were leaders who took what they found and adapted it to their needs. None of the cornerstones of their success, whether it be the slave army and administrators, the *timar* system, or state support of the economy, was unique to them. All were taken from others who had not made their systems perform so well. There was genius in knowing what to take and in making it work so well.

The other basis of Ottoman greatness, a habit of rule closely tied to eclecticism, can be called pragmatism. The sultans did what had to be done, even when the rules seemed to stand in their way. The Ottoman sultans were the heroes of Islam. Their private beliefs are mostly unknown, but they at least gave public evidence of being good Muslims. Yet they did not hesitate to deviate from Islamic rules when necessary. The best example of this is the child-levy which recruited the *devşirme*. Enslaving Christians who had not rebelled against Muslim rule was not allowed by the Holy Law, nor was the demand that the children convert to Islam. Nevertheless, the sultans not only committed the illegal acts, but made them the basis of their system of rule. It was a pragmatic system, not a theoretically legal one, even if it was accepted by pliant jurists, and it worked.

The Ottoman dealings with the kings and nobles of the Balkans can only be called pragmatic, as well. Less pragmatic Muslim rulers might have insisted that all military power be in the hands of Muslims; that was the Islamic tradition. Yet the Ottomans used Christian vassal kings to advance their cause and even gave *timar*s to Christian nobles, bringing those who might otherwise have rebelled into their camp. Bayezit I used Turkish Muslim fighters to attack in Christian Europe and Christian vassal troops to attack in Muslim Anatolia. Mehmet II hired Christian cannon-makers, because they made the best cannon, and included Christian models in his law codes. Pragmatism ultimately worked better for Mehmet than for Bayezit, but both were the most pragmatic of men.

The many other pragmatic actions of the Ottomans – the use of trading privileges to neutralize opposition from Italian city states, employing a mixture of warfare, marriage, fear, and diplomacy to overwhelm the Turkish principalities in Anatolia, allowing great power over their people to the Greek clergy, thus obviating a potential focus of rebellion, the political dealings with the Balkan princes, and many others – all demonstrate that the Ottomans were rulers willing to take all available means to success.

Does this mean that the sultans were cold, calculating men without real principle? Insofar as almost all successful rulers throughout history have possessed a certain cold calculation, the sultans surely manifested that quality. They were ruthless, but no more so than the other rulers of their time, less so than some. They cannot be called unprincipled. They consistently used their power to advance the rule of Islam, to them the greatest moral good. They took seriously the Islamic principle that justice was the essential quality of a ruler. Under their rule, Islamic and state law codes took the place of the often anarchic situations that had preceded their rule. Riches won in war supported many soup kitchens for the poor, hospitals, and libraries. As will be seen in the next chapter, they upheld a system in which marketplaces were regulated to protect honest dealing, merit played a great part in political advancement, and non-Muslims were guaranteed rights that Muslims and Jews never found in Christian lands. The sultans were men of principle, even if their main principle was that they should rule.

Chapter 4

The Ottoman State

Overleaf

The Siege of Rhodes. The miniature painting shows sultan Süleyman the Magnificent directing elements of the Ottoman army: Janissaries with firearms and pikes, the sultan's imperial guards with bows, cavalry with little to do in the siege of a city, and miners digging under the walls. (*Süleymanname*, Topkapı Sarayı Müzesi, H. 1517.)

The Ottoman State

The Ottoman government was not what you might think. When concepts have been shaped, as our concepts of the Ottomans have been shaped, by centuries of mythology it is difficult to understand the subjects of the myths.

Western images of Ottoman rule were shaped from afar. The Ottomans were too remote to be easily understood. To Renaissance Europeans, the Ottoman state was the mysterious instrument of the power of the sultan, the 'Grande Turke'. Terms such as Oriental Despotism were coined with a fanciful image in mind of brutal sultans, conquering all before them. To Europeans it seemed as if the Ottoman system was governed by the ruler's whim, and they delighted in images of large eunuchs ritually severing the heads of officials who had earned the sultan's displeasure, perhaps wishing that some of their own leaders could be exposed to the same treatment. The Ottoman government was not like that. Neither was it like the later Western image of a corrupt state where inefficiency led to ruin. Nor was it like another image spread in the West, this time spread by those who respected the Ottomans – a state where merit was all and a man rose to power only through his own abilities.

There was some truth in all these images, and others, of the Ottomans. The sultans indeed were great warriors who caused Christian Europe to tremble, but they were also able administrators who held their conquests for five hundred years through competent rule. Some of the greatest sultans, such as Selim I, were indeed cold and, when statecraft called for it, brutal. Others, such as Selim's father, Bayezit II, were religious and philosophical rulers more interested in internal improvements in the Empire than in conquests. Some officials were indeed corrupt, but were they any more corrupt than the Europeans who criticized them? (Casting the first stone might be difficult for anyone involved today in the granting of contracts for municipal construction projects.) On the positive side, the

Ottoman Empire at its height was indeed more of a meritocracy than was any European state of the time, but the son of a Grand Vezir was still considerably more likely to succeed in government than was the son of a peasant. In short, the Ottoman state was complicated, sometimes politically effective, sometimes not, and not always easy to understand.

Beginnings

The first government of the Ottomans was indistinguishable from the military. Following the old Turkish tradition of the naming of a leader, the *han*, the first Ottoman leaders took power because of their prowess as military commanders. Their political advisors were also those whom they put in charge of the troops. In a state that was very close to its nomadic roots, the distinction between minister of state and general was small or nonexistent.

As their conquests expanded, the Ottomans came into contact with more settled systems of government – the Byzantine Empire, with its Roman and Greek traditions, and the Islamic governing systems of the Arabs and Persians. Gradually the Ottomans evolved a governing system that was far from their nomadic roots. The ruler became more removed from the people, in the Middle Eastern and Byzantine style, and dependent on a bureaucracy. Court ceremonial more and more resembled Persian ideals; for the sultan and his retainers, silks replaced rougher clothes. But the Ottomans never completely forgot their Turkish nomadic roots. The sultan was always officially described as 'the Han, son of the Han', and on parade he and his main advisors could be identified by the horsetails on their standards, the mark of leadership among their Central Asian ancestors. Some Turkish military and leadership practices lasted until the end of the Empire, but the nomadic Turks in Central Asia had no treasury or taxation system fit for a great empire and indeed had few ideas on how to rule over farmers and merchants. For those principles the Turks had to look to the Persians, the Arabs, the Byzantines, and others.

Oddly, the Ottomans have sometimes been criticized for their borrowings from other cultures, the implication being that they had no governing genius of their own, but were forced to borrow that of others. It is true that the Ottomans were not creators of absolutely new forms of government. Most of what they adopted had been tried by others, sometimes many times until a successful form was found. The Ottoman genius was actually their ability to meld together, alter, and improve disparate systems to make a working government. The Ottomans were successfully eclectic, borrowing what they found was best and putting it to use. On reflection, it should be admitted that the ability to borrow the best from predecessors and other governments has always been the hallmark of a successful governing system. If something has proven itself in the governments of others, only a very foolish government would refuse to consider adopting it.

The Ottoman government was made up of Turkish, Byzantine, Persian, and traditional Islamic components, combined and modified to form a distinctive Ottoman governing system. The origin of the Turkish element is obvious, because it was the basic form of rule for the nomads who rode into Anatolia and ultimately created the Empire. Perhaps the most important aspect retained from the Turkish system was the idea of merit and ability as the basis for authority. In their harsh world, the nomads best succeeded when following leaders chosen for their leadership abilities. The Ottomans intentionally adopted a similar approach. In theory, if not always in practice, they expected high office to come to those who had first proven themselves at lower levels. (Considering the systems of advancement in place in Europe at the time, this is remarkable.)

The Byzantine element in the Ottoman state came with the conquest of previously Byzantine territories. It was convenient, often necessary, for the Ottomans to retain the Byzantine systems of taxation, land registration, etc., at first. They had no real record keepers or tax system themselves, but would need both if they hoped to keep their newly-won territories. The most obvious solution was the wholesale adoption of Byzantine records, Byzantine record-keeping practices, and even Byzantine bureaucrats. This was a temporary expedient, but it left its mark on the subsequent Ottoman system.

At the highest level, the Ottoman sultans were affected by the model of the Late Roman and Byzantine emperors as supreme rulers – detached rulers whose separation from other men was stressed, men to whom the populace would look in awe, fear, and respect. The emperors had also claimed universality of rule, a thing which the Ottoman sultans also came to claim for themselves. Mehmet II, the final conqueror of the Byzantine Empire, was known to use the title Caesar, as well as Han and Sultan. The only other possible models for the Ottoman sultan were the Seljuk sultans or the great Mongol leaders, such as Genghis Khan. The Mongols were no model for a settled empire, and the aloofness of the Seljuks from their people reinforced the Byzantine ideal.

From the Seljuks, as well as the Byzantines, the Ottomans took a tradition of an all-powerful, but removed sultan. They also adopted the Seljuk system of *vezirs* (government ministers) who were in charge of the state bureaucracy. Among the many governing ideas taken from the Seljuks and previous Islamic dynasties was the idea of a slave army. In theory, such an army was to be loyal only to its master, the ruler, whereas other troops might be loyal to their own region, their own lords, etc., and thus could not be completely trustworthy. The Ottomans took the old Seljuk practice and refined it into the Janissary Corps.

Islam provided the legal basis, the theological commitment, and the basic law of the Empire. The effect of Islam as it was practised in the Arab world became especially strong in the Ottoman Empire after Selim I's

105

conquest of Syria and Egypt. Istanbul became the new capital of Islam. The sultans became the conservative guardians of Sunni Islam. Islam so permeated the life and structure of the Ottoman court that the government was in many ways indistinguishable from the religion, which was, in fact, the Islamic ideal.

The Ottoman theory of government

Broadly speaking, modern governments, especially democratic governments, are expected to do for their people what the people want but cannot do for themselves. Therefore, governments provide schools, dispense welfare, regulate businesses, and set restrictions on all sorts of human behaviour. It is difficult to imagine a part of modern life that is not furnished, managed, controlled, monitored, or in some other way touched by governments. Neither in design nor in practice did the Ottomans have such a government.

The base of the Ottoman Empire was Islam. Religion was intimately bound up with the ideology and legitimacy of the government. At no time did the sultans claim to be rulers of a Turkish empire, even though they were themselves Turks, their empire was founded on Turkish soldiers, the state language was Turkish, and the sultans traced their lineage to Central Asia. Instead, their empire was always styled a *Muslim* empire, one of the line of Islamic empires that had included the Umayyads, the Abbasids, and the Seljuks. The sultans took their duties as the leaders of Islam very seriously. Their position bound them to protect Islam, its laws, and its holy places and to advance the cause of Islam in the world. It also bound them to respect the laws and traditions of Islam, including that which said that Christian and Jewish subjects of Islam were to be free to practise their religions. (This was quite different from the Christian rulers of contemporary Europe, who usually felt that all other religions should cease to exist.)

The functional theory of the Ottoman state was simple – the people paid the taxes, the sultan collected them. In return he protected the state and its people, defended Islam, and provided what other services he, the sultan, deemed desirable, such as military roads which might have civilian uses. Even though this seems unsatisfactory to modern minds, it was actually the pattern in most monarchies before modern times. The Ottomans were simply more honest in admitting their position. Until the nineteenth century, in the Ottoman Empire the rulers and the ruled were theoretically completely separate. Those who served the sultan were the *Ottomans* (in Turkish *Osmanlı*, 'those who are with Osman', the first sultan, and his successors), a group usually called the ruling class in English. 'Class', with its economic connotations in the West, is not a particularly good descriptor, because the basis of the ruling class was never economic. The term originally used by the Ottomans, themselves, was *askeri* ('military'), which denoted the military origins of the Empire and continued importance of the military. However, the *askeri* also contained many who were not at all military, such as religious leaders more at home with their theology books than with a sword. Whatever terminology is chosen, this upper class was considered to be separate from the remainder of the populace. All others in the Empire, the vast majority, were called the *Raya* ('flock', a term later applied only to non-Muslims), the flock whom the sultan protected from wolves and fleeced. They took no part in rule, nor did they expect to do so.

Lest the functional theory of Ottoman government appear too cold and callous, it must be remembered that the requirements of Islam greatly softened what might have been an unfeeling state. No matter how high his position, in the eyes of religion the sultan was a man like other men – a Muslim who had duties and responsibilities for which he would answer on the Day of Judgement. Like other men he would be held accountable according to the resources given him by God; the sultan had been given much, and thus he was expected by God to do much good. The sultan was bound by religion to be charitable, as were the other members of his government. Therefore, sultans, courtiers, and officials all built soup kitchens (*imarets*) for the poor, hospitals for the sick, fountains, and other constructions for the populace. Some of these charities, such as mosques built by sultans, benefited only Muslims. Others, such as wells or public fountains constructed in city neigh-bourhoods, benefited all. All Muslims and, for that matter, Christians, Jews, and others, were enjoined by God to advance justice in the world. Muslim legal theory spoke especially of the necessity and godliness of justice. As the one whose power allowed him most easily to advance justice, the sultan was under special obligation to do so.

There were also practical activities undertaken by the sultans and their governments which affected the people of the Empire. For example, good sense dictated intervention in the marketplace. If the markets of the Empire did not function well, tax revenues would have decreased. Thus it was that the sultan appointed inspectors (*muhtesibs*) of markets to guarantee accurate weights and measures, and to guard against cheating. It was in the sultan's economic interests to make sure that business functioned smoothly and accurately. It was also an extension of the sultan's duty to ensure justice. On a very practical level, it was felt that justice and econom-ic good sense were both best served by stable prices. Therefore, the sultan's government supported a stable economic system in which, in theory at least, craft guilds set fair prices. The vast majority of the Empire's people were farmers, and justice demanded that farmers be treated equitably. The practical interests of the sultan also dictated that the peasants be properly treated. Otherwise, the peasants would leave the land and the tax base would be lost. Justice and good sense thus worked together, at least in theory. In reality, as in all governments, sometimes neither justice nor good sense won the day. The responsibility was the sultan's.

The sultan

The Ottoman sultanate has long been part of the mythology of rule. From the time of the Renaissance, Europeans studied what they thought (with little information to go on) was the position of the sultan. Everything from his harem (often described in fanciful, unexpurgated tales) to his power of life and death over his followers fascinated the Europeans. As might be expected, most of what was 'known' about the sultan was nonsense, but the understanding that here were a man and an office of overwhelming importance was correct.

Ottoman sultans drew their power from the image of the great king that had existed since ancient times. From the time of the Babylonians to the Byzantines, the image of state power in the Middle East and Balkans had been of a monarch with unconditional authority who was chosen by God to rule. The symbol of the Ottoman sultanate was at the centre of all political life in the Balkans and almost all of the Middle East. He was the Han of the Turks, the leader of Islam, even the successor of Caesar by virtue of the conquest of the Byzantine Empire. A centuries-long tradition of rule carried with it a powerful prestige and prominence; the sultanate existed for so long that a government without the Ottoman sultan must have been unthinkable. It would be comparable to imagining the Roman Catholic Church without the Pope. This prestige was one important cause for the survival of the empire. Rebels might stage a coup d'état, exchanging one sultan for another, but they could not imagine ending the sultanate.

The sultan was the theoretical centre of the Ottoman system in a manner almost unknown in the West. The power of medieval European kings was fenced in by nobles' prerogatives. In later times, prime ministers were responsible to the parliaments from which they were chosen and to which they could quickly return. American presidents shared power with Congress and the Courts. In theory, none of these checks held back the power of the sultan. In fact the power of tradition and the Islamic establishment restrained even him, but in theory the sultan was the most absolute of monarchs.

The sultans also drew their power from the nature of their office. The greatest authority of the sultan came from his control of those who ruled. The system gave him absolute authority over appointments. All Ottoman civil and military officials served at the sultan's pleasure. Moreover, most officials were legally considered to be not free men, with rights guaranteed by the religious law of Islam, but slaves owned by the sultan, the *kapı kulları/devşirme.* This gave the sultan rights over their lives and property, and the punishment for disobeying his orders could be drastic indeed. Leaders of the Empire's religions, Muslim, Christian, and Jewish, were not his slaves, but they owed their appointments to him and could be replaced at any time. As long as he did not obviously contravene the law of Islam, the sultan could pass binding laws. He was the only one allowed to do so. Law thus emanated from him and was carried out in his name. More importantly, the sultan was the commander-in-chief of all armies. The right to make laws would have been of little use without the military power to ensure compliance with his wishes.

In practice, the powers of the sultan were considerably less than they were in theory. Much of his authority was of necessity delegated. He could not possibly oversee the actions of all those who spoke in his name. In a world where information was hard to collect and all records were kept by scribes who did not necessarily want their masters to know what was going on, the sultan could not know all that transpired. Information was always necessary for power, and information was limited. Those parties who ran the bureaucracy could make sure the sultan heard what they wanted.

The sultan was also constrained by tradition and law. Islam itself was a check on his absolute authority. He named those who led the religious establishment, wrote the law books, and sent out judges. However, the rules of Islam had been codified for centuries before the appearance of the Ottomans. The laws were such that the sultan had to obey. He could not change laws in areas in which modern governments routinely act, such as marriage, divorce, or inheritance. At best, as has been seen above, a powerful sultan could use his authority to bend the rules, if supported by the religious leaders he had named to their posts. Traditional methods of governing also had to be observed. Sultans who attempted to deny their traditional perquisites to the military could be, and occasionally in later years were, killed. If sultans did not act in the way expected by their followers, they could be deposed and another member of the Ottoman family put in their place.

Finally, the sultan's power was circumscribed by the size of his empire. The great distances between the capital and the provinces and the difficulty of communications left provincial governors with great independence. A governor in Iraq would only send matters of great importance to Istanbul for a decision, and then only if there was much time before the decision was needed. The ultimate sanction of attack by the Ottoman army kept the governor from revolting, but nothing kept him from being the *de facto* ruler of his province in most matters.

The 'ruling class'

Those who ran the Ottoman State have been called the ruling class. The term does not denote an economic class, but rather those who held power by virtue of their relationship to the sultan. They were the ones who exercised power in the sultan's name. As such, the ruling class were defined by what they did – defend the Empire and Islam and control revenues.

The leadership of the Ottoman state had at first come from the tribal chiefs who were the officers of Osman's and Orhan's army. They were chieftains of Turkish tribes who had freely associated with Osman because of his prowess as a leader. They and subsequent Turkish leaders have usually been called the Turkish notables, the aristocracy, or the Turkish nobility. ('Turkish nobility' is a confusing term, because of the association with European nobles, who were very little like the Turkish 'nobility'. The actual Turkish titles used to describe the leaders can be roughly translated as 'the boss'.) From an early date the Ottomans supported the notables and their soldiers by awarding them estates. The proceeds from the estates fed and clothed the Turks in a better fashion than they had known as nomads. The Turkish soldiers also lived off booty won in war, especially in the first two centuries of the Empire. They were thus anxious to heed the call to arms, often pressuring the sultan to go to war.

Until the fifteenth century, the leaders of the Turkish military were the most important men in the state after the sultan. They led the conquering Ottoman armies and became the Ottoman vezirs. However, the sultans feared their power and strove to balance it with a slave army.

As the Empire expanded and became a settled state, the sultans more and more depended on an old system of slave-soldiers and slave-administrators that had been used by the Seljuks and others. The theory was that while local or tribal leaders might be loyal to their followers or to their regions, slaves of the sultan would only be loyal to him. These slaves would be well-treated, put in positions of power, and dependent on the sultan for favour, advancement, and a good life. They were not usually bought in slave markets. The first were prisoners of war, trained fighting men or leaders who had been captured and were put into the sultan's service. Later, in the system called the *devşirme*, the sultans took children, selected for their talents and intelligence, from subject Christian families (the so-called child-levy). In a violation of Muslim principles, the children were converted to Islam, taught Ottoman customs and language, and tested carefully. Those who were judged to be most able were further trained to be administrators. The rest became the members of the Janissary Corps and other military units. The class of the sultan's slaves were known as the *kapı kulları* or, after the first days of the system, simply as the *devşirme*.

The word 'slavery' creates images in most minds of African slavery in the New World. Slavery in the Ottoman ruling class was very different, as was slavery in Islam in general. The *devşirme* were slaves who could rise to become the leaders of the Empire, even to the highest position below the sultan, the Grand Vezir. So with the disadvantages of their slave status came real power, often great wealth, and a comfortable life. On the other hand, the slaves of the sultan were completely in his hands. They could be deprived of property and imprisoned or even killed without trial if he

wished. They were entitled to little of the legal protection given to free
subjects by the law. [Captured]

At first the *devşirme* were a useful counter force to the Turkish
notables. The sultan could play one group off against the other. However,
the *devşirme* had great advantages over their rivals in their control of the
financial structure of the Empire (as will be seen below) and their closeness
to the sultan. In the fifteenth century, the *devşirme* began to take effective
control of the Ottoman administration, edging out the old Turkish leaders.
The sultan became as dependent on them as they were on him. The Turkish
leaders increasingly retired to their estates. In the coming years they and
their successors became true local lords, concerned with local problems first
and with the sultan's wishes second.

[margin: True blood Turkish leaders]

Rule in the age of Süleyman

Both the Turks and the Europeans have taken the Ottoman Empire in the
age of Süleyman the Magnificent as the exemplar of the Ottoman state. The
Westerners chose that age because it was as described, magnificent. The
Ottoman reign extended from the Arabian Peninsula to the border of
Austria and from the border of Iran into North Africa. What better time to
study a system than at the height of its power? The Turks chose Süleyman's
time partly for the same reasons, but more for the fact that it was at that
time that much of the Ottoman system was codified.

[margin: Turkish reason]

Historians have traditionally divided the Ottoman government of
Süleyman's time into categories – financial, military, religious, etc. – and
those categories are roughly followed here. These should be taken as functional definitions of positions. The Ottomans did not keep to them exactly,
nor were they closed categories. An Ottoman official might fit into the
category of 'the Military' at one point in his official life, then fit into the
imperial council at another. As has been seen above, a member of the religious hierarchy, such as Çandarlı Hayrettin might be a general and a high
administrator as well. Whether an Ottoman would have paid as much
attention to his change of category as we do is unknown. It would be well
to keep in mind that the system was fluid, much more fluid than most
modern systems of government.

[margin: Historical division of Ott.]

[margin: Ott Gov. very fluid.]

The palace

The leaders of the Ottoman Empire were attached to the sultan's palace.
Their places of deliberation, and for some of them their places of residence,
were within the vast palace that occupied the tip of the Old City of
Istanbul. The imperial palace of Topkapı did not conform to the Western

image of a palace. It rather resembled an extensive walled park with build-ings; 'imperial compound' might be a better term. Situated on the outcrop of land where the Golden Horn, the Bosphorus, and the Sea of Marmara came together, the palace hill rose above the shore. It was separated from the city by a high wall with one relatively small, easily defended gate.

The structure of the palace reflected the activities of those who worked within and their closeness to the person of the sultan. The outer courtyard, through which one had to pass to reach the sultan's chambers, mainly was the precinct of soldiers and officials who dealt with concerns outside the palace – the imperial architect, the head of the mint, and the like, as well as practical buildings such as the kitchens and the stables. The chamber of the Imperial Council opened off the outer courtyard. Beyond the enclosure was the sultan's personal domain, the inner courtyard. It con-tained the throne chamber, the treasury, and place for the officials of the sultan's personal service.

The sultan himself ruled from the harem, situated next to the inner courtyard, protected by imperial eunuchs who gained considerable power through ready access to the sultan and to the women to whom the sultan listened and whom he respected. (The mother of the sultan had a particu-larly high position and great influence, as parents frequently do over their children.)

The titles of those close to the sultan often belied their real power. The sultan's Swordbearer, for instance, was not a page who carried armour, but rather the official in charge of communication with the sultan. The Head of the Gardeners was indeed responsible for the palace gardens, but also for the defence of the shorelines in the capital region and policing the palace. The 'Lords of the Stirrup' (who were allowed to ride alongside the sultan's horse) included military leaders such as the *Ağa* ('Lord' or 'Master') of the Janissary Corps. What the titles did indicate was closeness to the sultan, those who rode by his side, such his falconer or his sword-bearer, and such closeness to the sultan meant power.

The Imperial Council

The sections of the Ottoman system that most corresponded with modern ideas of government were the Imperial Council and the Financial Administration, which can called the Ottoman bureaucracy. The bureau-crats who served the state were called the *kalemiye*, or 'men of the pen' – scribes. The executives of the Council and of Finance were responsible for the actual rule of the sultan over the Empire. They were the ones who over-saw the collection of taxes and the activities of government officials in the provinces.

The decision-making and deliberative body, somewhat the equivalent of the Cabinet in Britain or the United States, was the Imperial Council (called the *Divan-ı Hümayun*, which could be translated the 'Imperial Council' or the 'Imperial Sofa', indicating that the ministers literally sat on the sultan's divan when they met). The most important members of the Council were the *vezirs,* the chief officials of the sultan's administration, led by the Grand Vezir. While the sultan had originally presided over the divan personally, Mehmet the Conqueror and his successors had named the Grand Vezir to represent them. An opaque screen at one end of the divan chamber opened onto the sultan's chambers, and he might at any time hear the Council proceedings without being observed. The divan was thus not the place to engage in conspiracies.

Different officials met with the divan at different times, but it would usually contain the head military men of the Empire, as well as some leading members of the Islamic bureaucracy (see below) and the governors-general of Rumeli (Ottoman Europe) and Anatolia. There were also scribes who recorded the meetings, message carriers, and others who carried out the divan's business. The bureaucratic work of the Council was carried out by scribes, who kept records of its decisions and sent out official communications, such as appointments to government jobs and letters to foreign governments. The decisions of government went through their hands.

Finance

In Süleyman's time, the Ottomans had two treasurers, one for Ottoman Europe, the Treasurer for Rumeli ('Greek land', the Balkans), and one for Asia, the Treasurer for Anatolia. Under them were offices that kept track of all the income and expenditures of the Empire. The offices did exactly what one might expect – audited the Ottoman equivalent of tax returns, kept records of who owed what, and oversaw the expenditures, including salaries, for the various government departments. Their job was monumental. First a book-keeping system had to be created that would fit the financial system of the Empire. (Double entry book-keeping had not yet been invented and accounting as we know it did not exist. Some may count this as one of the glories of the age.) Because of the massive amount of financial data that had to be entered by hand in registers, added, and summarized for the Imperial Council and the sultan, the registers had to be kept in special codes that facilitated rapid entries. That meant that the financial scribes had to be specially trained in more than arithmetic. Theirs was the work of initiates, and the financial scribes were the only ones who understood the records (so perhaps they may be called accountants, after all). This made them indispensable and more than influential.

The taxes that the financial officers oversaw did not include a graduated income tax. The only thing close to it was a head tax collected from non-Muslims, in lieu of military service, according to their ability to pay.

113

Taxes were not so simple. They were collected on whatever things or activities could successfully be taxed. Customs dues were collected at ports, trade taxes from merchants. The primary taxes were on agricultural produce, with a special tax on the most important animal, sheep. Nomads paid taxes on the pastures they used, farmers on the lands they tilled. Various taxes were paid by individuals and every household in the Empire was theoretically supposed to pay a tax as a household.

Those sources of revenue that could be easily controlled (called *emanet*s), for example taxes on the markets in Istanbul, went directly to the treasury, collected by salaried officials. But relatively few taxes could be collected in that fashion. Collecting all the various taxes would have necessitated complete central government knowledge of almost everything that went on in the Empire – how many households there were, how many sheep, what goods passed through each port, etc. Indeed, the Ottoman financial scribes in the sixteenth century kept more complete records than any other country in the world – detailed lists of households and taxable properties. It was not enough. In the days before literacy was common and before adding machines or computers there could not be enough scribes to keep track of it all. Nor could information be collected and forwarded to the government quickly enough. Other solutions were found:

The timar

The *timar*, land given to soldiers to support their men, was developed long before the time of Süleyman. The Seljuks, the Byzantines, and others had previously used systems in which their supporters were settled on the land and supported by the land. In return for fighting for the emperor or sultan, leaders were allowed to collect taxes from an area and quarter their soldiers there. The system was used by the Ottomans both to settle down nomadic Turks and to defend the Empire.

The sultan distributed imperial lands (*miri* lands) to supporters, primarily Turkish military leaders, called *sipahi*s, who served as cavalry in the Ottoman forces. He also delegated the right to award *timar*s to his lieutenants in the provinces, the *sancakbeyi*s (governors, see below). The lands were the sultan's to dispose by right of conquest and tradition. Those who received the *timar*s paid no taxes for the land. Instead, proceeds from taxes of the villages in the *timar* were used to support a leader and his troops. In return for the support, the soldiers policed their region and served in the sultan's army whenever needed. *Timar*s varied greatly in size, the proceeds depending on the position and employment of the holder. A *beylerbeyi* (governor-general) could be granted a *timar* that produced fifty times the proceeds of one held by an ordinary *sipahi*.

Those who were given *timar*s were, according to Ottoman regulations, always members of the *askeri* class. This included Turkish notables and their descendants, military slaves (*kul*) of the sultan or of high officials, or members of the nobility of conquered states and their descendants. Therefore, *timar*s were held by Christians as well as Muslims, although these had generally converted to Islam by the time of Süleyman. No members of the *raya* class were to hold *timar*s. Nevertheless, despite the law, members of the *raya* were able to take *timar*s, and thus be assumed into the *askeri* class, through connections with provincial governors and bribery. Holding *timar*s, like membership in the *askeri* class, passed from father to son. Sons inherited smaller *timar*s, less than half the income, than those held by their fathers, although they could be granted more through service or political influence. *Timar*s were taken away for dereliction of duty; if a holder did not perform his duties, especially military duties, he lost his *timar* and even his membership in the *askeri* class.

By the time of Süleyman, *timar*-holding had undergone a great change because so many were awarded to members of the *devşirme*. As Turkish notable sons inherited smaller *timar*s than their fathers', much of the remaining land found its way into *devşirme* hands. Many Turkish *sipahi*s were legitimately or illegitimately dispossessed to make way for members of the *devşirme*. This fuelled the discontent and rebellions that arose at the end of Süleyman's reign and after.

[handwritten marginal note: Devsirme getting larger Timars fuel Rebelion and discontent for full blood Turks]

The tax farm

The *iltizam* or tax farm was based on an auction of the right to collect taxes from a specific portion of the sultan's property. In theory, whoever offered the highest sum to the treasury was awarded the concession. In fact, nothing as lucrative as tax farming was without a certain amount of bribery and the use of political influence. The tax farmer agreed to pay the government fixed sums at regular intervals. His own property or a rich guarantor stood as surety in case of default. He was then free to collect taxes from the property or other source of revenue, usually for a period of three years. A tax farmer might, for example, be given the right to collect taxes from a group of villages held as part of the sultan's personal reserve. He would give the treasury his agreed payments and send out his men to collect what they could. Some tax farmers would subcontract the collections to other tax farmers, particularly if the farms were far removed from the capital.

The tax farms were obviously subject to abuse. If a tax farmer was only to collect taxes for a few years, he had no personal interest in the long-term survival of the peasants in his region. He would be mightily tempted to overcharge the peasants. The sultan stood against this, and there were rules to protect the cultivators from the rapacity of tax collectors. This was not only altruism, for the sultan's men knew that land destroyed by the exactions of a tax farmer would not provide needed taxes in the years to come. When the central government was strong the rules that protected the peasants were properly applied, but when the central government was weak the peasants might suffer. The peasants on the *timar*s generally fared better, because the *timar* holder could often expect that his son and grandson would continue to control *timar* land and he would pass it to them in good shape. However, the peasants on both tax farms and *timar*s ultimately depended on the power of the central government. It was in the best interests of the government to make sure that the peasants were not overcharged too much. If they were, they would desert the land, and that meant no taxes flowing into the treasury. Therefore, while the government was strong, the peasants survived.

The term 'tax farm' is deceptive, because it implies to modern English speakers that the business was solely agricultural. In fact, many of the most lucrative tax farms had nothing to do with agriculture. Productive sources of revenue such as gold mines, trade monopolies on wine and other goods, and salt production were auctioned off to tax farmers. Customs collection, a most important part of imperial revenue, was routinely given as tax farms. The tax farmer acted nearly as a government official, calling on soldiers to enforce his collections and ships to stop smuggling. Many of these non-agricultural collections could have been put in the hands of salaried government employees. The customs dues of Istanbul were farmed out, for example, when there were many nearby officials of the treasury who could have collected them. The government obviously believed that private enterprise would give a better rate of return.

The vakıf

The Ottoman government allowed one legal method of avoiding taxes altogether, the *vakıf* or pious foundation. The principle behind the *vakıf* is familiar to modern economies – the rich may donate their property to a foundation that supports good causes, and the proceeds of the property are not taxed so long as they continue to be spent on charitable causes. Muslim pious foundations were much the same. Religion enjoined Muslims to be charitable, one of the pillars of Islam. Without charity, a Muslim could not hope to gain paradise. The *vakıf* was a way to realize charity effectively. Humans sometimes being other than charitable creatures, there were also practical benefits.

The essence of the *vakıf* was the removal of productive assets from the grasp of the tax man. In form, the *vakıf* came to the Ottomans almost unchanged from the Great Seljuk Empire. A rich merchant or government official would donate money, land, or property to create a foundation. Before it could be established, the foundation needed approval from an Islamic judge (a *kadı*, see below) and the government, but the donor was allowed to stipulate how the foundation's assets would be spent. He or she (and there were many rich female donors) named the trustees of the foundation, sometimes in perpetuity, the good cause it would support, and the general way in which it would function. Pious foundations were funded by economic levels of society from the middle to the highest. Sultans and high officials were prominent donors. Unlike other donors, the sultan could make donations of state lands, which were legally his.

The definition of a good cause that might be supported by a *vakıf* was broad. Almost anything that benefited society or religion was allowed. Because of this, foundations took over much of the creation and support of what modern societies would call civic improvements or welfare – activities that today are normally performed by the state, but did not fit within the Ottoman definition of government operations. For example, foundations supported soup kitchens for the poor and built and supported hospitals, libraries, public fountains, and wells. What might be built by governments in other lands, such as bridges, were constructed by foundations. Commerce was supported by the erection of caravansarays and other buildings. Religion was the greatest beneficiary: the great *medrese* complexes in Ottoman cities were supported by extensive *vakıf* endowments from sultans and vezirs, as were the great mosques. Smaller mosques and schools in provincial cities were built by pious merchants and governors. Endowments paid the tuition and support of students and some of the teachers (most *ulema* were paid state salaries). On a more personal level, foundations were also endowed to pay for prayers for the soul of the donor or for Quran readings to be made in his or her name.

In addition to city properties, agricultural land was turned into *vakıf*s. Here the sultan retained some rights of taxation, because the state claimed the right to tax peasant's labour, in practice a right often abrogated to serve a good cause. However, the most prominent foundations drew their support from enterprises in cities and towns. These were primarily bazaars and shops whose rents supported the foundations. For example, Mehmet II built the nucleus of the great covered bazaar in Istanbul and many other bazaars and shops to provide support for mosques and *medrese*s. The scope of the enterprise was immense: it has been estimated that in Süleyman's time 10,000 shops in Istanbul were owned by *vakıf*s. The shops in Istanbul and all over the empire were rented to all sorts of merchants and craftsmen. Only the most disreputable endeavours were usually, though not always, excluded. Large buildings such as warehouses (*han*s), bathhouses, and mills were also *vakıf* properties.

Were the foundations created solely for the purpose of saving the souls of the donors? No. There were also earthly benefits. One benefit was the care of one's family. A rich man or, especially, a high official knew that power and wealth were fleeting. Future governments might claim his property, before or after his death, and leave nothing to his descendents. However, if he created a *vakıf* and named his descendents as trustees, at a decent salary, he might ensure their economic survival. Both the good cause and the family would be well served. Foundations also gave their donors and his descendents, or other appointees to the job of trustee, considerable power. Any economic establishment on a grand scale carried with it power and the possibility of financial gain. Those who bought boat loads of grain for soup kitchens, hired hundreds of workers, rented numerous properties, or controlled many villages naturally could solicit bribes and favours. They could use their position to cultivate highly placed political friends. In some cities, foundations literally built and owned the entire commercial district, a position of great control. The leaders of religion, the ulema, in particular exercised control from a base of *vakıf* trusteeship. *Ulema* were either appointed as trustees in the initial deed or inherited *vakıf*s when the original family died out or proved derelict in their duties, for *vakıf*s were always supervised by government and the *kadı*s.

Of course, *vakıf*s were economic enterprises that could fail as well as prosper. If poorly administered or fraudulently milked of assets, they would go bankrupt and disappear. Sultans envied the wealth of foundations and sometimes managed, legally or illegally, to seize their assets. Mehmet II was particularly active in seizing *vakıf*s, claiming, often with justification, that many *vakıf*s had never been approved by the government and thus were illegal and subject to seizure. However, his actions aroused great animosity, and his successor, Bayezit II, returned the foundations to their supervisors. The great foundations of Istanbul, which supported the grand mosques and *medrese*s, existed well into modern times.

Irrespective of the intentions of their donors, or perhaps because of them, *vakıf*s filled a necessary part in Ottoman society. It is hard to imagine commercial life in the Empire without them. They allowed a form of capital formation and investment that did not exist in ordinary Ottoman economic life. Security of investment is a necessary element of a successful economy, and *vakıf*s provided security when it was all too often unavailable else-where. Best of all, they did much good, feeding the poor, ministering to the sick, building glorious religious edifices to feed the soul, and providing libraries to feed the mind.

Private property

The Ottoman sultan owned most of the land in his empire because of the 'right of conquest'. Ownership of land that had been conquered from Christian states was therefore his. However, much of the land that made up the Ottoman Empire had been in Muslim hands for centuries before the Ottoman conquest. State-owned lands in these conquests, which had similar systems to the Ottoman practice of state ownership, became Ottoman state lands. In the Arab lands and Anatolia, however, ownership of land according to Muslim law could not be legally overturned. Extensive estates had been granted to individuals by past Muslim rulers or had been legally purchased and passed down to descendants. These remained as private property (*mülk*), with normal rights to sell, bequeath to heirs, etc. under the Ottoman system.

The sultans also made grants of land for private ownership. These were usually lands that had been abandoned or were otherwise unproductive, and the grants were effective in turning such lands into productive, tax-paying assets. Some land registered as productive was also granted to high officials, although this was usually done for the purpose of allowing officials to create *vakıf*s in their names. Because the land converted to private ownership by the sultan was originally state land, the state was allowed to make stipulations with the grants. This included the provision that if the land was not put into production it would revert to the sultan. The legal conversion of state land to private ownership presented the opportunity for some corruption. Lands were deemed unproductive 'waste lands' because the government declared them to be so. The possibilities for illegal conversion are obvious.

The government could not claim ownership of private lands, and thus could not distribute it for *timar*s or rent it to tax farmers, but they could tax it. State revenues from private lands were not insignificant. In the provinces of Aleppo and Damascus and in southeastern Anatolia, in particular, taxes on private lands provided almost one-third of state revenues. Owners were also required to provide auxiliary troops to the armed forces in times of war.

The religious establishment

Islam was not a religion that could be properly practised simply by gathering with fellow believers and praying once a week. Islam intended to be a part of every aspect of a believer's life, including the government. For Muslims, all laws were ideally religious laws and the government was necessarily an Islamic government. The Ottomans recognized this by putting Islam at the centre of their government.

The sultan named the head of the Islamic administration of the empire, the *Şeyhülislam* ('Elder of Islam'). The job of *Şeyhülislam* reflected the nature of Islam, in which law was central. The leaders of Sunni Islam, the largest branch of the religion and that followed by the Ottomans, were actually the intellectuals of the religion. These scholars, called *mufti*s, applied the law of Islam (the *Sharia*) to legal situations. In effect, they wrote the law books and acted as advisors who told judges and political leaders what could and could not be done legally. The *Şeyhülislam* was the chief of the *mufti*s. He named the *mufti*s who went out to the provinces to issue legal opinions (*fetva*s) there. He also named the judges (*kadı*s) who sat on the official courts all over the Empire. In all areas of the Empire, these judges enforced the law of Islam and the law of the sultan, aided by the authority of the sultan's governors.

Both *kadi*s and *mufti*s were trained in a system of schooling that was for centuries the basis of education in the Ottoman Empire. Elementary education was provided in Islamic schools that were found in cities, towns, and sometimes even large villages. The education was very elementary, consisting primarily of memorizing of prayers and verses from the Koran. However, those marked as bright in the elementary schools were sent on to higher schools. The higher schools, called *medrese*s, were actually a series of schools, beginning in provincial towns and ending in Istanbul. If a student proved worthy at one level, he was advanced to a higher school. The highest was the grand *medrese* complex at the Süleymaniye Mosque in Istanbul. The training in the schools in many ways resembled the system taught in the classical world. Its emphasis was on rhetoric, philosophy, and language, as well as purely religious studies. As students ascended to the higher schools, their studies went more towards Islamic jurisprudence and theology. Those who succeeded in their studies became members of the learned class, the *ulema*, and became *mufti*s, judges, and instructors in the *medrese*s.

In addition to providing men of religion, the Islamic school system also trained those who became bureaucrats in other branches of the government. The schools were the primary source of literacy, so it was natural for their graduates to become scribes. Religious leaders of high rank also themselves took leading places in the bureaucracy. The men of religion were thus closely tied to the government as a whole. In times before Süleyman. members of *ulema* families rose to the highest offices, including Grand Vezir, and the political power of the *ulema* remained great throughout the Empire's history.

The bureaucracy

The members of the Ottoman bureaucracy were often closely allied to, but not necessarily members of, the *ulema*. Like other Ottoman governmental organizations, the bureaucracy arose as a practical and pragmatic tool of government, then solidified into an institution of government, often called the scribal institution. Originally, even Christian bureaucrats, who knew the taxation methods of conquered states, served under the Ottomans. By the time of Süleyman, however, membership in the bureaucracy had become centred in a ruling elite of freeborn Muslims, most of whom were themselves sons of bureaucrats or sons of members of the *ulema* or the *devşirme*. A person not of 'good family' might enter the bureaucracy through the Islamic school system, and a small percentage of the bureaucrats were from more or less humble origins.

After a prospective bureaucrat had passed through the middle level of the Islamic school system, at about age sixteen, he entered the bureaucracy as an apprentice. It was here that family connections helped the most, in finding a suitable first position. No amount of family connection could ensure success after that, because knowledge and political skill were essential to advancement and survival. A clever bureaucrat might advance to high position through a combination of competence, friendships with the mighty, and political skill. The other way to the top was through the religious establishment. High members of the *ulema* might themselves 'change hats' and be translated into the bureaucracy. Once again, friends and political skill were essential.

In keeping with the political nature of the bureaucracy, the power and relative importance of bureaucratic offices changed over time. Up to the time of Süleyman, the most important bureaucrats were the *defterdars*, or 'keepers of the registers'. They were led by a chief *defterdar*. Lower offices were divided into the sort of organizational table that is commonly seen in governments or businesses – offices with titles and responsibilities, held by occupants who were always striving to reach the next level of authority and income.

Most of the activities of Ottoman bureaucrats would be easily recognizable in a modern state, even if the methods of carrying them out differed. Ottoman bureaucrats kept records of the decisions made by officials and of how the decisions were executed. They recorded the internal workings of the government – who held which offices, who was hired, who was fired. Most importantly, they kept records of income and expenditure.

Provincial government

The basic administrative unit of the Ottomans was the *sancak* ('standard'), governed by a *sancakbeyi*. Sultans Murat I and Bayezit I created three *beylerbeyiliks* (the highest level of province, from *beylerbeyi*, 'governor-general') to oversee the *sancak*s of Rumeli (the Balkans), Western Anatolia, and Central Anatolia. As the Ottomans took new territories, they first created *sancak*s, then eventually organized the *sancak*s into *beylerbeyiliks*. The table lists those that had been created up to 1578, slightly after Süleyman's death.[1] Each *beylerbeyilik* was centred on a capital city, which held Janissary detachments to enforce central authority, religious judges, and bureaucrats to record taxation. *Sancak* administration was similar, but on a smaller scale.

The *sancakbeyi*s and *beylerbeyi*s led their administrative units in both peace and war, serving as heads of the administration as well as generals, in the traditional Ottoman fashion. Their authority was somewhat checked by

---

[1] Taken from Halil İnalcık, *The Ottoman Empire*, New York, 1973, p. 106, with slight changes.

Ottoman Beylerbeyliks, *to 1578*

Beylerbeylik	Capital
Rumeli	Edirne, Sofya, Manastır
Anadolu	Ankara, Kütahya
Rum	Amasya, Sivas
Trabzon	Trabzon
Bosna (Bosnia)	Sarajevo
Karaman	Konya
Kefe	Caffa
Dulkadır	Maraş
Erzurum	Erzurum
Diyarbakır	Diyarbakır
Musul	Mosul
Haleb	Aleppo
Şam	Damascus
Trablus-Şam	Tripoli (Lebanon)
Mısır (Egypt)	Cairo
Yemen	Zabid, San'a
Cezair-i bahr-i sefid	Gallipoli
Cezair-Garb	Algiers
Kars	Kars
Bağdat	Baghdad
Van	Van
Tunus	Tunis
Basra	Basra
Lahsa (al-Hasa)	al-Katif
Budin	Buda
Trablus-Garb	Tripoli (Africa)
Tamışvar	Temesvar
Şehrizor	Zor
Habeş	Suakin, Jidda
Kıbris (Cyprus)	Nicosia
Çıldır	Çıldır

officials of the central treasury, who watched the governor's transactions as well as the tax receipts, and by the Islamic judge, the *kadı*. The *kadı* enforced the Islamic law and the secular law (*kanun*) of the sultan. He too was expected to keep a watch on government officials, reporting transgressions to the central government. Due to the admixture of religion and law in Islamic states, the *kadı*'s power was great. It extended into the commercial sphere. *Kadı*s oversaw and notarized commercial contracts and heard legal cases of merchants. Their powers of oversight went to the highest levels: Two judges, the *kadıasker*s (military judges) of Anatolia and

Rumeli were given extensive powers over the military and the religious establishments in Ottoman Asia and Europe, respectively. Both sat on the imperial divan. Despite oversight, the *beylerbeyi*s or *sancakbeyi*s were in control of their provinces. They could even dismiss treasury officials and *kadı*s. However, the existence of those officials meant that Istanbul always kept a watch on the activities of the governors, and in Istanbul the treasury and the *ulema* both supported their administrators in the provinces, so the governors were forced to tread softly.

Extension of direct Ottoman control to all the regions of the Empire proved impossible. The area was too large and even imperial military power too limited for that. In provinces far removed from Istanbul such as those in eastern Anatolia and parts of the Arab region, different types of administration were accepted. Often, local leaders were left in control, sometimes remitting sums to the treasury, sometimes only sending men to fight for the sultan. Not all the *beylerbeyilik*s in the table were equally tied to the central government. Most of the provinces were under direct control, but provinces such as those in Eritrea/Western Sudan (Habeş) or the Arabian desert (Lahsa) were too far to be closely watched.

The military

The army

In the end it all depended on the soldiers. None of the elaborate structure of the Ottoman Empire could have survived had the military not been able to defend it.

The Ottoman Empire began as a military state and all the early sultans through the reign of Süleyman distinguished themselves as military leaders. Even as the Empire became more settled and administrative jobs more specialized, many bureaucrats were also soldiers. The Grand Vezir might direct the bureaucracy, but he was also called on to lead the army in the name of the sultan. Governors of Ottoman provinces had both civil and military powers. Members of the imperial divan were generals as well as administrators and advisors. This reflected not only the origins of the Ottoman Empire, but also the realities of a state that was always necessarily occupied with defence and conquest.

Long before the reign of Süleyman, the Empire had ceased to depend mainly on nomadic Turkish cavalry. Orhan, the second Ottoman sultan, organized a salaried army of foot soldiers (*yaya*s) and cavalrymen (*müsellem*s). At first, many, perhaps a majority, of the new standing army were Christians from the Balkans, although later they became an almost totally Muslim force. In the ensuing years, the sultans increasingly used

Turkish nomads for particular assignments, rather than as the mainstay of the army. The nomads became shock troops, attacking first to 'soften up' opposing armies, before the main attacks of other Ottoman troops, or raiders (*akıncıs*) who ravaged the territories of Ottoman enemies. Nomads were also settled in remote and hard-to-conquer regions such as Albania, where their very presence reinforced Turkish authority. Like the Great Seljuks, the Ottomans realized that they had to send the nomads to the periphery, where they could be useful, but not damaging to the Ottoman state in the way nomads tended to be. Better they raid others.

A number of other military functions were performed by freeborn troops. *Azabs, at first volunteers* but *by the time of Süleyman conscripts*, served primarily as marines and fortress guards. Others served as *derbend* ('mountain pass' or 'guardhouse') guards. Whole villages often served as *derbend* guards. Their purpose was to protect major roads, mountain passes, trade depots, and other areas of strategic and commercial importance. In exchange for tax exemption or the right to collect tolls, they provided a stable security force in their regions. Christians as well as Muslims served as *derbend* guards.

As the Ottoman state grew, many of the Turks settled down to become farmers. Those who remained as fighting men commonly became part of the *timar* system, supported by the proceeds from villagers' taxes and available for war when needed. Turkish leaders who had been granted *timar*s (*timarlı sipahi*s) kept their own horses and supplies and brought them and their retainers to campaigns. When called up, they were organized by provincial governors and sent to staging areas to be incorporated into the army. Eventually, the *yaya*s, *müsellem*s, and even *akıncı*s also passed from the status of salaried troops to become part of the *timar* system, from standing troops to 'militia'. The *sipahi*s, while still a major part of the Ottoman army under Süleyman, were also doomed as fighting units. They were armoured cavalry, bows and spears their weapons, and in the coming age of the musket such cavalrymen would be of little use.

The Ottoman army in the time of Süleyman

Kapı kulları *Forces*	*Local Forces*
Sipahi (Cavalry)	*Timarlı Sipahi* (Cavalry)
Cebeci (Armorers)	*Yaya* (Foot Soldiers)
Topçu (Artillerymen)	*Müsellem* (Cavalry)
Arabacı (Wagon Drivers)	*Akıncı* (Raiders)
Yeniçeri (Janissaries)	*Azab*
	Derbend

The best-known Ottoman soldiers were slaves of the sultan, the Janissaries. They formed the main part of the salaried standing army. Their precursors had originally been prisoners of war and others, including

Christians, who fought for the sultan, but the Janissary Corps eventually came almost entirely from the child-levy. Janissaries were trained from youth to be soldiers and initiated into one of the 101 battalions of the Corps. Expected to be always ready for battle, the Janissaries lived, ate, and slept with their battalions. They were not allowed to marry or take up other occupations until they retired from the service.

Until the seventeenth century, the number of the Janissaries was never great (30,000 is the figure most commonly given). However, they were marked by their discipline and their willingness to adopt new methods of warfare. They were probably the first standing army to uniformly adopt gunpowder weapons. Often their battles were won because of superior training and firepower. Auxiliary corps of armourers, artillerymen, etc. supported them. Like the Janissaries, these were slave soldiers. Other slave soldiers formed salaried cavalry regiments (like the cavalry housed on *timar*s, they were called *sipahi*s).

As was natural in any major army, the Ottomans also employed specialized armed units, both from the slave army and from the *timar* soldiers. These included quartermaster corps, military engineers, and other support groups.

The Ottoman army was a composite force which was formed of a salaried standing army and of units similar to the feudal levies of medieval Europe. Despite the tensions that such a system naturally produced, the units fought well together. It is somewhat surprising to those who view Christians and Muslims as forever opposing forces, but the early Ottomans managed very successfully to meld Christians into their armed forces. Unlike the Janissaries, these forces kept their religion but served the sultan, and did so very effectively. As long as the sultan and the central government maintained a high degree of control, the army was a unit. It was for long the most powerful force in Europe, perhaps in the world.

The navy

The Ottoman Empire was a land power, and the navy was definitely the second service. Not until the time of Süleyman did the leader of the navy, the Grand Admiral, take a place in the Imperial Council. The navy was not salaried by the central government. Its leaders were granted *timar*s, which they used to support their ships and men: Hayrettin Barbarossa was granted Algiers as his *timar*. Later Grand Admirals took Aegean islands as *timar*s. As the need for a navy increased, whole provinces were given over as *timar*s to the navy.

The organization of the navy was what might be expected, each large ship commanded by a captain (*reis*), organized into fleets commanded by admirals (*kapudan*). With the notable exception of Barbarossa's pirate sailors, Ottoman sailors were not primarily Muslim until very late in the

125

Empire's history, because the government relied on the best sailors in the Empire, and these were often Greeks or other Christians. The main battle vessels were galleys. As in the other Mediterranean countries' navies, many of the oarsmen were slaves captured in war and criminals sent to the galleys as punishment. Others came from drafts of oarsmen from villages which were relieved of other taxes in exchange for a levy of men for that purpose. (As galley oarsman was one of the worst employments ever devised by man, they would surely have preferred to pay their taxes.) *Azabs* served as marines, a critical position, because galleys fought at close quarters.

Merit and advancement

At its height, the Ottoman administrative system was based on merit. It rivalled the traditional Chinese civil service system in that regard.

Functioning as intended, the *devşirme* system was a model of meritocracy. The way to the top in the *devşirme* system was by proving oneself physically and mentally. Those taken in the child-levy had been selected for their physical grace, strength, and intelligence. During their training they underwent constant scrutiny. Only the most qualified were sent on to schools where they were trained to be officials and generals.

Turkish notables and their sons might prove themselves on the battlefield and be granted larger *timar*s and more authority, but by the time of Süleyman the *devşirme* had greatly encroached on Turkish notables' power. For those born Muslim, religion and the bureaucracy were the main paths to political power. The religious schools offered Muslims, even the occasional poor but intelligent Muslim, an opportunity to rise to power and authority. Learning was the key. The brightest and most hard-working advanced from school to school, perhaps rising to a place at the Süleymaniye Medrese in Istanbul. From there they might take high positions in the system that controlled both the law and religion of the Empire. Other freeborn Muslims, trained in the religious schools and the schools operated by the bureaucracy, took careers in the bureaucracy, as did members of the *ulema* themselves.

Despite its achievements, the Ottoman system was far from being a true meritocracy. The system that selected the best Christian youths for the *devşirme* also kept those who were born Muslim Turks from entering the *devşirme* ranks and having their chance to become Grand Vezir. *Timar* holders were by nature not selected purely by merit. With few exceptions, a Turk granted a *timar* had to be from the *askeri* class; villagers need not apply. The easiest way to gain a *timar* was to be the son of a *timar* holder. The administrative system did not necessarily select the best man to perform the duties of a particular office. The man selected was often the best politician, not the best technician. As in many systems where advancement is theoretically based on excellence, the merit shown by the highest bureaucrats might be merit in surviving the political wars. To enter and advance within the bureaucracy, the best knowledge was the knowledge that your father was a *vezir*. It was also true that sons of the religious leaders were usually the best prepared to pass the exams, attend the schools, and become members of the leadership themselves. Then as now, a word in the ear of a fellow professor might help one's son gain admission to a school. Once educated, highly placed relatives furthered one's career. Biographies of members of the *ulema* show many religious leaders who were the sons and grandsons of past religious leaders.

Nevertheless, and in spite of its flaws, the Ottoman system of government was based on merit to a surprising extent. Once in government, a junior official or soldier was able to prove his abilities by attaching himself to the 'party' of a powerful man. Successful leaders chose able deputies and advanced the deputies' careers, because it was in the interests of the powerful to have competent supporters. A good political sense and ability were the best qualifications for success.

The non-Muslims of the Empire

To the Ottomans, religious tolerance was both a practical and a legal necessity. Islamic law commanded that Christians and Jews (called *dhimmi*s, 'people of the Book', those who believed in the Bible) be allowed to practise their religions. The non-Muslims were legally bound to pay a special tax in lieu of military service, but could worship in their churches and keep schools, religious organizations and other elements of their religions. As an Islamic empire, the Ottoman Empire necessarily conformed to this Islamic law. There also was a practical basis for tolerance. The Ottomans ruled over a vast territory populated by members of different Christian sects. Even if they had wanted to force conversion, it might have proved impossible and certainly would have caused revolt. As long as his subjects accepted his rule, it was in the interests of the sultan to leave them in peace.

Throughout Middle Eastern history, religious institutions had provided many of the public services that modern citizens expect of the state. Religion was considered to be the most important thing in life, so schools were naturally religious schools, teaching that which was most important. Whatever their religion, all agreed that relations between people should be governed by God's wishes (though God's wishes differed from religion to religion). Therefore, how one treated his or her family, business associates, and neighbours was expected to conform to religious ethics, and this was often decided by religious courts. God had commanded that people love and help one another, so charity was part of religion as well, organized into welfare systems operated by the religious institutions. In short, religion was the essential factor in the actions that were most important to humans, so religions were integral to public welfare. Thus many functions that might elsewhere be considered governmental were in the Ottoman Empire carried out by religions.

The Ottoman Empire took the religious traditions of the Middle East and Balkans and codified them into law. Each religious group was named as a *millet* (literally 'nation'). The *millet*s were in charge of the education, welfare, and personal law of their members. Their leaders represented the needs of their people to the sultan's government. Sometimes, as was the case with the Greek Orthodox, the place of the *millet* was specifically recognized by law. Other *millet*s, such as the Jews, were simply recognized by tradition. As the centuries passed, more sects were officially recognized (such as the Greek Catholics or the Bulgarian Orthodox, who were recognized as separate *millet*s late in the Empire's history), but the *millet* system was an essential element of Ottoman government from an early date. Even before individual *millet*s were officially recognized, they had a *de facto* separate existence.

Because Islam was the official religion of the Empire one cannot really speak of a Muslim *millet*. Nevertheless, the Muslim community functioned in much the same way as the Christian communities, furnishing welfare, schools, places of worship, and the other services provided by the Christian and Jewish *millet*s for their own people. The Muslim organization undoubtedly had advantages. It drew a certain power from the fact that the leading members of the government, including the sultan, were among its members. The state was committed to the benefit of Islam. Thus in disputes between Muslims and members of other religions Muslim law took precedence, although the Muslim by no means always won the case.

It would be impossible to adequately describe the various *millet*s here. The major ones are depicted briefly below.

The Greek Orthodox

When the Byzantine Empire fell in 1453 the centre of the Greek Orthodox Church was shaken. The Church had been closely entwined with the Empire, each supporting the other and each a symbol of Greek identity. The state was now lost, but Mehmet the Conqueror had no wish to lose the centralized Church. Immediately upon his conquest of Constantinople he named a new Patriarch, Gennadius.

Gennadius was actually given more authority than previous patriarchs had held. Many of the powers given to the new Greek *millet* had previously been held by the Byzantine state or shared between Church and state. In the Greek tradition, which was very different from Roman Catholicism, the authority of each bishop was great; the Patriarch had little juridical control over local bishops. This had been especially true since the Turkish invasion had begun, because local Greek Christian communities had been cut off from central Byzantine authority. Now the power of the Ottoman state stood behind the Patriarch as he administered the Greek Christian *millet.*

Mehmet may originally have seen the Greek *millet* system as a way to systematize the administration of all the non-Muslims in the Ottoman Empire, but jealousies between the various Christian and Jewish groups would have made this impossible. Other groups soon had their own *millet*s. The Greek *millet* included the Orthodox populations of the Ottoman Empire. Greeks were called *Rum* by the Turks, following the old tradition of equating the Byzantine Greeks with the ancient Roman Empire. Although called 'Greek', many members of the Greek Orthodox Church were Slavs and Romanians, 'Greek' only because they were in the Greek Church. When the Arab provinces were conquered by the Ottomans, Arab Orthodox Christians became members of the Greek *millet*, listed in later censuses as 'Greeks'. To the Christians, Muslims, and Jews of the Middle East and Balkans, religion, not language, was the primary source of identity.

The Armenian Gregorians

The Armenian Gregorian (after St. Gregory the Illuminator, the evangelist of the Armenians) Church differed from the Greek Orthodox in that its members were all from one ethnic group, the Armenians. The original home of the Armenians was in eastern Anatolia and the southern Caucasus, but they had been migrating to other parts of the Middle East and elsewhere for centuries, and a small Armenian kingdom had existed in Cilicia. To the Armenians, their Church was a point of identification that kept them together through rule by various larger and stronger neighbours. The Armenian Church was considered heretical by both Greek Orthodox and Roman Catholics. It was monophysite, an early Christian belief that held that Jesus had only one nature, a divine nature. The Orthodox held that Jesus had two natures – divine and human. The Armenian Church was, therefore, persecuted under the Byzantines, always surviving, partly because of the remoteness of the Armenian mountains. Persecution by other Christians certainly helped to cement Armenian separation.

In the formative years of the Ottoman Empire the bulk of the Armenian population lay in areas under the rule of others. (In the Ottoman centuries, Echmiadzin, the main centre of the Gregorian Church and seat of the chief Patriarch, the *Catholicos*, was not under Ottoman control, except for very brief periods.) Mehmet II organized the Armenian community by setting up an Armenian Patriarch in Istanbul, whom he gave authority over the Armenian community similar to that of the Greek Patriarch over the Orthodox. However, much of the Armenian community lived far from the centre of the Empire. Armenian regions and villages were often virtually independent in their mountains. They ran their own affairs naturally, whether or not the *millet* system was in place.

The Jews

The centres of Jewish life in the Middle East, such as Palestine, Iraq, Yemen, and Egypt, all eventually came under Ottoman rule. Even in the time of Mehmet the Conqueror a significant community of Jews were Ottoman, remnants of the Jewish *diaspora* that had spread across the Mediterranean in Roman times. More than any other community, the Jews of the Mediterranean region had traditionally governed their own affairs. When Christian governments gave them orders it was usually to the Jews' detriment. In Islamic areas, the separation of Jews, Christians, and Muslims was ordained by the laws governing their status as protected 'people of the Book'. Therefore, in all the areas eventually ruled by the Ottomans the Jews were already a separate community. The Ottomans did little to affect Jewish status, other than to offer them a tolerance they had not known under Christian rulers. There was no perceived need to systematize the *millet* rules for Jews and, indeed, no formal charter for a Jewish *millet* was drawn up until the nineteenth century. However, the Ottomans treated the Jews legally much as they did other *millet*s.

Ottoman toleration drew Jews to the Empire from Eastern Europe and Spain and Portugal. The latter came in a great wave of forced migration when Ferdinand and Isabella of Spain and their successors forced conversion or exile on the non-Christians of Spain, a policy later followed in Portugal, as well. Along with some Jews already in the Empire they formed the Sephardic community. Ashkenazi (or European) Jews formed the other main part of the Jewish community.

The other millets

Although not always recognized officially within the *millet* structure, at least not until the end of the Empire, various Christian groups were *de facto millet*s. These included Nestorians, Syrian Orthodox, and Maronites. At first, Mehmet the Conqueror had attempted to put the smaller religious groups under the legal authority of the Armenian Patriarch in Istanbul, perhaps to balance the power of the Greek Patriarch. However, this system was unworkable. The smaller groups were frequently geographically removed from the centres of the Empire and in effect ruled themselves. Their religious leaders had great power.

From the eighteenth century, the Christian groups were greatly affected by Catholic missionaries, who drew members of the churches into Uniate churches that accepted the authority of the Pope, but kept their own liturgies. Greek and Armenian Catholics were among the new churches. The

Maronites of Lebanon converted in a body to papal authority. Members of other Christian sects, mainly Armenians, converted to Protestantism in the nineteenth century. In each case, the Ottomans recognized the new churches and their members as a new *millet*. This was sometimes necessary to keep the converts from persecution by members of the old church.

Ottoman tolerance in perspective

Although words such as 'non-judgemental' appear on scholars' lips from time to time, historians have always made comparisons that easily become judgements. The judgements are usually made in two ways – comparisons to contemporaries and comparisons to modern times. In the first, the political system, the riches, the art or almost anything else of one group is compared to that of another group living in the same period. In the second, they are compared to the situation at a much later date. The French political system in 1820, for example, can be compared to the British system in 1820 and very favourably compared to the Russian political system in the same year. However, the 1820 French system suffers considerably when compared to the French or British political systems in the 1980s (although not necessarily to the 1980s Russian system).

The same type of comparisons have been made of the Ottoman Empire. When measured against the religious freedoms in twentieth-century Canada, America, or Britain the Ottoman record appears to be very deficient. For most of the Empire's history, members of religious minorities were not allowed to serve in the army or share in central government. They paid a special tax. In some areas of the Empire, such as Yemen, Jews and Christians sometimes wore distinguishing clothing. Muslims felt superior and often acted accordingly. Until the end of the Empire the minorities, like the Muslims, did not vote in democratic elections. Compared to the state of the many different religious groups in modern Europe and North America, the state of Ottoman minorities was deficient in civil liberties.

[handwritten margin note: Ott. Religous tolerance not as good as it sounds.]

Such comparisons are worthwhile, because they allow moderns to evaluate their own freedoms. However, they do not tell us much beyond that. The concept of civil liberties was a developing one. The treatment of minorities in the sixteenth-century Ottoman Empire could not have been as developed as their treatment in some modern states. Better to compare the state of Ottoman religious minorities in the time of Süleyman to that of religious minorities elsewhere at the same time. For that, no better example exists than Spain.

Under Muslim rulers, medieval Spain had contained Muslim, Jewish, and Christian communities. Christian rulers had gradually conquered the Muslims until in 1492 the last Muslim stronghold, Granada, fell. The Spanish then proceeded to create a country with one religion. Muslims and

Jews were forced into exile or conversion. Those who were baptized but attempted to keep their old religious practices and beliefs in secret were persecuted by the infamous Spanish Inquisition. The expulsion of the Jews came at the height of Ottoman power. If they wished to religiously unify their empire, the Ottomans had their best chance then. Instead, they welcomed into their empire the Jews who had been expelled from Spain. From that day until this the Jewish community of Spain survived in Istanbul and elsewhere in the Ottoman Empire, speaking their own Judeo-Español language and keeping their religion.

Economic organization

Judging economies is a difficult business. More than the relative economic power of the state must be analysed. The real question is whether or not the people prosper, and this is most difficult to ascertain. For the Ottoman Empire, everything is made more difficult by the lack of information. While the strong Ottoman central government of the sixteenth century kept excellent records for its time, no one knew the average caloric intake of villagers or exact rates of inflation for local goods. Therefore, what is said of the Ottoman economy must be put in general terms. Historians must look at a wide variety of data – grain deliveries, what is known of taxes, production of textiles, etc. – and develop theories. Occasionally, although they do not often admit it, they are forced to guess – informed guesses, of course.

International trade

Information on the amounts of trade and production in the Ottoman Classical Age are limited. Because of the geographic position of the Ottoman Empire and the relative security of at least the first half of Süleyman's reign, trade was extensive, but amounts are only imprecisely known. It is known that trade produced a significant amount of the taxes that supported the government, but even that is hard to estimate. The Ottoman sultans definitely understood the place of commerce in the success of a state and, as will be seen below, acted accordingly.

The Ottoman Empire was at the centre of both sea and land routes between Europe and the Orient. The main land route from the East went through Central Asia to Tabriz in western Iran. From there it passed directly west across Anatolia to Bursa, İzmir, and Istanbul or southwest to Aleppo. Some caravans left the main east–west road at Erzurum, went north to Trabzon, then by sea to Istanbul. An alternate route from the East went overland to the north of the Caspian Sea to the Crimea, and from there by land to Ottoman Europe or by sea to Istanbul. From Istanbul, the main

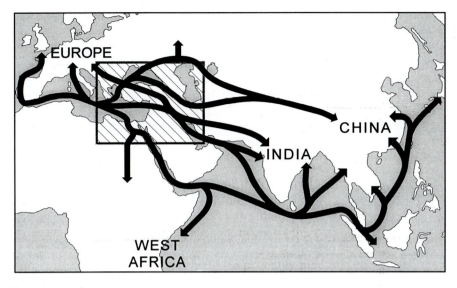

Eurasian trade routes.

highway went to Edirne. There, goods went north to Romania and Poland, west to northern Greece and Macedonia, or northwest to Hungary and Vienna or to the Adriatic Sea at Ragusa.

The sea route from the East went to Basra in southern Iraq, then up the Euphrates and overland to Aleppo. Alternatively, goods passed up the Red Sea, overland to the Nile and to Cairo, then up the Nile and overland to the Mediterranean. Until the Europeans forcibly disrupted this trade, it was exclusively the province of Muslim merchants.

International sea trade on the Mediterranean and Adriatic was mainly in the hands of the Italian city states – Venice, Genoa, and Florence. Boats took on cargoes in coastal Syria, Istanbul, İzmir, Alexandria, Ragusa, and smaller ports and transported them to Italy and then to the rest of Europe. The Black Sea had essentially been an Ottoman lake since the reign of Bayezit II. In the time of Süleyman, its trade was almost exclusively Muslim, with a small number of Venetian merchants and boats.

Placed as it was across the main trade routes of the medieval world, the Ottoman Empire was naturally enough much involved with trade. The sultans accepted as a duty the creation of a good environment for trade, because it benefited their subjects. This was in keeping with Islamic tradition that went back to the Prophet Muhammad, himself, who was a merchant. Since the time of the Arab Caliphates, Islamic rulers had deliberately fostered trade and cooperated with merchants. (Even the life of Sindbad the Sailor in the *Arabian Nights* shows the position of merchants and the fact that they had the ear of the Caliph.) The fact that merchants paid taxes, and successful merchants paid more taxes, did not escape the attention of the Ottoman government.

The two most prominent commodities that passed from Asia to Europe through the Middle East were silk and spices. The silk trade had passed through Anatolia since the late Middle Ages. From the fourteenth century, silk mainly passed from Iranian producers to the city of Tabriz, then on across Anatolia to Bursa. Italian merchants purchased silk in Bursa for transport to Italy and on to the rest of Europe. Silk went from Bursa by caravan to Aegean Sea ports. An alternative route to Italy went through Aleppo to the Mediterranean coast, then on to Italy. This route also came under Ottoman control in 1516.

The silk trade was extremely valuable to the Ottomans because silk was so desirable to the rich of Europe. Because silk was relatively light merchandise that could be easily brought to ports, and ports were easy areas in which to levy taxes, duties on silk were a major part of Ottoman state income. Moreover, the income from silk, unlike that from taxes on land, improved the Ottoman balance of payments. Silk brought in large amounts of European silver. The arrangement was purely beneficial for the Ottomans. The goods were produced in Iran, but Ottomans took a large amount of the profit as duty. Ottoman subjects were employed in the trade. There was very little expenditure to produce very large profits – an ideal financial situation. Tax on silk alone might produce 1 to 2 per cent of Ottoman state income.

The spice trade provided similar profits. The goods were once again produced in the East, but provided Ottoman profits and taxes. However, silk proved to be the most durable source of income when, later, Europeans developed other ways to obtain spices without passing through the Middle East.

The textile that was imported to the Ottoman Empire and that to a very limited extent counter-balanced the export of silk was wool. This seems odd, because in the Ottoman Empire the main domestic animal was the sheep, and much wool was produced domestically. The issue was undoubtedly quality. Italy produced the best quality woollen cloth. The cloth was desirable, not only in the Ottoman Empire, but further into Asia. The Ottomans claimed their share of the taxes on woollen goods that went from Italy, through the Ottoman dominions, into Iran and the East. The Ottoman Empire also sent the mohair produced in the Ankara region to Italy, where it was made into fine cloth, then re-exported.

The capitulations

The Ottoman Empire favoured international trade. Unless there were political reasons for hindrance, such as a state of war existing between the Ottomans and a trading partner, the empire allowed European traders relatively free access to its ports, as long as customs duty was paid. In fact, the Ottomans viewed the variety of goods brought into the empire by foreigners to be so beneficial that they granted special privileges, called capitulations (in this case a diplomatic term meaning an agreement between governments, not the common usage of 'surrender'), to trading partners. To a certain extent, Ottoman policies were the product of economic naïveté. The sultan's men do not seem to have considered that by fostering the trade of their rivals they might put themselves at a comparative disadvantage. This was understandable, given the fact that the balance of payments had for centuries been in favour of the Middle East. Throughout the Middle Ages, Europe had little to offer the Middle East, but wanted silks, spices, and grain. European gold thus came to the Middle Eastern states, and those states could not see that the situation would ever change. Besides, the clothing and jewellery brought in by the Europeans were appreciated by the rich, and some strategically valuable goods were imported, as well.

In addition to helping fill the markets, and the palace, with foreign goods, the Ottomans used trade privileges politically. Trading advantages were granted to friends, not to enemies. Countries such as France, sometime ally of the Ottomans against the Habsburgs, gained privileges; merchants from Habsburg lands did not. This could be a powerful weapon where the trading states of Italy were concerned. Trade advantages favouring European merchants were thus granted to the Genoese, the rivals of the Ottoman enemy, Venice, in the mid-fourteenth century.

The first capitulations, fourteenth- and fifteenth-century awards to Genoa, Venice, Florence, and Naples, stated that the Ottomans would allow specific amounts of goods into the Empire, sometimes guaranteeing purchases. The most important trading privileges awarded by the Ottomans were guarantees of rights to trade in the Empire, under imperial protection, and reductions in customs duties. Those who enjoyed special status under the capitulations changed status in an important manner. Under Muslim law, all not under the political control of an Islamic state were *ipso facto* enemies, with all the nastiness that entails. However, a special status of cooperation with infidels could apply, if they were friendly infidels. The capitulations stated that the holders were friends who should be well treated, and guaranteed freedom from attacks by Muslim pirates, in practice difficult to enforce. The amount of customs duty forgiven depended on the agreement reached with each country. Customs duties of 5 per cent were dropped to 4 or even 3 per cent, but duties varied among ports, and there were other fees on shipping, so it is difficult to evaluate exactly the benefit the foreigners received.

Part of the capitulations agreements were what today we would take as normal diplomatic practice. European consuls were guaranteed freedom of action and given imperial protection. The consuls were exempted from taxation and allowed free import and export of their own goods. This allowed them much of the unique status granted to diplomats today. However, in the time of Süleyman and before, foreign merchant communities were not completely free of Ottoman laws or completely under their own national laws (the principle of extraterritoriality). Instead, their position was analogous to that of the Ottoman *millet*s. Subjects of countries with capitulations rights were considered to be a separate community, with the *millet* rights of freedom of worship, the right to set up their own schools and welfare establishments, etc. The consuls/ambassadors were the heads of the communities. They had the right to apply their own national laws to most disputes between members of their community, just as the *millet*s had. As in the *millet* system, the ultimate authorities remained the Ottoman courts and the imperial divan. Disputes between foreign communities and between Muslims and foreigners were tried according to Ottoman rules and Islamic law, although the government might in practice give foreigners considerable legal latitude. Not until after the time of Süleyman did foreign communities claim full extraterritoriality – the right to have only their own national laws apply to them.

The cities with large foreign communities under the capitulatory regime during Süleyman's reign were Istanbul, İzmir, and Aleppo. Other cities were added later. In the cities, Europeans generally lived in their own quarters, with their own churches and civic functions. They also had their own commercial depots/warehouses. Members of the Ottoman Christian *millet*s functioned as intermediaries with the Empire outside the foreign quarters, serving as agents and translators. Contact with Muslims was minimal, a situation which probably appealed to both foreigners and Muslims.

In the time of Süleyman, only the Italian states and the French held rights under the capitulations. Soon after Süleyman's death in 1566, the capitulations were extended to other Europeans, including the Dutch and the English. Only the Habsburg lands were conspicuously absent. The capitulations had become an almost general grant of lower duties and special privileges to European trading partners. As trade conditions changed and European economies grew stronger, the capitulations would soon become a threat to the economic well-being of the Ottoman Empire.

Regional trade

It would be impossible to number all the types of goods that were traded within the Ottoman Empire. The most lucrative trade was, as might be expected, in luxury goods. Furs, jewels and precious metals, brocades, and other expensive items have always been marks of status. The sultan and high officials made sure that they had supplies of them from within and outside the Empire. A more constant trade, however, was in goods that served ordinary purposes – salt, cereal grains, meat, etc. Trade in these was constant, whereas trade in luxury goods depended on politics and fashion.

Some goods imported to Istanbul

From Anatolia	Grain, dairy products, animal products, olive oil, minerals, textiles, furs, fruits, nuts, opium, lumber and wood products.
From Ottoman Europe	Grain, salt, dairy products, iron, olive oil.
From Syria and Egypt	Grain, gold, sugar, spices, Black slaves, soap.
From Crimea and Environs	Grain, dairy products, salt, honey, animals and animal products, White slaves.

The best way to consider the goods traded within the Ottoman Empire is probably to look at the imports of Istanbul. Istanbul, one of the world's great metropolises, produced little of the food it needed and imported many other commodities. The table, by no means inclusive, lists some of the goods imported to the city. Besides basic foodstuffs, it includes raw materials for Istanbul workshops and luxuries for the palace and the rich.

A primary concern of the government was to supply Istanbul with grain at relatively low price. As empires had found since at least the Romans, it was within the power of the residents of the capital to riot and depose bureaucrats, generals, and even sovereigns. The populace of the capital had to be kept happy, or at least quiescent. That meant bread, although not circuses. A number of methods were used to achieve this end. Price fixing did not work very well, because people smuggled their grain out of the Empire rather than send it on to Istanbul at low rates. Forced sales worked better. For example, the princes of Moldavia and Wallachia were forced to provide a specified amount of wheat to Istanbul every year at fixed government prices. In times of famine, the government was not beyond using military force to take hoarded grain and ship it to the people of the capital. This might have caused suffering in the provinces, but the capital was fed.

Goods arrived in Istanbul following more or less the same routes described above for international trade and on local roads and coastal boats that travelled from port to port on the Mediterranean, Aegean, and Black Seas. Long distance carriers went from Egypt and Syrian to the capital.

The amount of trade within the provinces depended very much on the state of civil order and relative wealth of each region. Peasants never bought much jewellery or iron. The highest level of consumption they could hope for was some dried fruit, olive oil, or dairy products. Lumber was what they could cut nearby, not import from the forests of the Black Sea region. When they could, peasants bought small metal implements and weapons (buckets and knives, especially).

The economic picture was considerably different in the provincial towns. Many of these, particularly in western and central Anatolia and the Ottoman Europe, were tied into the empire-wide system of production. Carpets, for example, were made in a number of smaller cities. For this industry, wool and dye stuffs were imported, sometimes from a considerable distance. Tanners and textile makers exported their goods. And, on a smaller scale than the capital, each provincial city imported some food, usually from nearby farms. However, richer towns consumed some luxury goods and varied their diet with imports.

Guilds and production

In many ways, Ottoman guilds were what one might expect from knowledge of medieval European craft guilds. There were master craftsmen and apprentices, for example, and the guild regulated the quality of goods and prices charged. In other ways, the Ottoman guilds were distinctly Middle Eastern: there were merchants' guilds, as well as craft guilds. Most guilds were tied to mystical brotherhoods. Each had a sufi şeyh as spiritual guide, even though some had non-Muslim members. In Ottoman Egypt, the sufi şeyh was even the head of the guild. The Middle Eastern guilds were also more open than those of Europe. Some entered guilds without going through the normal apprenticeship procedures; friends and money probably helped.

The most important similarity between the European and Ottoman guilds was functional – a guild brought together those who made one sort of goods to ensure the benefit of all the craftsmen through quality control and price fixing. In the Ottoman Empire, the government cooperated with the guilds by supporting their monopolies.

Guilds in Ottoman cities were many and diverse. Most of the professions listed in the table had their own guilds (although one wonders how much economic power lay in the hands of the guild of mosquito net makers). The list of trades is drawn from an extremely detailed catalogue of more than 700 occupations in the seventeenth century drawn up by Evliya Çelebi.[2] According to Evliya, the corporate identity of craftsmen could be very specific – not just bakers, but bakers of a certain type of cake, not just weapon makers, but makers of one particular type of dagger. The diversity of craftsmen and merchants and their organizations is a bit overwhelming. Evliya estimated that there were a thousand and one guilds, which is

---

[2] Joseph von Hammer, translator, *Narrative of Travels in Europe, Asia, and Africa in the Seventeenth Century by Evliya Efendi*, vol. I, part II, London, 1846.

Trades and crafts of Istanbul (a selection)

apothecaries	eye doctors	rice merchants
architects	fan makers	rope makers
astronomers	fireworks makers	saddle makers
bakers of bread	fish cooks	sail makers
bakers of cakes	fishermen	sausage makers
barbers	flower merchants	scissors makers
bath attendants	fools and mimics	sheep butchers
bear keepers	fruit merchants	sherbet makers
beef butchers	fur merchants	ship builders
belt makers	garlic merchants	shoemakers
bird merchants	glue makers	sieve makers
blanket makers	goldsmiths	silk merchants
boat caulkers	horse dealers	singers
boat rowers	horse renters	slaughterers
booksellers	ink makers	slave traders
bow makers	jewellers	snow and ice merchants
brass flute makers	kettle merchants	soap makers
bridle makers	lance makers	speculators in grain
buffalo milkers	linen merchants	stationers
builders	lion keepers	stonecutters
butter merchants	locksmiths	sword makers
button makers	map makers	syrup makers
cage makers	match makers	table makers
camel drivers	millers	tailors
carpet merchants	mirror merchants	tanners
cave diggers	mosquito net makers	tar makers
charcoal sellers	musicians	tavern keepers
cheese sellers	musket makers	tent makers
circumcisers	nightingale merchants	thieves and footpads
coffee merchants	oil merchants	turban makers
coin stampers	old shoe merchants	upholsterers
cushion makers	opium merchants	vegetable sellers
dagger makers	painters	vinegar merchants
diamond cutters	parchment makers	wagon makers
dish makers	pearl merchants	watch makers
divers	pen makers	watchmen
drum makers	perfumers	water carriers
dung collectors	physicians	weavers
embroiderers	pipe makers	wine makers
engravers	rakı makers	wrestlers
executioners	razor makers	

stretching the definition of guild more than a little. Nevertheless, the variety of guilds was vast. One cannot help but appreciate a society where buffalo milkers and bear keepers were not only accepted as occupations, but organized into guilds.

The guilds were corporate entities that generally regulated their own affairs. The leader of each guild (the *kethüda*) was normally elected by the masters, who could also depose him. He represented the guild to the government. Other guild officials regulated internal affairs, including relations between members, or acted as experts who judged the quality of members' work. Some taxes were paid by masters through the guild.

The state did interfere with guilds, especially those that made goods that were essential for military purposes, but it more usually cooperated with them. The government officials most concerned with guild matters were the *muhtesib* and the *kadı*. The *muhtesib* was the official inspector of marketplaces, charged with making sure that weights and measures were honest and that no one charged more than the government-set maximum price. The *kadı*, or religious judge, adjudicated disputes between guilds, approved and sealed guild documents, and generally acted as a combination lawyer and administrative judge.

Both the state and the guilds were conservative. It suited both to keep the status quo. They came together over matters of price. The government supported the guild by setting reasonable prices for raw materials. It supported the consumers by setting maximum prices for finished goods. What might be called Ottoman economic theory held that truly free markets would be dangerous because too much might be produced, lowering prices and bankrupting craftsmen. Cheap goods would drive out quality. Alternatively, producers might gain monopolies and charge too much. Therefore, it was the government's duty to oversee prices and guilds. These are, in fact, the same arguments used for centuries in favour of state intervention in the marketplace all over the world. As has happened elsewhere, the rules proved hard to enforce. The politically well-connected frequently managed to produce or import cheaper goods without penalty. Restricting production proved difficult: the government tried to keep the number of shops static, but somehow more and more opened, sometimes double the allotted number.

As in the medieval West, masters owned their own shops. They produced goods using their apprentices, hired labour, and slaves. Depending on the craft, women as well as men were hired as labourers, although women were not allowed in the guilds. Apprentices served terms of at least three years. They were not only children, and were often much more skilled than the term implies.

The conservative economic system favoured by both the government and the guilds functioned fairly efficiently through the Classical Age of the Ottomans. However, it had potential problems that appeared later. Many have held that economic conservatism and limited production kept Ottoman entrepreneurs from evolving the type of new capitalism that led to economic development in Western Europe. This in turn put the Ottomans at the mercy of more developed European capitalism. Indeed, the word entrepreneur cannot be applied to legal production in the Ottoman Empire until centuries after the time of Süleyman. Some merchants might be called entrepreneurial, but not craftsmen.

For most of Ottoman history, the most entrepreneurial of Ottoman subjects were smugglers and other crooks. A look at the coastlines of Anatolia and the Balkans indicates the possible scope for smuggling. Such rugged coasts afforded many opportunities for small ships to sail into remote harbours and load illegal goods. Goods were smuggled to avoid customs duty or because export or import of some items was forbidden, and thus profitable. Most smuggling seems to have been exports. They included metals, sheep, grain, cotton, firearms, timber, fruit, wine, and almost every other kind of goods. By the nature of the crime, no records of the frequency and amount of smuggling were kept. However, the government often issued orders to provincial officials and customs tax farmers to curtail smuggling. Ship captains were ordered to deliver and pick up goods only at approved ports, with customs collectors in residence. Official concern indicates that smuggling must have been a problem.

The state and the economy

The Ottoman government did not have anything that might be called an overall economic strategy. Survival of the state, civil order, and, morally, the creation of a just Islamic society were the Ottoman goals. Any economic activities of the government were toward those ends. Ottoman governmental policy was based on the realization of discrete benefit, things that were considered good in themselves, without much consideration for the wider economic situation. For example, it was obviously good to have variety in the marketplace, so a large number of guilds were supported to ensure that they would continue to produce the variety they had always produced. Gold and silver, the only currency, were needed for buying and selling, so the government forbade their export. Stable prices were seen as beneficial to both sellers and buyers, so prices were fixed. Social disruption was a great fear, so guildsmen were virtually guaranteed employment and the government laboured mightily to ensure that supply and demand were not allowed to affect the provision or price of grain in the capital. Most important, the state always needed money, so it intervened to maximize its income.

Many government rules, particularly where guilds were concerned, had the effect of holding down production, but an abundance of manufactured goods was not seen to be particularly beneficial. On the contrary, the resultant lower prices would disrupt the guild system, and so such a situation was deemed undesirable. The Ottomans saw little need for an expanding market, the economic engine that led European capitalism to comparative riches. Instead, the Ottomans desired a stable market. The only large-scale government actions to increase production were in the areas of absolutely necessary commodities such as salt and precious metals, and of goods essential for military purposes.

With hindsight, one can see that the Ottomans should have been more concerned with their economy. The state might have spent more on infrastructure, building roads and bridges that would benefit trade, even if they had little or no military purposes, or financing the construction of a commercial fleet so that Ottoman goods could be carried on Ottoman boats, thus depriving the Venetians of middleman profits. The state might have made rules that expanded production, rather than curtailing it. However, the Ottomans had no understanding of the 'cycle of trade'. The Islamic Middle East had little tradition of government action to improve the civilian economy. Even the actions the Ottomans did take to regulate trade were not Islamic. Ottoman intervention in the economy was a triumph of perceived benefit over religious law. Islam did not sanction much interference in the marketplace by civil authority. The only regular intervention legally allowed a sovereign was his duty to enforce fair dealing by checking weights and measures, stopping fraud, etc. Even the collection of customs duty was legally questionable. Those who tried to justify government actions were kept busy with the art of casuistry, trampling the spirit of the law with convoluted reasoning. No moral qualms ever seem to have stopped the government from collecting taxes.

The Ottomans did not have a grasp of Keynesian economic principles. Nevertheless, the state did 'prime the economic pump' through its purchases. Providing palace luxuries for sultans, officials, and provincial governors kept many employed, but the major state expenditure was military. In the reign of Süleyman, more than 80,000 regular troops (*sipahis*, Janissaries, etc.) made up the army. Expenditure on their uniforms, saddles, tents, weapons, and sustenance was a major contribution to the Ottoman economy. Ship building, cannon and gunpowder manufacture, and fortress construction also provided employment and built up the economic infrastructure. Military expenditure can be viewed as an investment. The government invests its tax income in the military, from which in turn proceeds income – plunder, new properties, and new taxes from conquered territories. Despite certain moral problems with such purely economic analyses, that was the system upon which the Ottoman Empire up to the age of Süleyman was based. The economy expanded because the Empire expanded. It was obviously successful. The difficulty with military expenditure is that it can so easily turn unproductive. When the fortunes of war turn against you, your investment is easily lost.

Despite their lack of grasp of economic principles, it should not be thought that the Ottomans did not benefit trade and agricultural production. Whatever its other failures or benefits, for agriculture and trade alike, the primary benefit a government can bestow on its citizens is security. In the Ottoman Classical Age, security was the greatest benefit provided by the government.

Middle Eastern and Balkan trade depended on caravans on land. A strong Ottoman government provided protection for merchant caravans. It also attacked gangs of bandits and kept marauding tribes in check. Funds from *vakıfs* built and maintained hundreds of caravansarays to protect merchants at night (as a bonus, the caravansarays often made a profit for the foundations), and warehouses to protect property in cities. In regions such as the Arabian desert in which it was difficult to project military power, a strong, rich government could bribe the chiefs of nomad tribes not to attack caravans, knowing that the benefit to be gained far outweighed the cost of the bribes.

What was true on land was also true on sea. Sea trade was essential to the economic life of the Empire. Without it, not only would tax receipts suffer, but starvation would result. Istanbul could not feed itself. It depended on the navy to keep sea lanes open for shipments of grain. Much of the protection afforded was protection from piracy, a flourishing business in the Mediterranean. As bandits were a threat to trade on land, pirates were a threat by sea. The Ottoman navy protected Muslim trade in the Mediterranean and the Aegean. With mixed results, Süleyman even constructed fleets in the southern seas to protect Muslim trade in the Gulf and the Red Sea from the Portuguese, who appeared in the sixteenth century and attacked Muslim traders.

In the great days of power of the Ottoman central administration, there can be no question but that the government provided the security that led to increased trade and more bountiful agriculture. By defeating the Mamluks in Egypt and Syria and the various kingdoms of the Balkans, the Ottomans created what we might today call a great trade zone. In place of many different small states, each collecting its own taxes and providing varying levels of security, there was now one great empire that encouraged internal trade.

Chapter 5

Destabilization, 1566–1789

Overleaf

Princes walking in the harem, an indication of the confined upbringing of potential sultans. Earlier sultans spent their childhoods riding in the provinces, observing rough statecraft and learning the ways of rule. Later sultans took their exercise in confinement. It is no wonder that the quality of sultanate declined. (*Surname-i Vehbi*, Topkapı Sarayı Müzesi, A. 3593.)

Destabilization, 1566–1789

The middle centuries of the Ottoman Empire have traditionally been described as the period of decline. The concept of 'decline' comes from a favourite trick of historians – treating countries as if they were people. It has been strangely comforting for us to think of great human institutions as if they had a childhood, a period of vigorous growth, a maturity, then a decline to death. The difficulty with all this is that it does not fit reality very well. In human terms the Ottoman Empire grew very rapidly indeed in infancy. Its systems of government came to maturity fairly early, but the Empire perversely kept on expanding for 100 years after reaching maturity. 'Decline' then set in, and lasted for 250 years, followed by 90 years of 'rebirth', in which the dotard showed great vitality. The analogy to the rise and decline of human beings is fairly weak.

The main problem with the concept of decline is its descriptive weakness. Many would begin the period of Ottoman decline with the end of the reign of Süleyman the Magnificent. Ottoman decline is measured by the long, slow deterioration of the Ottoman central administration and the end of the conquests that had expanded Ottoman borders. This definition of decline ignores what may be the most important question of all – were the people of the Empire worse off or better off? An end to incessant wars of conquest might not have been bad for the people who would have died in the conflicts. Nor might all subjects have complained if the government weakened. Not everyone would have disliked the idea of an inefficient tax collector sent out from the capital, because such a tax collector might have been unable to collect his taxes. They would, however, have disliked the fact that an impoverished government could not pay for soldiers to protect them from bandits and civil disorder.

It is better to consider the events of the middle period of Ottoman history in their own right and to forget labels such as 'decline'. This has the added advantage of not forcing authors to explain how an empire could begin to decline in the sixteenth century and not die until the twentieth.

How, them, does one analyse the seventeenth- and eighteenth-century Ottoman Empire? Any state can be considered and evaluated either by comparison to other states or by seeing how well the state lived up to its own plans and ideals. The first evaluation asks how strong, wise, and effective the state was in comparison to its rivals. In the Ottoman case, this is usually a comparison to their European rivals. The other asks how well the Ottomans succeeded in keeping their empire as they themselves wanted it to be.s

The Ottomans and Europe

Like all other non-Western cultures, the people of the Ottoman Empire did not go through the Renaissance. Nor did they take part in the educational, scientific, philosophical, economic, and industrial revolutions that followed upon the Renaissance in Europe. There is no space here to consider whether Europe led the way to the modern age because of some inherent factor in European culture, because of luck, or a combination of the two. Whatever the reason, it is true that Europeans passed first into the modern technological age. All the great non-European empires, including the Ottomans, were left essentially outside of European development.

The elements of European development that most affected the Ottoman Empire were unquestionably military and economic. The Ottomans might have been able simply to ignore European intellectual development if it had been solely a matter of art, literature, and philosophy, but they could not ignore the presence of European armies at their gates, armies made stronger than their own through technology. They could and did try to ignore the effects of the new European economy, especially because economic matters were poorly understood. However, the conquering power of European economic superiority proved to be as devastating as any Western army to the Ottoman system.

Europe and the Ottoman military

Despite the fact that they had pioneered the modern standing army by creating the Janissary Corps, the traditional Ottoman army was primarily a cavalry force. This put it at a disadvantage when, beginning in the seventeenth century, military tactics stressed infantry in the field and strong fortification of cities. In many ways, though, the worst enemy of the Ottoman army was the Ottoman economy. Modern weapons of war either had to be built in factories that the Ottomans did not have or paid for with funds that were also unavailable. The kings of France, for example, could afford to equip their forces with the mobile cannon and advanced personal weapons that won wars. They could hire mercenaries, especially the Swiss, to fight for them. The Ottomans could not afford the latest weapons and often could not even pay their own soldiers. Intellectually, the Ottomans were at a loss to adjust to new military techniques. When no school in the Empire taught the calculus or modern engineering techniques, it can be no wonder that modern fortifications or artillery could not be built.

On the seas, the Ottomans were also hampered by their lack of ability to adapt to changes in military technology. The example of Ottoman defeat that is most usually cited is the Christian victory at Lepanto. In 1571 the navy of the Holy League (the Habsburgs, the Pope, and Venice) surprised the Ottoman navy in its winter quarters at Lepanto on the Gulf of Corinth and destroyed it. It is a bad example. Although defeated in that battle, the Ottomans had rebuilt their fleet in the eastern Mediterranean one year after their defeat and had regained their dominance there. The real problem was the type of ships the Ottomans built – galleys. Other Mediterranean powers were making the same mistake, building old weapons of war while the Atlantic nations were pioneering new ones. Naval power was in fact transferring to sailing ships (of the type familiar to fans of old pirate movies). It was the builders of the powerful modern sailing ships, first the Spanish and Portuguese, then the English and Dutch, who became the masters of the seas.

In the early modern period, Europe was rapidly developing the art of war. It was not only technology that increasingly set them apart from the Ottomans, but organization and tactics, as well. In the sixteenth century, European thinkers such as Machiavelli were already considering intellectually the practice of warfare. The seventeenth century saw a spate of more practical studies of warfare, such as studies on the machinery of war and on tactics. Notable were the development of a pyramidical structure of command (sergeants report to lieutenants, lieutenants to captains, captains to majors, majors to colonels, and on to field marshal) and drilling of men to achieve unity of action in the field. The Ottomans had neither. The structure of command, for example, was whatever the whim of the sultan, the Grand Vezir, or the commanding officer made it, and it could change very rapidly. Knowing whose orders to follow could become a real battlefield problem.

The one clear advantage the Ottomans had over their European foes was the calibre of their fighting men. Turkish peasants from Anatolia and Ottoman Europe became the backbone of the Ottoman armed forces. As will be seen below, the armed peasants could cause havoc at home, but they fought well against Ottoman enemies. The Ottomans could also count on the aid of their vassals, the Tatars of the Crimea. The Tatars, Turkish-speakers who lived in the Crimea and surrounding areas of what today is

149

southern Ukraine and southeastern Russia, had accepted Ottoman over-lordship in the sixteenth century to gain support in their constant conflicts with the Russians, Poles, and Ukrainians. Trained in the constant warfare of the steppes, they proved in many wars to be the mainstay of the Ottoman forces. The Turks and the Tatars can only be described as some of the strongest soldiers in history. Few men on earth could stand up to hard-ship as well as the Turkish soldier. Unfortunately, they had many hardships to endure. Nevertheless, the Turkish peasants and the Tatars were the ones who, by their strength, held the Empire's enemies off for so long. They almost made up in toughness what their government could not provide in advanced weapons – almost.

The limits of the Empire

The seeds of one Ottoman difficulty lay in past successes. The Ottoman Empire was plainly too large for close control from the centre. To under-stand how the immense size of the Empire might affect it politically, one needs to remember the difficulties of communications in times before the advent of telegraphs, telephones, or paved roads. Ottoman messengers, riding on horseback, might take weeks to reach outlying provinces; armies might take months. One can imagine a recalcitrant governor answering an order sent from Istanbul, which had taken weeks to arrive, with the reply, 'I don't understand your wishes. Please explain.' The added weeks needed to communicate might give enough time to organize a rebellion. The months it took the army to reach the governor would afford the time to prepare defences, draw local support and soldiers, and extend the revolt. Perforce, the distances involved in Ottoman administration meant that local governors had to have much independence. There was always the danger that a bit of independence might lead to the desire for more.

Militarily, distance thwarted the continuation of the conquests that had defined the Empire. For reasons of security and cost, the Ottomans could field only one main battle army. Sultans were seldom so confident of their authority that they could allow an underling to amass and retain a great army some distance from their oversight. That meant that the army was in practice restricted to one campaign season's march from Istanbul. It is perhaps no accident that the Ottoman borders in Europe and eastern Anatolia were that distance from the capital. The Ottomans did organize smaller regional armies, and these made conquests (for example, in the Ukraine), but the main army could not be used in two places at once.

The Ottoman conquests had also come up against enemies in both Europe and Asia who proved impossible to defeat. At first, the Safavids in Iran had held off the Ottomans primarily through 'scorched earth' policies, burning everything ahead of advancing Ottoman forces. For the Ottomans, conquest of a wilderness was no conquest at all. At the end of the sixteenth century, the Ottomans had managed to take lands in Georgia and Azerbaijan from the Safavids, only to have the Persians under the great Safavid, Shah Abbas the Great, regain all in the war of 1602–18. The Turks once again took Persian territory in 1725–27, then were driven out by another Persian ruler, Nadir Shah, in 1730. In the end, Ottoman–Persian borders remained essentially unchanged – many dead, much treasure lost, no gain for anyone.

In Europe, the Habsburg armies in Austria were part of a great European hegemony that could draw on support from near and far. Major conquests in both Europe and Asia had, by the end of Süleyman's reign, simply become too expensive. Soon after that, they became impossible.

The Ottoman people were hurt by the end of imperial expansion. While evidence is limited, it appears that in the seventeenth century the Ottoman Empire for the first time began to experience problems of over-population and large-scale unemployment. For a population geared to expand into new territories, a sudden stop to expansion must have had a disruptive effect. We know for sure that the seventeenth century saw an increase in the rebellion and banditry that are a common result of rural poverty and overpopulation.

The Ottoman economy

One of the primary causes of Ottoman economic inferiority cannot be blamed on any Ottoman deficiency – a change in trade routes from Europe to the East. For centuries the Middle East had been the middle region between Europe and the Orient. Trade passed on two-humped Bactrian camels across Central Asia or on lateen-sailed boats across the Indian Ocean, but the trade routes came together in the Middle East. Land routes from Asia ended at Istanbul or İzmir, sea routes in coastal Syria or Egypt, from which ports goods were trans-shipped to Europe. Middle Eastern merchants made fortunes from trade. The Ottoman government collected great amounts in customs dues and taxes. The transit trade was an important part of Ottoman personal and governmental wealth. It could not withstand the Portuguese discovery of an all-water route to Asia. Europeans were able to carry the goods of the East much more cheaply than before, keeping the transit profits for themselves and denying them to the Middle East. While the Middle Eastern transit trade did not quickly decline after the Portuguese discoveries, it did not increase as it always had. Once the Dutch and British, stronger opponents than the Portuguese, took over the trade, the Ottoman role in it was doomed.

Nor were the Ottomans at fault for another major blow to their economy, the European discovery of the Americas. The discovery and exploitation of the New World was geographically preordained to be made by European states on the Atlantic coast. Yet the Ottomans suffered for it. Most damaging to them was a by-product of the discoveries in the New World, inflation. Spanish conquest of South American silver mines and theft of their contents brought tremendous inflation to Europe. Because the availability of goods was limited, their costs rose as the money supply increased. After much disruption, the European economies settled down. Under the new European monetary equilibrium, prices were high; more silver bought less. The Ottomans had a fixed economic system. With government support, guilds and other suppliers set fixed prices for raw materials, goods, and wages. As European inflation increased, the price of raw materials outside the Ottoman Empire became much higher than within it. Raw materials were sucked out of the Empire, usually by illegal smuggling. Attempts to halt the smuggling led to corruption through bribery of the officials who were charged with stopping the smuggling, not to a stop in the illegal trade. The result was both unemployment and a lack of finished goods in the marketplace.

Eventually, prices in the Ottoman Empire rose to the world level, but not before great disruption to the Ottoman economy. The Ottoman government, reacting to the need to buy things that were more expensive than before, reacted as governments often do – they made things worse by adulterating the coinage. Reducing the amount of precious metal in coins was the equivalent of today's governments printing too many banknotes, and had the same result, more inflation. This caused further disruption in business and distrust of the government.

While they could have done nothing about the discovery of the Americas or the new European trade routes to the East, it can be said that the Ottomans were 'responsible' for the inflexibility of their economic system. This is true, but it is hard to see how they could have planned a system that could have responded to change and still have worked in the Middle Eastern environment. Their system was based on Middle Eastern and Balkan realities, not on anticipation that America would be discovered.

State income

Like most states, the Ottoman government always had a problem with income. There was never enough of it. Once the supply of relatively easy conquests had dried up, the Ottomans could no longer depend on resources from newly conquered territories to pay their bills. Instead, long wars with Austria and Iran exhausted the exchequer and paid back nothing in return. A more regular source of income was needed, but was hard to find.

The traditional taxes collected by the Ottomans were those sanctioned by Islamic law and practice: The *cizye*, or head tax, was collected from all non-Muslims. The *öşür* was a tax on agricultural produce. Both

Muslims and non-Muslims paid the *öşür*, the only exceptions being those who were exempted in repayment for services to the state. Other extraordinary taxes were levelled in time of emergency, *avarız* taxes. Another major source of income was the proceeds from auctioning off tax farms, which were theoretically given to the highest bidder for a three-year term. At various times, the state also claimed income from tribute, war booty, and the like.

As the need for income increased in the seventeenth century, the government did all it could to maximize revenues. The *cizye* had previously often been collected by household, now it was collected by individual and watched carefully, as were *öşür* taxes. However, watching carefully was not enough to bring in the needed funds. The government took steps that are not unknown in other countries. First, taxes were raised. This was done primarily by making the *avarız* taxes into regular taxes, collected every year, instead of special taxes. A limited form of 'graduated income tax' was implemented for these taxes in which taxpayers were divided into high, middle, and low incomes, with taxes adjusted accordingly.

Other methods to maximize taxes were more unusual. The government attempted, with much success, to change a basic part of the system of land holding. *Timar*s, land granted to *sipahi*s to support them and their men in exchange for military service, were converted whenever possible into tax farms. This made fiscal sense, because the military services of traditional cavalrymen were increasingly redundant. What was needed was money to hire musketmen. However, the traditional backbone of Turkish authority, the provincial *sipahi*, was being undermined. Tax farms themselves were auctioned first to one person then, sometimes before even a year was up, to another. The first tax farmer would have taken a chance that the crop would be good, would have sent out his men, paid for seed, etc., and awaited an expected good harvest. The sultan's men would then auction off the farm again, this time getting a better price than at first because the outlook was better for a good crop than could have been known six months before. The first tax farmer got his money back, but he had made nothing. The state got the extra income. Clever, but it drove down the auction price of tax farms, because an investor now faced risks from more than the weather. At a time when the Ottomans were anxious to convert as many *timar*s into tax farms as possible for the income, the policy backfired. It did, however, bring in more income for a while, and the Ottomans often needed income quickly.

It would be tempting to say that the Ottomans needed income so badly because the money was being misused. There was a great deal of expenditure on palaces, clothes, and the like, but surely not enough to bankrupt the state. The palace budget did take up one-fourth of the state expenditures, but this included much training and operation that would today be classified as military or bureaucratic. It is hard to tell if the palace took much more than it had in the glory days of the Empire. It is known, however, that military expenses were immense. As is demonstrated below, the nature of warfare had changed. Instead of calling on nomads who lived off booty or *sipahis* who lived off their *timars*, the sultan now had to outfit armies of foot soldiers who expected pay. As the technology of artillery and naval warfare improved, both became more expensive. Naval expenditure is an example. During the seventeenth and eighteenth centuries, warships were rapidly becoming larger and more deadly. In the 1670s, large European warships averaged 80 guns, 12 of which were 24 pounders. In the 1690s, they averaged 100 guns, 28 of which were 36 pounders. The ships of the 1670s on average carried 5,800 projectiles, those of the 1690s, 9,260 projectiles. Increased income was needed to pay the bill. The Ottomans did not have it.

Internal trade and economy

One of the problems with the decline of the Ottoman central administration in the seventeenth and eighteenth centuries is statistical. Once the greatest record keepers in the world, the Ottomans no longer kept track of things. For that reason, it is hard to know very precisely what the Ottoman economy of the period was like, though it is known with reasonable certainty that it was still largely self-sufficient. European goods were making increasing inroads, but what the Europeans had to offer was neither cheap enough or plentiful enough to overwhelm locally made goods. That would come later.

The continuation of self-sufficiency was largely due to the nature of human needs and to geography. Food, the most basic need, was produced in necessary quantities in the Ottoman domains. Only major droughts or civil unrest would cause starvation. This was more a tribute to the energy and skills of the farmers and herdsmen than to the economic system, but it meant that the most important articles of commerce were locally grown. Other countries, including the Europeans, could never grew enough inexpensive grain to compete locally (or usually in the world market, either) with the Middle Eastern farmer. The other basics of the ordinary person's life were all produced within the Empire's borders – building materials, cloth, many spices, furs, metalwork, coffee, sugar, etc. The exceptions – imported lead, tin to make bronze for cannon, etc. – were well within the amounts that could be financed by normal Ottoman exports.

The size and geography of the Empire insured that most production and consumption was necessarily local. European merchants might deliver goods to be consumed in port cities, but how many of these could profitably be transported on poor Ottoman roads across the mountains and through the deserts into the Ottoman interior?

The Empire was self-sufficient, but this was not all to the good, for the economy remained at best approximately at the same level as it had always been. Craftsmen, merchants, and farmers managed to produce enough for traditional levels of consumption, little more. In times of civil disorder, they produced less, as will be seen below. By contrast, western Europe in the eighteenth century was beginning to undergo the economic changes that would lead to the industrial revolution. Engineers were draining swamps and building dikes to increase arable land. Cottage industry was developing and driving out old guild methods of production. In England at the end of the eighteenth century, the first textile factories were coming into being. More food and new jobs were igniting rapid population increase. There was a steady growth of the middle class. In the Ottoman Empire, a middle class, mainly made up of Christian merchants who dealt with Europeans, was growing, but it was oriented toward international commerce, not production. The other forms of growth seen in Europe were not taking place.

Because the Empire was economically self-sufficient, the greatest barriers to trade were internal. Rebellions in the seventeenth and eighteenth centuries and the consequent lack of security in the provinces had a negative effect on trade. Wars with Persians, Austrians, Poles, and Russians also kept goods from crossing borders. It is known that the great eastern wars with the Safavids completely disrupted the silk trade. Incredibly, none of this ever stopped the merchants for long. The countryside was denuded of population. City populations in much of Anatolia were halved. Yet the caravans went on. After the worst Celali disruptions (see below) ended early in the 1600s, towns began to grow and kept on growing. Muslim, Armenian, and Orthodox traders kept alive the trade in cotton, silk, cereals, carpets, and other goods brought from long distances or from the interior. Despite rebellions and grave civil disorder, great herds of sheep still travelled across Anatolia to feed the people of western Anatolia and Istanbul. The great entrepôt of İzmir grew larger and more economically powerful as a trading centre – a port for Iranian silk and Anatolian produce and production alike. Obviously, the merchants were neither down nor out.

The development of Europe

While the Ottomans were suffering losses in even their traditional sources of national income, Western Europe was developing the economic system known as mercantilism. Judged by later theories of economic development, mercantilism had its problems, but it was extremely effective in encouraging the growth of European economies at the expense of economically traditional states such as the Ottomans.

Mercantilism was essentially a form of state-directed and ordered capitalism. Its primary proponent, Jean-Baptiste Colbert (1619–83), controller-general of finance to Louis XIV of France, built upon the theory that a country grew rich by exporting much and importing little. A self-sufficient state that sold goods to others and bought little attracted the gold of the others and kept its own. To that end, the French government built new industries to supply internal needs and to export. France's internal economy was strengthened through strict government supervision of manufactures and construction of an extensive system of roads and canals. Externally, France did all it could diplomatically and militarily to advance the sales of its merchants. Industry grew enormously.

Great Britain shared much of the philosophy of mercantilism, even though it depended more on the entrepreneurship of its merchants and less on state control. It too used the power of the government to advance the cause of trade. Laws (the Navigation Acts of 1651, 1660, and 1663) directed that most shipments to Britain be on British boats. British colonies exported raw materials and took finished goods from the home country, building British manufactures to a height that they could never have reached in their home market alone.

The key, as trading nations such as the British, the French, and the Dutch realized, was sea power. All three powers built extensive merchant marines. An expanded and modernized merchant marine, aided forcibly by the navy when necessary, fostered efficient and inexpensive trade. Success at trade bred more success. As trade grew, money was made and invested in more manufacture, more trade, and vastly improved armies and navies. For the Western Europeans, the result was riches and power.

The contrast with the Ottoman Empire was stark. The Ottomans neither knew nor applied mercantile principles. They did not have the state income to finance internal growth in manufactures, particularly as their funds were swallowed by wars, and would not have known how to do so, in any case. They did not have the sorts of water supply the British and French relied on to build their canals, nor the control over their provinces that would allow the construction of trunk roads. What 'merchant marine' the Ottomans possessed was mainly small boats that plied coastal waters. Even the trade between Ottoman Egypt and Istanbul passed to European ships. The Ottoman navy was feeble when compared to the ocean-going ships of the Europeans – smaller boats with less speed, fewer guns, and less efficient officers. In 1656, the navy suffered a major loss to the Venetians at Çanakkale. It was built up again, but only to the old standard. Naval decline relative to Europe continued. In 1770, the Russians capped the Ottoman naval disgrace. Not themselves known as the greatest seafaring nation, the Russians sailed a fleet around Europe, from the Baltic to the Mediterranean, to destroy the Ottoman fleet in its own waters in the battle of Çeşme (July 6, 1770).

The main economic disaster, of course, came from the Industrial Revolution. Like the Renaissance and the scientific revolution, the industrial revolution bypassed the non-Western world. European factories could produce higher-quality goods more cheaply. By the nineteenth century, the Ottomans found that traditional handcrafts could not compete with European imports. The result was unemployment, economic dependency, and commercial deterioration.

The difference between European development and Ottoman under-development is best exemplified by comparison with England. Simply put, the Ottoman Empire was a region of manual and animal labour. What rudimentary machinery there was in 1840 was little different from that of 1540. In England, the picture was quite different: Thomas Newcomen's steam engine appeared in 1705, James Watt's improved engine in the 1760s. In 1765, James Hargreaves and Richard Arkwright invented mechanical spinning machines. The two technologies were combined, and by the 1760s power looms had begun to appear. Other new industrial techniques allowed the production of massive amounts of iron. The iron was made into rails for the new railroads (after 1830) and more machinery to produce all sorts of goods. Among these goods were vastly improved and easily produced cannons, hand weapons, and military naval vessels. In the nineteenth century, the new industrial methods were to spread throughout western and parts of southern and eastern Europe.

European capitalism, the economic support of industrial production, had roots in the Renaissance, when banking families lent money to rulers and supported trading ventures, including the new trade with the East. By lending money at interest, the bankers increased their own fortunes and allowed entrepreneurial growth in the European economy. In the eighteenth century, banks and capitalists grown rich on the Asian and American trade were lending money to ventures all over Europe. Money was 'recycled', investing in one business, taking the proceeds from that to invest in another, all the while increasing production and riches. The Ottomans simply had no modern banks. (The Bank of England was founded in 1694; the Ottoman Bank was founded in 1856, by European investors.) Merchants and master craftsmen had money, but it was invested in their own endeavours or spent on personal pleasures. Commercial loans were minimal and usually short-term. Very few thought to invest in the western way. A clever Ottoman businessman might make much money, but he did not recycle it into the businesses of others, especially not into new methods of manufacturing. The limited capitalism of the Ottoman Empire was extremely conservative.

As European capitalism and the economy grew, education kept pace. Education began to increase rapidly in the seventeenth and eighteenth centuries in Western Europe. Schools appeared for even some poor children in Britain. Prussia began to make elementary education compulsory in 1717. By 1800, almost 90 per cent of the Scottish and 50 per cent of the English males were literate. Perhaps two-thirds of French males were literate. In the Ottoman Empire, although no one knows with any certainty, it is doubtful if 10 per cent of the population could read and write. In Europe, universities, which had been a part of European life since the middle ages, grew and expanded, educating the scientists who made the basic discoveries that allowed the creation of modern chemistry and physics, the building blocks of modern industry. Europe had the educated men who could imagine and create new methods and the skilled engineers and workmen who could bring them to industrial fruition. The Ottomans had no universities and what elementary schools existed specialized in religious learning.

Western Europeans possessed a banking system to channel money into economic development. They had, under mercantilism, generated extensive internal markets, strong manufacturing industries, good internal communications, and the most powerful commercial and military fleets on earth. They had, for the times, a well-educated populace. And, with the coming of the Industrial Revolution, they had the machines. The Ottomans had none of the above.

All was not lost economically before the nineteenth century. Until the beginning of the nineteenth century, the Ottoman balance of trade was still slightly in their favour. Silks, spices, and the other goods of the exotic East were still so desired in Europe that exporting them could balance the importation of tin, garments, watches, and the other goods that the Ottomans bought from the Europeans. Without the machinery that the Industrial Revolution was about to provide, the Europeans could not turn out goods much faster than could the Ottomans. However, all was prepared for the final act. The Europeans, particularly the British and French, had built up the economies and transport systems that would support the tremendous increase of inexpensive goods that the Industrial Revolution would produce. The Ottoman economy would prove to be unable to stand against European incursion.

Destabilization at the centre

All governments face the problem of ensuring that public servants work for the public good. The temptations of power are great. At one time or another, bureaucrats, military officers, politicians, kings, lords, or presidents have all enjoyed the chance to steal from the public whilst telling them that they, the masters, were naturally superior to the people. In fact, all wealth in the Ottoman Empire was based on the farmers who produced the necessities of life and on the craftsmen and merchants who brought goods to the marketplace. Until the advent of representative government and even after, the world's rulers and their officials took a tithe of production for themselves without reference to the wishes of those whom they ruled. The question was thus not whether the people *wanted* what the rulers provided, but whether the rulers provided what the people *needed*. In this the Ottomans were no different from any other rulers.

Modern governments attempt to assure the proper behaviour of bureaucrats and officials either through administrative regulations or political culture. Administrative rules define what each official in a state should and should not do. Penalties are set for violations. In a very broad sense, the American system of constitutional checks and balances is a structure of administrative rules, defining and dividing the powers of those in government and setting the executive, the judicial, and the legislative branches to watch each other. Although harder to define, a certain political culture can also help ensure effective government. In the British parliamentary system, for example, there are very few real checks on the power of the ruling party, yet there are no attempts to take over absolute rule or impose a party dictatorship. This is primarily due to the fact that neither members of parliament nor the public would consider such action and neither would condone them. This does not need to be written in a constitution. It is simply assumed that government does not work that way, and as long as that belief is dominant it is self-fulfilling.

The Ottoman government was based neither on the administrative rules nor the political culture found often in modern states. Instead, it was based on the person of the sultan. Certain traditions of rule and the Muslim Holy Law hemmed in the power of the sultan, but neither was a major impediment. As long as the sultan was capable and personally powerful, this system was a success. It allowed rapid adjustment to new situations and the kind of centralized command that wins wars. It was not so successful when the sultan was weak.

The sultanate

The advance of the Ottoman Empire until the time of Süleyman was tied to the greatness of its leaders, and the retreat of the Empire was tied to its leaders' weakness. More than other systems of government, the Ottoman system was dependent on the ruling abilities of the head of state. In theory and in practice, the Ottoman government *was* the wishes of the sultan.

From its first days, the Ottoman Empire had found difficulty in ensuring the orderly succession of good men to the sultanate. Other than the requirement that the throne go to a descendent of Osman, there was no set law of succession. The oldest son did not necessarily take his father's place. If the state was fortunate, the old sultan was able to place his most able son in a position of power before he died, ensuring the son's succession. The most evident example of this was Selim I, who killed all his sons but Süleyman. In addition to the brutality of such action, this strategy might not work if the old sultan made a poor choice. Süleyman himself arranged the death of his more able son, leaving the less able, Selim II, to take the throne.

159

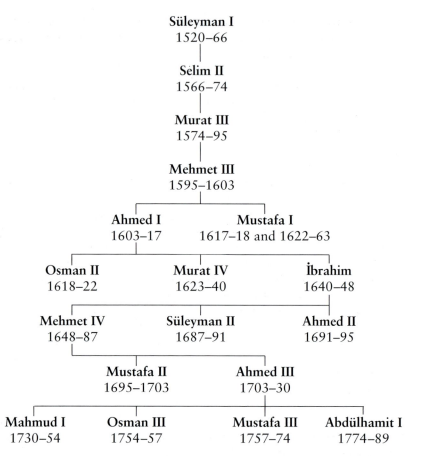

The other path to the throne was through conflict between claimants, sometimes through civil war. In the early days of the Empire, the sultan's sons were sent out as provincial governors and generals. As well as learning the ways of government, they mustered support for their cause. When the sultan died they rushed to Istanbul to be chosen by the military forces there, or organized armies in the provinces to attack their rivals. Selim I managed to gain enough support to be able to depose his own father. As a programme for ensuring the success of the most able, this type of conflict had its points. It did, however, waste the resources of the Empire on internal battles, and gave great comfort to the enemies of the Ottomans, who preferred to see them fighting among themselves.

The traditional Ottoman method for guaranteeing that a sultan would rule without threat from his brothers was also fraught with difficulties. That method was fratricide. Upon coming to the throne a sultan would immediately order the assassination of his brothers. From the accessions of Mehmet II (1451) to Mehmet III (1595) scores of unfortunate siblings were murdered 'to ensure peace in the world'. It is true that killing a rival was effective in removing a threat to the throne and in avoiding bloody civil wars that would have caused the deaths of many more than a few royals. But the sense of morality of even a hard-hearted ruling class was revolted by the practice. The powerful women of the harem were a particular factor in putting an end to it, as was the fear that killing off all claimants to the throne might leave the Ottomans with no sultan if a very young ruler (such as Ahmed I, who took the throne at the age of thirteen) died without off-spring.

The plan evolved by the Ottoman administration did away with the evil of civil war over succession and threats to the throne. It also led to worse abuses. Mehmet III (ruled 1595–1603) was the last sultan to be sent to the provinces for practical training. After him, all members of the Ottoman royal family were kept in the palace confines from birth, so that they could be watched and kept from organizing support in the provinces. Their training was whatever could be gained from palace officials, the women of the harem, and tutors. This was often an excellent classical education. Some prospective sultans became experts in poetry, music, and even the theory of statecraft, but practical training in government was unavailable, except for training in the ins and outs of palace intrigue. The name of the site of comfortable imprisonment in the palace – the *kafes* ('cage') – told it all. Brothers were no longer killed, which left them avail-able as pawns in palace intrigues.

Much has been written of the invidious effect of palace life on the potential sultans. Europeans loved to portray life in the harem as passing from one vice to another, leaving morally debilitated wrecks to take the throne. Since these conclusions were based on a remarkable lack of knowledge of the actual workings of the harem or the personal lives of its members, it is probably better to acknowledge that the most significant problem was lack of experience. To lead a great empire properly when one's practical knowledge only spanned the limits of one very small part of Istanbul was an impossible task.

The devşirme *and the harem*

When Süleyman the Magnificent died the *devşirme*, the powerful slaves at the centre of the Ottoman government, had already dominated the adminis-tration of the Ottoman Empire for more than 100 years. The path to high positions in government was through the clientage system. Young, able men attached themselves to rising leaders of the *devşirme*. As the leaders took on new powers they brought their protégés with them. If the leaders failed, there might be a chance for an able junior to switch sides and go over to his previous mentor's political enemies. This system fostered the creation of political parties that were based on individuals, not party platforms. As alliances were made and broken, the composition of the parties changed. Development of personal loyalties, mutual political favours, and a keen knowledge of the shifting sands of politics were necessary to personal success.

The Ottoman system had one very good side. It did ensure that those who rose to high office were extremely intelligent. Only very crafty politicians made it to the top. This merit system was remarked upon by contemporary Europeans, who saw it as a contrast to their own lands, where incompetents advanced, owing their preferment to birth, not ability. On the other hand, in the absence of the strong hand of a powerful sultan, the Ottoman system could quickly deteriorate. Bright officials would be forced to devote their time to protecting their own positions, and their lives, from the attacks of political enemies. In such times, little effort could be expended on governing. The system was also open to corruption. Extensive bribes were one way to guarantee the success of one's 'political party'. The temptation to recoup the cost of bribes from the government treasury was overwhelming, as was the temptation to reward political cronies with government jobs (a practice not unknown in the West).

The sultan in theory made the laws. In practice, especially in the times of weak sultans, government officials spoke with the sultan's voice. They exercised an authority unchecked by any constitution or other administrative measures. The 'political parties' that triumphed could, therefore, pass laws to dispossess, banish, or even kill their rivals and to ensure the monetary and political success of their own followers. If they then went on to collect unjust taxes or run the Empire badly, there was little to stand in their way.

Theoretically, the one who could do something about government failure was the sultan. As will be shown below, even he had to act within constraints, and sultans were killed when they went too far against the *devşirme*. However, the power of the sultan was so deeply embedded that he could bring about change and usually at least decide who would speak in his name. When the sultan was weak this gave a great deal of power to those who had his ear. Those who had greatest access to him were the members of his harem, particularly the women who were closest to him. Women of the sultan's harem were chosen for brains as well as beauty. They were women for whom the one great chance to express their native intelligence came in politics.

Through Turkish and Islamic tradition and human nature, sultans were close to their mothers. The sons of sultans were naturally emotionally removed from their illustrious fathers, not from their mothers. If the son rose to the sultanate, the power of his mother was great. This made the mother a focus of court intrigue. Sultans' mothers were leaders of palace factions and active participants in political battles, one of the main facets of which was the contest to see whose son would become the next sultan.

Based on pure intelligence, a government run by the women of the harem might have worked well. They were, after all, as clever or cleverer than the others in the political arena. The difficulty was their ignorance of the world. Because of their restricted existence, harem women seldom saw the situation of the world beyond the walls of the harem. In that they were very like the sultans. They knew the situation within the walls all too well, and they brought their considerable intelligence to bear on the conflicts they knew, but they could not factor military difficulties on the Hungarian frontier or economic problems of Anatolian merchants into their calculations. For that reason they cannot be considered to have been a positive political force. Their influence on the sultans was frequently negative.

The military

The Janissaries who charged in the final attack on Constantinople were the finest troops in the world. Selected for their strength and intelligence, they had been well trained, then kept as a regular standing army, always ready for warfare. The 'militia', the Turks who descended from the nomads who had created the Empire, were ready for each year's campaign season, serving under leaders whose *timar*s supported the troops. The army's weapons were the finest available, purchased from whatever source was best, whether Muslim or Christian. If the best cannon-maker was a European Christian, Mehmet the Conqueror bought his services. If European weapons appeared superior to those in the Ottoman arsenal, they were copied. The point was victory, and only that. The military served to that end.

As the Empire changed and military customs solidified, the old Ottoman traditions of military eclecticism and flexibility were gradually lost. The Janissary and other corps of slave soldiers, with their ties to the *devşirme* administrators of the Empire, became the dominant military presence. They were always greatly outnumbered by the levies of the Turkish militia. However, the militia was quartered in the countryside, living in villages or on *timar* lands. Their leaders, the Turkish notables, had retired to their lands when the *devşirme* took power in the capital. The Janissaries were in Istanbul in force, and they manned garrisons in provincial capitals, as well. This gave them, like the Praetorian Guard of old Rome, the power to enforce the will of their leaders, even against the will of the sultan. Instead of relying on the Janissaries the sultans began to fear them. The best evidence of this was the great sums of money the Janissaries were able to extort from the sultans. For example, when Süleyman's successor, Selim II, took power, he felt it necessary to distribute large sums to the Janissaries and other corps as 'accession money' (an old custom that originally had been a much less expensive part of the celebration of the new sultan's enthronement). The Janissaries felt that they could get more, and rioted until the sultan provided it. Future sultans found it necessary to empty the treasury on accession if they hoped to keep their thrones.

The Janissaries themselves degenerated from the mighty force they had been. They used their power to improve their personal lives, at the expense of the state. Under Selim II, they were allowed to enrol their sons in the Corps, changing forever the discipline of the old system. Instead of a regular army that kept to its barracks, the Janissaries were allowed to marry and, ultimately, even to take other employment while remaining on the Janissary payroll. Retaining their military pay, they became craftsmen or merchants. Janissary pay vouchers were distributed to political cronies who would provide no military service, but collected their pay. Away from the old discipline of the corps, the fighting quality of the Janissaries degenerated. Many found ways to send substitutes to fight for them in wars, remaining in the capital and working at their other jobs while the substitutes (almost always inferior fighters) fought for them.

Many of the *timar*-based Turkish soldiers often ignored the sultan's call to battle. Disaffected with the political situation in Istanbul and preferring not to fight for the glory of a state led by the *devşirme*, they simply stayed at home. Only if there was obvious benefit to them (such as the prospect of booty or the likelihood that a foreign enemy would actually destroy the Empire) or if the sultan could muster the force to threaten them if they did not fight, did they join in campaigns. Their style of fighting was in any case becoming obsolete in international warfare. Those who were called Turkish notables in earlier chapters increasingly had settled down to become local forces, often operating independently of the central government, sometimes opposing it, occasionally rebelling.

Notwithstanding all this, many Turkish soldiers continued to fight for the Empire, as had their ancestors. The Tatars of the Crimea were particularly valuable to the Ottomans as soldiers. But as time went on and the situation of the Empire deteriorated, more and more *timar* soldiers remained on their estates, continuing to collect their taxes, but not providing military service in return.

The city and the countryside, or the devşirme and the Turks

At times when prejudice against Turks was fashionable in Europe and America, it was common to hear the claim that the growth and vigour of the Ottomans was due to the *devşirme*, on the assumption that only those with 'Christian blood' (i.e., those born to Christian mothers) could have been so successful. The nonsense of such racist assertions needs no critique. Indeed, a counter argument can be made that the truly great times for the Ottomans came when they primarily depended on Turkish officials and administrators and that the *devşirme* through their political intrigues slowly sapped the strength of the Empire. Neither contention is worth much. Both groups contributed to the Empire's greatness and the *devşirme* were Turks in culture and language, the only variables that really counted. It was nevertheless true that there was a real division and clash between the *devşirme*-run establishment in Istanbul and the Turkish leadership in the provinces.

In the capital, the antagonism between the native Turks and the *devşirme* evidenced itself in conflict between the Turkish cavalrymen (the *sipahis*) and the Janissaries. Sheer numbers and political clout usually ensured that the Janissaries had the upper hand in the capital. For example, in 1603, *sipahis* and members of the *ulema* revolted in Istanbul against *devşirme* domination, forcing sultan Mehmet III to change his policies, but a Janissary counterattack defeated them and returned government policies to the status quo.

Although little is known of the thoughts of the Turks of Anatolia, it seems that they felt frustration at the state of the government in Istanbul. As the *devşirme* took control, it could not be said that the government reflected the makeup of the Turkish population. Those who ruled were different from the subjects. When famine struck and peasants were not aided, when taxes were raised to fight far off wars that only seemed to take men and money from Anatolia, not give any benefit, or when any government function failed, the Anatolians must have felt alienation all the more. This surely contributed to rebellion, as will be seen below.

The deterioration of centralized power in Istanbul naturally had its effects in the provinces. From the perspective of the provinces, it seemed that taxes were paid in and little seen in return. Ordinary functions of government, such as the suppression of banditry and patrolling of trade routes, were not carried out. The social contract between governor and governed was not being fulfilled. The result was protest against the government and a desire to have more effective local control. Loss of central control was also an opportunity for local governors and other officials who wished to increase their own power. They could exploit the public dissatisfaction with the central government and gain local support for local control, in their hands. As the decline continued, governors and strongmen increasingly became all but independent. Tax payments from their regions dwindled. For the people of some provinces, their personal situation was sometimes improved. It was better to have a good local ruler who knew the region than bad rule from Istanbul. Of course, not all local rulers were good ones, and conflicts between local strongmen damaged life for all. Ultimately, the weakening of the state led to foreign wars and foreign domination that few wanted.

Rebellion and decentralization in Ottoman Asia

Revolt in Anatolia and elsewhere in the Empire was not just an occurrence of the Ottoman middle centuries. The great sultans of the Classical Age faced revolts large and small. The rules of both Bayezit II and Selim I were opposed by Shia Turkish nomad rebels in eastern Anatolia. Since the time of Selim I dissatisfaction with Ottoman rule in Anatolia had taken the form of Celali revolts. Originally the name of a group of rebels (the followers of a man named Celal) who had sided with the Safavids against the Ottomans, the name Celali had come to signify popular uprisings of the Anatolian peasantry and tribesmen against the central government. Their revolts, like Muslim revolts since the days immediately following the death of the Prophet Muhammad, took on religious, as well as economic and political colouring. The rebels often had ties to mystical Islamic brotherhoods or even Shia preachers. The rebellions often expressed the Anatolian Turks' rejection of the domination of the *devşirme* in Istanbul. Celali revolts in southeastern Anatolia had been put down by the army of Süleyman the Magnificent, but only with great difficulty, and only after the Ottomans had made concessions to local notables to secure their help. They began once again in the early 1600s, joined by disaffected Turkish soldiers, and simmered through much of the seventeenth century, breaking out when the government was weakest.

Revolt and civil disorder were not simply a matter of rebels taking advantage of a weak government. Civil disruption was in the nature of rule in the Middle East and the Balkans. There was no way to avoid it, because in any human society a certain proportion of the populace will always believe it can runs things better than those they believe to be the fiends or fools in high office. Modern societies largely avoid problems with rebels by showing force to those who might plan rebellions: police are on street corners or drive by often. Soldiers are housed in barracks in or near cities, where their potential force can be seen and appreciated. If a revolt does break out, good roads and helicopters can deliver force quickly, before it can spread. This is very important. If a revolt is not quickly contained, it appears to potential rebels that it might be a success, and they join in. The revolt becomes all the more difficult to contain.

The type of force the central government can deliver also does much to deter rebellion. If the state has planes, bombs, tanks, heavy machine guns and artillery, and is known to be willing to use them on its citizens, rebels armed with hunting rifles will think twice about opposing the government. This admittedly does not always save the state. The government of the Tsar, the Soviet Union, and the modern Russian Republic have all proved willing to use maximum force on rebels, but the Tsar and the commissars are gone. Nonetheless, without their guns, they would have faded long before they did.

Without the guns or the helicopters, traditional Middle Eastern governments could not rapidly deploy against rebels. A great Middle Eastern empire was forced to keep its main army in one piece – when not fighting, close to the capital – and under loyal generals. To divide the army for long would have been folly. Generals would have decided they should be sultans. This happened often enough in the Roman and Byzantine Empires for the Ottomans to have learned the lesson. The Ottomans only partially solved this problem with *sipahi*s, members of the ruling class living in the provinces, supported by their *timar*s, who were expected to keep local order. Because of the nature of weapons and warfare, the *sipahi* and his trained men were a stronger force than any group of rebel peasants, but the system was never completely effective. Nomadic and semi-nomadic tribes were themselves militarily strong and never had been completely bent to the sultan's authority. The geography of the Empire, covered with mountainous regions where small groups of rebels could hide and organize, always contributed to revolt. Nevertheless, the Ottomans dealt successfully with rebels. Then the military and political environment changed. Central power declined and new forms of warfare, based on musket-carrying infantrymen, made successful revolt more possible, and therefore more likely.

The Celali revolts

The background to the seventeenth-century revolts of Anatolian Turks demonstrates the confusion of factors that led to the decline of Ottoman power.

First, there were local economic factors that opened the way to rebellion. Many scholars have long held that the population of Anatolia rose precipitously in the 1600s, and that this led to mass unemployment. This may be so, or politics or changes in trade patterns may have been a more significant factor. In any case, it is certainly true that there were many poor in Anatolia – dispossessed peasants or those who were looking for any route out of rural poverty. Contemporaries remarked on the great number of men unemployed and wandering through the countryside. They were fertile ground for rebellion.

A world economic crisis, precipitated by a flood of silver from the New World and the inflation it caused aggravated the situation. The state, as seen above, was economically wounded. On a local level, those on fixed incomes suffered, as they always do in times of high inflation. A 1593–1606 war with Austria, called the 'Long War', caused more hardship. Taxes were increased to pay for war just at the time when the economy was deteriorating.

Alienation between the provinces and the centre in Istanbul, ruled by leaders who, as *devşirme*, shared little with the Anatolian Turks, must have also had a part in stirring rebellion.

The Ottoman government, in an attempt to cope with changes in methods of warfare, unwittingly contributed to its own problems. At the beginning of the seventeenth century, the Ottomans could see that the art of war had taken a turn against the type of armies that had won the earlier

167

Ottoman wars. Ottoman armies now had to stand against Austrian armies that depended on massed firepower from foot soldiers. Large cavalry units were increasingly superfluous. As a result, the *sipahi* cavalry gradually disappeared. By the middle of the century, fewer than 10,000 remained.

The Ottomans took two steps to modernize their army. First, they increased the supply of firearms to the Janissaries. However, there were never enough Janissaries to make up the needed numbers of soldiers and the Janissary units were themselves losing their cohesion and fighting ability, as seen above. As a second option, the Ottomans turned to the mass of Turks in Anatolia. It was a time when firearms were becoming generally used in the countryside. Relatively easy to produce, muskets had taken the place of bows and arrows. Unlike those who shot the bows that had been the traditional Ottoman weapon, musketeers did not have to be expert marksmen to use their weapons effectively. A peasant could quickly become a musketman. Great numbers of the Anatolian Turks were unemployed or underemployed, and they either had muskets or could be given them and easily trained in their use. They were enrolled and trained in the Ottoman forces, both by the central government and by local governors, as salaried soldiers, called *sekban*s.

Had the government been able to pay the salaries of the *sekban*s consistently, all might have been well. The *sekban*s proved to be good soldiers in war, effective against the European armies. However, the Ottomans could not pay the price. Although they tried, they could not rapidly convert enough *timar* lands into tax-paying sources of cash. State control was not adequate to create a well-ordered tax system, so the *sekban*s were sometimes not paid during war. After the war with Iran ended in 1590, tens of thousands were discharged from military service, when common sense would have indicated that it was better to keep them as a standing army than to set militarily trained, unemployed men loose on the countryside. But without money for salaries, there was no choice. The *sekban*s left government service, often still in their units under their own captains. They turned their military skills to survival at the expense of the people of Anatolia. The *sekban*s were the backbone of rebellion against the government. Their rebellions were all the more difficult to put down, because they were just as much trained soldiers as were those who were sent against them. They were joined in rebellion by the superfluous multitudes of Anatolia, also poor and unemployed, also possessing guns.

The best-known of the Celali rebels was also the most dangerous to civil peace in Anatolia. Kara Yazıcı ('Black Scribe') was a leader of *sekban* troops who, when ordered to put down rebels in southern Anatolia, instead joined their revolt and became its leader. An Ottoman general, Hüseyn Paşa, sent to defeat Kara Yazıcı, actually joined him in revolt. By the year 1599 Kara Yazıcı had amassed an estimated 20,000 armed men in his service. In that year, his forces defeated an army sent against them and held

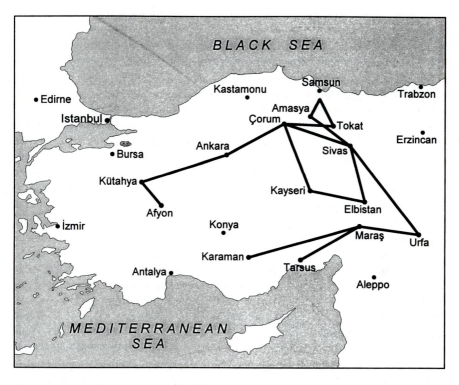

The marches of Kara Yazıcı and Deli Hasan.

---

out against another army that besieged him in Urfa. His forces then moved north toward Sivas and Çorum.

Kara Yazıcı and his lieutenants were not simply bandits. They craved the respectability of entry into the Ottoman ruling class (the *askeri*). This allowed the Ottoman government to 'buy them off' with official appointments. In 1600, Kara Yazıcı was made a governor (*sancakbeyi*) in north central Anatolia, first in Amasya, then in Çorum. Official sanction made little difference to the Anatolian peasants and townsmen unfortunate enough to come into contact with the plundering rebels and bandits who called themselves 'soldiers of the governor'. A famine in Anatolia led the *sekban*s to plunder more to feed themselves at a time when the peasants had less to lose.

Kara Yazıcı remained an Ottoman official for less than a year. His men caused such havoc that the government finally disowned him. He rebelled once again. One Ottoman force sent against him was defeated. Another chased him across central Anatolia and finally defeated him at Kayseri in 1602. Kara Yazıcı and his men escaped north, however, to the mountains north of Tokat, where he died of natural causes.

Kara Yazıcı's death was not the end of the troubles. His brother, Deli ('mad') Hasan took over his army. In 1602, he rode south, where he joined with other Celalis, swelling his force. He defeated one Ottoman army at Tokat, sacking and burning the area, moved to Çorum, where he defeated another army, then on to beseige Ankara. The rich of Ankara bribed him to leave. Moving to Kütahya, he put an Ottoman army under siege in that city, finally wintering in Afyon in 1602–03.

Ottoman political cleverness succeeded where Ottoman armies failed. Like his brother and many other Celali leaders, Deli Hasan felt himself to be an unrecognized leader, an Ottoman who was held down by officials in Istanbul. When the government raised him to official status and sent him and his army to Europe as an Ottoman general, Deli Hasan made his peace and joined the war against the Austrians in Europe. His forces alternately fought bravely and caused disruptions. Deli Hasan himself seems to have conspired with Ottoman enemies. He was executed in 1606.

The map indicates the disaster brought to Anatolia by Kara Yazıcı and Deli Hasan. Tens of thousands of men passed through much of Anatolia, raiding farms and merchants, producing nothing, but taking the produce of those who did, leaving destruction behind them. And Kara Yazıcı and Deli Hasan were by no means the only Celalis who plagued the region. The devastation the Celalis left behind and fear of what they would do caused what was called the 'Great Flight' of both leaders and peasants to Istanbul and other safe areas. Much of Anatolia was left without culti-vators or merchants. Worse, many whose livelihoods had been destroyed themselves became bandits, preying on those who still had farms or businesses. Traditional authority in many provinces ended when the *timar*-holding *sipahi*s fled to Istanbul to escape the Celalis. In the capital, the Anatolian *sipahi*s themselves became a threat to the government, revolting unsuccessfully in 1603, as mentioned above.

The Ottoman government managed to survive the Celali disruptions. Indeed, it showed great cleverness in dealing with them, as it had done with both Kara Yazıcı and Deli Hasan. The Ottomans were extremely pragmatic. Rebel *sekban*s were hired to hunt down other rebel *sekban*s. Assassination and bribery proved effective in dealing with Celali leaders. Ultimately, this ended the Celali threat to the state, but devastation was still left behind in Anatolia.

Other rebellions followed in the seventeenth century. Ottoman gover-nors were among those who rebelled. The revolts were put down with difficulty, using the same combination of politics and force that had broken Deli Hasan. Anatolian nomadic and semi-nomadic Turks were prominent in the revolts, as were many others who called for a change in Ottoman rule – not an end to the reign of the sultans, but an end to the *devşirme*-run central administration. The revolts continued into the eighteenth century. When relative peace finally came, it was not due to a reassertion of central government control, but because of the spread of rule by local Turkish leaders in much of Anatolia, as will be seen below.

Degeneration of Ottoman rule in the provinces

The Ottoman Empire was too large and too diverse to be ruled directly. Effectively governing an area that included most of the Middle East, Balkans, and North Africa would have demanded rapid communications, a large skilled bureaucracy, the ability to quickly deploy military forces throughout the empire, and other tools of administration that only became available in more modern times. Therefore, in effect the Ottomans, like other empires before them, allowed most regions of their empire to be ruled by local governors. All but the most important decisions were made by local officials. The central government kept control by changing governors often, sending spies to watch over governors who might revolt or keep too much of the tax proceeds, and by the constant threat of intervention from the main Ottoman army.

All regions of the Empire were less centrally ruled than is true in modern states. Nevertheless, some were kept under much closer control than others. When the Ottoman system was working efficiently, some regions were closely monitored by imperial bureaucrats, who drew up detailed statistical and administrative reports. With this information, the sultan could keep a close watch on the provinces most important to him. To such provinces, the sultan's government sent out governors who were officials of the central administration, primarily *devşirme* officials. Their loyalties were expected to be to the centre, not to the areas they ruled. They were considered to be less likely to conspire with locals to frustrate the sultan's tax collectors or to declare local independence.

Other provinces, particularly those with mountainous or desert terrain, could not be easily ruled from the centre. Such regions had in fact always been largely ruled locally, no matter which empire claimed nominal control. The Ottomans often named the most powerful of locals in these provinces to positions of authority, because they held authority in any case. As Ottoman governors, these leaders were expected to send levies for Ottoman wars and forward taxes or tribute to Istanbul, but in practice they often provided neither. The Ottomans were usually happy if they did not declare independence and caused a minimum of trouble. Good behaviour was ultimately contingent on the power of the Ottoman army. It would take quite a bit of aggravation before the Ottomans would resort to mounting a major campaign against Kurdish or bedouin chiefs, but the possibility was always there.

The Ottoman system of projecting governmental authority into far-flung provinces was probably the only one possible. However, it had one major flaw. If the military power of the central government diminished, locals who had been held in check mainly by the threat of military intervention might revolt. For the people of the provinces, this could mean disaster. When autonomous Ottoman governors, local notables, or tribes fought to fill a power vacuum crops were destroyed, villages were destroyed, and people died. Thus the decline of the Ottoman military and Ottoman administration was not only a political matter. For nearly two centuries, the weakness of central authority opened the way for local forces to seize power. The central government necessarily opposed this. The result was a series of rebellions and civil wars that gravely damaged many previously productive regions of the Empire. Ottoman Syria is given here as an example.

Upheaval in Syria

Ottoman Syria illustrates the dilemma that was at the heart of Ottoman rule in the provinces. The Ottomans naturally wished to continue their rule in Syria, but the methods that were essential to this were themselves a cause of decay.

In Syria, the large region that stretched from the southern border of Anatolia to Egypt, Ottoman governors ruled directly over cities and major agricultural areas. Local leadership was accepted in the deserts and mountains. The Ottomans could not control such areas effectively without major military actions. Large armies would have been needed to capture bedouin tribes and force them into obedience or to enter the mountain redoubts of tribesmen. About such matters the Ottomans were very practical: as long as the mountaineers or bedouin did not cause too much trouble, the Ottomans left them alone. If the government could collect taxes from them, it did so; if not, not. The major concern was that the tribes should not disrupt commerce, attack tax-paying villages, or organize revolts against the government. The Ottomans were not above bribing tribal leaders to ensure good behaviour. They were also willing to play tribal politics, giving their support to a weaker chief, for example, in a conflict with a stronger. In this way they retained a 'balance of power' in which no one leader grew strong enough to oppose Ottoman rule.

One Ottoman policy of curtailing a governor's power by limiting his term in office ultimately worked against its purpose – the continuance of central government authority. In the Arab world, the policy was excessively applied. Governors in seventeenth-century Damascus, for example, averaged little over a year in office. This indeed kept them from developing their personal power, but it also left a power vacuum to be filled by local forces. Sometimes these were originally central government forces who had blended into the local society and power structure. In the late sixteenth century, the Janissaries of Syria had begun to allow local Arabs to buy places in the Janissary Corps. This theoretically illegal practice opened military power to local citizens and made local families part of the 'central government forces'. When new Ottoman forces were sent to Syria in the eighteenth century, partly to oppose the power of the older Ottoman forces, they too eventually became localized. Different groups of supposedly Ottoman soldiers struggled among themselves for power.

The power over which the various forces contended was seldom absolute. Like the Celali leaders described above, the local leaders in Syria did not question the ultimate sovereignty of the sultan. They wanted to become governors or de facto rulers so that they could have the day-to-day power over their regions, including the all-important ability to collect taxes. Even if the sultan had to receive his share, much money still would stick to the hands of the tax collectors. As important was the guarantee of the dominance of one's family. If a local leader took over practical operation of the provincial government, he could advance his own family and friends and diminish the power of his enemies' family and friends.

The problem for the Ottoman state was not that Syria would become independent. Ultimately, the Ottoman army and the divisive conflicts of local forces ensured that independence was a practical impossibility. The real difficulty was the civil disorder brought about by internal conflicts. Less business could be done and fewer crops produced while the countryside was in uproar and different forces were invading cities. Practical rule over seventeenth-century Aleppo is an example of the problem. At the start of the century, Aleppo was immersed in a virtual civil war between the 'localized' Janissaries from Damascus and the Ottoman governors of Aleppo. The Damascus Janissaries had seized the city at the end of the sixteenth century, had been evicted by the Ottoman governor's forces in 1599, then returned, put the city under siege, and retook Aleppo. A new governor, Nasuh Paşa, allied himself with a Kurdish chief, Husayn Janbulad, in 1602 and attacked the city, driving out the Damascus Janissaries. Fearful of Husayn's power, the Ottoman government convinced Nasuh Paşa to break with him. However, while Husayn's and Nasuh's forces fought, the Ottomans changed their mind and named Husayn as governor of Aleppo. After more fighting, a peace was arranged and Husayn began to rule in Aleppo in 1604. In 1605 he was beheaded for treason, but his tribe revolted. Ali Janbulad, nephew of Husayn, allied himself with other rebels in Adana and Lebanon and held out until 1607, when he was finally defeated by an Ottoman army. The Janissaries of Aleppo and Damascus then resumed their internal struggle for power.

The type of conflict seen in Aleppo may in fact have aided Ottoman sovereignty. All the forces were too busy battling against each other to secede from the empire. Ottoman attempts at balancing opposing forces and the shifting of Ottoman support can be viewed as a clever tactic at a time when Ottoman armies were more than busy with wars in Europe and

Iran. The effect of the battles cannot have been as salutary for the people of Aleppo and environs.

For the people of Syria, what was needed was stability of rule, whoever the ruler. The relatively long governorship of yet another Nasuh Paşa in Damascus from 1708 to 1714 provided a breathing spell for populace and commerce alike. Nevertheless, Nasuh Paşa was killed by the Ottoman government, which feared his power. After a period of near-anarchy, Syrians found that real local control could provide the best government. From 1725 to 1730, Ismail al-Azm, a member of a prominent local landholding family who had previously been governor of Trablus, served successfully as governor of Damascus. Members of his family took other Syrian governorships. But the Azms' power and success were again a threat to the centre. They too were deposed. Another Azm, Asad, provided good government for a long period, 1743–57, and his relatives again took high positions in Syria. After them, the situation degenerated once again, with excesses from both bedouin and local Janissaries. From the events in Syria, it is impossible not to deduce that actions of the central government, while perhaps necessary to ensure Ottoman rule, were not in the best interests of the region.

Ottoman attempts at reform

With hindsight, one can say that the seventeenth-century Ottoman Empire was in need of radical reform. The old Ottoman system increasingly did not work because it could not work. It was not fitted to the changing world. The Ottomans could not have been expected to see this. Like most other states, they did not have the ability to stand outside of their traditions and history and view their problems objectively, nor did they have the information needed to make a proper evaluation. They knew too little of Europe to appreciate that Europe was gradually equalling, then surpassing them in power.

All of this does not mean that the Ottomans did not see that they had problems. They knew that something was wrong when the Empire's armies and institutions did not show their traditional vigour. Many realized that changes were needed. Those who saw the need of change and laboured to implement it are usually called traditional reformers. It is not a title they would have recognized themselves. They would surely have considered themselves to be only government officials, notables, or sultans who tried to make the Empire function properly. They key to traditional reform is the word 'properly'. What bound the traditional reformers together was their image of a properly-functioning empire, an empire that functioned as they imagined it always had – following the traditional Ottoman system that had been so successful in the past.

After Süleyman

Soon after the death of Süleyman, observant Ottomans already might have seen that the old power of the Empire was threatened. They could see that the rulers after Süleyman were not especially able. His son and successor, Selim II (1566–74), for example, has gone down in history as a drunkard rather than as a ruler. Nevertheless, the Ottoman bureaucracy managed to rule the Empire so that few, if any, of those not intimately involved with the government could see any problem. The Ottoman system was so strong that it could take a considerable battering before showing great effects.

Sultan Selim's reign had signal military successes. A rebellion was defeated in Yemen, leaving the Ottomans in control of the Red Sea. Ottoman control of the eastern Mediterranean was bolstered by the conquest of the island of Cyprus in 1571. The armies of Selim's successor, Murat III (ruled 1574–95), attacked in the East. In long wars with the Safavids (1578–90), the Ottomans took all of Azerbaijan and lands in the Caucasus. Wars with the Habsburgs in Central Europe that began in the reign of Murat III and continued into the reigns of Mehmet III (1595–1603) and Ahmed I (1603–17) were inconclusive, but the Ottomans retained all their territory in Europe (treaty of Sitva Torok, 1606). Celalis who revolted in Anatolia were eventually either put down or bought off. Even though the Safavids managed to regain their territory in the East, Ahmed I kept the old Ottoman borders. Again, the hypothetical observant Ottoman might have seen signs of trouble in the fact that after generations of war the Empire had remained largely as it was, within its old borders, but no one was quite so observant.

The real debacle came on the accession of Sultan Mustafa I (1617), the brother of Ahmed I. Some of his predecessors might not have been brilliant, but none was as mentally deficient as Mustafa. Ahmed I had been young and childless when he took the throne, and his brother Mustafa therefore was not killed. Even when Ahmed had sons, it was thought dangerous to leave the sultanate in the hands of a very young boy should the sultan die. Mustafa lived on, separated from the world, but alive. It seemed the break with tradition had been wise when Ahmed I died in 1617. Ahmed's oldest son, Osman, was only thirteen years old, so Mustafa was advanced to the throne. Sultan Mustafa was mentally deficient. It cannot be known how greatly stories of his insanity were exaggerated by his enemies (or, more precisely, by the enemies of the parties that supported him, since Mustafa was but a pawn). It is known that he was incompetent to rule. From descriptions of the symptoms, he is often described as a paranoid, overwhelmed by fear that he would be deposed or murdered, in itself not a sign of madness, considering his circumstances. His mental problems were probably exploited by his advisors as a method of controlling him. In any case, it was those advisors (perhaps better styled manipulators) who actually ruled. If his manipulators did play on his disease, it was counterproductive, because their enemies were able to use Sultan Mustafa's mental state as an excuse to depose him in 1618, after a reign of but a few months. Harem intrigues played a part in the decision, a triumph for the mother of Osman, Mahfiruz.

Osman II

Osman II (1618–22) had plans for reforming the government, but, as a young teenager, was not particularly temperate or politic in carrying them out. Osman's advisors immediately began a policy of increasing his, and their own, power. Osman not only banished from power those who had supported Mustafa, but also some of those who had been his own supporters and expected to have a controlling interest in the government because of their support. The powers of the religious head, the *Şeyhülislam*, to appoint judges in the Empire was curtailed. The Grand Vezir and other vezirs were replaced. It became obvious that Osman planned to rule as his great ancestors had ruled.

Osman II had little time to put many political reforms into effect. Most of his short reign was occupied with a war with Poland, which ended badly for the Ottomans in October 1621. At the end of the war, Osman turned his attention to affairs in Istanbul. The sultan blamed the army for the failures in Poland, just as the army blamed him. His reputation with much of the military was poor. Nevertheless, Osman's government began to take measures to improve the efficiency of the Janissaries – increasing workloads and training, instituting harsh discipline, and restricting practices that were harmful to the martial spirit. Even then, Osman did not view his military improvements as sufficient.

Osman II never described his plans satisfactorily, but his enemies, who now included many of the most powerful men in the Empire, believed they knew what he had planned. They believed that Osman and his advisors had developed a radical plan of reform. The power of the *devşirme* was to be crushed, perhaps the *devşirme* system ended completely. The military support of the *devşirme*, the Janissary Corps, was also to be eliminated, or at least replaced as the core element of the Ottoman military. In place of the Janissaries and the other elements of the slave army, Osman planned to recruit a fighting force primarily from among the Turkish peasants of Anatolia.

If implemented, such reforms would strike at the heart of the system of government that had come to control the Ottoman state, including the power of the *devşirme*, the ladies of the harem, and the religious leaders of the *ulema*. Osman's plan took a stand against all that was essential to the *devşirme*-run system of Ottoman government. It saw the old system as damaging to the Empire and to the sultanate and planned to replace it with one where Turkish influence was stronger. For the first time since the time of sultan Mehmet II it appeared as if the native Turkish element might be in ascendancy. It was even rumoured, probably with some justification, that Osman planned to remove the capital from Istanbul to Anatolia in order to escape the pernicious influence of the capital and the *devşirme*. The intent to return to an Empire more like the early Ottoman Empire is obvious.

How much of this scheme was genuinely intended and how much might actually have been implemented will never be known. Perhaps the most meaningful thing about the plan was that it was believed. Whether or not Osman would have carried out the project, it is significant that the old guard saw that reform would destroy their position and that they would fight to continue their privileges. As might be expected, those who were to lose their positions if Osman's reforms were carried out were none too pleased. His enemies included the powers of the old regime – the Janissaries, the leaders of the *devşirme*, most of the high religious leaders, and anyone whose personal fate was tied to the continuation of the old system.

If Osman's reforms were to succeed, he had to remove himself from the power of those who opposed him. In 1622, he announced that he would travel to Mecca and Medina to make the Muslim pilgrimage, the first sultan ever to do so. It did not escape the notice of his enemies that his journey would be through Anatolia, where he could gather strength from Turkish forces (including *timar* holders, governors, and soldiers) and put his plans for a new Turkish Empire into effect. The pilgrimage might be abruptly discontinued at a new capital. Before any of this could happen, Osman's opponents revolted, killing first those who supported him, then assassinating the sultan himself. Osman had failed. He was replaced by Mustafa, whose second reign (1622–23) proved more disastrous than his first.

Murat IV

The desire of many in the ruling class to have an extremely weak sultan is understandable. The principle of 'while the cat's away the mice will play' applied. The theory of Ottoman government assumed that power resided in the hands of a strong sultan. In the absence of a watchful, powerful sultan, personal power was waiting to be seized, and there were many who wished to do just that. However, the Turkish leaders in Anatolia stopped the charade of government. Soon after Mustafa's second accession to the throne, governors in the provinces began to refuse to recognize his authority. They sent in no taxes to Istanbul. The governor of Erzurum rose in revolt, naming the misrule of the *devşirme* and murder of Osman II as causes for rebellion. Other provincial leaders followed. With the treasury empty and the future of the Empire in doubt, the leaders in Istanbul had no choice but to depose Mustafa once again.

Mustafa was replaced by his nephew Murat IV (ruled 1623–40), a son of Ahmed I. Murat IV began his reign while he was still a child. Real power was in the hands of his mother, Kösem, who used her position to engage in constant political battles within the administration. Meanwhile, the situation in the Empire deteriorated. Revolts broke out in eastern Anatolia, Yemen, the Crimea, Syria, Egypt, and elsewhere. Most damaging, the great Safavid Shah of Iran, Abbas I, took advantage of the Ottoman disarray and invaded Iraq, taking Baghdad in 1624. Unsuccessful Ottoman attempts to recapture Baghdad were hampered by the need to fight internal and external enemies at the same time. The army soon broke into feuding groups which attacked each other and generally forgot the Empire's enemies, sometimes allying themselves with rebel bands. Indeed, the soldiers themselves, through constant raiding and looting, became the main threat to stability. Ultimately, public order broke down all over the Empire, even in Istanbul. It appeared that the Empire might dissolve from internal decay.

The prospect of the imminent demise of the Ottoman Empire finally overcame the self-interest of rebels and bureaucrats alike. Without the Empire, all of their positions would have gone. Rather than lose everything, they rallied behind the sultan. In 1632, Murat, now twenty-two years old, actually took charge. With the agreement of all political forces, he placed his own advisors in high position and began to rule.

Murat IV was the exemplar of what has been called traditional reform. His reform of the operation of the Ottoman state stymied Ottoman enemies, reinvigorated the Empire for a time, and allowed it to continue much as it had been for centuries, a strong, traditional Middle Eastern empire. Murat's reforms did not, however, change the fundamental flaws that were to make the Ottomans the prey of European imperialists.

Murat and his advisors could not help but see the decay around them. They assumed that it had resulted from a failure to keep to old Ottoman standards. Reformers saw that everything had been better during the reign of Süleyman the Magnificent and drew the obvious conclusion. If things were to be as they had been in the reign of Süleyman, the system of government and its officials would have to be as they were then. The solution to governmental decay was to become better Ottomans, to return to the values of the Empire at its height. This Murat began to do with a vengeance.

Murat's primary solution for problems of bribery and malfeasance in office was execution. Provincial governors, Janissary leaders, and officials of the bureaucracy were all held to a high standard. Those who fell from grace were killed. Thousands were so punished. In the Empire, rebels and bandits were ruthlessly eliminated, sometimes by government-supported vigilante actions. Murat redistributed the *timar*s of rebellious subjects to those who were more loyal and managed through threat, if loyalty was not enough, to ensure that the *timar* holders kept to their duties.

Murat's crusade to reinvigorate his empire had elements that can be seen in modern societies. Like many a modern reformer, Murat believed that the greatest downfall of his people was moral laxness. He saw foreign substances, which in his day were coffee and tobacco, as the leading edge of depravity. The shops in which coffee and tobacco were consumed were potential hotbeds of seditious talk, so they were closed. Both substances were forbidden. Other lapses from morality were strictly punished, and woe betide the artist or poet who offended religious or political propriety. It was a bad time for sin.

Murat's reforms worked, at least as long as he was sultan. Celali revolts in Anatolia were put down mercilessly. A renewed army was able to defeat the Safavids and retake Baghdad in 1638. The northern borders were held against Polish incursions. Civil peace throughout the Empire was greatly improved. For contemporaries, it may have appeared that the glory of the Ottoman Empire as it had been under Süleyman had returned.

The failure of traditional reform

In fact, the situation of the Ottoman Empire was very different from what it had been one hundred years before. Murat had made the system work as well as it could, but what was needed was another system.

The disarray of the Ottoman government in the years before Murat IV had not been due to the sudden appearance of corrupt men. Very seldom in history has political disaster been caused by personal evil. Usually it is the opposite – a poor system encourages corrupt and incompetent men to rise in government and makes it impossible for the best men to triumph. Murat punished the corrupt and bought time for the Ottoman state. He did not change the basic system, which was the same at his death as at his accession.

If Murat's style of reform was to continue, the sultan who succeeded him would have had to be equally forceful and competent, a hard man like Murat who would stop at nothing to assure competent government. Yet the method of selecting sultans that had produced rulers such as Sultan Mustafa remained. The sultan who followed Murat, İbrahim (1640–48), was cut from the old mould of incompetence. Shortly after he took the throne, Murat's reformers were forced from office, sometimes killed. The treasury was soon empty. Bribery returned as an integral part of government. In the palace, the old harem rivalries returned in full force. Provincial leaders once again took power in their own territories, sending little money to the central treasury.

If traditional reform is judged by its own standard – whether it was able to return the government and society to traditional Ottoman values – it was in the long run a failure. It was also unsuccessful in what was to become a more important area – the relative strength of the Ottomans and

Europe. It was not enough for the Ottomans to return to their strengths of the days of Süleyman. The world had not waited for them to get their house in order. While the Ottomans were at best remaining as they were, the European nations were advancing in technology. If the Ottomans were to keep pace with Europe, and survive its pressures against them, they would have to change. The reforms of Osman II would probably not have succeeded any better in the long term than those of Murat IV. Osman's intention to bring the Empire back to traditional Turkish virtues, while more palatable than Murat's harsh defence of Süleyman's system, would also have surely failed. He would have created an Empire with all the virtues of the first Ottomans, the strong Turkish warriors who conquered all in their paths. They would have been the military and political virtues of the fourteenth century, not the seventeenth. The European enemies of the Ottomans, on the other hand, had seventeenth-century military and political systems.

The Ottomans had a difficult time seeing the need for fundamental reform. They had much seeming justification in thinking they were superior to all others, with little to learn from Europeans. Until the end of the seventeenth century, the Ottoman Empire in Europe remained intact. No significant territories were lost. The Ottomans could be pardoned for thinking that the Europeans were not able to retake Süleyman's conquests, even a century after they had been made. They could not know of the changes in European education and economy that would ultimately defeat them. The sense of superiority that comes with military conquest was strong in the Ottomans. Without clear proof, they could have had no reason to suspect that Europe was pulling ahead.

It should be remembered that even in the seventeenth and eighteenth centuries the Ottoman Empire was still a great power. It ruled over vast territory in Europe, Asia, and Africa, much larger than that of any potential European rival. The large number of troops the Empire could bring to battle could often overwhelm its enemies, even when an enemy's technology and tactics might be superior. Rulers and peoples all over Eastern Europe and western Asia still showed the Ottoman sultan the mixture of fear and respect that is the due of great emperors. Three hundred years after their beginnings, the Ottomans were still a force in the world, although not the force they thought they were. The worst aspect of traditional reform was that by bringing the Ottomans to something resembling their old form it hid the real nature of the problems. Reform made the Ottomans feel that, like Süleyman's armies, they could ride against the Europeans and win.

The road to Vienna

The years following Murat IV's death in 1648 showed clearly the defects of the Ottoman system. Murat's mother Kösem, also the mother of the new sultan, İbrahim, was arguably the most important person in Istanbul. Her intelligence and political ability, as well as her position as mother of the sultan, made her a decisive force in Ottoman government, even though her knowledge of the world outside the harem walls must have been limited. She was particularly able at forging alliances with those who held power in the imperial palace – vezirs, members of the *ulema*, and courtiers. Kösem managed to rid herself of Murat IV's last Grand Vezir, Kemankeş Kara Mustafa, a competent reformer and rival for power, in 1644. He was replaced with a much less competent, but much more pliable, successor. However, nothing could be done to make Kösem's son İbrahim appear fit for power. He was such a poor specimen that even those who might have personally benefited from weak imperial oversight, such as the leaders of the Janissary Corps, saw his continued rule as a danger. In 1648, he was overthrown in a Janissary revolt. His seven-year old son Mehmet replaced him. For the next three years, palace forces led by Kösem and Turhan, the mother of Mehmet IV, vied for control. Kösem, backed by some Janissary leaders, wished to force Mehmet IV from the throne, because Mehmet was dependent, like most children, on his mother, Kösem's enemy. Turhan was supported by the palace eunuchs and other harem forces, and the Janissaries were brought over to her side. Finally, in 1651, Kösem was assassinated. Turhan took charge.

All of this intrigue may appear confusing, but the reality was an even more muddled stew of intrigue. Palace forces vied for power, changing sides as they calculated who might win. The sultans were little more than tools – İbrahim was a fool; Mehmet IV was a child. Mehmet was relegated to childish pursuits and never really trained for rule. During his long reign, he scarcely ruled at all.

For seven years, from Kemankeş Kara Mustafa's death to that of Kösem, the Ottoman Empire had been in disorder that mirrored the turmoil at its centre. Once they had triumphed, Turhan and her friends did little to change the situation. Grand Vezirs came and went, ten in eight years, leaving disaster behind. Illegal taxes were levied, then wasted. Not until disaster almost overwhelmed them were those in power willing to put the own interests second to the needs of the Empire.

Just as in the time of Murat IV, in the middle of the seventeenth century disorder in Anatolia led to a resurgence of the traditional Ottoman system. Celali revolts had been a major factor behind the acceptance of Murat IV by the Janissaries, who feared Celali successes. Put down or bought off by Murat, Celalis rose once again after Murat's death and by 1650 held much of Anatolia in their sway. Beset by these internal enemies, the Ottoman centre also reeled from attacks by the Venetians, who destroyed the Ottoman fleet in the Aegean Sea, took islands at the mouth of the Dardanelles, and menaced the heart of the Empire. The real rulers of the Empire, Turhan and the others in the palace, looked for a saviour.

181

In 1656, the Ottomans turned to a Grand Vezir who would apply the strictures of traditional reform in the manner of Murat IV. Mehmet Köprülü was a member of the *devşirme* noted for his abilities, a veteran of the political warfare inside the palace administration. Despite his seventy-one years, he attacked the Empire's problems with great energy. Afraid that continued catastrophe would threaten her own position, Turhan gave him a free hand, herself retiring from active participation in the government. The sultan had never really begun to participate.

Through executions and banishments Köprülü rid the central administration of those who would oppose him and cemented power in his own hands. The military heads who had failed against the Venetians and Celalis were executed. Those who were corrupt, as well as many whose only crime may have been to oppose dictatorial rule, were ruthlessly killed. Tens of thousands were said to have died in Köprülü's purges, but the budget was balanced and the military brought up to their old standard.

Mehmet Köprülü was militarily successful against the Venetians, the rebels in Anatolia, and revolts in Ottoman Europe. By ridding the administration of the members of other parties, he was able to put into effect what might today be called a dictatorship. His administration was ruthless but effective. When he died in 1661 power passed into the hands of his son, Fazıl Ahmed Köprülü, who was Grand Vezir for the next fifteen years. Those years were among the best ever experienced by the Ottoman state. Enemies having been removed by his father, Fazıl Ahmed was able to rule more pacifically. Fazıl Ahmed was a successful warrior, defeating the Venetians and taking Crete from them, holding off the Habsburgs in Hungary and Transylvania, and conquering part of the Ukraine. As had been the case under Murat IV, the Empire appeared strong. Hindsight tells us that this was not so. The conquest of Crete from Venice, never really opposed by a major force, took years and demonstrated a great deal of military ineptitude. Venice was a spent force, maimed by changes in trade patterns that damaged her traditional strength, which was economic. The Austrian Habsburgs would soon prove themselves more than a match for the Ottomans in Hungary.

The debacle came in 1683. Fazıl Ahmed Köprülü had died in 1676, to be replaced by his foster brother, Kara Mustafa, as Grand Vezir. Kara Mustafa kept up the Köprülü tradition of harsh but effective rule. However, he and his advisors came to believe that the Köprülü reforms had succeeded in making the Ottomans once again strong enough to battle against the best in Europe. He tried to do what Süleyman had failed to achieve – take Vienna and crush Habsburg power in Central Europe. The attempt was unsuccessful, and the extent of the failure shows the difference between the position of the Köprülü Empire and that of Süleyman. Although Süleyman failed to take Vienna, he nevertheless retreated with an intact army. He retained his power and possessions. The Ottoman Empire still stretched nearly to the gates of Vienna. When Kara Mustafa retreated, the Ottoman army was harried by the Habsburgs and their allies, the Poles. The army tried to make a stand at Gran, where it was defeated and virtually destroyed. Süleyman had left a stable structure of defences in Europe. Kara Mustafa left disarray and a defenceless frontier. He was executed on the order of the sultan.

In 1684, the Habsburgs followed up the Ottoman loss with attacks into Ottoman territory. Joined by Venice, Poland, Russia, and other European states, the Austrians took Ottoman Hungary with little resistance. War continued on many fronts until 1699. Then, in desperate straits at home and on the battlefield, the Ottomans signed the treaty of Carlowitz. In it they gave up Hungary and Transylvania to Austria, as well as the Ukraine to Poland and islands in the Aegean, the Dalmatian Coast, and the Morea to Venice. Russia received a foothold on the Black Sea that was to signal further ambitions against the Ottomans. For the Ottomans, it was the worst disaster since Tamerlane and one from which they would never really recover. For the Europeans, the myth of Ottoman invincibility was over.

After Vienna – further attempts at reform and further dissolution

Although crippled, Ottoman power did not disappear after the debacle of Vienna. The Ottomans were able to rebuild their army, although not to its previous size. This had its benefits, because a large number of unqualified Janissaries were struck from the rolls. While there was conflict, including one short civil war, between political forces, the Empire managed to stay out of foreign wars until 1710. Then, to the astonishment of all, especially Tsar Peter the Great, the Ottomans defeated the Russians at the battle of the Pruth (July 20, 1711). In 1715, the Ottomans were able to drive the Venetians from southern Greece. However, once again overconfidence was the Ottoman undoing. When the Austrians came to the aid of the Venetians in 1717–18 they inflicted major defeats on the Ottomans. Under the terms of the treaty of Passarowitz (July 21, 1718), the Empire lost even more lands to the north. The Austrians claimed Serbia and its capital Belgrade, what little remained to the Ottomans of Hungary (the Banat), and western Wallachia.

The Tulip Period

As was ever the case with the Ottomans, defeat led to reform. What ensued was one of the strangest examples of traditional reform, the Tulip Period. Sultan Ahmed III who took power in 1703, in the wake of the disaster at Carlowitz, was fortunate to have as Grand Vezir Nevşehirli Damad İbrahim Paşa, a consummate politician who knew the Empire needed both change

183

and a period of respite from war. He also decided that the Europeans had something that deserved to be imitated, a startling admission for an Ottoman. Ambassadors were sent to European courts. They sent back incredulous reports on the wonders they saw – baroque palaces, impressive gardens, and grand balls at which women danced with men! This led to the first 'westernization' of the Ottoman Empire, but superficial is the kindest word for the result. The sultan, who preferred show to substance, led a grand adoption of things French. Ottoman officials adopted Western dress and sat in European-style chairs. Grandees had their pictures painted in the French fashion, often by European painters imported for the purpose. Palaces and gardens in the French fashion were constructed all across Istanbul. The period took its name from the importation and ubiquitous planting of tulips. Growing tulips, considered a sign of Western ways, became a sign of sophistication. Many a *paşa* became a tulip horticultural-ist. It was a time of parties and entertainments in what the Ottomans thought was the European fashion. The ordinary people of Istanbul must have thought the aristocracy had collectively gone mad.

All was not frivolous. The Ottoman reporters from Europe had not been concerned with social life only. They reported on fortifications, army organization and training, and factories. Some matters of importance were copied from the Europeans, in particular the printing press, which now produced the first printed books in Ottoman Turkish. These included scientific books which for the first time made European science available to readers of Turkish. It can also be asserted that any opening to the West, no matter how silly, would eventually be beneficial. However, the immediate result of Tulip Period was a popular uprising. Poor people in Istanbul saw that new palaces and European finery were increasing while they often went hungry. Taxes were increased, at least some of which went on expensive imports of unnecessary fripperies from Europe. Prejudice against the works of the infidel West was already present, and the excesses of Ahmed III seemed to confirm all the fears of religious and cultural conservatives. Military events added to public displeasure – a long war with Iran, which had gone well at first, turned against the Ottomans in 1730, and Ottoman territory in the East had been lost. Finally, in September 1730, a popular revolt in Istanbul (the Patrona Halil Revolt) claimed the head of İbrahim Paşa and forced the sultan to abdicate.

Ahmed III's successor, Mahmud I (1730–54), was able to make some practical reforms of the Ottoman military. In a war against Russia and Austria (1736–39), the Ottomans were able to regain what they had lost in the treaty of Passarowitz and make slight gains against the Russians. Iran was defeated and the old Ottoman–Iranian borders restored. The Habsburgs, previously the most potent of the Ottoman enemies, had entered a long period of military decline with their loss of Spain to the French Bourbons in the War of Spanish Succession (1701–14). France, and not the Ottomans, was now the power that most threatened Habsburg possessions. The redirection of Austrian military activity to the north and west and the general Austrian military decline meant that the Ottomans felt less threat from that quarter. However, Russia was growing ever stronger and would return to decisively defeat the Ottomans later in the century. No fundamental changes had been made in the Ottoman military. At best it could hope to remain at its old strength while its European enemies grew ever stronger. Even this hope was forlorn. Continued degeneration of the Ottoman administrative situation, especially in the Balkans, meant that not even the old levels of strength could be upheld.

The ayans *of Ottoman Europe*

The degeneration of the Ottoman administrative system was well demon-strated by the emergence of a system of independent rule by military lords in parts of Anatolia and, especially, the Ottoman Balkans. These *ayans* ('notables') were sometimes members of locally prominent families who developed the authority of their families when central authority declined. Although they existed into the nineteenth century, their rule was actually close to the medieval European ideal of government – autonomous lords who accepted the overlordship of their sovereign and sometimes fought for him in wars, but were jealous of their own prerogatives. More often, the *ayans* were freebooters – rebellious Ottoman officials, leaders of armed bands, or even bandits – who gathered around them armed men and took over areas of the European empire. Some of them are listed in the table.[1] There were a number of others. The areas ruled by the *ayans* were a significant part of Ottoman Europe in the late eighteenth century. One of

The most important *Ayans*

Veysioğlu Halil Usta	Dimotica
Dağdevirenoğlu	Eastern Thrace
Tokatcıklı Süleyman Ağa	Western Thrace
Yıllıkzade Süleyman Ağa	Silistria, Deliorman
Nazır Ahmed Ağa	Dobruja
Tirsiniklioğlu İsmail Ağa	Nikopolis, Sistova, Rusçuk
Pasvanoğlu Osman Paşa	Vidin, Sofya
Buşatlı Mahmud Paşa	Northern Albania
İbrahim Paşa	Northern Epirus
Tepedenli Ali Paşa	Southern Epirus

---

[1] Taken from Stanford J. Shaw, *Between Old and New*, Cambridge, Massachusetts, 1971, pp. 227–8.

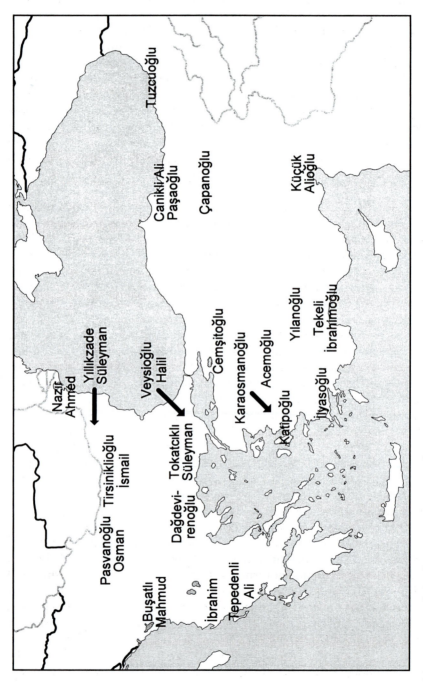

Primary *ayans* and *derebeys.*

the two most important of the *ayan*s was Pasvanoğlu Osman Paşa (the other was Ali Paşa of Yanina). He can serve as an example of Ottoman decay. The fact that Pasvanoğlu legally claimed the highest title of Ottoman government, *paşa*, indicates his status in the confused administration of the Ottoman Balkans at its lowest point.

Pasvanoğlu Osman ('Osman of the Pasvanoğlu family') was a member of a minor landholding family who had turned to banditry. He must have been good at this, because he was able to attract a large band of fellow renegades to his standard. He seized control of the town of Vidin and turned it into a haven for bandits and ex-soldiers, forming his men into an army and building his treasury through raiding. In 1795, he declared open revolt against the Ottoman government. His forces took much of northwest Bulgaria, as well as raiding and ravaging Ottoman Romania and Serbia. In 1797, the Ottoman army managed to defeat Osman's forces and keep him to the Vidin area, but not until his men had ravaged far into east and central Bulgaria. A major Ottoman army put him under siege in Vidin in 1798, but Osman was saved by the withdrawal of Ottoman forces to fight a war against Napoleon, who had invaded Ottoman Egypt that year. The Ottoman sultan, Selim III, unable to stop Pasvanoğlu Osman, instead pardoned him and named him governor in Vidin, in effect legalizing all of Osman's crimes.

In 1799 and 1800, Osman's forces spread destruction in northern Bulgaria, fighting the armies of other *ayan*s. Taking advantage of the Ottoman withdrawal of men to fight the French in Egypt, Osman raided into Serbia in 1800, even briefly taking Belgrade. His allies seized Serbia in 1801. Ottoman armies sent against Osman were often as dangerous to the populace as was Osman. Often unpaid, and often recruited from the same type of bandits who had joined Osman, they raided at will. The result was disastrous for the Empire and its subjects. The Serbian revolution of 1804–13, for example, was largely a result of the poor protection, from *ayan*s and Ottoman soldiers alike, afforded Serbia by the Ottomans.

Pasvanoğlu Osman died of natural causes in 1807. During his lifetime, he and his allies had managed to ravage much of the land in Serbia, central and northern Bulgaria, and southern Romania. As raiders who lived off plunder, his soldier/bandits often raided the same areas again and again. Not only did the Ottoman government lose the tax monies that Osman did not forward to Istanbul, but he destroyed the commerce and agriculture, and thus the tax revenues, of many other regions, as well. Interestingly, the Ottoman subjects who seem to have suffered least from Osman Pasvanoğlu's depredations were the people of Vidin, itself. Perhaps to keep a secure base, perhaps because he saw himself as a 'just king' of Vidin, he ruled there fairly well. The people of Vidin certainly did better than those of the surrounding areas.

None of the other *ayan*s of the Balkans was worse for the region than was Pasvanoğlu, but they were not much better. Their internecine wars destroyed farms, impoverished cities, and weakened the Ottoman state. They were a cause as well as a symptom of Ottoman administrative decline. Their power demonstrated that by the year 1800 the Ottoman state did not actually rule most of its territory. None of the *ayan*s proved individually to have sufficient power to break free and become truly independent. In fact, most probably did not consider the possibility; declarations of independence such as Pasvanoğlu's were rare, and even his may have been more bargaining ploy than true intention. It was a dangerous world beyond the Ottoman borders, and the *ayan*s knew it. Alone a local ruler could never stand against invaders from Europe. They had to stand together against external opponents such as the Russians. The only banner that could unite them was the flag of the sultan. Therefore, when the Russians invaded, the *ayan*s sent their men to fight. In the 1806–12 war, *ayan*s' forces were the majority of those who stood, admittedly not very successfully, against the Russians. It was a weak state, and they wanted it to remain that way, but it was their state.

The derebeys *of Anatolia*

The independent local leaders in Anatolia were usually called *derebey*s ('lords of the valley'). Like the *ayan*s of Ottoman Europe, in the eighteenth century they were virtually independent. There were, however, great differences between the *ayan*s and the *derebey*s. When one looks at the history of the *ayan*s, the picture is one of glorified bandits who manage to claim a great deal of power and to use that power badly. The picture of the Anatolian *derebey*s is of more truly local rulers, concerned with local conditions and ruling as something close to medieval lords, not rebellious bandits. These pictures are perhaps not completely fair to either group, but they are close. *Ayan* leaders were individuals who on their death passed on

The most important derebey *families*

Küçük Alioğlu	Payas, Adana
İlyasoğlu	Milas, Menteşe
Tekeli İbrahimoğlu	Antalya
Tuzcuoğlu	Rize
Cemşitoğlu	Bilecik
Acemoğlu	Uşak
Yılanlıoğlu	Isparta
Katipoğlu	İzmir
Karaosmanoğlu	Western Anatolia
Çapanoğlu	Central Anatolia
Canikli Ali Paşaoglu	Northeast Anatolia

authority to whichever of their lieutenants or rivals was strong enough to claim it. The list of *derebey* families in the table[2] demonstrates a very different situation in Anatolia. Note that what is listed are *families* of lords, usually passing authority from father to son. This in itself is a sign of more stable rule. Masters are less likely to destroy productive resources for quick gain if they know their children will be succeeding them. For peasants and city dwellers alike, long-term rule is almost always preferable to short-term, 'grab what you can and run for it' rule.

The *derebey* families did fight each other, but they were much less likely to engage in the type of pillage that characterized Pasvanoğlu Osman, and they were more likely to support the sultan in international wars. For many Anatolians, the situation under the *derebey*s must have been an improvement over the past. Surely it was better to have one local lord who provided protection than it was to live under constant threat of Celali attack or the equally nasty efforts of undisciplined government soldiers. Based on the security of life of their 'subjects', the rule of the *derebey*s must be accounted a success.

Derebey rule in Anatolia was also rule of Anatolian Turks by Anatolian Turks. Some of the *derebey*s had come directly from Turkish nomad families. Others were local notables with long histories in their regions. As such they were surely more knowledgeable than any Istanbul bureaucrat could ever be about the status and needs of their regions. They were probably also more pleasing to the local citizens. The Turks of Anatolia, like any other humans, must have preferred leaders who were geographically and culturally close to them, and that surely could not be said of the bureaucrats and politicians in Istanbul. In many ways, the situation in Anatolia at the end of the eighteenth century resembles that at the end of the Rum Seljuk Empire – local Turkish lords, much removed by culture and politics from the high life of the court, each governing his own 'principality'. The first sultan, Osman, and his successors had come from such a system. There was much that was good about autonomous regional rule. Unfortunately, the world of the nineteenth century would not allow an empire weakened by regional autonomy to survive. Only a unified empire could stand against the enemies that surrounded the Ottomans.

At the end of the eighteenth century, *ayan*s ruled in much of Ottoman Europe, *derebey*s in Anatolia, independent governors in Syria. Mamluk rule had even reappeared in Egypt. What did that leave to the sultan? Not much. The sultans only actually had direct control over the areas closest to Istanbul. This did not mean that the various autonomous lords did not recognize the sultans as their sovereign. They did, and even sent him some money and troops when needed, but never enough to advance the power of the state or to win wars. Mainly, the sultan was recognized as the symbol of

---

[2] Taken from Shaw, p. 215.

the Muslim Empire, standing against the Christians who threatened the state. It was this that kept the Empire alive during the weakest days of the central government. No one could imagine a different political environment – there had to be a sultan. This allowed the sultan to survive and to play one autonomous lord off against another.

Survival of the Empire

The Ottoman Empire was by no means doomed in 1699. Looking back at the turn of the eighteenth century one can say that the Empire was on the road to extinction. Ultimate destruction would not have appeared to be a certainty to observers in 1699. After the Peace of Carlowitz the Ottoman Empire continued to lose land slowly. There were not what can be called major losses until the 1770s, and the majority of the territory in Ottoman Europe remained in the Empire until 100 years after that. Occasionally, traditional reforming measures managed to invigorate the Empire yet again – the Persians and even the Russians were sometimes defeated. The Ottoman Army was still a formidable force, primarily due to the endurance and fighting ability of the ordinary Turkish soldier. Yet Carlowitz had demonstrated that Europe was militarily superior.

The lesson that seems obvious to us today was that, if they hoped to hold their own against Europe, the Ottomans had to emulate Europe. To do so meant not only changing an army, but altering a way of life. Once the Ottomans set upon the path of radical, Europeanizing reform, there was no part of their society that could escape change. A new army was certainly needed, but a new army depended on new weapons. New weapons depended on new factories, which depended on new methods of production and educated workers, which in turn demanded a European-style educational system. European schools needed textbooks, which were in European languages, so those had to be learned. Etcetera. The decision to truly reform was a decision to change everything. Perhaps it should be no surprise that it took the Ottomans almost 100 years after Carlowitz to make the decision to really change.

Another lesson for those who look at the Ottoman Empire in its period of 'decline' is the opposite of the one usually taken. As has been done above, historians naturally study what was wrong with the Ottoman Empire (just as today's newspaper columnists prefer to write of what is wrong with politics, society, or any other topic). It is too easy to forget that in 1683, when the campaign to Vienna failed, the Ottoman sultans had already ruled for 400 years, and that more than 200 more years would pass before the Empire ceased to exist. Few states could claim such longevity.

The tenacity of the ordinary farmer and merchant should not be forgotten. Throughout the seventeenth and eighteenth centuries, despite civil disruption, the degeneration of government, and high taxation, commerce continued. For example, the merchants of Ankara, living in an area heavily beset by Celali disorders, were virtually bankrupt in 1600. The population of the city of Ankara declined and peasants fled the province for safer regions. Yet twenty years later the merchants had reconstructed economic life. They built fortified city walls for protection and went about business within. Caravans left for İzmir with mohair from the Angora goats raised in the region. The merchants thus kept not only themselves, but herdsmen, land holders, and the economy alive.

Despite decay in the palace and fragmentation of rule, the Ottoman Empire did not collapse from within. Its institutions were sufficient to see it through. What ultimately brought it down were the forces of European imperialism, fuelled by an irresistible European economy. This was not only true of the Ottomans. Of all the non-western countries, only Japan can be said to have withstood the force of Europe, and Japan had the benefit of relative isolation and lack of concentrated European attack while it developed, a breathing space that was never afforded the Ottomans. In fairness, the Ottomans should be compared to the other great empires attacked by Europe – India, China, the Aztecs, etc. None of these was able to match the Ottoman feat of survival. When considering Ottoman faults it is instructive to look at a map of the world in the late nineteenth century, 300 years after the onset of Ottoman 'decline'. In a world ruled by the imperialists of Britain, France, Russia, and Germany, the Ottoman Empire stood out as holding to its independence, however fragile it may have been. Considerations of decline should never blind one to the greatness of Ottoman rule.

Chapter 6

Imperialism and Nationalism

Turkish prisoners of war after the defeat at Plevna in the Russo-Turkish War of 1877–78. For an idea of the relative impoverishment of the Ottoman forces, note the footwear of the Ottoman and Russian soldiers. (*Illustrated London News*. January 12, 1878, supplement.)

Imperialism and Nationalism

The nineteenth-century Ottoman Empire attempted to survive in a world in which imperialism was triumphant. All over Asia and Africa, British, French, German, and Russian armies were finishing the conquest of non-European peoples. By the end of the century, India was the possession of the British, as was much of Africa. France had taken much of North and West Africa. Russia had conquered Muslim Central Asia and the region of the Caucasus Mountains, as well as Christian European countries such as Poland and Finland. All of East Asia was under European control, except Japan and the interior of China. All the great non-Western empires but one had succumbed to European finances and firepower.

Alone among the old Asian empires, the Ottoman Empire managed to survive and keep its independence throughout the 'imperial century'. This success is often overlooked in the light of obvious European economic and military superiority over the Ottomans. It should not be. The survival of the Ottoman Empire for so long was a tribute to Ottoman administration, diplomacy, reform, and military prowess, all in the face of overwhelming odds.

During the nineteenth century the Ottoman lands were whittled away, particularly by Russian attack, but the Ottomans managed to live on. Their situation can be compared to that of a noble family, fallen on hard times, which manages to hold on by selling off old family treasures, one by one. The Ottoman treasures were stolen, rather than sold, but the situation was nonetheless similar. Like the impoverished family, the Ottoman's economic situation was always grim, and they stood to lose all, but somehow did not. Also like many a person fallen on hard times, the Ottomans could not afford to fail, because they had family that depended on them. The Ottoman family was the millions of Turks and other Muslims in and outside of the Ottoman Empire who depended on the Ottomans for survival, sure that if the Ottomans failed, they would die. They were correct, for the

Ottomans' enemies were intent not simply on taking their lands, but on expelling the Turks and other Muslims who lived in them. In the end, the inhabitants of the Ottoman Empire paid an awful price for the covetousness of others. From 1800 to 1922, millions died in the wars with Russia, civil wars between Muslims and Christians brought about by European intervention, and forced exiles of whole populations.

The contraction of the Ottoman Empire

The Ottoman Empire had begun to lose territory 100 years after it had reached its greatest power and extent. In the late seventeenth century, it quickly lost its northernmost territories in Europe. Then the threat to the Ottomans somewhat subsided. The Europeans were more concerned with wars in Western Europe. After the debacle of the second siege of Vienna and subsequent losses to the Austrians, there were no major Ottoman losses for more than half a century. During that time a new enemy was gaining power, Russia.

Imperial Russia

In modern times, Russia has been the greatest threat to the Turks. Rising as it did at the time when Ottoman power was on the wane, Russia expanded at the expense of the Ottomans. Until the end of the First World War, the Russian and Ottoman Empires were constant enemies. (It was an animosity that was to be renewed after the Second World War, when Stalin threatened the Turkish Republic, which responded by joining NATO.) For the Turks and other Muslims of the region, Russia was more than a political enemy. Russia was a threat to their survival.

The first significant Ottoman losses to the Russians came during the reign of Catherine the Great (1762–96). During her reign, the Ottomans were for the first time driven from territories in which the population was predominantly Muslim. Catherine's forces fought the Ottomans from 1768–72, and in the peace of Küçük Kaynarcı (1774) were given Ottoman territories on the Black Sea. The Crimea was declared 'independent', but was under Russian control and was annexed by Russia in 1783. In the treaty, the Russians also declared their right to intervene in support of Greek Orthodox Christians in the Ottoman Empire, a stipulation that was to be a thorn in the Ottoman side for another century.

Further Ottoman losses to the Russians came in 1792 and 1812, when more Ottoman territory on the northern Black Sea was forcibly transferred.

In the region of the Caucasus Mountains, Russian expansion had begun before the start of the nineteenth century. Under the guise of coming to the aid of the Georgians, the Russian Empire absorbed Georgia in 1800. It then set upon a policy of subjugating the Muslim lands in the region. First to fall were the predominantly Turkish provinces of northwestern Iran. These provinces, on the west coast of the Caspian Sea, were primarily populated by Turks, mainly Shia Muslim in religion, with minorities of Armenians. They were nominally under the rule of the Persian Empire, although in most affairs autonomous under local rulers (*han*s or *khan*s). By the turn of the nineteenth century the Russians in the Caucasus were militarily strong enough to defeat the *han*s and their Persian overlords. One by one the khanates were taken by the Russians, using their own troops and Georgian mercenaries and aided by local Armenians. The culmination of the Russian attack came in the war of 1826–28, in which the Russians defeated the Persians and took the last of the khanates, Erivan. In the war with the Ottomans (1828–29) that followed the Persian war, the Russians took territory on the eastern coast on the Black Sea. They spent the next forty years cementing their control of the Caucasus region, battling against the local Muslim population, which continually rose against them to gain their independence.

The Ottoman Empire gained a brief respite from its losses to Russia when the Russians lost the Crimean War (1853–56) to the Ottomans, Britain, and France. However, the only Ottoman reward for victory, and the great expense of the war, was a small amount of land at the mouth of the River Danube. Russia again defeated the Ottomans in the war of 1877–78. The defeat was massive. The peace treaty signed in Berlin in 1878 awarded much of northeastern Anatolia to the Russians. In Ottoman Europe, a separate Bulgarian state was created, which Russia assumed would be its client state in the Balkans.

Other losses

The other traditional enemy of the Ottomans, Austria, was less of a threat. Through much of the nineteenth century the Austrians were occupied with the nationalistic aspirations of their Hungarian and Slavic subjects and in resisting revolution in and out of their Empire. They were deeply involved with European politics in the Napoleonic and post-Napoleonic times, and militarily involved with Prussia, to their detriment (Austrian defeat in the war of 1866). This left little time for adventures in the Ottoman Balkans. Indeed, in some ways the Austrians balanced the threat from Russia. Austria-Hungary was a state led by Germans and Hungarians, neither of them Slavic peoples, but a state that controlled many Slavs. The Russians, on the other hand, were Slavs They were sometimes champions of pan-Slavism (the desire to have one, unified Slavic people and state), sometimes supporters of the independence of Slavic peoples. This made the Austrians wary of Russian intentions. They had no wish to see Russia's influence over the Balkan Slavs expand. The Russians thus had to fear Austrian intervention when they attacked the Ottomans.

The only Austrian occupation of Ottoman territory in the nineteenth century came as a result of the Russo-Turkish War of 1877–78. The Russians agreed to Austrian occupation of the Ottoman provinces of Bosnia and Herzegovina as the payment for Austrian nonintervention in the war. The Congress of Berlin (June 13–July 13, 1878), which adjudicated border changes after the war, confirmed the Austrian occupation. In 1908, the areas were formally annexed to the Austro-Hungarian Empire. While the lands gained by the Austrians were not particularly extensive, they later assumed great importance. By incorporating Bosnia and Herzegovina into their Empire, the Austrians took in many more Slavic-speakers and incurred the wrath of Serbian nationalists, who wanted the two territories for a Greater Serbia. It was the action of one of those Serbian nationalists in assassinating Austrian Archduke Francis Ferdinand in the Bosnian capital of Sarajevo (June 28, 1914), that sparked off World War I.

The other nineteenth-century Ottoman losses to great European powers came in North Africa. In the nineteenth century, Tunisia and Egypt were nominally Ottoman provinces, but were in fact autonomous. The French seized Tunisia, which was ruled by an independent Muslim governor, the Bey of Tunis, in 1881, in part to make sure that Italy did not take it. The Ottomans were only paid tribute by the real rulers of Egypt, Muhammad Ali (see below) and his descendents, and had small say in most state matters. It was therefore not a real territorial loss for the Ottomans when Egypt was seized in 1882 by the British. The loss of prestige was worse. The Ottoman sultan attached great importance to his position as leader and defender of the Islamic peoples. Seizure of Muslim countries such as Egypt was a blow to the pride of all Muslims, the beginning of a dislike and fear of the West that was to continue among many Muslims for more than a century. The island of Cyprus also came under British sway, although with at least grudging Ottoman approval. It was given to the British 'to protect' in exchange for British support against the Russians after the Ottoman defeat in 1878.

Italy was the last of the Western powers to seize Ottoman lands before the First World War. In 1911 Italy attempted to seize the Ottoman province of Tripoli (the coastal region of present-day Libya). The Ottomans, greatly outnumbered and with insecure supply lines, fought a guerilla war, aided by the Libyan Arabs, but were forced to sue for peace when the Balkan wars broke out (see below).

Geographic losses

The table lists the areas in the slow but steady dismemberment of the Ottoman Empire. The areas in the table are approximate, because it is

Area of the Ottoman Empire in miles and kilometres (000s)

	1675	*1750*	*1850*	*1900*	*1914*
Europe					
Square miles	450	320	200	80	10
Square kilometres	1,170	830	520	210	30
Asia and Africa					
Square miles	1,020	1,020	940	830	680
Square kilometres	2,640	2,640	2,430	2,150	1,760
Total					
Square miles	1,470	1,340	1,140	910	690
Square kilometres	3,810	3,470	2,950	2,360	1,790

Comparison to Modern States

	Turkey	*United States*	*United Kingdom*	*France*	*Germany*
Square miles	300	3,680	94	210	140
Square kilometres	780	9,530	240	550	350

sometimes hard to discern where the Ottoman Empire ended, especially where Ottoman power trailed off into the desert. In the table, the Mediterranean and Aegean islands are all included under Europe. It should be noted that not all the areas included were really under direct Ottoman control. Regions of North Africa in particular were very loosely held, and often were in fact autonomous. Also, the size of the Empire's holdings in Africa and Asia make those regions appear much larger than their populated areas. Desert took up a good portion of the holdings in Africa and Asia. Unfortunately for the Ottomans, the regions lost in Europe in the 1800s were some of the most productive, whereas some of the least productive regions, such as most of Iraq and the borderlands of the Arabian desert, remained until the empire's end.

The Ottomans and the Europeans

Cynicism is the historically accurate way to view relations between states. History teaches that when a man proclaims his friendship and hugs you in the street he is probably picking your pocket. Like most countries in history, the Ottomans had no real friends. Statesmen in European capitals might personally have respected the Ottomans, wished them well in their reforms, or pitied them their losses to Russia, but European leaders were concerned with their own countries' benefit, not that of the Ottomans. The only time the Ottomans could count on the support of a European power was when it was in that power's own interest.

Throughout the nineteenth century, the country that most stood by the Ottomans was Great Britain. The reason was the balance of power. Britain always worked to deny supremacy to any one European power. This often meant that they would support the Ottomans, because defeating the Ottomans, or at least defeating them too badly, would give too much power to the victor. Therefore, when Napoleon invaded Egypt in 1798 the British joined forces with the Ottomans to defeat him. The British, along with the French, allied with the Ottomans against the Russians in the Crimean War. If Russian had become too powerful this would have been a threat to the balance of power. Although domestic feeling kept them from aiding the Ottomans in the 1877–78 Russo-Turkish War, the British did ensure, at the Congress of Berlin (1878) that Ottoman losses were somewhat lessened, in exchange for which they received Cyprus. The British occupied Egypt in 1882, but the Ottomans could still count on them to support the integrity of the Ottoman Empire in all those areas that the British could not practically take themselves. That all changed in 1907. Britain and Russia agreed to the Anglo-Russian Entente (August 30), and the two empires grew closer. British policy went from opposing Russian expansion to supporting Russian plans as a bulwark against the new power of Germany. The enemies of the Russians became the enemies of Britain. Thus did the balance of power turn against the Ottomans.

When the Ottomans lost their traditional 'friend' they did not gain new friends from the ranks of their traditional enemies. The position of the Austrians and Russians concerning the Ottoman Empire was that of two wolves who each wanted to devour a tasty morsel, but who were each afraid to take their attention from the other long enough to eat, afraid that if his attention lapsed he might be the next dinner. The Empire survived at least partly because of their rivalry.

After 1907, the only country the Ottomans could remotely trust was Germany. Germany was too far away from the Ottoman Empire to harbour immediate intentions of territorial gain at Ottoman expense, but wanted to use the Ottomans as a force to keep the Russians in check. The Germans also saw the Ottoman Empire as a conduit for German economic penetration of the East. The Germans ultimately took the place of the British as the supporters of the Ottoman Empire.

Economic imperialism

In the nineteenth century, Western Europeans had long seen the relation between national power and national wealth. In France and, in particular, England, international politics and the expansion of trade were joined together. This resulted in wealth for the Europeans, but often worked to the detriment of less developed countries. Disabled by their lack of economic expertise and military power, the Ottomans were relegated to the position of exporter of raw materials to European factories and importers of modern goods. Although village industries such as weaving remained economically strong in their own regions, industries that had produced textiles and other manufactures on a large scale had long been in decline. The mills of England could produce many basic goods and ship them far more cheaply than the goods could be produced in the Middle East. Other, more advanced goods, such as new cannon, warships, and modern machinery for factory production, were simply beyond the technical ability of the Ottomans to produce. The Ottomans could not protect themselves from what was, in effect, economic warfare.

Relative poverty did not mean that the Ottoman Empire had no need of expensive modern goods. The Ottoman Empire took out its first European loan in 1854, to pay the costs of the Crimean War. Borrowing soon became a bad habit. Just as it has for many modern governments, for the Ottomans borrowing appeared to be a fairly painless way to develop their country. In theory, the state could borrow money to set up industries or to create a better economic climate to increase the country's wealth. For example, a textile mill could be built on borrowed funds, then the debt paid off by the proceeds from the cloth made at the mill and sold. Railroads would theoretically improve the economy and thus 'pay for themselves', European advisors, imported books, imported machines, etc. would all 'pay for themselves'.

Of course, it did not work that way. The theory of borrowing your way to riches only works if you have a good plan, you follow it, and you have luck. The Ottomans had some good plans, but in general they were poor capitalists. For example, until 1874 the Empire taxed the internal movement of goods and thus made it difficult for its own factories to buy raw materials from its own farms. Like many a modern individual with a new credit card, Ottoman rulers and officials spent some of their borrowed funds on non-productive purchases – palace decorations, European finery, and the like. However, the main difficulty lay in the assumption that new production could pay off the debts. It could not. Neither the workforce nor the managers were skilled enough to compete with European factories, nor did they have enough time to learn. The debts became due before they could make enough to pay them off. The Ottomans then had to borrow more to pay the interest on the first debts. As they borrowed more, the cost of borrowing went up. In order to lessen their risks, European investors insisted that their expenses and much of the loans' exorbitant interest be paid in advance, deducted from the initial amount received by the Ottomans. The result was that the Ottomans sometimes received only half of what they borrowed, although they had to repay the whole sum. In

1865, for example, the Empire took out a loan of 40 million lire (approximately £36 million or $173 million), but only received 20 million, exactly half of what was to be repaid with interest. Saddest of all, the 20 million lire they did receive went to repay earlier debts.

Even had the Ottomans known exactly what to do with their credit, they had the bad luck to need the money elsewhere. Much of what was borrowed by the Ottomans clearly could not be put to productive use. Even though there had been little significant improvement in their tax base, the Ottomans were faced with the need to spend ever more on defence. Too much of the government income, whether from taxes or borrowing, had to be spent on guns. Defence was the primary consideration of the state – it would do little good to develop the economy of a region only to hand that region over to the Russians or others. Yet that is what happened again and again. When the Russians seized Ottoman territory the Ottoman Empire lost economically many times over. Great expenditures were completely wasted on non-productive war. For example, Ottoman Bulgaria was one of the showpieces of governmental reform: northern Bulgaria was the first province to be reorganized by nineteenth-century Ottoman reformers. State revenues were spent to develop the region. Yet Bulgaria, like other provinces where much investment had been made, was lost and, as far as the Ottomans were concerned, all the investment was wasted. With the loss of territories went businesses, productive farms, and tax revenues, particularly in Ottoman Europe. Irrespective of the justice of the conflict, the Ottomans, as losers, found that they were forced to pay war indemnities. After the 1877–78 war, for instance, the Congress of Berlin ordered them to pay slightly more than 800 million francs to the Russians. It was impossible to pay massive amounts for defence and still contribute enough to needed economic development. The old saying, 'you can't have both guns and butter', was especially true for the Turks, and the Turks could not ignore the need for guns.

Another problem for the Ottomans was the insurmountable barrier that the capitulations put in the way of economic development. The capitulations were arrangements between the Ottoman government and the European powers that had existed since the time of Süleyman the Magnificent. Under their terms, European merchants were given preferential tax and customs treatment in the Ottoman Empire. They paid very low amounts to the Ottoman government (through most of the nineteenth century, a 5 per cent import duty), sometimes less than the taxes and duties that Ottoman manufacturers paid. At first, the Ottomans had granted preferential treatment to reward their allies and to encourage trade. The deal was almost never reciprocal. In the days of their greatest might the Ottomans saw no need to develop Ottoman trade with the Europeans. Later, when they were weak, the Ottomans had no way to enforce customs equality with the Europeans. Worse, they could not abrogate the capitulations, because they were too weak to withstand European military pressure. The Europeans made it plain that they would defend the capitulations with force. Ottoman trade was at a permanent disadvantage.

The capitulations made it impossible for the Ottomans to employ the most basic measures to protect their industries. The protective tariff was an accepted means to protect a developing country's economy. The United States, for example, was able to develop its own industry by forcing British manufacturers and others to pay such high customs duties that local manufactures became cheaper than the imports. When local industries were highly developed, *then* tariffs could be cut. This the Ottomans could not do. Goods from European factories were naturally less expensive than goods from new and relatively inefficient Ottoman factories, but nothing could be done to protect the local products.

Other special arrangements went hand in hand with the economic capitulations. Europeans ran their own post offices in the Ottoman Empire, ensuring better communications for them than were available to Ottoman businesses. Europeans also enjoyed extraterritoriality in the Ottoman Empire – the right to apply their own laws to their nationals, rather than the laws of the Ottoman Empire. They thus had special laws and courts that applied only to them. Ottoman business regulations often did not apply to the foreigners. If foreign citizens committed a crime, civil as well as mercantile, they were tried in special European courts, not Ottoman courts. In addition, many members of Ottoman minority groups were allowed to buy or were granted foreign citizenship and its advantages, even though they never had left the Ottoman Empire. Not only were the Ottomans unable to pass laws favouring their own, they were forced to accept laws that favoured others.

For the Muslims and Jews of the Empire there was another disadvantage. Perhaps naturally, European merchants chose Ottoman Christians to act as their middlemen in the Empire. Some of the preference for Christians was psychological – the nineteenth century was a time of strong religious feeling in Europe and America, and Christians were preferred by other Christians. Part of the reason for the preference was practical. The Christians of the Ottoman Empire had been in contact with Europe for some time. Missionaries and governments had long been in communication with them. Many more of their numbers spoke European languages, often learned in missionary schools, and knew European ways. Few Muslims knew either. Therefore, it was practical for the Europeans to deal with Ottoman Christians. Whatever the reasons, the system made it very difficult for Muslims and Jews to partake of the benefits of increased trade. As will be seen below, this had more than an economic result. It drove an economic wedge between the Ottoman religious communities.

The result of European economic penetration was a decline in domestic manufacturing. With very few exceptions, no Ottoman craftsmen could stand up to the inexpensive alternatives from Europe. The production of cloth was a good example of the degeneration:

> In 1862 the British consul in Aleppo stated that in the proceeding ten years the number of looms in that city had fallen from 10,000 to 2,000 and output from 4 million pieces to 1.5 million. In 1868, a government commission reported that, during the preceding 30–40 years, the number of cloth-making looms in Istanbul had fallen from 2,750 to 25; of brocade looms from 350 to 4; and of upholstery silk looms from 60 to 8. In Bursa, already in 1838 manufactures of cotton and silk were 'on the decline'; in 1843 some 20,000 pieces of cloth were produced, but by 1846 output had fallen to 13,000, and by 1863 to 3,000.[1]

All was not gloom. At the end of the Empire, in the periods of the Abdülhamit II and the Committee of Union and Progress, to be seen in Chapter 9, the Ottoman Middle East was able to make sizeable economic gains. The Empire remained an exporter of raw materials and importer of finished goods, but better communications, transport, and government support at least allowed the export of more raw materials. The government favoured industrial development, cutting import dues on machinery, etc. for domestic manufacturers. They realized that if duties for foreigners could not be cut, reducing duties for domestic manufacturers was the only alternative. By the First World War, 17,000 workers in Istanbul and İzmir were working in mechanized factories – a small figure compared to Europe, but a start. Some industries could succeed because it was far cheaper to produce finished goods, such as olive oil, close to where the raw materials were grown. Some, such as oriental carpets, could not be matched in the West. Nevertheless, Europeans were still dominant in the Ottoman economy. Only after World War I, in the Turkish Republic, when the capitulations had finally been dismantled, could the Turks really begin to control their own economy.

The nationalism of the Ottoman minorities

Exposure to Europe had more than an economic effect. As their economic and cultural connections to Europe grew, the Christian minorities of the Ottoman Empire also imbibed European political philosophy. The nineteenth century was a time of nationalism in Europe and the Americas. Italy

---

[1] Charles Issawi, *An Economic History of the Middle East and North Africa*, New York, 1982, p. 152.

and Germany were each unified under nationalist philosophies. Ethnic groups in large empires began to crave separate states of their own. The nationalist creed called for a people and a state to come together – a separate state for each ethnic group. Like many other philosophies, nationalism came to the Ottoman Empire from Europe.

Nationalism and the idea of the nation are difficult to define, because both are essentially arational. For various reasons, which might have included common language, common life styles, common religion, a respect for a mythologized history, or economic bonds, people believed that they were specially tied to other, similar people in one 'nation'. The nation, then, existed in the minds of those who believed in it. With that belief came a sense of superiority over other humans – 'My nation is best.' Nationalists uniformly believed that their nation deserved a state of its own, and nationalists were often willing to fight for that state. Much political philosophy was written that spoke of 'the soul of the nation' or 'the mind of the nation', as if such unprovable entities really existed. Scholars, newspapermen, and politicians all praised the national will as a justification for war.

The Ottoman Empire had its own traditional type of 'nationalism', the *millet* system. Indeed, the term *millet* is often translated into English as 'nation'. However, the Ottoman nations were religious, not ethnic, groups. Members of *millet*s such as the Greek Orthodox were from diverse ethnic groups. Some who were Greek Orthodox in 'nationality' were Greeks; others were Arabs, Bulgarians, Serbs, etc. Other *millet*s, such as the Armenian *millet*, contained only one ethnic group. All were identified by their religion. The nationalism that was imported from Europe was unlike the old Ottoman system. Whereas the *millet* system had accepted and fostered religious separation, the new nationalism stressed political separation. Because the Ottoman Empire contained so many distinct ethnic groups, successful nationalism could only mean the dissolution of the Empire.

Why nationalism developed in the Ottoman Empire

Although it was very different from European nationalism, the Ottoman *millet* system did contribute to the development of nationalism among the Christian minority groups of the Empire. Ottoman minorities were used to thinking of themselves as separate. They operated their own schools, courts, and welfare systems. They were used to living separately, often in particular quarters of cities or in their own villages. Even more important, they saw that members of their own ethnic group were not the ones that ran the Empire. This was undoubtedy a cause of resentment. There was a natural human desire to run their own affairs. Separation and resentment made the adoption of nationalism easier.

Distinct languages also helped the feeling of separation. In America, the state schools that taught only in English and a resolute decision to accept only English in public life forced different ethnic groups to assimilate. The Ottoman Empire's tolerance of diversity had the opposite effect. No attempt had been made to force Ottoman subjects to speak Turkish – in 1800 a large majority did not speak it as their first language and perhaps most Ottoman subjects did not speak it at all. Serbs spoke Serbian, Greeks spoke Greek, Bulgarians spoke Bulgarian, Arabs spoke Arabic. With a distinct language went a distinct culture. Centuries of living side-by-side had blurred the ethnic divisions, but they still existed.

Contact with Europe and America was the catalyst that turned traditional minority separation into nationalism. At first the contacts were economic. In the Balkans, Orthodox Christian merchants had long controlled commerce. This was partly due to the fact that Turkish Muslims, although they had long been traders in Anatolia, were more concerned with the military, the government, and agriculture than with trade. It was also a matter of continuing tradition. Orthodox merchants, both Greeks and Slavs, in Ottoman Europe had been the traders of the region long before the Turks arrived, and they and their commercial networks survived changes in government. When trade with the rest of Europe increased dramatically it was natural that the Orthodox merchants be involved in it. European goods were cheaper, but Europeans knew little of how to trade in the Ottoman Empire. The Orthodox became the 'middlemen' who sold British or French goods to the Ottoman Empire and sold Ottoman agricultural goods to the Europeans. In theory, Muslims might have performed as middlemen, as they had done in other regions for centuries, but Europeans preferred dealing with fellow Christians, and Christians had more experience and better connections. Greeks and Armenians took the same position in Anatolia that the Orthodox took in Ottoman Europe.

With the European trade came wealth. As the nineteenth century advanced, increased trade meant richer Ottoman minorities. It also meant that the minorities were closer and closer to Europe. Their new wealth supported European-style schools where European languages were taught. The linguistic skills allowed members of the minorities to read of and to assimilate European doctrines such as nationalism. The sense of superiority that was inherent in nationalism was fed by the economic success of the minorities. In the thinking of the nineteenth century and long after, 'richer' was equated with 'better'.

The West fed the fires of nationalism in many ways. Missionary schools, primarily operated by American Protestants, offered a fine education to tens of thousands of Christians, not to Muslims. The schools also became a gathering place of revolutionary nationalists – students who learned nationalist doctrines and a sense of Christian superiority in the schools and translated them into action, first in student groups, then in armed revolt. Bulgarian revolutionaries, for example, openly credited the American college in Istanbul, Robert College, for its place in their successful revolution. The president of the college, Cyrus Hamlin, was given a Bulgarian medal. Traditional Ottoman tolerance of separate Christian religious education, Ottoman desire to learn from the advanced teaching techniques brought by the Americans, and fear of European reprisals if they closed Christian schools forced the Ottomans to accept the situation.

Economic, educational, and religious ties allowed Ottoman minorities to migrate to the West. There they organized nationalist revolutionary groups and campaigned for support for their plans. Support was easily gained, because the populace in the West had held a negative image of the Turks since the Middle Ages, when Turks were considered a threat to the existence of Christianity. It was natural for Western Christians to feel a certain brotherhood with their fellow Christians in the Middle East and the Balkans, especially since they knew very little of the Muslims. Other than an occasional ambassador, there were very few Turks in the West. Therefore, the image of the Ottoman Empire that was seen there came from historical prejudice and the opinions of Ottoman minority groups. Support for minority nationalism in the West became a force behind the dissolution of the Ottoman Empire.

The sense of ethnic identity that sustained nationalism was also fostered in Europe. In the eighteenth century, before minority nationalism had developed, a distinct intellectual life for the minorities developed outside the Ottoman boundaries. Within the Ottoman Empire the Christian minorities had developed little in the way of national literatures or philosophies. Like the Turks, Arabs, and other ethnic groups, they had not begun to write the type of national poems, novels, histories, and dictionaries that were being written in the West. These came to them from the outside. Armenians, for example, first developed modern Armenian books in Venice. Greek books were published especially in Vienna. Armenians, Greeks, Serbs, and other ethnic groups all developed their languages, wrote poems and histories, and compiled dictionaries of their languages in European countries at a time when it seemed most of their people in the Ottoman Empire had little national identity. These first intellectual steps toward nationalism were then imported and propagated.

Political and military support for minority nationalism

The most significant European support for nationalism was military support. Despite the intellectual and economic causes for national separatism, it is doubtful if nationalist revolutionaries would have been successful had they not been backed up by European armies.

The Greek revolution of 1821, perhaps more based on religious than nationalistic distinctions, was by itself a failure. After initial successes against the old Janissary-led Ottoman army, it had foundered when sultan Mahmud II asked Muhammad Ali, the governor of Egypt, for help.

207

Muhammad Ali's troops had almost completed the defeat of the rebels when Europe intervened. In 1827, the French, British, and Russians took the side of the Greek rebels. At Navarino they destroyed the fleet that was necessary to supply the Ottoman soldiers in Greece, despite the fact that all three European countries were at peace with the Ottoman Empire. Englishmen took command of the Greek army and navy. The Ottomans could not fight all Europe. They were forced to withdraw and a new Greek kingdom was proclaimed and a European prince, Otto of Bavaria, took the Greek throne in 1832.

Greece expanded through further European intervention. Thessaly and parts of Epirus, in central Greece, were given to the Greek kingdom by the Congress of Berlin in 1878. In 1897, when the Greeks attacked the Ottomans in an attempt to gain more land, and were defeated, the Europeans kept the Ottomans from gaining anything but a small amount of land and a small indemnity. In 1898, the European powers, acting as 'honest brokers' in deciding a Greek revolt on the island of Crete, named Prince George of Greece as governor of the island, thus effectively ceding it to Greece. Formal union with Greece came in 1908.

In Serbia and Romania, Ottoman authority was first diminished, then ended completely, by Russian intervention. Military threat from Russia forced the Ottomans (the treaty of Bucharest, May 28, 1812, and the Convention of Akkerman, October 7, 1826) to make Serbia and the Romanian principalities, Moldavia and Wallachia, virtually autonomous and to accept that Serbia and Romania were under Russian protection. Under the terms of the treaty of Edirne (September 14, 1829), which followed the Russian defeat of the Ottoman Empire in the 1828–29 war, Serbia and Romania were made autonomous. In 1866, the powers forced the Ottomans to remove their few remaining troops from Serbia. Both Serbia and Romania were made fully independent after Russia defeated the Ottomans in the 1877–78 Russo–Turkish War, as was Montenegro.

The Bulgarian revolution of 1876 was put down by the Ottomans. Despite this, an independent Bulgaria was created when the Russians defeated the Ottomans in 1878. Once again, the new nation was created by Russian order after the Ottomans lost the war.

Other parts of the Ottoman Empire that later became independent countries were also created by the Europeans, although at first the Europeans claimed them for themselves. As seen above, Cyprus was taken by the British as their price for supporting the Ottoman side in the peace conference (the Congress of Berlin) that followed the Ottoman defeat by the Russians in 1877–78. After a conflict broke out between Maronite Christians and Druze in 1860, France invaded Lebanon and did not leave until the Ottomans agreed to make Mount Lebanon (smaller than today's Lebanon) virtually autonomous in 1861. The French seized Tunisia in 1881, the British Egypt in 1882, and the Italians Libya in 1912, creating separate states.

Each of these European incursions into the Ottoman Empire made the Empire weaker, lowered its tax revenues, and made it harder for the Empire to reform and survive.

Turkish nationalism

Turkish nationalism always involved a fundamental conflict in political philosophy. Turkish intellectuals had read European political works. They had lived as revolutionaries in Europe and had been imbued with European ideas, including nationalism. Yet they were also intent on retaining intact a multi-ethnic Empire. Many of them wished to strengthen their 'Turkishness', but were afraid of alienating non-Turks. In the matter of language, for example, the Turkish nationalists, like all other nationalists, felt that their country should have one language, Turkish. But what to do about the fact that the Arabs and others did not wish to adopt Turkish? They also had to face the almost overwhelming problem that most Turks in the villages thought of themselves primarily as Muslims. Any national identification among Turks before the First World War was weak.

The strongest driving force behind Turkish nationalism was opposition to European intervention and to the plans of the minority nationalists. Turks had been declared by others to be 'the enemy' that must be defeated. In response, the Turks began to think of themselves as a group that must stand together. To combat the prejudices of Europeans they began to look into their own history. Pre-eminent among the Turkish nationalists was Ziya Gökalp (1876–1924), a sociologist who was active in the Committee of Union and Progress (see below). Ziya, his companions, and his followers looked to Turkish folk culture and history for inspiration. They found Turkish identity in traditions that came before or stood outside of Islam and Ottomanism – the political traditions of the Central Asian Turks and the first Turks who had come to Anatolia, old Turkish folk tales and music, a 'pure' language uncorrupted by Arabic words, etc. They were generally secularists, intent on diminishing the place of Islam and replacing its predominance with Turkish nationalism.

The government of the Committee of Union and Progress, which took power in 1908–9, was affected by the ideas of Ziya Gökalp. Although very few laws were passed that actually made the Empire more Turkish, government support was given to a number of nationalist initiatives. An unsuccessful attempt was made to develop a new Turkish alphabet and end writing with Arabic characters. The school curriculum began to demand Turkish instruction even in non-Turkish regions of the empire. The state, which could affect commerce through its buying power, expected financial dealings to be made in Turkish. Whenever possible, the Turkish language was expected in government dealings.

During the First World War Turkish nationalism intensified, but it was not until the creation of the Turkish Republic that it can be said to have triumphed. After the war, when the Arab provinces had been detached from the Empire the new Turkish state, much more ethnically homogenous than the Ottoman Empire, became truly nationalist in character.

The nationalism of other ethnic groups

Nationalism developed more slowly among Arab Muslims than among the non-Arab Christian minorities, just as it had among the Turks. The Arabs were part of an Islamic Empire, just as they had been for centuries, and the call to nationalism faced many obstacles. By nature, nationalism was an affront to the cherished idea of unity in Islam. Thus many of the Arab nationalists were in fact Christian Arabs, who by nature did not identify with the Islamic nature of the Ottoman state. Until very late in the Empire's life, Arab nationalism was primarily literary and ethnic, stressing the greatness of Arabic language and culture. Only in organizations in Cairo, under British protection, and in a few isolated cells in Ottoman cities was political independence for the Arabs seriously considered.

Arab apathy to nationalism changed somewhat when the Committee of Union and Progress government began to give evidence of Turkish nationalism. Some Arab intellectuals fled to Paris and breathed new life into Arab newspapers and nationalist organizations that had existed in a small way for a decade. Secret and public groups also sprang up in Syria and Lebanon. They advocated varying positions from reform of the Ottoman system to autonomy. Decentralization of rule was their dominant theme. During World War I more radical sentiments emerged, and a number of Arab revolutionaries were hanged as traitors. Some saw the rebellion of Sharif Husayn in Mecca as a chance for an Arab kingdom. However, these cannot be considered to be popular movements. As an example, when the British took Palestine from the Ottomans during the First World War they called for Arab volunteers to fight against the Ottomans; only approximately one hundred Arabs from all of Palestine volunteered.

Armenian nationalism was unsuccessful, partly for demographic reasons and partly because it could not gain enough European support. The Armenians were spread through Anatolia and the Caucasus, a majority only in small, widely separated regions. Surrounded by Muslim majorities, it was difficult for them to revolt with success. When Armenian revolutionaries did act, beginning in earnest in the 1890s, the effect was bloody. Thousands of Turks were killed in the first phase of revolt, then thousands of Armenians killed when the Ottomans put the revolt down. The hope was that Europeans would intervene on the Armenian side, but they did not. Eastern Anatolia, the site of the revolts, was not particularly valued by the Great Powers. Russia, having taken a large part of the Ottoman East in 1878, which it was still assimilating, was beset by troubles from its own revolutionaries and from European politics. It aided in Armenian organization, weapons, etc., guided by the wish that fighting the Armenians would weaken the Ottomans, but did no more. Not until the First World War were the Russians willing to fight once again in eastern Anatolia, and then it was to take the region for themselves, using Armenian revolutionaries to advance Russian ends.

Other ethnic groups in the Ottoman Empire were largely untouched by European-style nationalism. Many, such as the Kurdish tribes or the Nestorian Christians in eastern Anatolia, were indeed independently minded, but they always had been. They had never looked politically beyond the leadership of their own tribes or religious leaders and were in no way nationalistic in the European sense. The Jews of the Empire supported the Ottoman state throughout its existence, with the exception of the Zionist Jews in Palestine, who had come to the Middle East from Europe with firm nationalist ideals.

The alliance of imperialism and nationalism

Nationalism was a potent force against Ottoman survival, but it was imperialism that devastated the Ottoman Empire. Although nationalist revolutionaries created situations that caused Great Power intervention and ultimately the creation of new national states, in no case was nationalism alone enough for success. Even in bad times, the Ottoman Empire as a whole was stronger than any of its parts that wished to secede. Another factor was that the revolutionaries did not necessarily represent popular feeling, even among their own people. Throughout history, farmers have usually wished simply to be left alone. They make poor revolutionaries. In the revolutions, therefore, the sides were the revolutionary nationalists and their European supporters against the Ottoman state. It is doubtful if the majority of the non-Muslim population took either side.

The losses of the Ottoman Empire were the result of European strength and Ottoman weakness. The Ottomans were buffeted on all sides by Europe. European economic might put the Ottomans at a great commercial disadvantage. The capitulations made it certain that the Ottomans could never catch up. Military attacks from Russia and European support for revolutionaries within the Empire cost the Ottoman Empire lives and treasure just at the time when they most needed both to advance reform.

The cycle was unending. Money was needed for reform, but it was spent on defence and reparations after wars were lost. The forces of imperialism were too strong to resist.

None of this was uniquely Ottoman. As stated at the beginning of this chapter, the Ottoman losses were only a part of a world-wide triumph of European imperialism, and the Ottomans fared better than most. Unlike the peoples of India, Africa, Southeast Asia, or Central Asia, the Ottoman Turks at least ended the nineteenth century with a state. The costs in human life were great, as will be seen below, and in World War I imperialism was to exact an even greater toll.

In 1800, three vast empires controlled Eastern Europe and the Middle East – Russia, Austria-Hungary, and the Ottoman Empire. All three have today disappeared. The Austro-Hungarian, Ottoman, and Russian Empires all died in the First World War, although Russian imperialism continued, in the guise of the Soviet Union, for another seventy years. The questions they left behind are still with us. Imperialism is today justifiably condemned, but is nationalism therefore a better solution to political rule? Should every ethnic group have its own state, or is that a sure path to destructive national competition and war? It is instructive that of the three empires only the successor of the Russian Empire, the USSR, dissolved due to internal pressure, and the result of the dissolution of the Soviet Union will not be known for many years. The dissolution of Austria-Hungary and the Ottoman Empire led to wars in the Middle East and the Balkans that have not yet ended.

Chapter 7

Environment and Life

Tokat: shops and houses built around an easily defended citadel, now in ruins. Such defences were an essential part of Anatolian cities. (Albert Gabriel, *En Turquie*, Paris, Paul Hartmann, 1935.)

Environment and Life

The Turks were not restricted to Turkey. In the Ottoman Empire, Turks lived in significant numbers throughout Anatolia, the Balkans, the Caucasus, and what is today Ukraine and Russia. Despite that, the largest and most dense concentration of Turkish population in the Ottoman Empire was in Anatolia, in the area of today's Turkish Republic. It would not be possible to consider here the environments of all the areas in which Turks lived, much less the varied environments of the far-flung Ottoman Empire, which they ruled. Therefore, the following exposition mainly has been restricted to Ottoman Anatolia.

Most of Anatolia is high land. The median altitude is well over 3,500 feet above sea level. When one goes inland from the Mediterranean or Black Sea one very soon comes to high hills or mountains. The land rises from the shore very precipitously in some places, such as the Black Sea region. In other areas the rise is more gradual, but continuous. While it is not usually described as such by geographers, most of Anatolia resembles much of California. Like California, it has dry hills with few trees. There is, however, considerable geographic variation between regions.

Central Anatolia is a high plateau, flat compared to eastern Anatolia. Nevertheless, there are few places on the plateau that do not seem hilly or even mountainous from the ground. In fact central Anatolia appears to be a series of broad valleys surrounded by high hills. The land can be best described as steppe grassland. By the beginning of the Ottoman Empire, the plateau had already been almost completely deforested.

Northern Anatolia, the Black Sea region, is a narrow strip of land along the coast. With few exceptions, tall hills or mountains rise very close to the shore. They often come right to the sea, making it impossible to construct long distance roads along the coast. Human habitation centres on the shoreline and in the valleys of rivers and streams that flow into the Black Sea. The eastern part of the region is more forested than

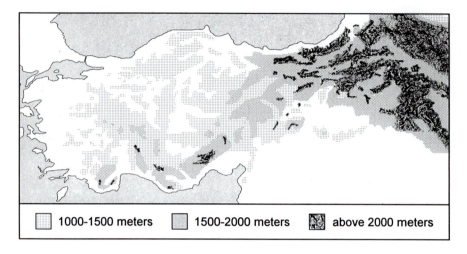

| | 1000-1500 meters | | 1500-2000 meters | | above 2000 meters |

Elevation of land in Anatolia.

any other part of Anatolia, with extensive evergreen and deciduous forests and brushland. That region resembles the Pacific northwest of America or the west of Canada, with hills, rhododendrons, and evergreen trees in abundance.

Southern Anatolia lies on the Mediterranean and stretches inland a short distance from the sea. In some areas, the rise of land from the sea to the higher elevations is similar to that on the Black Sea, although the shoreline is often deeper and the valleys wider. As in the north, most of the coast is cut off from the central plateau. Communication runs through a few river valleys. The plain that runs deepest inland is in the region of Adana, where a large fertile plain is cut off by highland to the north, east, and west. The mountains of the south support forests, although they are far less extensive than in the north.

Eastern Anatolia is very rugged and mountainous terrain, extremely difficult to traverse. Mountain ranges run through it, with some significant peaks (e.g., Mount Ararat, over 16,000 feet high). Valleys are narrow. Rivers have for centuries etched themselves deeply into the high terrain, often leaving steep gorges with no valleys at all. The population traditionally settled mainly in the few broad high plains between mountain ranges.

Western Anatolia is the most hospitable to large human settlements. The Marmara region to the north is part of a relatively low-lying area that extends around the Sea of Marmara from the foothills of the central Anatolian plateau to the foothills of the mountain chains in the Balkans. The Aegean region stretches farther inland from the sea than the coastal plains of either the Black Sea or the Mediterranean. Broad river valleys stretch up to the central plateau. Due to the ease of communication, mild

216

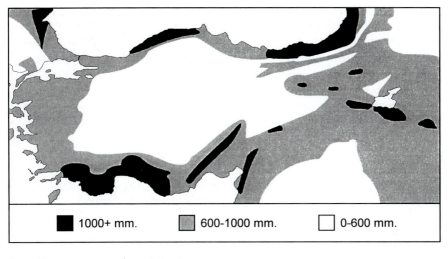

1000+ mm.   600-1000 mm.   0-600 mm.

Anatolia: mean annual precipitation.

weather, and good conditions for agriculture, the Marmara and Aegean regions can be considered to have been the best in Ottoman Anatolia.

Rivers (see map on pp. 14–15) in all but the southeast are minor, useful for irrigation but seldom for large-scale transport. They nevertheless mean life to a region with scant rainfall. Western Anatolian rivers are particularly valuable for irrigation, as they meander across their flood plains, covering much ground and allowing farmers easy access to water. (The word 'meander' comes from the classical name for the River Menderes, whose two branches flow back and forth across the southwest into the Aegean Sea.) Rivers that drain into the Black Sea and the Mediterranean are generally short, cut through the coastal mountains to the sea, with the exception of the region near Adana, where rivers run through a plain with marshes and river deltas, and the long Kızıl Irmak river system in the north. In the east rise both the Tigris and the Euphrates, which flow south through Iraq. In Ottoman times, they had limited use for irrigation, because they and their tributaries flowed through the narrow, deeply etched valleys mentioned above. Some smaller rivers in central and eastern Anatolia drain into lakes, the Tuz Gölü ('Salt Lake') near Konya and Lake Van near the Iranian border, both of which are closed and do not in turn drain into the seas.

Climate

Not all the Middle East is desert. It is not even all hot. The seas that surround Anatolia and the Anatolian terrain combine to make an extremely variable climate. The Mediterranean coast has mild winters and hot summers, with high humidity. The Black Sea coast winters are also mild and its summers fairly hot, but it experiences more rain than elsewhere in Anatolia. Perhaps the best overall weather is in the Aegean and Marmara regions. Winters are mild, summers hot in the day but cool at night. On the vast central plateau, winters are much colder and more snowy than on the coasts, while summer temperatures are little different.

The great extremes in climate come in the east. Winter is extremely cold, with snow that stays on the ground for one-third of the year. (For comparison: the average temperature in Kars in February is −12 °C, in Erzurum −7 °C, in Minneapolis −8 °C, in Moscow −8 °C.) It is an inhospitable climate for humans and domestic animals, one of the worst in all Eurasia. In winter, travel is often impossible due to snow that closes mountain passes and makes even travel between neighbouring villages very difficult. In summer, the weather is hot in the southeast, cooler in the northeast, but dry all over the east. Cities such as Urfa and Diyarbakır have many days of freezing temperatures in winter and blazing heat in the summer. The temperatures in the southeast routinely rise above 38 °C through much of the summer (average temperatures in August: Adana 28 °C, Diyarbakır 30 °C, Urfa 31 °C, Miami 28 °C, Dallas 30 °C, Cairo 28 °C).

Rainfall on the Black Sea and Mediterranean coasts is considerable by the standards of the Middle East. The highlands of the east receive much more rain than the central plateau. As seen on the map, the regions of significant rainfall make a rough rectangle around central Anatolia, areas of which can be called arid. (Annual precipitation in central Anatolia is similar to that in Los Angeles, that is, very dry: Ankara 387 mm, Konya 323 mm, Los Angeles 308 mm.)

Anatolia: Temperatures (in degrees Centrigrade) and days with snow

| City | Temperature in February | | Temperature in August | | Average days with snow |
	Average	Lowest	Average	Highest	
Adana	10.3	−6.6	28.1	45.6	0
Ankara	1.0	−24.2	23.3	40.0	22
Busa	6.0	−25.7	23.9	42.6	10
Diyarbakır	3.6	−19.1	30.5	45.9	13
Edirne	3.8	−18.9	24.1	40.8	17
Erzurum	−7.0	−27.5	19.6	34.0	114
İzmir	8.5	−8.4	27.3	42.7	0.3
Kars	−11.6	−37.0	17.3	34.6	108
Konya	0.1	−26.2	23.0	40.0	21
Sivas	−3.6	−34.4	19.7	37.6	62
Trabzon	7.4	−7.4	23.2	38.2	8
Urfa	5.1	−12.4	21.4	46.2	3
Van	−3.6	−28.2	21.7	36.7	78

−20 °C = −4 °F   0 °C = 32 °F   20 °C = 68 °F   40 °C = 104 °F

Travel by land in Ottoman Asia

Cities en route	Hours
Istanbul to Kastamonu	150
Kastamonu to Sivas	82
Sivas to Diyarbakır	89
Diyarbakır to Mosul	90
Mosul to Baghdad	108
Baghdad to Basra	100
Istanbul to Basra	**619**
Istanbul to Eskişehir	62
Eskişehir to Afyon	32
Afyon to Konya	48
Konya to Adana	70
Adana to Aleppo	70
Aleppo to Damascus	94
Damascus to Beirut	12
Beyrut to Jerusalem	36
Istanbul to Jerusalem	**424**
Istanbul to Afyon	94
Afyon to İzmir	54
Istanbul to İzmir	**148**

The land, transport and communication

Travel in Anatolia, and in much of the rest of the Ottoman Empire, was far from easy. Navigable rivers were few, so people and animals had to walk. Unless one travelled straight west from the Aegean Sea, it was virtually impossible to move inland without climbing over at least one mountain range. Eastern Anatolia was one mountain chain after another. That meant that the relatively rapid travel possible in fairly flat places like most of Europe beyond the Ottoman borders, a few Alps notwithstanding, was impossible in Anatolia. Outside of Anatolia, prospects for travel were only slightly better. While the mountains in the Ottoman Balkans were lower than those in eastern Anatolia or northern Iraq, they were still a significant impediment to travel. In Greater Syria and Arabia, there were mountains, but it was deserts that presented the worst problems.

To gain an idea of the difficulties of communication and travel in a vast empire where roads were less than developed, consider the journeys of Ottoman postal riders in the mid-nineteenth century, as recorded in official documents. Their routes can be considered to be the fastest normal times in which journeys in the Empire could be made, transferring riders and horses and never stopping. In earlier times, the journeys would not have been any faster, although, later in the nineteenth century, steamships and railroads made trips much shorter. (Travel by steamship to Samsun, for example, cut more than 100 hours from the trip to Baghdad.) Routes other than those listed might have saved some time, but the journeys would always have been long. Travelling by land, it theoretically took an official letter 619 hours to go from the capital to the Empire's farthest reaches in Basra. It never was really that fast, because riders did not in fact jump from their horse and hand the message to another rider who was ready to carry on. Some days should be added for waiting for horses, some diversions, and the occasional meal.

No other travellers went as fast as official couriers. Travellers had to sleep, and would not have stayed on horseback all day. Not even the back-sides of provincial officials were strong enough for that. Assuming eight hours of fast travel each day, the trip from Istanbul to Basra would have taken 77 days. Merchant caravans, walking with their animals would take twice as long or more. Even land trips to cities relatively near Istanbul, such as the trading city of İzmir, took weeks. A wise man took the boat. Sailing ships made journeys to coastal cities more quickly and with greater comfort. However, most of the Empire was not on the coast; horse and camel were the best modes of travel, walking the most common one.

The distances in the Ottoman Empire help explain many political aspects of the empire, such as the virtual autonomy of provincial governors in most periods. They also explain some of the economic problems of the Ottomans. Economic integration of such far-flung territory, where travel took so long, was a formidable task. It should be remembered that the factors that made journeys so long – mountains, dry plains, and deserts – also made transport all the more difficult. As evidence, note the diagram drawn by Mark Sykes of part of a trip through Anatolia. Unlike most maps, which

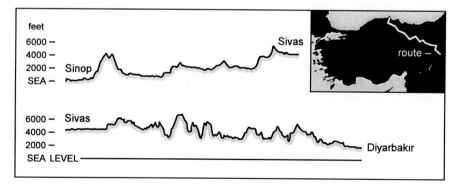

Roads from Diyarbakır to Sinop, elevations.

display a journey *across* a region, Sykes' map displays his journey *up and down*. Although the diagram appears as if he were mountain climbing, Sykes remained on the road – the distinction between climbing mountains and travelling on Anatolian roads was sometimes small.

Ottoman crops and animals

Sometimes the most basic and most important information on the history of a people is hardest to find. It is much easier to find the name of every vezir in the Ottoman court than to find out what Anatolian farmers' children ate for dinner. Yet, for the children at least, what was for dinner, if anything, was much more important than who was Grand Vezir. For most of Ottoman history information on agriculture and animal husbandry is scarce and anecdotal. The first attempts to actually estimate the numbers and variety of Ottoman crops and livestock did not come until near the end of the Empire. However, much of what was recorded then must have been generally true for earlier periods, excepting New World crops such as maize (corn) or tomatoes. Agriculture in traditional societies was by nature conservative. When, in the nineteenth century, the Ottomans attempted to introduce new crops they met with only limited success. Nevertheless, it should be noted that the descriptions given here have been taken from the very end of the Ottoman Empire.

Crops

As was true all over the world, the main crops in the Ottoman Empire were cereal grains, which accounted for approximately 80 per cent of the cultivated land. The main cereal crop, wheat, was grown all over the Empire. The Turks ate quite a lot of bread. In Anatolia, the largest area of wheat cultivation was on the north central plateau. The same region was the largest cultivator of barley, which was the second crop in Anatolia, with other grains (millet, oats, etc.) in much smaller amounts. Potatoes were grown in the northern Aegean and Marmara regions (near Bursa), to a lesser extent on the Black Sea, and barely anywhere else. Thus the Anatolian farmer was primarily a wheat farmer, producing the daily bread in much the same way and on the same land as millennia before. At the end of the Empire, the Ottoman government tried to vary and extend agriculture, especially introducing corn and rice, with some success, but Anatolia remained primarily wheat land. Like the Ukrainian, Canadian, or American (e.g., Kansas) steppes, Anatolia was a natural place to grow grasses such as wheat. While rice was prized as food throughout the Ottoman period, appearing in soups, meat dishes, and many other applications, it

221

Population and agricultural production, percentages of totals in Anatolia, by region, 1910

	Humans	Wheat	Rice	Grapes	Olives	Cotton	Tobacco
West	26.7	20	1	55	64	37	34
Centre	35.7	45	19	25	*	4	22
East	10.7	15	50	3	*	3	6
South	10.6	13	7	13	36	56	2
North	16.3	7	22	4	*	*	36

* less than 1 per cent
  some rounding error

was never grown in Anatolia in sufficient quantities and much was imported.

Among non-cereal crops, olives were prominent. They were grown especially in the Aegean region. Beans were grown all over, but especially near the Black Sea. Fruits, usually of very high quality, were grown in the Aegean and Mediterranean regions and not much elsewhere. The only sizeable exceptions were grapes, which were cultivated all over Anatolia, and melons, which grew along watercourses even in otherwise rather barren districts. Green vegetables were not as common as in modern times.

Through most of Ottoman history, the regions that produced the crops that might have varied the Anatolian diet were effectively cut off from the centre and east of Anatolia. Farms on the Mediterranean coast might have grown bumper crops of peaches while farmers 100 miles inland had never seen a fresh peach. The culprit was the terrain. Until the coming of the bulldozer and dynamiting passes through mountains for roads, it was often impossible for crops to travel inland over the mountains. Moreover, because land transport was much more expensive than sea, it was far cheaper to ship fruits or vegetables hundreds of miles to Istanbul by boat than fifty miles inland by cart or camel. Because of that, only western and coastal Anatolia had ready access to a varied diet. The climate and rainfall there made it possible to grow more kinds of foodstuffs and the terrain allowed the foods to be transported. In much of the rest of Anatolia, variety in eating was virtually unknown.

Geography also shaped the amount of production of various crops. Wheat was naturally produced more in the great plateau of central Anatolia, which was naturally grassland. Rice, on the other hand, demanded more water, and so was found in regions with more water than the dry centre of Anatolia. Fruits were produced in regions that had the proper climate and land, but, equally important, in those where transport was available to get the crop to market fairly quickly. Wheat might store easily and last well on long trips from central Anatolia, but peaches would not. The table identifies the percentage of population in five growing regions of Anatolia and the percentage of key crops in those regions. It must be noted that these are statistics from a time when transport was better than ever before in Anatolia. That meant that many regions of western Anatolia that were near railways, for example, could produce crops that they had not been able to produce before.

Anatolia produced non-food crops from the earliest times. In Ottoman times, silk was imported from Iran, later produced in Anatolia, woven (especially in Bursa), and exported all over the world. Nineteenth-century European merchants encouraged the production of agricultural 'raw materials' for European factories and stores. Opium was grown in the Aegean and central provinces (Konya, Ankara, etc.) and sold to the British, who shipped it to China until c. 1850, then to Europe and America. Nineteenth-century farmers grew tobacco, the most important export crop, in the Aegean and Black Sea regions and to some extent in the east (Diyarbakır). Cotton was grown in considerable quantities on the plains near the city of Adana. Another major export 'crop' was silk cocoons and raw silk, a very important cash crop until the nineteenth century, but still a significant source of income until the twentieth century. Grapes and raisins should also be considered a cash crop, because they were a main export to Europe.

Animals

Like their Central Asian ancestors, the Ottoman Turks kept sheep as their primary meat animals. Goats were also kept in large numbers. At the end of the Empire, the Ottomans recorded ten times as many sheep and goats as cows in Anatolia, and there is no reason to believe the situation was much different earlier. The raising of sheep and goats was spread all over Anatolia. As might be expected, goats were a more prominent part of the livestock in regions where their natural capabilities were suited to

Population and farm animals, percentages of totals in Anatolia, by region, 1910

	Humans	*Cows*	*Goats**	*Sheep*	*Fowl*
West	26.7	25	24	19	31
Centre	35.7	37	37	43	23
East	10.7	22	11	19	5
South	10.6	3	23	12	14
North	16.3	14	5	7	27

* not including Angora goats
  some rounding error

broken terrain and scrub bushes. Sheep and goats were the most useful of domestic animals. They produced milk and meat and their wool clothed the Turks and was woven into carpets. In addition, wool and mohair were substantial exports.

After sheep and goats, all other animals were far less important. Anatolians raised many chickens, primarily for eggs. They were put in stew when they were too old to produce. Turkeys, despite their Western name, were virtually unknown. While cows were not as common as in the west, in some areas such as the northeast cows were raised for beef. Water buffaloes also provided meat similar to beef. Milk cows could be found in all regions. Pigs were forbidden by religious law to all Muslims and so were not raised except in some Christian communities.

Animals naturally provided much of the protein consumed by the Turks. This usually came in the form of milk products – milk, butter, cheese, and yogurt. Yogurt and goat cheese were important sources of protein, because they would not easily spoil in the absence of refrigeration. Meat was a lesser source of protein. Most peasants consumed it only on special occasions or when an animal had outlasted its useful life as a provider of milk or wool.

By region, the production of animals for food was spread fairly evenly over Anatolia. Exceptions were easterners, who seem to have had few eggs, and southerners, who did not often see a good steak.

The use of animals for transport was second only to their use for food and clothing. Camels were the mainstay of the caravans which carried most Ottoman goods in the early and middle periods of the Empire. Not until the later nineteenth century did the coming of railways begin to lessen the use of camels and donkeys as transport animals. In the nineteenth century, although not as common as in the Arab world, camels were still used to transport goods in Anatolia, particularly in southwestern and south central Anatolia. There were very few camels in northern and eastern Anatolia. In general, the further south one went in Anatolia, the more one found camels. However, donkeys and horses were much more numerous than camels everywhere in Anatolia. On farms, the most common work animals were donkeys, oxen, and, to a lesser extent, mules, water buffaloes, and camels.

Nomads

As the Ottoman Empire passed from a nomad principality to a settled state, the importance and number of nomadic tribes greatly diminished. The settlement of nomads was partly a function of the sort of economic factors that caused the decline or disappearance of nomadism all over the world.

Expansion of agriculture naturally claimed lands once used by nomads. It may be also that nomads simply began to prefer a more settled and certain life. Government opposition helped to force nomads to make the transition to farmers. Centralized governments by nature preferred agriculturalists to nomads, because farmers were more promising sources of tax revenue. The Ottoman government shared this view. Taxation of herds was one weapon that reduced nomad tribes. Another was bureaucratic preferment of agriculturalists over nomads in matters of land-holding and rights-of-way for nomadic wanderings. In the late nineteenth century, the Ottoman government took their opposition one step further, forcibly settling many nomads against the tribes' wishes. Nomads in southern Anatolia in particular were settled in this way, placed on farms in newly-drained lands that had been swamps, now grew cash crops, and had a high incidence of malaria.

Whatever the reasons for the change, it is indisputable that the Turks of Anatolia began as nomads and became farmers. Even those who remained in their nomad tribes no longer shared the lifestyles of their Central Asian ancestors. The Anatolian nomads who are called *yörüks* (or *yürüks*), were 'two-pasture nomads.' They moved twice a year, from their summer to their winter pastures. In summer, they lived in tents, in winter in either houses or fairly rude shelters made of reeds or other materials. Until railways and steamships took over much long-distance transport, *yörüks* were at the centre of the long-distance hauling of goods in the Empire.

Unless government power in an area was particularly weak, Ottoman forces did not allow the nomads to engage in their traditional occupation of raiding settled agriculturalists. However, they did share another part of the basic nomadic economy with their ancestors – they lived off their animals. Turkish nomads kept vast flocks of sheep and sometimes goats from which they took wool, milk, and meat. In their summer pastures they might grow some crops, but were more likely to trade animals or animal products for other foods. The nomads were skilled in textile making and carpet weaving, and much of the tradition of Turkish carpet-making arose from nomads' textiles. They also occasionally took government jobs, such as fighting, hauling goods for the army, serving as guards of strategic regions, and cutting wood on state lands.

The relationships between nomads and settled peoples and nomads and the state were always strained. Nomads had to be kept under surveillance by government officials and soldiers, particularly when they moved to new pastures, or they were likely to revert to old habits of raiding. It was difficult to collect taxes (which they paid in sheep, hides, and fleece) from them. They were often not the most orthodox of Muslims, retaining many religious habits considered heterodox by the Sunni majority. Nomads were always 'the other,' those who rejected the lifestyles of their fellow subjects.

Villages

Villages in different regions were formed on different patterns. In the eastern Black Sea region, for example, houses were sometimes spread relatively far apart, but the usual village configuration was of houses built close together. Farmers did not live among their fields, as has been common in North America. More like the Europeans, they lived in the village and went out to their fields. The reasons behind this were political, social, and environmental. Living close together provided protection. It allowed the village to put up a common front against dangers. Cooperation in matters such as house building and harvesting was facilitated by nearness to neighbours. The neighbours upon whom one could rely were often family members – cousins, nephews and nieces, uncles and aunts, and parents and children. And the social aspects of closeness were prized. Men gathered together in tea houses or homes. Women visited each other's homes, and family members watched each other's children. Religion also demanded closeness. Islam is a congregational religion whose members are enjoined to pray together. For all these reasons, Turks preferred a compact village life.

Villages were usually built along a road ('animal track' might be a better term) or path that bisected the village. Commonly, this path ran out of the village to other villages or to a larger road. Largely out of fear of bandits, Celalis, and travelling soldiers, the villages were seldom sited on the main roads themselves. That was the extent of planning. Houses were built wherever the builder found a suitable site. As many of the house yards were walled, paths between the houses meandered along the sides of the walls and houses. Travel along the paths was thus seldom in a straight line.

The village centre was not markedly different from other neighbourhoods. It might feature a small store, a tea house, and a mosque, but these were constructed out of the same materials as the other buildings and were practically indistinguishable from them. There were no government buildings *per se*. Village leaders, those who settled disputes and represented the village to the government, fulfilled their positions from their homes. The elders met in the home of the *muhtar* (mayor), whose job it was to represent the village to the government, but who was himself only the most respected of the farmers. No one was a full-time worker at anything but farming, herding, or housekeeping, although there were some who also took on specialized jobs. Thus the barber cut hair in the tea house, then went off to his fields.

Around the village, an area of open land would be owned communally and used for grazing. There would be a small cemetery. Well-to-do villages might have possessed a small building used as a Koran school for children and a one-room guest house for visitors. On the whole, though, a village was a collection of houses or housing compounds. For any needs other than the most basic, villagers travelled to the local market town.

Land holding

Until the nineteenth century, very few peasants actually owned their land. Through custom and the 'right of conquest', much land was the property of the sultan. It was administrated either by *timar* holders, who enjoyed the proceeds of the land in exchange for military service, or by tax farmers, who paid a fee to the government in exchange for the right to collect from the peasants (see Chapter 4). Although there was land that had, legally or illegally, been turned into private property, this was seldom held by peasants, but rather by landlords. Much land was held by Islamic pious foundations (*vakıf*s), who were in theory to use the proceeds to support charitable causes. The central government recognized the differing rights of *timar* holders, tax farmers, and pious foundation administrators. Peasants were legally only using the land. Under an 1858 Land Law, many peasants were able to register lands in their own names, paying taxes to the state rather than a tax farmer.

In practice, theoretical ownership probably made very little difference to the farmers. They paid most of their surplus to someone. Whether they paid taxes on land they owned or paid to a pious foundation administrator, a tax farmer, a *timar* holder, or an owner cannot have meant much to them. What counted was how much they were forced to pay. Many have theorized that peasants who had long-term landlords, especially landlord families who lived in the region for centuries, were better off than those whose tax farmers changed often, because short-term holders wanted to collect as much as they could as quickly as possible, before they were replaced by another. This makes sense, but is unproven.

Housing

Climate was the factor that most determined the types of Anatolian houses. Turkish houses were adapted to the rainfall patterns and extremes in temperature found in Anatolia. The houses also reflected the relative poverty of many in Anatolia and the lack of the building material most used in the world, wood. Finally, Turkish houses reflected the social and religious systems of the people. They were, in other words, designed to fit into their complex environment, and did so very well.

In Anatolia, as elsewhere, the form of housing depended on the environment. Because the climate was on average dry and wood was scarce, the most common building material was mud brick. (It is no accident that mud brick, *adobe*, was also the building material in the dry southwestern region of America.) Mud brick was made by pouring a solution of wet mud and straw into wooden forms. The forms were left in place while the mud partially dried, usually for one day, then taken away. The bricks dried on the ground for a further week or more. In building interior and exterior

The need of a new coat of whitewash allows the form of construction of this mud brick mosque to be seen.

walls, the same mixture used for the bricks served, when mixed with straw, as mortar. Courses of mud brick were laid on a foundation of stone, if possible. Because of the relative weakness of the bricks, the walls were thicker than fired brick walls would be, and only were built up to a height of one or two stories.

A house's roof was laid on poplar poles which were held firmly by mud brick mortar. These were covered with woven reed matting, then straw or other material that could be arranged to make a flat surface. The builders poured great quantities of the mud mortar on the roof, then topped this with a layer of clay soil to repel water. The roof was stamped by foot or rolled with a cylindrical stone into a hard, flat surface that would shed water and protect the house from heat. Only the richer houses had tiled roofs.

The window and door openings of the house were framed in rough wood. Then the entire surface of the new house was covered with layers of the mortar. Inside, more mortar was stamped into the floors of each room and rolled smooth, the floors made hard by the addition of alum. At the end of their job, the builders sometimes added a 'whitewash' of special earth and water to the house, leaving a distinctive colour and a surface somewhat more resistant to the elements than the normal mortared mud brick. This whitewash layer was renewed periodically.

The main advantage of mud brick construction was its cost. Nothing is cheaper than earth. In a region that had been deforested a millennium ago, there was little wood for building, and building stone was neither readily available nor easy to use. Thick mud brick walls also made rooms cool in summer. Therefore, mud brick construction was ideal for Anatolia and much of the rest of the Middle East. The disadvantage of mud brick was its impermanence. Floors, ceilings, and walls demanded careful attention. Whitewash had to be renewed many times each year. If layers of the 'mortar' that covered the wall were not scrupulously replaced, the brick would quickly wash away in rainy seasons. Moreover, the brick walls broke easily when subjected to lateral, shaking forces like those in earthquakes, allowing the heavy earthen roofs to collapse. Much of Anatolia is in earthquake zones: an earthquake that heavily damaged Ankara and other cities in 1668 was felt all over north and north-central Anatolia. İzmir was destroyed by an earthquake in 1688, Istanbul badly damaged by one in 1756.

In areas such as the Black Sea region, where wood was more plentiful and rainfall greater, more wood could be used in houses. Mud brick would wash away more quickly in rainy climates, and flat roofs would not shed rain quickly enough. Therefore, in the Black Sea and other regions with high rainfall, sloped roofs were covered with wood shingles or ceramic tiles. Sometimes builders made solid houses out of stone, but the amount of labour needed for such a dwelling made stone houses relatively uncommon. Where stone was used, houses would commonly be two storied, with a stone bottom floor and a wooden top floor, with a sloped roof. Kiln-fired brick was uncommon anywhere in Anatolia.

The forms of houses

To a Turk, family privacy was essential. Except in the very poorest areas, it was rare to find a Turkish house that did not have at least two rooms –

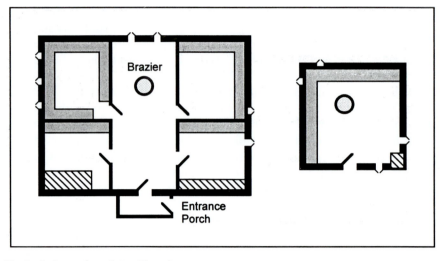

Typical plans of modest village houses.

one that could serve as a 'public' room where guests could be received and at least one other that was reserved for the family. The latter room is usually called the *harem*, a word that translates best as 'sacred' and 'protected'. (The Western fantasy of dancing girls lounging around a pool in the harem, peeling grapes for the master, is, like most Western fantasies, far from the mundane reality.) Houses from the peasant's mud brick dwelling to the palace of the sultan were divided along this public-private axis.

The form of the Ottoman Turkish house was very different from that of the houses found in Western Europe or North America. As can be seen in the figures, the hall was a very prominent part of most Turkish houses. In the West, halls were narrow corridors used to connect rooms, but the Turks used large halls as living space. The central hall in a house was usually larger than any other room. It connected to the outside, and thus could be used as a public space, reserving the rooms that opened off the hall for the family. When the family was alone, the hall was a large space in which they could gather together. Some families, though, used the hall as a large storage room, doing all their living in the smaller rooms.

The hall in many homes was in fact a large porch that ran across the front of the building. Other homes had halls as centres of the building, with rooms opening on two or three sides. In some homes, the hall was actually outside (see plans of a larger village house), not cut off by doors, but connecting the rooms. The halls of such homes functioned as an outdoor living space, protected from the elements by the same roof that covered the rooms.

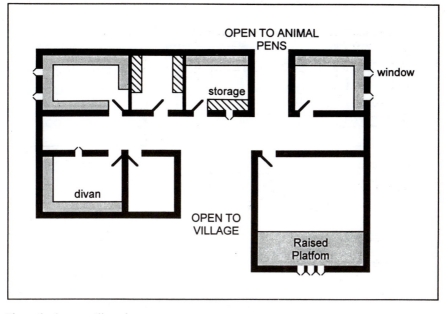

Plan of a larger village house.

The poorest villagers, including those who had no family to help in the construction of larger houses, might live in single-roomed houses (see plans of modest village houses). These served all the functions of home life – sleeping, relaxing, meeting with friends, etc. One-room houses were particularly well suited to areas of Anatolia with very cold weather. They were naturally easy to heat; a quilt stretched over a brazier of hot coals, then over the lower bodies of the family members seated on low *divan*s would often be used. One-room homes were sometimes dug into hillsides, in order to take advantage of the heating and cooling effects of natural insulation. Such houses were dug out, then the house front formed from mud brick or mortared stone. The inside walls and floors were plastered with mud mortar. While single-room houses cut into hillsides had definite disadvantages, not the least of which was lack of light, they were strong and snug in snow country. This was particularly valuable in eastern Anatolia, where snowfall often covered normal houses for much of the winter. The hill houses had no fear that walls or roofs would collapse from the weight of the snow.

A common form of house in high and wet country was two-storied (see plan of a two-storey house). The second floor of those houses followed the normal pattern of Turkish houses, but the bottom floor was unique. The ground floor was used throughout the year for storage. In winter, animals were kept there. The arrangement was necessary for their survival, because they would have frozen in the open or in unheated barns, and

231

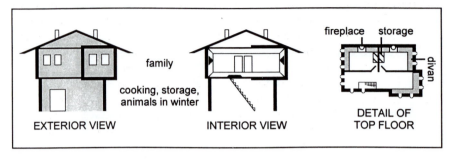

Plan of a two-storey village house.

would have been difficult to milk. When inside they not only were protected from the weather, but provided heat from their bodies for the household.

The humans in a two-storied house lived on the top floor, under a peaked roof that shed snow better than the flat roof of other houses. The floor was reached by stairs or a ladder from the ground floor. Because the second floor was protected from the view of strangers, two-floor houses could have more and larger windows. Their interiors were brighter, more filled with light.

The difficulty of a two-storied house was its inflexibility. A one-storied mud brick house could be easily extended. New rooms could be added to old to accommodate new family members. Whole houses could be constructed next to one another and joined by high walls into a family compound. Two-storied houses were not so easily extended. Moreover they were naturally more expensive and difficult to build. They demanded more wood, and so were mainly seen in forested regions.

Furniture and furnishings

Today we have difficulty imagining houses without chairs and beds. Floors are for walking on; furniture is for sitting or sleeping on. Clothes are kept in cupboards (with wooden doors), wardrobes, and chests of drawers. None of these were seen in Ottoman Anatolia, except in the houses of the rich. The problem was wood. It was so precious that the household use of wood was almost always structural. What little wood a villager could afford held up the roof or went into the doors of the house and its rooms. In most villages, tables were rare, chairs almost nonexistent.

The function of today's wooden furniture was taken up by the building itself. Seats, beds, and storage were built into the walls of the house, made of the same brick that formed the walls, or the floor was employed. If the inhabitants could afford them or they wove them themselves, rugs were placed on the floors. The most ubiquitous element was the *divan*, a low outcropping from the wall, approximately 2 feet (60 cm) or more wide by 2½ feet (75 cm) high that was covered by cushions or rugs. It served for sitting and, if wide enough, for sleeping. More often, household members slept on the floor or on raised mud brick platforms. Bedding was kept rolled up during the day, then brought out at night. Quilts and thin mattresses provided warmth above and below the sleeper. Both were typically stuffed with wool or, for the very poor, straw.

Living was thus closer to the ground than in the modern West. In addition to the lack of wood, and its expense, cultural factors must have been at work to cause this. Until late in the Empire, when European ways were copied and French-style furniture appeared in profusion, sultans and vezirs also lounged on divans and even slept on platforms or floors. The cause might lie in the Central Asian background of the Turks, who did not carry French Provincial furniture for use in their tents, or it may be that Westerners are the strange ones, inventing the need for chairs where no real need exists.

Storage in village houses was literally built into the walls. Small niches or large spaces were allowed for in the house construction or later dug into the mud bricks. If wood was used, it was as doors for the storage areas. Of course, in regions such as the Black Sea where wood was more available, cabinets were seen more often. However, most of Anatolia had little wood for such purposes. Clothes were hung on pegs or folded in storage places.

Villagers warmed themselves with fireplaces built into the walls or with *mangals*, braziers which held hot coals from fires (see plans). Villagers covered their earthen floors with flat weave rugs (*kilims*) or sometimes woven carpets. In general, clothes provided much of the warmth of the villagers, indoors and out. Shutters and textiles or skins hung over windows and doors kept out chill drafts. Glass was virtually unknown. Given the lack of wood and glass, it is hard to see how any other system was possible.

The animals

Housing for animals was as important as for people, for humans depended on their animals for survival. Cold weather in much of Anatolia necessitated protection for animals, and this was often provided by turning the ground floor of a two-storied house into a winter stable. It was more common for separate mud-brick buildings to be built for animals. Rooms/stables/barns for animals might be added to houses, sharing a wall with the house, with separate entrances at the back of the human habitation. Stables were often placed in the yard of a house, forming parts of a wall that defined the yard. In very cold, mountainous areas such as the Anatolian east, small stables or barns were sometimes dug into hillsides, as were human houses. It was by no means unknown for animals to winter in the same small homes as their masters, if the family were especially poor. The warmth provided by the beasts and the knowledge that animals and men were ensuring each other's survival compensated for the smells.

In milder weather, animals were kept in pens or yards made of mud brick, wood, or stone. However, sheep were often in the pasture with family members or hired shepherds to guard them, aided by fierce Turkish sheep dogs which, unlike British sheep dogs, guarded rather than drove the sheep. Goats were frequently seen roaming free near the house, eating what they could find (as goats will). Pens were most in use for donkeys and other beasts of burden.

Peasants stored crops on the bottom floors of houses or in buildings that were part of the housing complex. The storage was often rudimentary, because much of the year's harvest was sold or paid in taxes before the onset of bad weather. In general, storage buildings appeared more ramshackle than houses. Some types of storage would have appeared strange to foreign visitors. Hay, for example, was often simply stored on the roof of houses or stables during the central Anatolian summer. There was little rain to damage it and storing it high kept it from the animals.

The family compound

While many or most of the houses in villages might be single houses, open to the village road, some were part of more complex compounds. This was particularly true of the houses of richer farmers and those with many children. The compounds might contain one human dwelling or a number, because a farmer's sons might live with their family under the same roof as the father and mother or under separate roofs. Even if the latter were true, it would not be proper to think of the dwellings as truly separate, because family members would actually live and sleep in all the buildings and eat communally.

The figure is representative of the type of family compound found in Ottoman Central Anatolia. It would have been the house of a relatively well-to-do peasant family or even a minor landlord. As was common, but by no means universal, cooking was done away from the house, for fear of fire. Stable areas were constructed along different plans depending on usage, with wide openings into covered sheep enclosures and closed barns for horses or donkeys. Chicken coops would often be found in the compound, as would fruit trees. Toilets and storage for dried manure chips, to be burned in fires, were as far from the house as possible, for obvious reasons. Compound walls were mainly constructed of mud brick or stone.

Compounds were not usually separated from other types of housing in a village. Two neighbours' compounds might share a wall. The houses to the sides of a compound might also be houses with open yards, not compounds. In a typical central Anatolian village, family compounds were mixed in with single buildings, large compounds and small houses, side by side.

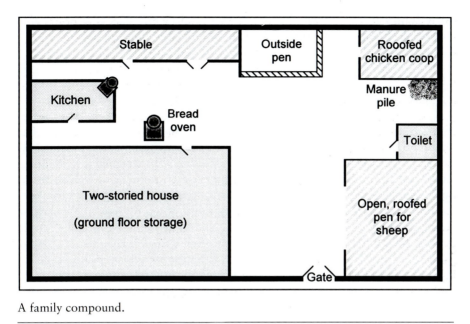

A family compound.

The building system in context

The wonder of the Ottoman Turkish houses was their conformity to the strictures of their environment. Most of Anatolia lacked what most cultures would have considered to be the essential basic building material, wood. Lack of wood or coal for the very hot fires needed to make fired brick also made such brick scarce. Yet sound houses that provided adequate shelter were constructed. The lowliest and cheapest materials were adapted to fit the need of villagers who had intelligence and tradition and little else with which to work.

The materials of home building were not peculiar to the Turks. All the cultures of the region had used similar methods from prehistoric times. As they did in many things, the Turks developed the common architectural heritage to match their particular needs. These included the desire to ensure the privacy of the family and the need to conform to the physical environment. While the methods were inexpensive, they were not easy to realize. The traditions of home building that had been worked out for centuries demanded cooperation and forethought. Family members and friends had to gather together to make a new house. Certain villagers were experts on building different parts of the house. The roof of a mud brick home, in particular, demanded an expert's touch. Planning well ahead was essential. Knowing they would need roofs for future houses, families began generations before the wood was needed to grow, tend, and water the poplar trees that were essential for roof poles. Women began to weave the textiles for their future houses when they were young girls. All was done as it had always been done, generation after generation.

Towns and cities

Villages were connected to the outer world through market towns. The market town was a centre of both commerce and government. It was usually the seat of the district government, a judge to enforce Islamic law, political and financial officials of the Ottoman state, and a number of Janissaries or other soldiers in the earlier period and rural police (gendarmes) in the later period. A villager could take his surplus to the town for sale and purchase agricultural implements, farm animals, and other necessities. If he could afford them, bolts of cloth, jewellery, and such luxuries were also available. The town was also the site of travelling markets, which brought goods from the wider world. Villages were normally situated within a day's walk of the town. Many villagers, in fact, could walk to the town, transact their business, and return home by nightfall.

Certain features were common to all district centres – a congregational mosque, a public bath, a government building or buildings, a market square – others depended on the region. Olive oil presses were obviously not a feature in the northeast highlands, where no olive trees grew, and Christian churches were only found in areas where the population was religiously mixed. As an example of a market town, the following are the buildings found in the market town of Beyşehir, near Konya in central Anatolia, in 1892, as recorded in the Ottoman yearbook (*salname*) of the Konya province:

> 595 houses, 149 small shops, 27 large shops, 5 warehouses, 9 coffee houses, 8 bakeries, 2 mills, 1 slaughterhouse, 1 public bath.

> 5 mosques, 12 small mosques, 4 religious elementary schools, 1 dervish (mystic) lodge, 5 tombs of holy men.

> 1 government building, 1 courthouse, 1 barracks, 2 military storehouses, 4 public water fountains (providing the town's water supply).

Beyşehir was typical of a fairly large market town. It would be a mistake to think of any of the above as being grand. Even the larger mosques were fairly small by city standards. The government building held few bureaucrats,

---

Opposite: A street scene in İzmir. (Thomas Allom, *Constantinople and the Scenery of the Seven Churches of Asia Minor*, London, 1838.)

and the barracks few soldiers. In poorer areas to the east the number of shops would have been less, but government buildings, courts, mosques, slaughterhouses, warehouses, baths, bakeries, coffee houses, and schools would have been present.

The physical structure of the market towns also varied by region. In the richer west and north, stone was used for some government buildings and wood was more commonly seen in many houses and stores. Mud brick was used in all regions, however. Town houses were little different in form from village houses, although on the whole they were larger and grander. Two-storey buildings were more common.

Streets in most market towns were normally unpaved, winding and, to Western eyes, narrow. Without lorries or cars, there was no necessity for wide roads. Camels and donkeys did not need them. Paths in residential sections of the town had been formed by chance settlement, based on where the citizens had built the first houses, not on any plan. However, one or two main streets were typically wider and rather straight. Winding residential streets came off the main roads.

The market towns were part of a chain of political authority that went from the village to the town to the city and finally to the capital in Istanbul. In practice, the power that generated from the sultan ended at the market town. The government's power was represented in the town by soldiers, administrators, and judges, but the villagers had to come to the town to avail themselves of the benefits of government.

Provincial cities

The cities of the Ottoman Empire included most of the great Eastern cities of antiquity – Damascus, Aleppo, Cairo, Jerusalem, Baghdad, Athens, Salonica, Smyrna (Ottoman İzmir), and of course Constantinople (Istanbul). Like the Middle Eastern and Balkan empires that had come before it, the Ottoman Empire was intensely urban. Until the commercial and, later, industrial changes that shaped modern Europe, Ottoman cities were larger and grander than any in Western Europe.

The cities of Anatolia often had long and illustrious histories. Konya had been the capital of the Rum Seljuk Empire, Bursa the first real capital of the Ottomans. Cities such as Trabzon (Trapezus, Trebizond), Kayseri (Caesarea), İznik (Nicaea) and İzmir (Smyrna) had been Ancient Greek or Roman cities. One city, Antakya (Antioch) was still laid out in a grid pattern of streets inherited from the orderly streets of the Roman military camp it had once been. The heritage of the cities was evident in many of them. Konya, for example, was filled with Seljuk mosques and holy tombs, including the tomb of the most famous of Turkish mystics, Jelal al-Din Rumi,

Ottoman provinces and provincial capitals, 1899

Anatolia and E. Thrace	Other
Erzurum	Kosova (Uskub)
İzmit	Selanik (Salonica)
Adana	Yanya
Ankara	İşkodra
Aydın (İzmir)	Manastır
Bitlis	Çatalca
Haleb (Aleppo)	Cezair-i Bahr-i Sefid
Hüdavendigâr (Bursa)	Bağdat (Baghdad)
Diyarbakır	Basra
Sivas	Hijaz (Mecca)
Şehir Emaneti (Istanbul)	Suriye (Damascus)
Trabzon	Beyrut
Kastamonu	Mosul
Kale-i Sultaniye (Biga)	Yemen
Konya	Bengazi
Mamuretülaziz (Harput)	Trablusgarb (Tripoli)
Van	Kuds-i Şerif (Jerusalem)
Edirne	Cebel-i Lubnan
	Zor

founder of the Mevlevi mystical sect, the so-called whirling dervishes. The presence of such sites meant a constant influx of travellers and pilgrims.

Most of the Ottoman Turks were farmers, but Ottoman cities definitely held higher social status than did rural areas. Middle East tradition had based government, religion, the making of art, and the writing of literature in cities long before the advent of Islam. Islam itself was formulated in cities. The great theologians who set the course of Islam lived and worked there, and cities were the sites of the *medrese* schools that educated members of the Islamic religious class, the *ulema*. There was no tradition of religious centres 'in the wilderness', such as the important Greek or Coptic monasteries from which bishops were drawn. As in other regions, economic life in the Middle East and Balkans naturally was directed from cities.

In Anatolia, the largest cities were Bursa and İzmir in the west, Trabzon in the north, Erzurum, Van, and Diyarbakır in the east, Adana in the south, and Ankara, Sivas, and Konya in the centre. They and other, somewhat less important, cities were the centres of Ottoman provinces. Officials in the towns reported to governors in the cities. The governors themselves reported directly to Istanbul.

The first Ottoman provinces would be properly called military governorships. The sultan ordered officers (*beys*) to govern regions of the new empire. The *beys* were identified by the standards (*sancaks*) that

239

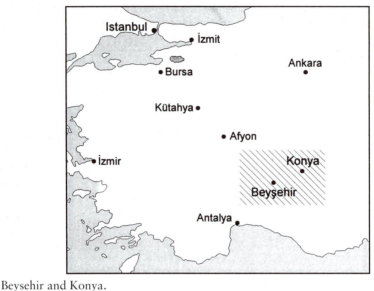

Beysehir and Konya.

represented their authority. Thus they were styled *sancakbeyi*s and their provinces called *sancak*s. *Beylerbeyi*s (governors-general) were appointed over the *sancakbeyi*s in Anatolia and the Balkans. The Ottoman provinces with large Turkish populations in the Ottoman Classical Age had capitals in cities such as Edirne, Kütahya, Ankara, Amasya, Konya, Sivas, Trabzon, Erzurum, and Kars. With some additions, these remained the most important cities in Anatolia and eastern Thrace throughout Ottoman history. Nineteenth-century provinces (*vilâyet*s) were governed from the same cities. Provincial organization changed over the centuries, as did provincial borders, but provincial capitals were still the large cities (see the table of the Ottoman provinces, in 1899).

The political life of cities reflected political life in Istanbul. Each Ottoman governor was a small sultan in his province. In times of peace, he was the ultimate civil authority, overseeing the bureaucracy and taxation. Distance and difficulties of communication with Istanbul meant that relatively few decisions were ever referred to the central government. Regulations did come from the centre, but their implementation was often up to the governor's discretion. If he did poorly, he was replaced, but while in office he held real authority. In times of war, the governor was the chief general. He organized the province's military and often led them into battle himself.

While the authority of governors was diminished by nineteenth-century centralizing reforms, the provincial cities still remained regional centres of power. Capitals contained visible signs of the power and authority of the government. These included the governor's palace and buildings for the provincial bureaucrats. In addition to headquarters for the provincial police force, the gendarmerie, there was a garrison of gendarmes and, in some provinces, a garrison of regular army soldiers as well. Cities often developed around a fortified centre that contained government buildings.

The form of Ottoman cities

Much of the decription given above of the physical form of the market towns was true of the Anatolian cities, as well, but on a larger scale. A comparison of the nineteenth-century town of Beyşehir with the provincial capital city of Konya, for example, shows fifteen times as many houses in Konya, thirteen times as many shops, and many more coffee houses, bakeries, and public baths. Buildings were, on average, somewhat larger. Yet the functions of the buildings in the city and the town were roughly the same. The major differences were in storage, transport, and communication facilities, and government presence. The city was naturally the centre for goods that made their way to and from the towns and off from the city to other areas. The city of Konya had a telegraph office in 1892, Beyşehir had none. The city was also more cosmopolitan. Beyşehir only had Islamic religious buildings, but Konya had one Greek Orthodox and one Armenian church and a Greek and an Armenian school. Konya had five libraries, Beyşehir none.

Much more than in villages, housing in cities obviously reflected differences in the economic position of the inhabitants. The well-to-do were likely to have two-storied houses that held both public rooms for entertaining and private rooms for the family. The poor who lived near the city centre often lived in one-room 'apartments'. The alternative for the poor was to live outside the main city neighbourhoods, in the 'suburbs'. There they could live in housing of the type seen in villages. However, the penalty was a long journey on foot into the city for work. In larger cities, distance made such commuting impossible. Consequently, city neighbourhoods customarily contained housing for all economic groups, from the rich to the working poor.

Districts in traditional Ottoman cities often were populated by people with common interests or backgrounds. Sometimes the largest group in a neighbourhood would be devotees of a particular dervish convent that was the main feature of the area. Other neighbourhoods were made up of people who had come from villages in one region. Ex-villagers who were already in the city found work and housing for others who wished to migrate, and these naturally lived together for companionship and cooperation. Large families, expanded over generations, also naturally lived in the same part of the city. Members of guilds and their families, or others who worked in the same jobs lived with their families in areas close to their bazaars. The close ties between neighbours meant that the neighbourhoods were organized by family, regional, or business ties, and thus had an internal cohesion. They provided a sense of belonging that otherwise would have been lacking in the large city.

Commerce

Shops in cities can be placed in one of three categories. The first type were simple shops that stood alone and were often grocers or the like – shops that catered to the needs of their neighbourhoods. Some work places also stood alone, particularly trades that were noisy or smelly, such as slaughterhouses or tanneries. The second type was a street or streets of shops, one next to the other, called a *çarşı*. These shops, craftsmen's work places, stores selling the same type of goods, or both, also might be together in a closed compound with a large gate which was closed at night. The third type, a covered bazaar or *bedestan*, gathered together many shops of similar or different types under a roof. *Bedestan*s had usually been constructed by a pious foundation or by a sultan or local lord. In Anatolia, the *bedestan*s were frequently pre-Ottoman establishments. They were typically the property of a foundation which charged rents to support the *bedestan* and some charitable purpose. Larger cities might contain all three forms of commercial shops. The commercial heart of the city was normally in the centre, close to the government buildings.

*Bedestan*s were a normal feature of large and some small cities. In large cities, the *bedestan* would have a number of streets of workers and merchants, a small covered city. Some *bedestan*s were devoted to one craft, but most had a number of crafts and materials for sale, typically, with each craft gathered together in its own area. In Middle Eastern climates, which were often very hot in summer, sometimes cold and snow-filled in winter, and sometimes both, the benefits of a covered market are evident. However, the main reason for covered markets was their security. They were closed at night and guarded by watchmen and Janissaries in the earlier Ottoman period, police in the later period. Merchants might store their goods in their shops or in warehouses/manufactories (*han*s), which were often large, with many rooms rented out on long or short leases. Bulk goods, such as cotton or foodstuffs, were especially stored in warehouses. *Han*s varied in size, shape and function, but if there was a typical *han*, it was square, with a large central courtyard and often two or three stories. Craftsmen and merchants stored their goods and used their shops as small 'factories' for producing their wares.

Covered and open markets are still a feature of Middle Eastern cities today. Then and now, they might sell cloth and clothing, gold, silver, and jewellery, spices, carpets, and copper pots, among other goods. One feature of Ottoman times – slave markets – is not seen today. Craftsmen might make goods in the markets or make them elsewhere and only sell them there. Larger *bedestan*s contained most of the necessities of life – mosques, restaurants, inns, as well as the goods sold in the shops.

Much of the production of goods in Ottoman cities depended on the availability of raw materials and transport and on local needs. Thus the presence of great flocks in central Anatolia determined that weaving of woollen goods should be done in central Anatolia. Cotton growing in the south and western regions of Anatolia meant cotton weaving in those regions. Metal working naturally took place in towns near the mines of northern Anatolia. Much normal production, however, was carried out everywhere. Occupations such as butcher, baker, and candlestick maker were needed in all regions.

Markets and Çarşıs, Central Anatolia, late sixteenth century

Raw Materials, Animals	Textile Trades	Leather Trades
	felt makers	saddlers
grain	workers in cotton	shoemakers
fish	weaving of goats' hair	slipper makers
wood	dyers	tanners
rice	workers in linen	
fruit	thread market	**Miscellaneous**
salt	weavers	turners
grape syrup	cleaners of cotton wool	wax makers
chestnuts	linen drapers	makers of roofs
cotton	silk mercers	makers of bowls
goats' hair	taffeta makers	general stores
reed mats	dealers in angora wool	camel drivers
soap	dealers in coarse wool	second-hand goods
horses	tailors	carpenters
sheep	skull-cap makers	spinning wheel men
cattle	cap makers	workers in stone
	makers of saddle cushions	bowstring makers
Foodstuffs		
grocers	**Metal Trades**	
bakers	kettlemakers	
savoury pastry makers	blacksmiths	
drug-sellers	farriers	
helva makers	goldsmiths	
butchers	swordmakers	
cookshops	needlemakers	
syrup makers		

Information exists on the types of businesses in central Anatolia in the sixteenth century. The table[1] lists, without indicating their frequency, which is not known, some of the types of existing markets – all owned by *vakıf*s. Some of these were markets set off by themselves, others were *çarşı*s, or streets in which the commercial activity took place. There were undoubtedly other types of markets and certainly many other types of business and manufacturing. Unless counted under 'weavers', carpet makers and stores should have been seen, for instance, but are not listed in the source. However, the table does indicate the scope and peculiarities of the business of Anatolia. Some of the trades and markets were only found in specific areas. Fish markets were naturally found on the sea coast, for example. Others, such as grain dealers and grocers were found almost everywhere. Some goods, often economically important, were specific to the regional culture. The savoury pastries were a common food – *börek*, which is cheese, meat, etc. baked in layers of thin dough. Grape syrups and other syrups were important for making sweets. Skull-cap makers and markets were common, probably because Muslims often wore skull-caps in mosques and elsewhere. In praying, Muslims touch their foreheads to the ground, so brimmed hats were seldom seen.

As markets and customs changed, the latter very slowly, the frequency of some trades changed as well. Nonetheless, a list of markets in the nineteenth century would have been surprisingly similar to that in the table, though some new types of shops would have been added. More people were literate, so paper sellers would have been in evidence. The existence of the printing press meant books and bookstores. In some cities, implements and clothing from Europe would be sold by merchants, where previously craftsmen had sold their own manufactures. Gunpowder sellers replaced sword makers. Some crafts, and their markets, died out. There was not much call for bow-string makers in the late nineteenth century. Most of the professions were still needed, for they filled basic human needs.

Istanbul

To the Ottomans, Istanbul was a separate category of existence. Partisans of Paris, San Francisco, New York, or London will understand what Turks meant when they said 'the City', and expected to be instantly understood as speaking of Istanbul. To its inhabitants, life outside of the city was half a life, or less. The Ottomans did not even use the designation 'Istanbul' in government pronouncements. On official documents the city was labelled *Der*

---

[1] Excerpted from Suraiya Faroqhi, *Towns and Townsmen of Ottoman Anatolia*, Cambridge, 1984.

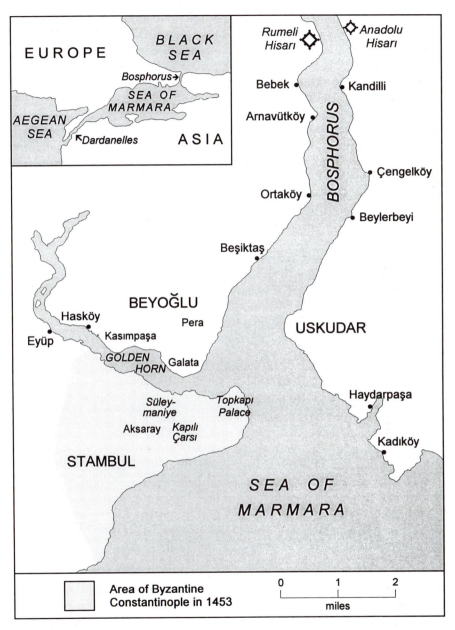

Istanbul.

Saadet, which poetic Victorians translated 'Abode of Bliss' (and which sounds considerably better than 'House of Happiness', another possible translation). The city thus did not really have a name, only a description of felicity.

245

The real Istanbul encompassed both bliss and anguish. Like all other cities, it had a large portion of poor and hungry within its walls. Beggars were common, drawn to the city from impoverished villages or dispossessed by civil disorder. To a modern European, although not to a medieval or early modern European, the streets would have appeared dirty. Yet it was also stunningly beautiful, gifted by nature and embellished by man. Istanbul was situated where the Bosphorus flowed into the Sea of Marmara, on the border of Europe and Asia. The Golden Horn, which opened to the west at the mouth of the Bosphorus, provided one of the best harbours in the world. Both sides of the Bosphorus and the north of the Golden Horn were hilly, with valleys running to the water. From the city, forests could be seen across the Bosphorus, on the hills in Anatolia. Other forests stretched north of the city to the Black Sea. The climate was good. The Sea of Marmara and the Bosphorus helped to moderate the weather of Istanbul, giving the city breezes that cooled the summers and making it warmer in winter than the lands in either northwest Anatolia or Thrace.

The region between the Golden Horn and the Sea of Marmara was well suited for both defence and trade. A settlement had been founded there as early as the seventh century B.C. It became the capital of the Eastern Roman Empire, named Constantinople after Constantine the Great (306–337). The successors of the Eastern Roman Empire, the Byzantines, ruled from the city until 1453. As the Byzantine capital, Constantinople was fabled for its riches and splendour. It was surely the greatest city in Europe during the Middle Ages.

At the time of the Ottoman conquest in 1453, Istanbul was a shell, deserted by most of its population, the remnant of the mighty Byzantine Empire. To the city within the walls (the Old City, the ancient Byzantine capital, often called 'Stambul' by Europeans) was appended the suburb of Galata, across the Golden Horn, a thriving community of European traders. Mehmet II came upon a city that had fallen on hard times, and he and his successors set upon the task of building its splendour. A population of craftsmen, workers, and merchants was imported, whether they wished to come or not. The city that resulted was marked by its natural beauty and its architecture.

The water

Some cities, such as Venice or San Francisco, cannot be properly perceived without the waterways that are a part of them. Istanbul was and is such a city. The Sea of Marmara, the Golden Horn, and the Bosphorus were integral to the Ottoman city of Istanbul. They were the main avenues of transport and communication within the city, and first rowed, later steam-powered boats constantly plied them all. Shipping was the life blood of the city's economy.

In addition to its aesthetic benefits, the water also afforded the best method of transport in the city. The Sea of Marmara and, especially, the Bosphorus and the Golden Horn were the primary arteries of the city. Before the advent of steamships, boats were rowed or sailed up and down the Bosphorus. A large guild of ferrymen took passengers across and up and down the Bosphorus and the Golden Horn. High officials of the Ottoman government had their own boats, beautifully decorated, each rowed by twenty men. Lesser mortals had fewer oarsmen, but they still arrived at their destinations more quickly than they could by land. Cargo boats with lateen sails sailed from shore village to shore village and on to the city. In 1851, the first steamboat ferries arrived, soon providing rapid transport to all sections of the city, and putting many oarsmen out of work. Travelling on the open deck of a ferry was a joy, especially when compared with the alternative – horse-drawn carriages on hot, dusty streets.

Fishing villages stretched up the Bosphorus and on the Marmara shore. Typically, each had a small port area, a small commercial street along the water, and another commercial street that extended away from the shore. On the Bosphorus, the villages' main streets stretched up into the hills that flanked both sides of the strait. Many had existed since Byzantine times. As the city's population grew, particularly in the later nineteenth century, the city borders expanded and encompassed nearby villages. Eventually, many of them became 'dormitory communities' for Istanbul. Workers took ferries into the city for work.

Houses in Istanbul were built with the water in mind. Palaces of the sultans were built on or overlooking the water. Pashas and merchants kept summer houses up the Bosphorus. Because the city was built on hills, the water was never far from sight. It was a city of porches and balconies. Much of the Asian and European sides of the Bosphorus, halfway to the Black Sea, were lined with wooden houses that had balconies with wide windows that were opened to draw in the breeze from the water. In Topkapı, the palace of the sultans, was a particular covered balcony from which could be seen the Bosphorus, the Marmara, and the hills of Asia, one of the most beautiful views on earth. Sultans in the palace grounds and poor men on the shores both enjoyed the views of the water.

Monuments

Next to Haghia Sophia (Ayasofya), the great church of Justinian, which had been converted to a mosque on the conquest of the city, the most notable inheritances from antiquity were the grand aqueduct of Valens, the open space of the Byzantine hippodrome, and the great wall of Theodosius. Triumphal columns erected by the Byzantine emperors rose in the city. The Theodosian wall, the Golden Horn, and the Sea of Marmara defined the Old City; outside the walls stretched great cemeteries to the west. The great

A contemporary postcard of an Istanbul street. Note the sign in Turkish, Greek and Armenian.

mosques commissioned by Mehmet II, Ahmed I, Süleyman, and later sultans established the Islamic character of the city, as did mosques, *mescid*s (smaller prayer halls), and other Islamic buildings. Evliya Çelebi, the seventeenth-century traveller, wrote that there were more than 15,000 mosques and *mescid*s in Istanbul. While Evliya was more than prone to exaggeration, Islamic structures were surely numerous.

As mosques marked the Islamic character of the city, so did government buildings mark it as Ottoman. Ottoman palaces and government buildings symbolized the place of Istanbul as centre of the Ottoman state. Pride of place went to the imperial palace of Topkapı. Structures such as the arsenal, barracks, and the imperial dockyards spoke of Ottoman power. In the nineteenth century, imperial palaces of great beauty were constructed up the

Bosphorus, as were large schools. In the Old City, a grand central post office, a railway station, and administrative buildings were constructed in contemporary European styles. Across the Golden Horn, in Galata, embassies and European-owned banks built new and often architecturally distinguished buildings – ominous but attractive symbols of European control.

From a boat entering the Golden Horn, the greatest of the Ottoman monuments could be seen on the point of the Stambul peninsula on the hills of the city. The Topkapı Palace stood on the left, behind it the great mosque of sultan Ahmed. To the right of the palace was the great Ayasofya mosque. The mosque of Süleyman, one of the most beautiful buildings in the world, and the mosque of Mehmet the Conqueror rose from hills further up the Golden Horn. Another great mosque was on the shore of the Horn, below the others, the Yeni Valide mosque, named not after a sultan, but after the mother of Mehmet IV. The other buildings of the Old City were mainly of only one or two stories, so the view of the monuments was unimpaired.

Areas of Istanbul were often designated by their monuments – 'Beyazıt' (Bayezit) for the environs of the mosque of Sultan Bayezit, 'Tophane' for the cannon foundry/arsenal, 'Fatih' ('Conqueror') for the neighbourhood of the mosque of Mehmet II. Throughout the Ottoman period, as now, those who dwelled in Istanbul were surrounded by its history.

City streets

Many of the streets of traditional Istanbul would have looked forbidding to modern Western eyes. The Old City, the area within the walls built by the emperor Theodosius, was particularly 'Middle Eastern' in its street plan – narrow streets with many turns, no grid pattern, and many *cul de sac* lanes. Maps of the Old City of Istanbul in the early nineteenth century look much like maps of the streets of Cairo or other Middle Eastern cities of the time. For example, the street map[2] on the following page is a section of the Old City, the Aksaray district, *c.* 1850. Although one cannot tell it by the scale of the map, the streets are almost all narrow, some only wide enough for two pedestrians to pass each other. The streets wind in no discernible pattern. Someone who did not know his way could easily be lost.

What is seldom considered is that city structures like that shown in the map were not inefficient – at least not until changes in forms of transport made them so. Today we assume that relatively wide streets are essential – there must be room to park vehicles and still let traffic pass. In the cities of the Ottoman Empire there were naturally no cars. Narrow, animal-drawn carts did exist, but were not the usual method of carrying goods into residential areas. Deliveries were more often made by human beings, who carried goods on their backs. Thus city neighbourhoods had

---

[2] The map has been adapted from Zeynep Çelik, *The Remaking of Istanbul*, Seattle, 1986, p. 54.

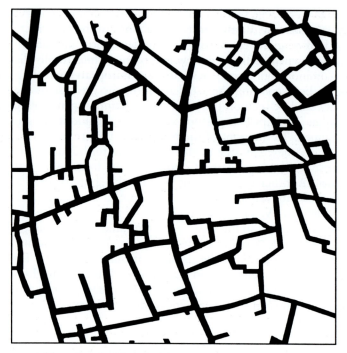

The Aksaray neighbourhood of Istanbul.

little need of broad streets. On the contrary, cost and distance factors made narrow streets preferable. Unlike in the countryside, land in the city was at a premium. Moreover, the normal mode of going from one place to another was on foot. Broad streets would have increased the size of the city, making it that much farther to walk to get anywhere. There were also savings from paving as little ground as possible. Most streets were unpaved or covered with gravel, but many were paved with flat cobbles, a labour-intensive undertaking.

The winding nature of the streets and the many *cul de sac*s were not the product of any city plan. Rather they were the result of streets spreading between houses after the houses were built. Istanbul had been populated for more than a millennium, and houses had been built over old streets, new paths cut when houses were torn down, etc. The result was the mosaic that appears in the map. However, such streets had a practical benefit in providing protection for those who dwelled in them. Neighbourhood security was primarily in the hands of the residents. When a stranger appeared windows opened and people watched. Short, closed streets facilitated this self-policing. Privacy was ensured by the difficulty of passing through residential areas to get from one part of the city to another; the main roads were a surer route. Narrow streets could even be closed by

gates at night. In short, roads that might appear dark and dangerous were
in reality safer than wide streets might have been.

In the nineteenth and twentieth centuries, all this changed. Wider
carriages, increased loads of goods, and eventually the motor car demanded
wider thoroughfares. The government wanted straight roads to facilitate
the passage of goods and municipal vehicles, especially fire engines. The
opportunity for rationalized roads along the European or American pattern
came from devastating fires that broke out in the city. Most of the Old City
was constructed of wood. Wooden buildings, built close together, were
always at risk of fire. From the early seventeenth century, major fires
burned large sections of the city in almost every decade. Maps of Istanbul
always showed large deserted areas, neighbourhoods that had been
destroyed by fire. When whole districts burned the nineteenth-century
Ottoman government replaced them with straight streets, more or less on a
grid pattern. Few of the old neighbourhoods remain today.

Buildings

Istanbul lay on the trade routes from the forested regions of the Balkans
and the Black Sea. Wood for building was far more plentiful than in most
of Anatolia and was used to construct Istanbul houses. Houses of many
levels of society, from the middle to the richest were built of wood. Some of
them had stone bottom stories; some were all board. The poor sometimes
lived in homes of mud brick, especially on the outskirts of the city. The rich
might live in houses at least partially made of stone or fired brick. However,
most of Istanbul was housed in wood.

The inside arrangement of Istanbul houses would appear similar to
that of Anatolian village dwellings. If there was a typical Istanbul house, it
was two- or three-storied and most of the living was done on the upper
floor(s). These consisted of a large hall from which rooms opened. On the
lowest floor, which was at street-level, were the kitchen, storage areas, and
possibly rooms for living. It was very common for at least one room to
project out over the street, with a view of the Bosphorus or Marmara if at
all possible. Obviously, such houses were not for the poor.

The poor might live, more closely packed, in houses that were not
easily distinguishable from the outside from single-family dwellings.
Rather than many rooms, the poor family would occupy one. The very
poor could not afford to live in the centre of the city, so they inhabited the
suburbs.

It was common in Middle East cities for the well-to-do to live close to
the centre of a city and the poor to be relegated to the suburbs. There were
no fast roads to carry the rich to their work; therefore, living close to one's
business or government work was a privilege. The poor were forced to
walk the distances into the cities. Istanbul was no different, except that the

251

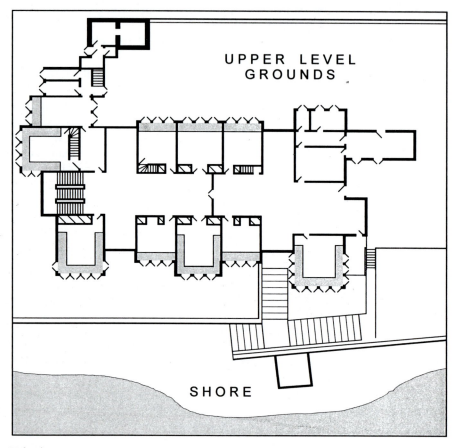

Yalı plan.

Bosphorus and Marmara allowed some of the rich to live a distance from the city and to be rowed in from their residences.

The great houses on the Bosphorus, called *yalı*s, were the architectural culmination of the Ottoman house. With doors and windows that opened almost directly on the waterway, they signified the Ottoman love of the water. Some were used as year-round dwellings, but many were summer houses. In the nineteenth century, European embassies bought or constructed *yalı*s, as well, and used them as summer embassies. The most famous of these was the British summer embassy at Therapia. It was especially valuable, because the British had built their embassy on a hill directly above the main centre of cholera and other diseases in Istanbul, the Kasımpaşa district, known as 'the worst sewer in Europe'. It was good to get away from that

Opposite: Ottoman Residences (*yalı*) on the Bosphorus. (William H. Bartlett, illustrator, in Julia Pardoe, *Beauties of the Bosphorus*, London, 1838.)

neighbourhood in summer. Many of the *yalı*s were moderately-sized buildings, still much larger than most of the city's dwellings, but many were
palaces. Ministers of state, the 'old families' of the empire, and even some
European families long resident in Istanbul owned or rented the greatest
houses. The *yalı* in the picture and diagram was one of those. It had large
public and private rooms, grounds with trees and shrubs, and a great
numbers of windows. When the windows were opened the breeze from
the Bosphorus flowed through the house. Then and now, one of the most
satisfying pastimes for those who lived by the Bosphorus was sitting by the
window, feeling the breeze, and watching boats pass.

Buying and selling

The centre of the commercial life of Istanbul was in the covered bazaar
(Kapalı Çarşı) in the centre of the Old City. The economic foundation of
the Istanbul covered bazaar was laid by sultan Mehmet II, the conqueror of
Istanbul. Mehmet built more than 800 shops in the central location that
was to become the covered bazaar, mainly shops of cloth merchants and
tailors. Profits from them supported the *vakıf* endowments made by the
sultan. Most of these shops were probably made of wood and were not all
gathered into one roofed market. It was after a great fire in 1701 that the
Ottoman government rebuilt the market in stone and masonry, covering it
and creating a small commercial city.

From the fifteenth century on, the market expanded and the number
of shops continued to grow. There were so many shops, indeed, that no one
was able to count them accurately. By 1701, there were approximately
3,000, and perhaps more than 4,000 at the end of the nineteenth century.
In addition to shops, the covered bazaar contained a communal bath, a
mosque and a number of smaller prayer halls (*mescid*s), fountains, a school, a
number of warehouses, coffee houses, and restaurants. The market was
entered through 18 gates, and it contained 61 streets. Most of the streets
were small and many were very narrow. It was a vast warren of little shops
whose goods spilled out into the streets, watched over by thousands of rug-
sellers, cloth-sellers, and other merchants. Losing oneself in the covered
market was not unusual.

As in the markets in other Ottoman cities, merchants in the covered
bazaar were segregated by trade. Goldsmiths, shoemakers, carpet merchants, and those who sold coats, furniture, jewellery, furs, cutlery, old
clothes, cosmetics, hats, and almost any other kind of goods gathered
together in their own sections of the bazaar. To Europeans and Americans,
the covered bazaar was a wondrous place, the exotic Orient for which they

---

Opposite: A main thoroughfare in the Grand Bazaar (*Kapalı Çarşı*) in Istanbul.
(Bartlett, in Pardoe, *Beauties of the Bosphorus*.)

always searched and seldom found. They spoke of it in terms worthy of the Arabian Nights. Witness the comments of one visitor, captivated by, of all things, shoes.

> The shoe bazaar is one of the most resplendent of all, and possibly fills the brain more than any other with wild longings and riotous desires. It consists of two glittering rows of shops, which make the street in which it is situated look like a suite of royal apartments or like one of those gardens in the Arabian fairy-stories where the fruit trees are laden with pearls and have golden leaves. There are shoes enough there to supply the feet of every court in Europe and Asia. The walls are completely covered with slippers of the sauciest shapes and most striking and fanciful colors, made out of skins, velvet, brocade and satin, ornamented with filigree-work, gold, tinsel, pearls, silken tassels, swan's down; flowered and starred in gold and silver; so thickly covered with intricate embroidery as to completely hide the original texture; and glittering with emeralds and sapphires....
> [There are] tiny slippers of white satin on which ardent lover's kisses will be showered; and it may be that yonder pair encrusted with pearls will some day stand beside the couch of the Padishah [sultan] himself, awaiting the feet of some beautiful Georgian. But how, you ask yourself, is it possible for any feet to get into such tiny receptacles? Some of them seem intended to fit the houris and fairies – long as the leaf of a lily, wide of the leaf of a rose, of such dimensions as to throw all Andalusia into despair; graceful as a dream – not slippers at all, but jewels, toys, objects to stand on one's table full of bonbons or to keep billetsdoux in. Once allow your imagination to dwell upon the foot which could wear them, and you are reduced to an insane desire to behold it yourself, to stroke and caress it like some pretty plaything.[3]

The covered bazaar indisputably catered to the specialized interests of all sorts of buyer.

Other covered markets were found in other sections of the old city. The Mısır Çarşısı ('Egypt Market') was two long covered streets near the Golden Horn. It had the distinction of being the most interesting-smelling market in Istanbul, specializing in spices as well as other produce from Egypt. A wood market also stood along the Golden Horn. Other markets, such as a dried fruit market and a flower market, were situated at different places over the centuries. Shops near the various *han*s of Istanbul sold the products – copper work, baskets, wooden products, etc. – that were made there. Other markets, selling all manner of goods, were in reality travelling

---

[3] Edmondo de Amicis, *Constantinople*, Philadelphia, 1896, pp. 142–4.

emporiums in which merchants sold goods in various parts of the city on different days. These specialized in anything that could be carried – foods, perfume, clothes, sweets, buckets, ropes, knives, cheap rugs, and almost anything else that could be imagined.

A changing city

Istanbul naturally reflected the changes in the Ottoman Empire over the centuries. When Mehmet the Conqueror took the city it was made up of the Old City, bordered by the great walls to the west, and the Genoese suburb of Galata. Settlements on the Bosphorus and across the sea in Asia were separate from the city and each other. Farms and open land came between the Bosphorus settlements and Istanbul. A major suburb, Eyüp, was up the Golden Horn from the city. Üsküdar, directly across from Istanbul, was a large city in itself. The situation changed as the city grew and the suburbs became integrated with it. Estimates of the early population are very imprecise, but Istanbul may have grown from approximately 200,000 at the death of Mehmet II to perhaps 500,000 in the middle 1500s and 700,000 by 1700. (In order to make comparisons, these figures include the populations of the surrounding regions, areas that would become part of the city later. The city proper had half to two-thirds as many people.) Growth was partly due to immigration, partly to expansion of the city's boundaries. Houses, shops, and manufacturing buildings filled in the open spaces between Istanbul and Eyüp and up the Bosphorus. Across the Bosphorus, Üsküdar grew in the time of Süleyman the Magnificent and boats, rowed by a guild of ferrymen, constantly travelled between Europe and Asia. (In the nineteenth century, steam ferries took their place.) As Europeans came to Istanbul in large numbers, Galata developed north onto the hills the Europeans called Pera. By 1900, nearly a million people lived in Istanbul and its suburbs.

There is little precise information on the composition of the population of Istanbul or their lifestyles. Early population registers listed 80,000 households in the city *c.* 1525: 46,000 Muslim, 25,000 Christian, and 9,000 Jewish. The government only took a fairly detailed census of the city late in the empire's history, the Istanbul City Census of 1886.

The table overleaf lists the population of Istanbul as it was recorded in the late nineteenth century. Muslims were the single largest religious group in Istanbul, but they were not a majority. Because the Ottomans registered population only by religious groups, information on ethnic groups is unavailable. The Muslims in the table included Albanians, Bosnians, Arabs, Kurds, and others, although most were Turks. Some of the Greek Orthodox were Slavs, not Greeks. Under 'aliens' were included many Christians and some Jews, actual lifelong residents of Istanbul, who had managed to obtain foreign passports or whose families had kept their

Istanbul by religious group, 1886

	Population	Per cent
Muslim	384,910	44.1
Greek	152,741	17.8
Armenian	149,590	17.1
Uniate Catholic	6,442	0.7
Bulgarian	4,377	0.5
Roman Catholic	1,082	0.1
Protestant	819	*
Jewish	44,361	5.1
Aliens†	129,243	14.8
Total	873,565	

some rounding error
* less than 0.1 per cent
† foreign nationals and unknown

original citizenships over generations. A number who worked in the city but were listed in population registers elsewhere or who lived in 'Greater Istanbul' but not within the census borders were not included in the totals. The *de facto* population of Greater Istanbul was probably 100,000 higher.

Istanbul had a very fluid population. People in search of work, military men, public officials, merchants, students, and many others moved into and out of the city. In addition, a large number of refugees had settled there. The Istanbul City Census of 1886 listed 63 per cent of Muslim, 55 per cent of the Greek Orthodox, and 55 per cent of the Armenian residents of the city as having been born outside Istanbul. Of the major population groups, only the Jews were almost all (95 per cent) born in the city. Unfortunately, there is no record of how many of the 'aliens' were born in the city or in the Ottoman Empire.

Since Istanbul was the capital, a large proportion of its population was employed by the state. In 1886, 6 per cent of the male Ottoman subjects in the city were public employees; 38 per cent were students, a very high percentage. Only 33 per cent were listed in the census as being in 'business or labour'. However, there were certainly a further number who were at least occasionally employed but did not want the census taker (or the tax collector) to know.

Chapter 8 . . . .

Turkish Society and Personal Life

Turkish Society and Personal Life

Under the subjects of architecture, geography, and meteorology, much has already been written above on the Turkish society of Anatolia. Human beings always adapt themselves to their surroundings. This is as true of their social relations as it is of their building techniques. The most obvious example of this is the rural–urban difference noticed in all societies. Everything from crime to eating habits changed when peasants come to the city.

Consideration of the physical world in which the Turks lived says much about their lives. For example, the mud brick house was used to maximize the value gained from available materials. Family structure also optimized benefits to family members. What the family maximized was survival. Turkish families stressed the need for family members to work together and stick together. In a difficult environment, a villager needed to count on someone during the hard times. Family cohesion meant that someone would help feed the family if the harvest was bad or watch the crops and guard the family when men went off to war. Family members would support each other in village disputes or conflicts over scarce resources. The environment also demanded that the number of children be maximized. Children meant that more hands were available for the harvest work. Children were 'social security', because they would care for their parents when they grew old. Another example of optimization was respect for old age. Turks showed a respect for age that would astound the parents of teenagers in the West. Elders were listened to and their advice was followed, because it was sound. Little changed in the world of the Turkish peasant. The old had learned of droughts, locust swarms, tax collectors, and other such plagues by living through them. Experience was a valuable teacher, and it was a survival skill to pay heed to the wisdom of the old. Thus what seems like good manners was also common sense.

Of course, environment did not determine everything. Turks had children because children are wonderful in themselves, an expression of love, not only because they were thinking of their retirement income. The old were respected because of a natural affection for those who raised you and, hopefully, taught you well. Environment was an important factor in shaping human society, but it was only one of many factors.

Marriage and the family

In understanding traditional Turkish marriages, or indeed any relations between the sexes in history, modern readers are at a disadvantage. The tendency to view ancestors as slightly bad or invincibly ignorant is always present. Nowhere is this as true as when modern men and women look at relations between their grandmothers and grandfathers. Women were unquestionably not treated as equals by men in bygone days, and it is easy to turn historical comparisons from those days to this into moral judgements. It is less easy, but probably more just, to recognize that both men and women were bound by the cultural values they inherited, even while one affirms that those values might sometimes have been wrong. This should be kept in mind when considering Turkish culture long ago. It should also be remembered that the ancestors of modern American or European men and women were not paragons when it came to equality between the sexes. (Some may even be willing to admit that real equality has not quite arrived today.)

As was true in all Muslim societies, every Turk was expected to marry. Celibacy was considered to be an unnatural state that no reasonable person would freely choose. Homosexuality, while present, as in any society, was religiously condemned. Ideally, the young were to marry at an early age, sometimes soon after puberty. The Turkish concept of sexual desire, especially among villagers, was practical. If the young were left unmarried, it was likely that their sexual desires would find an outlet outside of marriage. This, it was felt, would cause all sorts of social and moral evils. Parents were especially concerned with the sexual purity of their daughters. Islamic tradition held that women's sexuality was a strong force that could only be held in check through constant oversight by men, first a father, then a husband.

Traditionally, almost all marriages were arranged by the parents of the young people. The primary considerations of marriage were economic – a 'good marriage' was one in which parents could arrange for a mate of equal or higher social and economic status, but other factors were not omitted completely. Mothers, in particular, looked out for the happiness of their children in non-economic concerns. Physical attractiveness was not ignored. In general, men were prized for their abilities as a 'breadwinners' and women for their proficiency in housekeeping and child care. Strength was appreciated in a man, homemaking skills in a women. Virginity was demanded of previously unmarried women. Thus Turkish society valued the same qualities held most high in almost all traditional societies.

Some marriage customs varied by regions or by groups. All groups of Turks considered marriage to siblings, parents, grandparents, aunts and uncles to be forbidden, as it was in Muslim law. Some also felt that marriage to first cousins was forbidden or at least undesirable. Perhaps they in some way understood the potential genetic problems of inbreeding, or perhaps they just believed that marriages to strangers would increase social and economic contacts and support for the family, because marrying into another family brought the families closer and led to cooperation in work or in village conflicts. However, other groups of Turks felt that marrying cousins on the father's side was proper and even made the best matches. Some considered it best for a son to marry his father's brother's daughter. This was primarily to ensure the conservation of land in the family. No one outside the family could claim a share of their land when the father died if the children were all married in the family. How often this form of marriage took place between cousins in fact is unknown. The fact that it was an ideal does not mean those who were to be married would agree to it.

Customs varied, but there was a normal procedure that was followed in arranging marriages. It was in theory the job of the young man's father to initiate marriage arrangements. He decided that his son was old enough to marry and began to look for a suitable match. In reality, women spent much time considering marriage prospects for both sons and daughters long before their children were old enough to marry. In villages, in particular, all eligible partners in the region would have been considered for years before marriage was ever formally proposed.

The man's family sent intermediaries, usually uncles or other relatives, to strike a marriage bargain. They discussed what would be expected of the spouses and their families in a very practical way – praising the accomplishments of their child, the benefits to be brought to the other spouse, what sort of house the new bride would come to, what she would bring to the house in the way of linens and pots, and other important subjects. Included in the negotiations was bargaining over the sum to be paid by the man's family as the bride settlement (*mehr*). According to Islamic custom and law, a sum of money was to be paid by the husband when he took a bride. Part of this was to be kept in trust for the bride, to support her if the groom died or divorced her, although many parents simply took the daughter's bride settlement as their own, considering it to be payment for the loss of their daughter's labour. Factors such as family wealth, physical beauty, and the abilities of the prospective spouses affected the amount of the settlement. To Westerners brought up in a romantic tradition, such negotiations may seem cold, but they were essential. It was felt that successful marriage rested upon exactly such practical considerations (and, considering that money problems are listed as the greatest cause of friction in modern marriages, such calculated practicality may have been at least somewhat justified).

It was also essential that the families come to agreement *as families*. The happiness of the couple was not the only consideration. Turks expected that marriage would bind two families together, not just a man and wife. Members of the two families would help each other and look out for each other's interests. A properly constructed marriage made cooperation between families all the more likely. In fact, marriage itself could in many ways be considered a contract between two families.

After the practical matters were concluded, social forms took over. The women of the two families came together, exchanged gifts, and discussed the forthcoming marriage. The bride to be was formally introduced to her prospective mother-in-law. In a traditional sign of respect, she kissed her mother-in-law's hand and served tea, a symbol of recognition that she accepted the authority of the older woman into whose house she would come. The relationship between the two women bound the two families together. Women of both families celebrated the forthcoming marriage and their new familial relationship.

Finally, on the wedding day, men of the two families met and formally agreed to the marriage contract in the presence of witnesses and a man of religion. The entire village celebrated with a feast and dancing, a celebration that often lasted for days, with women and men celebrating separately. The bride was formally escorted to her new home. Her husband and new family welcomed her. As in Western tradition, consummation was the seal of the marriage. The bride was considered to have passed into the new family. She was called 'our bride' by her new family members, signifying that the marriage was a thing of families, not only individuals. Only occasionally was the situation reversed and a husband came into the home of the bride's family. This was in the case of poor men who married into families with no sons, an arrangement sanctioned by the economic necessity to have young men in a household.

After marriage, the bride remained close to her own relatives, even though she had passed into a new family. Children were in effect brought up by the families of both father and mother. Women exchanged 'baby sitting' with their sisters and mothers, as well as with the women in her own house. Brides often remained particularly close to their brothers. Brothers were men a married woman could meet with often, joke and discuss serious issues with, and with whom she could act in a normal way, unrestrained by the social conventions that separated a woman from male companionship outside her marriage family.

Human ingenuity can find a way around the most rigid social systems. In the case of Turkish marriage, there were obviously times when the system broke down. Young people fell in love, even when such things were not considered proper. No one could keep the sexes completely apart when young men and women passed in the street or worked in the fields or sneaked looks at each other in secret. Usually, love triumphed through the intercession of family members, especially mothers, who convinced husbands and fathers that marriages should be arranged between the two sweethearts. When this was impossible, another way existed, *kız kaçırma*, 'stealing a bride'. *Kız kaçırma*, which might more properly be called elopement, played upon the prejudices of the community. Village opinion insisted that a man who seduced a virgin should marry her, and held that any man and woman who spent a night together must have had sexual intercourse. Therefore, a way around either parental disapproval or perhaps lack of money for the bride settlement lay in 'abduction'. The young man would sneak away with his beloved and leave her with a relative overnight. Despite the lack of any real sexual activity, that was enough to guarantee marriage, if not parental approval. There was danger in this, because the anger of the woman's father and brothers might lead to violence. More often, however, love conquered all but an angry pair of new in-laws. Even these usually came round when grandchildren appeared.

Polygamy

One major difference between marriage customs in Islamic and Christian cultures was polygamy (more properly polygyny). Islamic law allowed a man to marry four wives, if certain conditions were met. The main condition was equality of treatment. Religious law did not allow a man to overtly favour one wife over another: their clothing, living space, rights to sexual intercourse, etc. were to be equal. However, human nature must have made this difficult, if not impossible.

Polygamy seems to have been fairly rare among the Turks of the Ottoman Empire. Statistical evidence is meagre, but what data exists suggests that in normal times less than 5 per cent of women may have been in polygamous unions. The main reason for this was probably social – the preference of both women and men for monogamous unions and the reluctance of parents to arrange a place for a daughter as a second wife. Economics was also a deterrent to polygamy: the bride settlement could be a large expense and marriages themselves were expensive. Marrying meant capital outlay. There was also a certain expense in running a larger household. In addition, the Turkish cultures of Central Asia had been monogamous before coming into contact with Middle Eastern traditions. Whatever the reason, most Turks were obviously by preference monogamous.

Why then did polygamy exist among the Turks at all? Modern ideas on marriage in the West and in the Turkish Republic have rightly turned away from polygamy, but it would be a mistake to believe that polygamy had no social utility. The most common type of polygamy was probably part of the social welfare system that bound Turkish families together.

265

When a man died it was the duty of his brother to look after the surviving family. As will be seen below, the brothers had often lived with their families in the same household. The wives of the two brothers had been companions, their children had played together. Given the expectation that all women of child-bearing age be married and the family's desire to keep an inheritance in the household, the most natural solution was the marriage of the widow to the brother. This type of polygamous marriage thus kept the fabric of the family and of society together. Polygamy also had a benefit to the society as a whole, because it helped sustain the birth rate. At various times in Ottoman history, wars caused a great mortality among Turkish males. In a purely monogamous society, this would have necessarily meant that women would have been without husbands, and thus without children, as well. The population would have declined, with disastrous results for the village and the society as a whole. Polygamous unions were commonly entered into when the first marriage proved to be sterile, in the hope that the second union would produce offspring. Children, as will be seen below, were essential for survival.

It must also be admitted that some polygamy, particularly among the rich and powerful, was a matter of a man simply wanting more than one woman. This might be considered analogous to the practice of some European or American men taking mistresses, with the difference that second wives enjoyed far greater legal protection and social respect than did mistresses.

Divorce

In theory, divorce, like marriage, was governed by well-defined Muslim laws. In the Holy Law, a man was allowed to divorce quite easily: he had to only to say words of dissolution three times for the marriage to be ended. Three times were stipulated so that ordinary arguments, in which harsh words were said, would not automatically lead to divorce. It is one thing to say, 'I don't want to be married to you' in the heat of anger, and another to say the same words formally, three times, knowing the result. A woman could not simply divorce by repudiation. She was forced to go to an Islamic judge for marriage dissolution. She had to demonstrate that her husband had violated the marriage contract in specific ways, especially by denying her support or sexual relations.

As in many other things, in matters of divorce, the law was not the final word. Among villagers, the vast majority of the Turks, men did not divorce so easily, nor women with so much difficulty, as the Islamic law implied. From limited knowledge and studies from periods after the end of the Ottoman Empire, in which little had changed in village life, it seems that both women and men in fact initiated divorce. When a man divorced his wife, she left his (or his family's) home and returned to her father or other male relative. If the wife wished to divorce, she simply left on her own. The husband was then forced to formally divorce her if he wished to remarry. However, most separations were just that, what modern courts would call 'trial separations'. More often than not they ended in reconciliation.

Many factors in society stood against divorce. Primary was the fact that marriage was a family affair, not only an arrangement between one man and one woman. A husband might not like his wife, but if she was a good mother and worked well with other members of the extended family, the family would do much to stop any talk of divorce. Much had been invested in the marriage – not only emotion, but expense. Clothing, bedding, pots, and other household goods had been purchased; a house had been built. Among a generally poor people, such goods were not easy to give up. Public shame was also a factor. If a man or woman caused a marriage to dissolve for what fellow villagers thought was a bad reason, the entire village would censure him or her, and public shame was not easy to live with in a closed society. As in the West until recently, perhaps the most common reason antagonistic couples stayed together was 'for the children'. Much could be and was forgiven for one who was a good father or mother, even though not necessarily a good husband or wife.

The reasons for divorce were mainly the same as in any society – incompatibility, ill treatment, including physical abuse by the husband, financial problems that led to altercations between spouses, adultery, and failure of one or both parties to keep to the basic expectations of marriage, especially not doing the work the family needed from either husband or wife. To these were added another reason for a husband to divorce, the 'failure' of the wife to produce a son. Sons were greatly desired and needed for financial security, to carry on the family and support the old folks. Turkish villagers were no experts in genetics. Like others (Henry VIII comes to mind), they blamed women for not producing sons. Thus a man without sons might try another wife. Popular feeling held that it was morally better, if financially possible, to take a second wife, continuing to support the first one, but divorce caused by a lack of sons was not uncommon.

The incidence of divorce is unknown. Throughout the Ottoman Age, the government never kept records of either marriages or divorces. It is known that few divorced people remained unmarried. According to Islamic rules, a divorced woman was supposed to wait 100 days before remarrying, but this rule was routinely broken. Remarriage often came soon after divorce. The entire society was based on married life and the family. It was widely felt that a man could not live without a woman, because he could not take care of himself. While such sentiments might not have been absolutely true, in practice they were accurate. Society so divided men's and women's work that neither could live very successfully without the other. Therefore, a man had to remarry, which meant that wives had to marry as well, or there would not have been enough women to go around.

267

The Turkish family

A description of the Islamic Turkish family can take many directions. A Muslim, including Turks in villages and cities, would usually describe the relationship between husband, wife, and children from an Islamic viewpoint. The relationships between the sexes were decided by tradition and law. Marriage was, after all, a contract entered into under the rules of Islam and ordered by those same laws. To a Muslim, its structure and function was ordained by God. More secular analysts have stressed the practical nature of Turkish marital relations. Marriage was society's mechanism to guarantee the birth of and proper care of children, to make sure that the old were cared for, and to conserve property in the family. An economist, when he decided to summarize his ideas, might say that marriage maximized utility for the Turks. Note that in none of these concepts is the idea of 'love matches' mentioned. Love is a hard concept to analyse. Sadly for romantics, love between marriage partners was a secondary consideration. There undoubtedly was love between spouses in Turkish marriages, but survival was the primary reason for marriage. Marriage helped not only the Turkish people to survive, but individuals as well. In this Turks were no different from most other people throughout history.

The normal family in most of the modern world is a nuclear family, comprising father, mother and children. The nuclear family can also be called the Western ideal, so much so that the term 'family' is usually taken to mean mother, father, and children, unless otherwise stated. This was not true among the Turks of the Ottoman Empire. There, the ideal can be said to have been the extended family, a family in which more than one related parent–children group lived together in the same household.

Turkish extended families took on many different forms. In one form, three generations of males, along with their wives and daughters, lived in one house or on one compound of houses. An example is the household of Şaban (see diagram), who lived in the Black Sea region of Anatolia in the 1840s, and whose family was registered by the Ottoman census-takers. As listed in the Ottoman registration of his village, Şaban was an elderly grandfather with two surviving sons. The registrar described him as a farmer, of small stature, with a white beard. His two sons were married, and they and their children formed part of Şaban's household. In all, seven males were in the household. They were probably joined by an equal number of females – wives and children. However, the Ottoman registrars in the 1840s did not include women in their records, because the records were primarily kept for purposes of military conscription and because it was thought to be a violation of the sanctity of the family to enter the home and count the women. Not until later in the nineteenth century did the Ottomans began to enumerate women, as well.

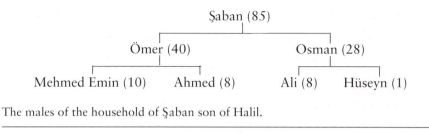

The males of the household of Şaban son of Halil.

The convention behind the extended family was simple – sons did not move out of the family home. Instead, brides moved in with the husband's parents' family. In such cases, the extended family remained together until the grandfather (or other oldest male) died. At that point, they often would split up into different households, each led by a son. Sometimes they remained together after the grandfather's death. Two or three brothers kept together the household, which was actually two or more nuclear families joined together. In the areas of Anatolia for which family structure has been studied, this form of extended family was more common than the 'three-generation' family. Given normal family rivalries, the benefits of such an arrangement must have been great for it to have been common. Another reason for such families was the fact that women sometimes brought up young children after the father died. The mother was in fact the head of the household as the children grew up and that arrangement remained in place after the sons reached their majority.

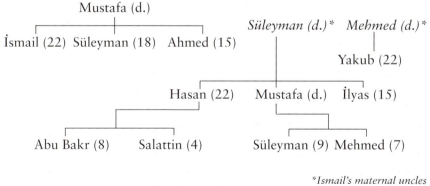

*Ismail's maternal uncles

The males of the household of İsmail son of Mustafa.

Occasionally, other relatives joined the household. These included cousins, nephews, nieces, elderly relatives, divorced or widowed sisters and daughters, and other kin. The family of İsmail was an example of the latter. İsmail was only 22 at the time of the registration, perhaps a registrar's guess rather than a precise age, but he was obviously young to head a large household. One can theorize that his father, Mustafa, had died, leaving İsmail, the oldest male, as the household head. In fact, in such cases İsmail's mother may have been the ongoing authority in the house. The mother's family moved in with İsmail and his brother. As inheritor from his father and oldest male of the original family, İsmail was considered the head of the household, but his cousins (sons of İsmail's dead uncles) were also adults. (İsmail and Yakub may have been married, but had no male children.) Women included, the household of İsmail may have included 20 people.

The primacy of the extended family was based on trust. In Turkish and other Middle Eastern societies it was assumed that brothers, sisters, a mother, or a father were the ones a person could depend on. The closer the family connection, the more reliable the bond. This explains much of why brothers stayed together in the household even after their father's death. Simply put, family members took care of one another. The extended family provided 'welfare' to its members. The sick or the old would be taken care of by young, healthy grandchildren or great nephews. Work would be shared. There would always be someone to help with heavy chores, such as threshing or house building. For women, the arduous labours of child care, weeding crops, and cooking could be shared. Perhaps the most important benefit of the extended family was psychological. There were always those upon whom a person could rely. Security was found in the family.

The extended family also had a positive effect on the population and thus on the survival of the Turks as a group. Throughout the Ottoman times, Anatolia and the other areas of the Empire were areas of high mortality. Like the rest of the world before modern sanitation and medicine and increased agricultural production, Turks were likely to die in great numbers of disease or sometimes of hunger. Added to this, especially in the nineteenth century, was the great loss of men in the Ottoman wars with the Russians. If young Turks had married late and had children along a 'European' pattern, the population would have decreased, because not enough children would have been born to keep up population numbers. However, the extended family allowed many to marry early, and thus have more children than they might otherwise have done. Young married couples did not have to be economically self-sufficient before they could marry, as they were usually forced to be in Western Europe or America. Instead, they were part of the economy of the extended family, which gave work to the couple, fed them and their children, and even provided baby sitters. (As an example, see Hasan in the household of İsmail. Even though Hasan's age is surely understated, he still was obviously a young father with two sons and an unknown number of daughters.)

Despite the obvious benefits of the extended family and societal preference for it, it was not the norm. More households were not extended than extended. As in Europe and America, a majority of families were nuclear. In the Black Sea region and the city of Istanbul, the only Ottoman area for which extensive studies have been made, relatively few of the families were extended. Cities, to which young men migrated for work, naturally had fewer extended families. Dwellings in cities were also less amenable to extended families than were family compounds in the country-side. However, two-thirds of the Black Sea families were nuclear. Some of these were households which had broken up at the death of a grandfather and which would later develop into extended households as sons married and had children. Some were the product of economic necessity, such as the need to travel away from one's home village for work. Others may have been nuclear households set up by couples who were economically secure and preferred to live alone with their children, perhaps because they did not like their relatives.

Male and female

The theoretical dominance of males in traditional Muslim societies is in-contestable, but, as might be expected, there was much variance between theory and practice. The universally-held theory in Muslim countries was that women were physically and intellectually weaker than men. They could not be counted on to make the right decisions for a family. Of course, such judgements were made and transmitted by men. The reality of family decisions was quite different. Anthropologists did not make detailed studies of relations between the sexes in the Ottoman Empire. However, studies were made of Turks in more modern times, but before the egalitarian philosophy of the Turkish Republic and the effects of technological change took hold. There is every reason to believe that the findings of these studies were true of Turks in earlier times, as well. What they found was that men and women had different spheres of authority in which each made decisions and each had actual control.

The forms of relations between the sexes among the Turks made it appear as if men were absolute masters in all things. Women obeyed direct commands from husbands and acted in a subservient fashion before them in public. Men held most property and even rich women could only engage in business through male intermediaries. The public face of each family was male; in public, men did all the talking. Men whose wives were obviously outspoken or who 'ruled the roost' were made the butt of jokes (as were such men in the not too distant past in the West). Both men and women subscribed to a belief in the necessity of male dominance. However, it would be an error to equate form with substance in relations between the sexes.

271

Authority in the family and the separation of the sexes

The image of Turkish women that comes from a superficial description of their position in traditional Turkish society is one of weak and subservient females, waiting for men to make decisions, anxious to follow orders. Yet no one who has lived among Turks, whether in Ottoman times or today, has found the words 'weak' or 'subservient' to apply to Turkish women. 'Strong' or 'assertive' come more readily to mind, but the ways in which these qualities were exercised in traditional society were quite different from what a Westerner might expect. In some ways, the concept of male dominance that was the ideal of Turkish society was accurate, in other ways it was false.

The bald statement of cultural norms can hide the inner workings of any society. The acceptance of theoretical male dominance hid the fact that family decisions were often just that, decisions made by a family group that included women. In matters of marriage described above, for example, the appearance was that marriages were arranged by men. Men made the official selection of mates and bargained over the bride price. However, women were intimately involved with the actual decisions. A bride was, after all, to come into the women's part of the family. She had to be acceptable to the women of the family, especially to the oldest woman, who would guide her life much more than would the bride's husband. To assume that males would ignore women's wishes in selecting marriage partners for sons and daughters would be to assume that the men were more than a bit mad, wholly unconcerned with domestic peace in the home where they too had to live.

While this type of female 'consultative authority' was a real female power, the most important female authority rose out of the nature of traditional Turkish society. In Turkish tradition, a man's primary duty was to support and protect his family, while a woman's was to manage the home and raise children. The origin of this dichotomy was older than history and existed in almost all societies. In Middle Eastern cultures, the separation of male and female duties was found in an extreme form. It has been said that man's world was 'public', woman's world was 'private', and that the two only seldom met. This is too extreme, but the separation between the domain of women and the domain of men was substantial.

In villages and sultans' palaces alike, Turkish women and men had their own spheres of life and work. The division of work in Turkish villages was all but absolute. There was 'men's work' and 'women's work', and the two were not mixed. Men organized the ploughing, sowing, and harvesting, built the houses, went to the market towns, and dealt with government officials. They were the representatives of the family in relations with other families. Almost all other family functions were the province of women – child rearing, feeding and sustaining the family and tending the crops and the animals. There was remarkably little communication between the male and female spheres. Women dealt with women and men dealt with men.

Outside the family circle, male–female friendships were considered undesirable and were virtually unknown: men gathered, talked, and worked with men; women correspondingly gathered and dealt with other women. Each had their own circles of communication and authority.

The division of labour made men and women absolutely dependent on each other. A man did not cook or care for babies so he needed a wife or daughter to care for him. Conversely, a woman did not defend the family property, deal with government officials, or usually bring crops to market, so she needed a husband, brother, or son to care for her. A woman's sphere of control was inside the house, a man's was outside. Was such division of labour necessary or necessarily desirable? Of course not. Another social system could surely have been constructed that would have given both women and men more scope to develop their talents and interests. However, like nearly all other traditional societies, the Turks developed a system where the husband represented and defended the family – a situation that undoubtedly derived only from man's greater physical strength. All else followed from that basic activity.

The question of male and female authority must be seen in the context of this division of labour. One must also consider what 'authority' really means. Is it theoretical position in society, status, or is it the power to make decisions? In modern societies, authority is often defined as power to affect politics and the economy. Women have asserted their right to power in government and the workplace. In a traditional Turkish village, those questions seldom applied. The general powerlessness of peasants left little scope for the assertion of authority over either government or economic life. Turkish men did have theoretical authority in relations with the political and economic world outside the home. Men gathered together to decide how the village would deal with the tax collector or counter bandit raids. This authority was real only insofar as villagers had actual freedom to affect events. In reality, they had very little chance to do anything but what they were told.

Because of the division of labour, men had effectively abdicated the chance to have any great effect on the most important things in life. The real benefit that men held was not authority, but relaxation. In most villages at most times, men simply did less work than women. Men worked very hard during the seasons of ploughing and harvest. They also had the hardest and most damaging work of all – fighting in wars. But when they were not fighting, sowing, or harvesting, men's work was much less. Women were responsible for child care, cooking, sewing, baking, laundering, and the other household tasks that never ended. Women also did the traditional sustaining agricultural work – milking cows and goats, weeding in the fields, caring for domestic animals, baking manure in the sun for fuel, etc. Their actions determined whether children lived or died, whether crops failed or grew, whether home life was comfortable or miserable – areas in which real and important decisions were made daily. Men might go off to the tea house to relax. Women had no such luxury. Women made the basic decisions in life because they were there, whether in the home or the fields, when the decisions had to be made. If men had wanted to make those decisions, they would have been forced to be in the fields or the home, and they had no wish to do so. Was there great inequality? Yes, but the greatest inequality in village life was in labour, not real authority.

Relations between men and women in cities, among the upper classes, were very different from in villages. A rich woman's authority can be said to be less important than that of a poor woman, because it was less critical. A village woman's decisions on caring for a sick cow might mean triumph or disaster for her family, but family survival was not dependent on the actions of rich women. They could, however, exercise authority over a veritable army of servants. Servants provided the labour that women did for themselves in the villages. Child care was largely in the hands of teachers and nannies. Rich urban women were free to enjoy themselves, but in a restricted way. They took carefully chaperoned trips to parks for picnics, listened to musicians, and met often to take tea and sweets. They did have more opportunity than a villager of either sex ever saw to affect political decisions, but it was only through personal influence on their husbands. The case of the women of the harem and their great effect on government is the best example of this. Because most upper-class women were essentially uneducated, though, it is difficult to believe that they had much effect on political decisions. In the nineteenth century, however, it was the city women of the upper and middle classes that began to partake of the freedom of modern society. These women could attend the new schools for females that were created by Ottoman reforms. They learned European languages, and could read the latest philosophies and political treatises. Although they were not in the court or politics, they prepared a generation of daughters to take a real place in Turkish political life after World War I, when women in the Turkish Republic eventually took up places in parliament, the universities, and business.

Although no one would say that women were a dominant part of Ottoman commercial enterprise, women were a distinct part of the economic life of the empire throughout the Ottoman centuries. They traditionally spun wool and cotton for sale and performed other basic handicraft tasks in villages and, especially, in nomadic tribes. In the later empire, when textile production expanded, the work of tribal women was an important part of the 'putting out system' in which entrepreneurs used their labour to produce yarn and carpets. Turkish women of the lower economic classes, along with women of the Christian minorities, became a part of urban manufacturing life in the empire in the nineteenth century. They took places in factories in western Anatolia and Istanbul. Textiles were particularly the province of female labour, as was the case in Europe. Whether or not this economic integration of females was on the whole beneficial is a matter of debate. Women in textile factories were breaking old stereotypes, but they were also working for low wages under often poor conditions.

Richer women were sometimes capitalists. They inherited wealth from husbands and family and invested it in commercial ventures. Judicial records from both early and late periods show women as business owners of considerable enterprise. Because of social strictures, women could seldom operate businesses themselves: it was not possible for female merchants to set out on long caravan trading journeys. However, female investors could control their endeavours through male employees. As legal holders of land and property, women were often registered in Ottoman records as buying and selling goods, entering into contracts, and bringing cases in court. Unquestionably, women were legally part of 'the system'. What will probably never be known is how much the presence of female owners in property registers and court records indicates genuine female control. Were they in charge or only the legal owners of endeavours actually operated and controlled by male members of their families? Probably both were true.

Religion and society

The most important factor in male–female relations, and perhaps the hardest for modern secular-minded readers to understand, is the importance of religion in the workings of traditional Turkish society. Men and women did not act as they did or accept inequalities and hardships simply because they had been taught to do so. They accepted the world as they found it because they did not expect it to last long. They believed they were on earth briefly before they passed to paradise. The way to ensure that they arrived in heaven was to act properly. Women and men who acted improperly were not simply liable to the censure of their fellow villagers, they were also going to hell. In the minds of villagers and most city people there was no distinction between 'religious' and 'secular' activity. Islam was a religion that permeated all of life. Being morally good meant doing everything properly, from praying five times a day to showing proper deference to elders. Socially correct action was also morally correct action. The problems and inequities of life were tolerated because the goal was so much more important than the difficulties of the journey.

Rearing children

The separation of boys and girls began at a young age. Boys were treated differently from girls almost from birth. As they grew, boys were given more latitude than girls. Boys were more likely to find their childish pranks responded to with a smile, girls with a reprimand. Cultural assumptions of

275

male superiority were taught to both sexes by such adult behaviour. Nevertheless, the upbringing of both boys and girls was similar in the early years. Both lived and developed in the family atmosphere created by the women who governed the house. It should not be thought that the preference shown to boys indicated that fathers gave poor treatment to their daughters. Quite the contrary – Turkish fathers were much more likely to show affection to the daughters than were their contemporaries in the West, where such displays of affection were not as culturally accepted. The sexes were treated differently emotionally. Mothers tended to 'spoil' their sons, fathers to treat them sternly. This was reversed with girls. The closest relationships in the family were often mother–son and father–daughter.

A cultural value that was thoroughly inculcated in Turkish children was respect for age. This was not simply respect for the elderly. Older brothers and sisters were also to be respected and obeyed. This carried on throughout life. Older brothers, in particular, held status and authority. When fathers died they took over the first place in the extended family. Their authority could affect marriage decisions, divisions of responsibility in the family, and the work and duties of their siblings. (It may also have been one of the reasons for the breakup of extended households.) Obedience to elders was one of the central values of the culture and it was taught to the young.

To villagers, the most important values passed to children were religious. Heaven and hell were real to Turkish villagers. Their actions in life would decide which was to be their place for eternity. All believed that following the laws of Islam was essential, even though there was sometimes confusion over what Islamic laws were. Local traditions and heterodox beliefs were ubiquitous and commonly believed by villagers to be a part of Islam. Beliefs reinforced the social system, giving divine sanction, for example, to family organization, the relationship between the sexes, and the imperial power structure.

In villages, if schools existed, they were for males only, and what was taught was intended to help students gain entrance into heaven, not to be of much practical use on earth. The teacher was the religious leader of the village, or occasionally a travelling religious teacher. The primary course of study was memorization of prayers and verses from the Quran. As the schools were not supervised by orthodox religious leaders, what was taught was an admixture of Islamic canons, folk beliefs, and often beliefs of mystical groups. Literacy was not required and was seldom attained. In rare circumstances, a boy might be recognized as a particularly able student and would be sent on to a religious school in a market town or city, but such occurrences were very rare indeed.

The actual education of a young male came at the hands of his father and other relatives. He learned the traditions of farming, house building, and stock-rearing through observation and the guidance of older men. His tutelage did not encourage innovation. What was taught was the tried and true, the methods that had served his people for millennia. This was the only way. Villagers lived very close to the subsistence level. It was known that the old ways worked, whereas experimentation could lead to disaster. Education can thus be compared to apprenticeship. Like apprentices in crafts, young village boys both learned and worked, and through work they became proficient farmers themselves. Young boys were given easy tasks such as watching sheep, then, as they grew older, put to work sowing, harvesting, and performing other more difficult tasks, always under supervision until they learned. Education began at a very young age. For example, boys of six or seven would accompany their fathers to the threshing shed where they would sit as weights on the sledge that was drawn over the wheat to separate it from the chaff. Praise came to those who did their small tasks well, censure or spankings to those who did not apply themselves to their duties.

Like the education of boys, that of girls was an apprenticeship system. They learned to cook, sew, and care for animals by first watching and then assisting the women of the family. One of the main duties of young girls was child care. One of the most common sights in a Turkish village was of a young girl, only seven or eight herself, carrying a younger child on her back. Older girls were given authority over their young charges, and were expected to need little parental supervision when they watched the babies. Girls were taught that what was expected of them was proper and modest behaviour, which included sexual abstinence until marriage and chastity after. Although it stressed morality, their education was not prudish. Sex was discussed and girls were told it should be a pleasurable experience.

It was expected that both boys and girls would do real work at young ages. They matured quickly. Both sexes were considered to be adults, and acted as adults in what moderns would call the teenage years.

Life and death

In the modern West, populations remain the same or grow only slightly because mortality and fertility are both low. Couples have relatively few children, but they live a long time. The Ottoman Turks had a different schedule: couples had many children, but they often died young.

Birth

The average Turkish woman, one who lived through her entire reproductive life (approximately age 15 to 45), had six children. As an average, this figure includes many who had few children and many who had a large number. However, most women would have had many children. Birth control was not completely unknown, but few effective techniques were known and, in any case, its use was frowned upon. Abortion existed, but was dangerous, illegal under religious law, and its incidence is unknown. In many periods of Ottoman history, the factor that most inhibited births must have been the absence of the husband. Wars took away Turkish men for considerable periods, and many never returned. Many wives must have waited long for husbands, finally remarrying when they felt their husbands must be dead.

Bearing children was considered not only a woman's duty, but her glory. A woman's status was enhanced by bearing children, especially sons. Children were not the sort of economic drain that they often are to modern families. Families with more sons could grow more food, watch over more sheep, and actually live better than families with few sons. Therefore, even the poorest benefited from having many children.

As in most of the world's traditional societies, having male children was considered imperative. Men and women without sons were pitied, and sometimes made the butt of jokes. Part of the reason for this was the sort of prejudice most societies have shown in favour of males. That prejudice, however, was based on practicality. Daughters left home and became part of another's family. Sons stayed in the family. They helped with sowing and the harvest and, when their parents grew old, sons provided the only 'social security' available to villagers. Sons stayed and took care of their parents, daughters left and took care of the parents of their husbands. Therefore, sons were valuable. It also did not escape the attention of fathers or mothers that males had a higher status in society. Put bluntly, both men and women had been taught that males were better than females. Those who wanted respect and a better life for their children might very practically wish for sons.

Death

There is very little hard evidence on what killed the Ottoman Turks, other than warfare. The only real statistics on causes of death were compiled in Istanbul and some other cities at the end of the empire. These indicate that the most common killers of young children, from birth to age five, were diseases of the intestines and the pulmonary system, the diseases that killed children in all pre-modern societies. A great number of children died of what were only called 'convulsions', probably the result of fevers caused by illnesses treated easily today with remedies available on pharmacy shelves. Measles and smallpox were both common causes of death among children.

In cities, from young adulthood through middle age, the most common cause of death was another that is much less seen in modern cities, tuberculosis. One-third to one-half of the recorded deaths of young adults

278

in Istanbul at the end of the nineteenth century were from tuberculosis and its complications. Smallpox also claimed many, although it was much worse among children. Typhoid killed as many adults as did smallpox, approximately 5 per cent of the young adult deaths were caused by each. Deaths at all ages from intestinal ailments were much more common than is seen in the modern world.

Those who managed to live through the diseases that assailed them in youth and middle age died of roughly the same diseases that strike modern man in old age – heart disease, strokes, kidney problems, urinary tract infections, ulcers, and cancer. Cancer was less a cause of death than today: most people did not live long enough for cancer to develop.

Causes of death in rural areas were doubtless somewhat different from in cities, but there is little evidence of what peasants died from. Because of poor food and water, intestinal ailments must have been more common, tuberculosis less common. As in other societies before modern times, most deaths in Turkish villages, towns, and cities alike were deaths of children. Children were particularly susceptible to the intestinal diseases, such as dysentery and giardia, that were the most frequent cause of childhood deaths.

The underlying factor behind deaths of the Turks in the countryside – the vast majority of the Turks – was not lack of medicine; it was lack of good food and water. Great famines such as the one that struck Anatolia in 1873–74 could kill tens of thousands at one blow, but the constant mortality from malnutrition was a worse killer. People whose diets were primarily made up of carbohydrates, with few vegetables, fewer fruits, and limited protein, were naturally susceptible to disease. Water carried the most common diseases, and there were no water treatment plants. Ignorance of the nature of disease was in itself one of the causes of death. As seen above, water-born intestinal diseases were the main killers of children. Parents had no idea what caused these deaths. Therefore, little effort was made to made to provide sanitary water supplies. If the water had no smell and looked clear, it was considered good. In fact, it was common for mothers to wet a finger with water, then put it into a baby's mouth as a pacifier. Children naturally died of such kindly treatment.

There are no statistics on death of women in childbirth, but there is reason to suspect that it was not as great as might be thought. Childbirth was guided by midwives and experienced mothers, practical experts who probably knew more about the subject than did the doctors of the time. Turkish women gave birth in a squatting position, much more effective and less likely to cause complications than the more modern habit of giving birth while lying down.

Mortality from epidemic diseases was severe. Data on deaths from bubonic plague and other epidemic diseases are not even remotely precise, but they do demonstrate high mortality. Bubonic plague was endemic in

Number of years in which plague appeared in Ottoman cities, 1701–1844

City	Weak	Moderate	Strong	Terrible	Total
Istanbul	77	6	5	6	94
Salonica	32	8	7	4	51
İzmir	52	11	8	7	78
Aleppo	8	6	5	6	25
Alexandria	39	13	3	4	59
Cairo	19	5	5	6	35

the Near East long after it had died out in Western Europe. Major plague epidemics struck until the 1840s. Minor outbreaks lasted in eastern Anatolia into the 1890s. Plague was present in Ottoman cities so often that it was almost a common disease. Contemporaries were so overwhelmed by the disease that they described it in horrific terms, estimating, for example, that in the great epidemic of 1786 one-third of the population of Istanbul died. While this was certainly a wild exaggeration, it is evident that great numbers died. The disease spread along trade routes and the paths of pilgrims to and from Mecca, so coastal cities[1] suffered the worst mortality, the interior less. The worst plagues did strike heavily into the interior, and many died. Western Anatolia, Egypt, and northern Syria reported plague epidemics most often, but the apparent pre-eminence of those areas may have been the result of poor reporting in the other regions. All areas of Anatolia undoubtedly suffered from the plague. Plague was passed by pilgrims from Mecca, and pilgrims came from all parts of Anatolia.

The great nineteenth-century cholera epidemics struck the Middle East and Balkans with ferocity, each epidemic killing hundreds of thousands. Cholera's system of delivery could not have been better designed to spread the disease. Typically, Muslim pilgrims brought the disease from its 'home' in India to Mecca when they made the pilgrimage. Muslims from other lands contracted the disease there and brought it home. Anatolia suffered particularly badly in the great epidemics of 1847 and 1865.

Typhus epidemics struck the Ottoman Empire in times of warfare and mass migration. The years 1864 to 1880 were particularly bad for the disease. Refugees from Russian conquests in the Balkans and the Caucasus died in great numbers from typhus and other diseases and spread typhus wherever they settled in Ottoman Anatolia and Syria. Other diseases that were called epidemics in the West, such as smallpox and typhoid, were always present in the Middle East and thus are more properly called endemic diseases. Malaria was endemic in the swampy areas of the Adana

---

[1] The table is excerpted from Daniel Panzac, *La Peste dans l'Empire Ottoman, 1700–1850*, Leuven, 1985, p. 216.

The Structure of the Ottoman Turkish Population (percentages)

| | Turkish Population | | | | England and Wales, 1891 | | United Kingdom, 1992 | |
| | 18th century | | Late 19th century | | | | | |
Ages	Male	Female	Male	Female	Male	Female	Male	Female
0–14	34.8	34.8	38.2	38.0	36.1	34.1	20.3	18.4
15–29	26.6	26.3	26.8	26.6	27.2	27.6	23.0	21.1
30–44	19.8	19.4	18.4	18.1	18.4	18.5	21.7	20.5
45–59	12.7	13.1	11.2	11.5	11.4	11.9	17.2	16.6
60–	6.1	6.4	5.4	5.8	6.9	7.9	17.8	23.4
Birth rate (/000)	49.3		47.5		31.4		13.5	
Death rate (/000)	43.7		33.3		20.2		10.9	
Life expectancy*	22.4	25.0	30.0	32.5			73.5	79.0
Infant mortality†	42.8	36.2	33.4	28.8	14.9		0.7	

* At birth, years.

† Deaths 0–1 divided by births, percentages.

Source, Coale and Demeny Stable Population Tables. Mitchell, *European Historical Statistics*. United Nations, *1993 Demographic Yearbook*.

province (Cilicia), parts of Greater Syria, and other regions that were favourable to the anopheles mosquito that spread the disease.

The structure of the population

The Turkish nomads who rode into Anatolia could probably expect longer lives than the farmers of Anatolia. This was not only due to their military dominance or to the fact that losers in war are more likely to die early than winners. They also had a healthier lifestyle. Their flocks gave them needed protein, and they could find or take what other food they needed. Peasants, on the other hand, were slaves to conditions on their farms. Unlike the nomads, they could seldom ride to new lands in times of famine or search out new water supplies. They were also much more likely to have needed sustenance taken by bandits or tax collectors.

The lifestyle of the Turks changed when they became peasants themselves. In the glory days of the Ottoman Empire, they probably did fairly well. Early Ottoman records indicate that the Turkish population rose fairly rapidly in the Empire's first two hundred years, an indication that life was good. That changed. Particularly after the sixteenth century, personal survival was difficult in the Ottoman Empire. A high birth rate only allowed the size of the Turkish population to stay where it was. Each year, slightly more children were born than the number of people who died of natural causes, but wars and civil unrest caused extra deaths that brought the population roughly into balance. Then, in the middle of the nineteenth century, conditions changed and the population began to grow. The reasons were political, not medical. Briefly put, increased central government authority and the relative peace that came with it made for better conditions of life. More crops could get to market, banditry could be suppressed, and civil unrest was lessened. In times of famine, at least some relief supplies could reach the starving.

The table above indicates what the Turkish population looked like in the eighteenth and at the end of the nineteenth centuries. The figures are approximations. Actual populations varied considerably. For example, in western Anatolia, where crops were better and the government had better control, people lived longer than they did in eastern or central Anatolia. Malaria affected some regions, Russian military invasions affected others. Migration affected everything. However, the figures do give a good approximation of the structure of the Turkish population. Figures for England and Wales in 1891 and the United Kingdom in 1992 have been included for comparison.

In the table, life expectancy is an average of how long a person will live after birth, but the statistic is greatly affected by infant mortality. In the eighteenth century, approximately half of those born would have died before the age of five. If a Turk lived past the age of five, he or she could expect, on average, to live almost to the age of fifty.

Note that the structure of the Turkish population and the English and Welsh population were very similar at the end of the nineteenth century. There was approximately the same proportion of children and the middle aged in the two groups. The reasons for this age structure were different in each population. In Great Britain, both birth rates and death rates were low; Ottoman Turkish birth and death rates were both high. This led to populations that appeared similar, but whose dynamics were very different. Put another way, there were fewer children in England and Wales because fewer were born, fewer in the Ottoman Empire because so many died young.

Chapter 9

Reform, 1789–1912

Overleaf

A meeting of the Chamber of Deputies of the first Ottoman Parliament. Although it was a real step toward democracy, the parliament was more form than substance. Deputies from the various *millet*s sat next to one another, but often represented their individual desires and those of their *millet* rather than those of the Empire. Real power remained largely in the hands of high officials and the sultan. (*Illustrated London News*. April 14, 1877, p. 345.)

Reform, 1789–1912

According to popular psychology, the first step to a cure is recognizing that you have a problem. The Ottoman Empire had a psychological problem, or at least a problem of lack of perception – it did not realize that it was falling ever more behind Europe. It took the Ottomans quite a while to recognize their situation and their peril. Three centuries later, one can look back at the Empire and wonder why the Ottomans did not realize their predicament in 1699. In that year they lost Hungary and other lands in a humiliating treaty forced upon them by Christian powers that they had once dominated. Should that shock not have been enough to awaken them? It seems not. Real reform of the Ottoman system was to wait for more than 100 years.

In the eyes of eighteenth-century Ottomans, the losses of 1699 could have appeared to be a temporary setback. The losses might have been due simply to the overreaching ambition of the Grand Vezir or to the difficulty of fighting at such a great distance from Istanbul. Both explanations were true, if not complete. They could easily have blinded the Ottomans to the true nature of their difficulties. An even more convincing reason for the Ottoman blindness is the nature of self-deception. Radical reform, the sort needed in the Ottoman Empire, disrupts the lives of many, particularly those in power. Rather than risk changing an entire political and social system, human beings will naturally find ways to explain away their difficulties. Judging by modern history, the Ottomans have not been alone in adhering to a government policy of wishful thinking.

Actually, some eighteenth-century Ottomans were slowly beginning to appreciate the military and economic superiority of Europe. In 1718, Sultan Ahmed III formally recognized the need to improve the Empire's forces to meet the superiority of the European armies. A small number of Ottoman travellers and ambassadors reported on European ways and technological pre-eminence. A few European military advisors were

Ottoman Europe in 1789.

imported. Yet reform was entered into only at great peril. The aforementioned Ahmed III, for example, lost his throne because he was perceived as having too great an affection for things European. Some Grand Vezirs who flirted with European ways were executed. Obviously, the Ottoman ruling class, not to mention the Ottoman people, had not been convinced that reform was needed.

Modernization, westernization, and development

The Ottoman Empire was only the first of many nations who were to face the problems of reform. Throughout the twentieth century so-called Third World countries have tried to partake of the economic and military strength of the West. The terms used to describe this process have indicated a certain confusion among reformers, a confusion mirrored in the reforms themselves. The term *modernization* has been used, because all nations wish to be modern, whatever that word means to them. To most, it has seemed to mean being so rich that one's country is in the forefront of economic advancement and, therefore, national power. The word carries no sense of how that is to be brought about. Nor is the word *development* particularly descriptive; countries can develop their resources and industries and still be far below the standards of richer nations. Such terms have little descriptive meaning.

The term *westernization*, on the other hand, is descriptive. It means 'becoming like the West', that is, becoming like the nations of Western Europe and North America. The word is often unpopular because it implies much more than improving one's economy. Commitment to the concept of westernization assumes that to be as rich and powerful as the West a country must learn to live and think like the West. Few countries have ever wanted to do that. People who have wanted excellent medical care, consumer goods, and strong armies have not usually wished to think and act like Germans or Americans in order to get them. Indians or Iranians, for example, have wished to remain Indians or Iranians in culture and religion, but to somehow become *rich* Indians or Iranians. The problem is how to manage it. Western riches developed in the specific context of the cultures and history of Western Europe and America, collectively called 'Western culture'. Economic development was part and parcel of that culture. Could countries pick and choose from Western culture, taking only technology and economy and leaving behind philosophy and traditions? The term *westernization* thus neatly defines the problem – how did a country become as rich as the West and still keep its soul?

The Ottoman Empire was one of the first countries to come to grips with the problems of westernization. As Ottoman reform expanded one can see the Ottomans being dragged further and further into emulation of the West. Few sultans or reforming bureaucrats wanted their empire to become 'westernized' in culture, but they were all forced to take steps to bring that about. A new army demanded European advisors, new weapons, and a new financial system to pay for it, all along European models. A new economy demanded more expert advisors from Europe and new systems of organization, as well as new technologies. The European experts brought the outside world to the Ottoman Empire. They were naturally seen and emulated in spheres other than technology. Europeans brought with them European

287

books, closer communications with Europe, and a galling sense of superiority that goaded Ottoman nationals to copy them, if only to best them someday.

The most momentous change came with European education. Textbooks on trigonometry and calculus, needed for military engineering and artillery, were written in European languages, especially French, the *lingua franca* of nineteenth-century Europe. The directions for operating new machines and repair manuals were in European languages. European military tactics could only be studied in European books on tactics and military history. Therefore, the Ottomans could only understand European techniques if they could read European languages. But students who could read military texts could also read novels. Worse, from the standpoint of the Ottoman establishment, the students could read political philosophy. The new opening to the West brought with it philosophy, literature, and history, not only technology. For students, it was a short step from volumes on technology to volumes on revolution.

The history of the Ottoman Empire in the nineteenth and twentieth centuries is a history of the conflict between the new ways and the old. Westernization was necessary if the Empire was to survive, but westernization carried with it ideas and practices that were inimical to the traditional Ottoman and Muslim ways. Traditionalists reacted against this, sometimes in open revolt. Even confirmed reformers were afraid of going too far.

Sultan Selim III

Sultan Selim III ascended to the throne in 1789. Although he had been raised in the palace harem, his education was more complete than that of the sultans before him. Selim had at least some training in European thought. In his youth, Selim had been allowed occasionally to leave the palace and had received tutelage in European ways, including access to

Mustafa III		Abdülhamit I	
1757–74		1774–89	
Selim III	Mustafa IV	Mahmud II	
1789–1807	1807–8	1808–39	
	Abdülmecid I	Abdülaziz ——	Abdülmecid II
	1839–61	1861–76	*Caliph* 1922–24
Murat V	Abdülhamit II	Mehmet V	Mehmet VI
1876	1876–1909	1909–18	1918–22

European writings. He seems to have grasped the low state of the Empire better than had his predecessors.

When Selim took the throne the fortunes of the Empire were at a particularly low point. In 1774 the Russians had secured a significant position in the Ottoman Empire in the peace of Küçük Kaynarcı. The Crimea, which had provided some of the best Ottoman soldiers, had been detached from the Ottoman Empire, and was soon to be taken over completely by the Russians. Russia gained naval bases and trade rights on the Black Sea, and it was obvious that they would be back for more. When Selim took the throne in 1789 the Ottomans had once again been at war, with both Russia and Austria, since 1787. The only bright spot was the preoccupation with revolutionary France that kept the Ottomans' opponents busy in other regions.

Selim gathered around him a group of reformers. The reforms they advocated cannot be called radical: all elements of Ottoman society except the army and the treasury were to be untouched. Their perception only extended to the military problems of the Empire. Like the traditional reformers of past centuries, they seem to have assumed that military reform would have been enough. The Köprülü vezirs, for example, had vastly improved the Empire's army while leaving the underlying political system intact. However, Selim's reforms were different from past reforms in that he adopted European models for the army. In that area, he recognized that success demanded emulation of Europe. His reforms can be viewed as an intermediary step between Ottoman traditional reform and the Europeanizing reforms that would follow.

The new army

Selim was a cautious reformer. Drawing on the recent defeats of the Janissaries, he convinced key members of the religious and civil establishment that some European ways might be tried. European weapons and some European instructors were imported to train the soldiers outside of Istanbul. The new regiment they formed was called the *Nizam-i Cedid* (the 'newly ordered' corps). They were dressed in modified European-style uniforms and schooled in European methods of war. The new techniques seem simplistic when compared to a European standard, but they were revolutionary to the Ottomans. They included drill, to help the soldiers act as a unit, and a pyramidical structure of command, each soldier taking orders from a superior up to the commander. All was paid for through a special treasury created from confiscated lands and other sources.

The *Nizam-i Cedid* was successful. Selim was unwilling to make use of it against the traditional enemies of reform in the Empire, but it did serve well at the battle of Acre (1799), where Napoleon's advance into the Ottoman Empire was repelled. Napoleon had invaded Egypt in the previous year, spreading the conquests of the French Revolution into the Middle East. As his forces attempted to advance their control into Ottoman Syria, British and Ottoman forces, including Selim's new troops, defeated the French. The reforms had obviously been a success, if only a tentative one.

Housed in barracks near Istanbul, the new corps was potentially a force that Selim could draw upon to defend his reforms and himself against his opponents, had he been willing to use it. He was afraid to do so. Civil war is a horrible thought for any ruler. The image of Turks fighting Turks instead of resisting foreign enemies was perhaps abhorrent to Selim III. He was probably also more concerned for his personal welfare than for reform. The underlying reasons for his lack of will probably will never be known. Whatever the reasons, Selim abandoned his reforms when they met strong opposition.

Rebellion

Opposition to the new army was sure to surface once its implications were realized by conservatives. What was the use of a new army if it was not to replace the old army? The Janissaries and other traditional corps were not very good soldiers, but they had many supporters. Whether from philosophy or self-interest, bureaucrats, politicians, and many religious leaders agreed that they had much to lose if the old system was dismantled. They were willing to go along with change only if it was not fundamental. Selim's reforms cannot really be called radical, but they did threaten the power base of the conservatives. Without the Janissary-led military, the conservatives would have no way to enforce their views, and it was obvious that the new army meant the eventual demise of the Janissaries. They might be forced into new, modernized units or replaced entirely. If that happened, the power base of conservatism would be destroyed. When this became apparent the conservatives, led by the Janissaries, revolted in 1807. They demanded that the new army be disbanded and reforming members of the government be eliminated.

Selim III had two options. First, he could escape to the barracks of the new army and call upon his supporters in the provinces to assist him against the rebels. As central authority had waned, local leaders, the *ayan*s, had taken effective control of much of the territory of the Ottoman Empire, as seen above. Many of the *ayan*s of the Balkans, who were situated on the front lines against the Russians and Austrians, supported Selim's reforms. Although others were against any assertion of central government control, many governors and independent local leaders would have come to his aid. Second, Selim could give in to the rebels' demands, hoping to save his own position. He took the latter course. His reforming Grand Vezir was given over to a mob to be torn apart. The *Nizam-i Cedid* was disbanded.

The events that followed the destruction of the new army showed that there were those who favoured reform, but that the power of conservatism was great. On the dissolution of the *Nizam-i Cedid* many of the reformers and new soldiers escaped to the protection of local lords in the Balkans. In particular, the *ayan* lord of Rusçuk, Bayraktar Mustafa Paşa, supported them, organizing a committee of *ayan*s who opposed the new Ottoman government. Some of these lords had previously opposed Selim, and their actions may have indicated opposition to whoever was in power in Istanbul and thus in a position to curtail their autonomy. Nevertheless, they saved many reformers.

Selim himself survived the coup d'état, but was deposed and replaced by his cousin Mustafa IV. However, led by Bayraktar Mustafa, the Balkan lords marched on Istanbul in 1808 to reinstate Selim. Mustafa, fearing his own death, attempted to kill the only other members of the Ottoman house who might become sultans, Selim and Mustafa's brother, Mahmud, so that he would perforce remain as sultan. Mahmud escaped; Selim did not.

When the lords' army entered Istanbul it was Mustafa's turn to die. Mahmud was named sultan, with actual power in the hands of the lords. However, most of the *ayans*' force returned to their lands after their victory, leaving Istanbul lightly garrisoned. Another revolt overthrew their rule. Bayraktar Mustafa was killed, and the opponents of reform were once again in power. Sultan Mahmud II was allowed to live, as the only remaining member of the royal family, but the forces of conservatism were in control.

The lesson of the reign of Selim III was the necessity of military power standing behind a reforming sultan and the need of a sultan with strong resolution. Selim's reforms had not changed the old order. Selim had tried to create a parallel army that at least at first would coexist with the Janissaries. This did not work, because it left the conservatives with a military force that could be used against the reformers. Moreover, Selim lacked the determination, or perhaps lacked the personal courage, to stand up to the power of the conservatives. Any future successful reformer of the Empire could not repeat his mistakes.

Sultan Mahmud II

Mahmud II was a man of incredible patience. He spent the next eighteen years after the conservative triumph in making friends. Submerging his true feelings on reform and acting like a conservative sultan, he gradually filled government posts with those who had personal loyalty to him. Many potential supporters received financial preferment from the sultan. Religious leaders, in particular, were favoured with the sultan's largesse. Schools and mosques were built and conservative religious principles upheld. Many who might have been Mahmud's natural enemies were thus made into his supporters, and Mahmud developed a reputation as a pious sultan. The Janissaries, on the other hand, spent those years making enemies. In wars against the Russians and Greek rebels they proved to be poor fighters, sometimes refusing to fight at all. They extorted money from the government and the people of Istanbul and the provincial towns. Janissaries even burnt houses in Istanbul to indicate their displeasure at being asked to fight the Russians, showing their power to inflict damage if they were opposed. All this drove many who would have supported them to oppose them. Mahmud meanwhile cemented his authority in the provinces, using politics, trickery, occasional force, and a policy of divide and conquer to end much of the power of the local lords. Even conservatives could see that he was an effective ruler.

Mahmud II finally moved against conservatism in 1826. Rather than attempt to publicly create a new army at first – Selim's mistake – Mahmud had slowly built up and modernized certain traditional corps of the Ottoman army, particularly the artillery and units that rivalled and hated the Janissaries. Now he announced that the Janissaries would have to reform. A modernized military unit would be formed from a select group of the best Janissaries. Anyone could see that the traditional Janissary system was threatened. On June 14 the Janissaries revolted.

Mahmud stood firm. Rather than give in to the Janissary demands, he called upon reliable military corps and upon the people of Istanbul, who proved to be fed up with the Janissary excesses. Mobs appeared in the streets, but they were loyal to the sultan. The Janissaries, who had expected a repeat of Selim III's collapse, were stunned. They retreated to their barracks. There they were surrounded and attacked by Mahmud's loyal artillerymen, their barracks set aflame, and the Janissaries inside killed. Similar scenes were enacted in the provinces. Many Janissaries died; most conveniently forgot that they had ever been Janissaries and became regular subjects of the sultan.

The fall of the Janissaries was the essential beginning of radical reform of the Empire. Conservative forces could still call upon much popular support, conservative bureaucrats and officials could still block reforms, but the enemies of reform no longer had the military power to enforce their demands. After 1826 the army became the tool of reforming sultans and vezirs. By the next century it was to become a primary agent of westernizing reform.

The Reforms of Mahmud II

Compared to later reforms, the reforms of Mahmud II appear to be small stuff. He began publishing the first newspaper in the Empire, but it had a small circulation, primarily among officials. New secondary schools, intended to train officers and officials, were founded, but most schooling, and all primary schooling of Muslims, was still in the hands of the religious establishment. Primary school training more closely resembled medieval schooling than the European standard of the time. Courts were still traditional religious courts. The economy was still very weak. New-style factories did not appear. Too many traditionalists stood in the way of reform and Mahmud and his reformers had no real idea of modern economy, industry, or politics. Nevertheless, Mahmud was a great reformer.

Mahmud's place as a reformer was established by the changes he made in the government infrastructure. The changes he made in the military and government administration were the base of later reforms.

The sultan began to organize the government along European lines, with ministries and ministers that had set duties and set areas of government that they controlled. Regular salaries were paid to bureaucrats. The old system, which had existed in the Middle East for millennia, was based on payment for services rendered. Government officials were often paid a fee (called *bahşiş*) by those who had used their services. Payment of set salaries was obviously much less open to corruption. Previously the system of making laws had been loose, with all laws theoretically coming from the sultan and his divan. Now legislative bodies were appointed. Something resembling a cabinet was created, formed from the ministers and high officials who represented their departments, rather than, as in the old divan, only being an advisory board that had small connection with the daily workings of government. The key word of the administrative reforms was centralization. Provincial armies were put under orders from Istanbul, not from the provincial governors. A new postal system kept Istanbul informed on provincial affairs. In order to centralize taxation and military conscription, new registers of the population were begun. Not all the reforms functioned effectively or were fully implemented, but the work had started.

Military reforms were essential. With the death of the Janissary Corps the Ottoman military was left without a core. There were still a great number of soldiers in units that had not been disbanded and in provincial garrisons, but these were not trained in modern warfare. They were divided into small 'armies', without a central army that would be the mainstay of defence. An army had to be built quickly. It was constructed more or less along European lines of authority, into both a standing army and a reserve. Unlike the old Ottoman system, authority in the new army passed down in a pyramidical structure of command. The sultan's government drafted conscripts and accepted volunteers into the new force, training them in European tactics and giving them European-style weapons whenever possible. European advisers, of whom the Prussians were best, began to assist in training. However, transforming an entire military system was slow and expensive work. By some counts the armed forces required more than half of the government's yearly expenditure. Even then, it would take years of training and much more expenditure before the army reached a high level of expertise.

The predicament was that the Ottoman army had little time for development. As will be seen in the next two chapters, the Ottoman Empire was being assaulted from Europe just as it was attempting reform. The Russians attacked the Empire in 1828, long before the new army was even partly trained or organized. European intervention defeated Ottoman forces in the war for Greek independence in 1828. The worst defeats came at the hands of an Ottoman vassal, Muhammad Ali, the Ottoman governor of Egypt. (He is also known by the Turkish form of his name, which he probably used himself, Mehmet Ali.) Like many previous leaders of Egypt, Muhammad Ali was virtually independent. With the aid of France, he had modernized his armed forces before the Ottomans. In 1831 and again in 1839, the Egyptian army advanced far into Anatolia. Only European intervention saved the Empire from him, because the European powers had no wish to see what they viewed as a stronger presence in control of the Ottoman Empire. From 1831 to 1840 Muhammad Ali controlled many of the Ottoman Arab provinces, theoretically as governor, actually as ruler, and was only dislodged by European action. The wars dealt a double blow to the Ottoman Empire. Provinces and their tax revenues, much needed for reforms, were lost and the new army was decimated in battle before it could be trained. Due to these catastrophes and to the drag of traditionalism the new army was never fully developed during Mahmud's reign. Nevertheless, radical change had begun and would continue until a more respectable force could emerge under later sultans.

The new bureaucrats

One of the most intractable problems for any government reformers is the question of manpower. Who will supervise and carry out reforms? In any system of government it is one thing for the central government to issue an order and quite another for lower officials to carry it out. Bureaucrats can defeat reform through ignorance; they can simply not know how to make change. They can also work very slowly, 'lose' orders, 'forget' rules, conspire to defeat the spirit of the law while carrying out the letter of the law, and obstruct change in all the other ways known to bureaucrats. For the Ottomans, this was an immense dilemma. From the highest to the lowest levels of government, officials had no idea what reform meant. They had all been trained in the old system and knew virtually nothing of European ways. Many were still imbued with the idea of Ottoman cultural superiority. Moreover, Europeans, who were often properly viewed as enemies of the Ottoman state and way of life, were disliked. It was very hard to emulate those who were both despised and feared. Learning from one's enemies is always wise, as the reformers knew, but before the Ottomans could learn they had to overcome their prejudices.

Mahmud once again took the first steps to change. He began with language. Ignorance of European languages was the main factor that held back Ottoman learning of new ways. Ottoman bureaucrats were not poor at languages; they customarily had a command of Arabic and Persian as well as of the intricacies of Ottoman Turkish, but those were not the languages they needed to know. Mahmud switched the linguistic orientation of the government. Government offices were each instructed to open training schools in European languages, especially French. The most successful of these was the Translation Office (*Tercüme Odası*) of the Foreign Ministry, established in 1833. That office not only produced translators, but served as a training school for bureaucrats who developed a Western orientation. Language became a door opening onto European culture for Ottoman bureaucrats and high officials, and graduates of the Translation Office soon became the leading executives of the state.

In general, Mahmud's changes in the bureaucracy only took hold slowly. Younger bureaucrats were trained in new ways, but older bureaucrats stood above them and often stymied change. Gradually the younger men took charge. They were led by reformers, often trained in the Translation Office. The process was slow.

Pay close attention

The age of the Tanzimat

Mahmud II died in 1839 and was succeeded by his son, Abdülmecid I. Soon after his accession to the throne, Abdülmecid was convinced by the sorry military state of the Empire to support the reformers who had risen under Mahmud II. He relied on the leader of the reform faction of the bureaucracy, Mustafa Reşit Paşa.

Mustafa Reşit Paşa had begun his career under the old Ottoman system. His first advancement in the Ottoman civil service came as a result of family connections, but he soon became part of the new system. He was nevertheless the prototype of a new type of Ottoman bureaucrat because he knew what westernization entailed from personal experience. While in his twenties he had seen Muhammad Ali's reforms in Cairo. In his thirties he travelled widely in Europe, serving as Ottoman ambassador in both Paris and London. He returned to Istanbul to become foreign minister to Mahmud II. He was thus a combination of the old and the new – a politician who understood the politics of the traditional Ottoman bureaucracy and a reformer dedicated to change – both an Ottoman and a westernizer.

Throughout his service to the government, Mustafa Reşit developed a circle of protégés who shared his vision of reform. Collectively, these have been known as the 'Men of the Tanzimat' (in Turkish, *Tanzimatçılar*, literally 'those who put things in order'). Mustafa Reşit's two principle aides and colleagues, Ali and Fuat, were representative of the reformers. They at first worked under Mustafa Reşit, then alongside him, finally succeeding him as leaders of reform when he died in 1858. Their lives were typical of those of the Men of the Tanzimat. Both had begun their schooling in the traditional Islamic school, the *medrese*. Both had learned French as their introduction to the ways of Europe, Ali in the Translation Office, Fuat in the imperial medical school, and had served in Ottoman embassies in Europe. They had risen through the Ottoman bureaucracy by the usual means, attaching themselves to powerful men who brought them along as they advanced. Like Mustafa Reşit, they were men of both the old and the new worlds, as were the other Men of the Tanzimat. On the one hand, they were traditional Ottomans who had risen through Ottoman methods, on the other hand, they were reformers who knew European ways and planned to emulate them. This made them, not schizophrenic, but surely committed to retaining as much of the traditional ways as possible while they did what had to be done to reform the Empire.

The mentality of the Tanzimat reformers presented them with unique problems. They saw and respected the European way, but they also respected their own traditions. They had no wish to turn the Ottoman Empire into a pale reflection of Western Europe. Like all the reformers before them, they wanted an improved and successful Ottoman Empire, with Ottoman customs, Ottoman religious practices, and Ottoman government. This meant that truly radical reform was difficult, if not impossible. In theory, a government and economic system modelled on Britain or France might have been a success, but it would never have worked in reality. Neither the reformers nor the people of the Empire wanted to be English, American, or French. However, with each reform the state went further from its traditions.

Tanzimat reforms

Soon after taking power, on November 3, 1839, Abdülmecid proclaimed his reformist intentions in a public declaration, the *Hatt-ı Hümayun* of Gülhane, before assembled members of the government and foreign ambassadors:

> ... Full of confidence, therefore, in the help of the Most High, and certain of the support of our Prophet, we deem it right to seek by new institutions to give to the provinces composing the Ottoman Empire the benefit of a good administration.

> These institutions must be principally carried out under three heads, which are:

1. The guarantees ensuring to our subjects perfect security for life, honour, and fortune.
2. A regular system of assessing and levying taxes.
3. An equally regular system for the levying of troops and the duration of their service.[1]

The imperial order went on to describe necessary changes. In the financial sphere, taxes would be regularized so that inequities were abolished. Tax farms would be abolished, because they had become the property of men of 'the most violent and avaricious passions'. Justice was to be guaranteed to individuals through a new penal code, and personal property was declared to be inviolate. Bribery and inefficient bureaucrats were to be restricted by higher salaries and new bureaucratic codes. Military conscription was to be applied equally to Muslims who were eligible to serve and a military council created to organize the armed services. A judicial council was to meet with other government officials 'in order to frame laws regulating the security of life and fortune and the assessment of taxes'.

It was a very clever document, proclaiming that the changes the sultan described were in fact a return to old Ottoman ways. This was not strictly true, but presenting reform as tradition was effective public relations. The true significance was that for the first time, a sultan had declared publicly that reform was needed and would be implemented. Subjects were declared to be possessors of rights, not only tax-payers. Change was to be the order of the government. The sad part of the document was the incredibly naive belief that 'the result, which by the help of God we hope to attain, can be obtained within a few years'. Reform was to prove to be considerably more difficult than that.

The essence of the Tanzimat reforms was a changed idea of the state. The traditional Ottoman state provided protection from foreign powers, fostered religion, and kept civil order. Schools, welfare, commercial enterprise, and other social activities were left to individuals or to the *millets*. Unlike the old, the new government was to be involved in many areas of human life. It adopted the Western philosophy that a state was to do for its people what the people wanted or needed and could not do for themselves. This brought the government into areas where no Ottoman government had ever entered before. If the people needed jobs, the state would help the economy. If they needed better justice, the state would reorder the justice system, previously left to religious judges. If the people needed roads, bridges, or water pipelines, the state would build them, not leave their construction to the vagaries of private charity. The new system was a major redefinition of what a state should be.

---

[1] quoted in J.C. Hurewitz, *Diplomacy in the Near and Middle East*, vol. 1, Princeton, p. 114.

The greatest success of the reformers was in government administration. The government was slowly reorganized along European lines. Administration was divided into ministries, including a Foreign Ministry, an Interior Ministry, a Finance Ministry, and others. This was essential. The older system had assumed that trained bureaucrats (scribes) would be able to deal with whatever management the state required. However, generalists, trained in the old scribal system, could never understand the various specific needs of different parts of modern government. To understand, one need only imagine how well a scribe would function first as an accountant, then as a superintendent of schools, then as a bureaucrat in the police department, then as an inspector of weights and measures, then as a diplomat. Efficiency demanded that a bureaucrat be trained and develop his skills in one ministry, mastering one line of work. When such a bureaucrat advised the government there would be at least some assurance that he knew what he was talking about.

Administrative change also reached to the highest levels of government. A Council of Ministers met to advise the sultan and approve the actions of the ministries and lower organs of government. Here the system diverged from European forms, with accompanying difficulties. Each of the ministers and other officials, such as the head of the army or the head of the Islamic establishment (*Şeyhülislam*), was largely his own boss. In a parliamentary system such as that of Britain all the ministers are members of the ruling party or coalition parties. They are responsible to the Prime Minister and to the discipline of the Party. Each of the Ottoman officials was responsible only to the sultan. There were no western-style political parties, only 'political parties' tied to individuals, as described above. Therefore, the Grand Vezir had to 'play politics' constantly. Often a conservative opponent of reform might head one or more ministries, doing what he could to stand in the way of reform. A reforming Grand Vezir would have to compromise with him, not simply give orders. The sultan, too, had to placate political factions. All this slowed the pace of reform, but the reformers had little choice. Attempting to change the entire system overnight would have led to violent conservative reaction and, most probably, an end to reform.

It is the nature of government reform that its results often are only seen many years after the reforms are begun. The classic examples of this in the Ottoman Empire were reforms in transport and communications. When Mahmud II took office Ottoman communications were essentially as they had been in the time of Süleyman, perhaps worse, because the bandits who preyed on merchants and messengers had been better kept in check in Süleyman's time. The Tanzimat began to build modern roads and telegraph lines. Railways were slowly constructed. A postal system was created. Although the work took decades and the Ottomans were forced to depend on Europeans whose goals were seldom the same as those of the government, especially for the development of railways, the rewards were still substantial.

Not only were new markets opened up for merchants, but eventually the ability of the central authorities to govern was greatly improved. Orders sent by telegraph were received almost immediately by provincial governors. Troops sent by rail or steam ship could nip revolts in the bud, before they spread.

Education was an area in which reform advanced successfully, although slowly. The traditional Muslim educational system was not suited to the modern world. The problem was not that the schools were religious. The problem lay in what the Islamic schools did not teach – technical subjects such as trigonometry, calculus, biology, chemistry, and foreign languages. While no reformer had the power, and perhaps not even the desire, to close the Islamic schools, the reformers realized that trained manpower was the basis of modernization. New schools were needed.

Under Mahmud II, technical schools had been opened. These schools were usually attached to government departments, but taught basic subjects such as mathematics, science, and language. The first real Ottoman medical school, for example, was a military school, as was the first engineering school. Middle schools (*Rüşdiye*) were opened for young boys who had passed from the traditional Muslim elementary schools. The middle schools trained boys in technical subjects so that they would be ready to study in more advanced technical schools and become engineers and other professionals. Teachers came from newly created teacher training schools. Not until the end of the Tanzimat period, however, had sizeable numbers of students passed through the schools. Schools were costly and teachers were scarce. As was the case with all reform, it took time for the system to develop: a few teachers were trained, who in turn taught students, who in turn became teachers, who in turn taught more students... . Developing a large educated class took many decades. By 1867, less than 3 per cent of the population was enrolled in the new schools, and 90 per cent of these were in elementary schools, slowly working their way up the new educational ladder.

The effect of the schools was to create an educated elite. There were too few schools for a general system of modern education. The greatest success was in the training of the military and the bureaucracy. It was these men who led reform.

The greatest failure of the reformers was in the area of economics. The Men of the Tanzimat were never able to maximize government revenues or institute authentic financial reforms. Indeed, they were never able even to collect the taxes due under the old system. The power of the central government was developing, but it was still not enough to ensure that everyone paid their taxes. The system of tax-farming was known to be inefficient and wasteful. Assigning trained bureaucrats to collect taxes in the provinces was far better. However, trained bureaucrats were not available in sufficient numbers. Therefore tax-farms were only slowly abolished.

Before agricultural taxes were properly assessed and collected an accurate knowledge of land holdings and agricultural production was essential. In 1858 a land registration law was passed. It took so many years to collect the information and register the land that the work was still not done by World War I. Thus even when the Ottomans knew what had to be done they did not have the resources to do it.

Often the Ottomans did not know what had to be done. Much of this was due to the simple fact that the leaders of the bureaucracy did not understood economics and trade. Part of the problem was cultural: Ottoman officials were trained to administer a system of collecting taxes and spending them. They did not come from merchant families and had no desire for themselves or their children to become businessmen. Large-scale trade in the Empire was mainly in the hands of non-Muslim minority groups, with whom the Europeans preferred to trade. Muslim merchants existed, especially in the provinces, but they were not of the group that became government officials. Few in the Ottoman Empire could have understood the economic systems of world trade. Where would they have learned? It took many years and many bitter experiences before the Ottomans would begin to understand the world market.

Even had the Ottomans been able to collect all the taxes and run the government with absolute efficiency, this would probably not have been enough to finance economic reform. The money was needed elsewhere. The Ottoman Empire was under constant threat of attack, especially from Russia. The short-term needs of defence overrode the long-term needs of economic development. It would have done little good to create a new economy for the benefit of invaders who would come in and seize it all. Often that was exactly what happened. The money spent to develop Ottoman Bulgaria, for example, was a total loss, because Russian armies took Bulgaria.

As with education, in economic matters the Ottomans were forced to try to do everything at once. Industrial development depended on trained manpower, modern machines, a commercial network, adequate financing, a credit system, good transport, etc. It did little good to build a factory unless modern machines could be imported. Trained workers were needed to run the machines. The goods from the factory would rot if there were not roads and railways to deliver them to consumers or merchants to sell them. Finally, the goods had to appeal to the consumers; they had to be good value. All this was too much for a poor country to achieve.

The capitulations were a major impediment to Ottoman economic reform. Without the factories, trained manpower, and commercial systems of the Europeans the Ottomans could not compete. Europeans could bring cheaper, better goods to the Empire than the Ottoman manufacturers could produce. In many other countries, a system of protective tariffs had been put in place to protect budding industries. Large customs duties on imports made them more expensive and local goods more competitive. Local factories were able to grow. But the capitulations made a protective tariff an impossibility for the Ottomans. The European states forced a system of low tariffs on the Ottomans. Under terms of treaties sometimes signed centuries before, nineteenth-century Ottomans were not in control of taxes on imports into their country. European navies and politics enforced the capitulations. If the Ottomans unilaterally ended the capitulations, they would risk major war. In addition, the Ottomans depended on the good will of Great Britain to hold off Russian plans to dismember their empire. How could the Ottomans stand against the British, the main economic beneficiaries of the capitulations, when they needed British help for their survival?

Sultan Abdülaziz

Mustafa Reşit's reforms had been carried out and expanded by Ali and Fuat Paşas, his successors. Holding office as Grand Vezir and Foreign Minister at various times, the two had cemented power in their own hands. However, when Fuat Paşa died in 1869 and Ali Paşa in 1871 they were not succeeded by powerful reformers. Ali Paşa, in particular, had been too authoritarian a leader to allow any strong contenders for his power, and thus there was no one who could succeed to it. Instead, sultan Abdülaziz (1861–76) was able to assert his own authority. The Men of the Tanzimat, no democrats, had kept power at the centre of government. Under them, centralized power was a tool of the bureaucracy, but it could equally be the tool of a sultan. By changing Grand Vezirs often and placing his own supporters in key posts, Abdülaziz took charge.

Abdülaziz did not deliberately frustrate reform. His government made changes in central and provincial governing systems and other minor reforms. But Abdülaziz did slow the pace of reform. This was not necessarily an error; a breathing space to assimilate changes already made was not necessarily a bad thing. His real problem was financial. The Men of the Tanzimat had never been great economists, as described above. After Ali's death in 1871, the economic problems that had been looming for years finally threatened to destroy the state. Abdülaziz proved unable to take the decisive steps that were necessary to avert bankruptcy.

The predicament was debt. Since the Crimean War, when the first foreign loans had been contracted to finance the war, the Ottoman Empire had borrowed from European bankers. Loans were needed to finance the government, largely because so much was needed to pay for military defence, leaving too small a sum to finance reform. The assumption was that money could be borrowed to pay for development and that new government income would come in because of the reforms. The new income would pay off the debts. It did not work that way in reality. More and more was borrowed and not repaid. Abdülaziz kept spending money, including lavish personal expenditures on palaces and the like. When austerity was needed he continued to spend.

Faced with impending disaster, the Ottoman bureaucracy united to act in their own interest and the interest of the Empire. They hesitantly began to take the next step in reform, constitutional rule and the beginnings of democracy.

The Ottoman constitution

Reading European political tracts and associating with Europeans affected a new generation of Ottoman political thinkers. Usually trained in the Ottoman bureaucratic schools, they developed a respect for European political institutions, not just the desire to use Western technology and administrative techniques. They were convinced that the Ottoman Empire would never be truly modernized until it had adopted a democratic government and a constitution. Gathering secretly in Istanbul, the reformers joined in the Young Ottoman Society in 1865. At first in Istanbul, then in exile in Europe, these reformers, called the Young Ottomans, propagandized against the governments of Ali Paşa then, when Ali died in 1871, against the increasingly autocratic rule of sultan Abdülaziz. Their weapon was the newspaper. When their writings were censored in Istanbul they sent newspapers printed in Europe into the Ottoman Empire through independent European post offices not under Ottoman control. Throughout the reign of Abdülaziz their influence increased. Their calls for a change in the system of rule had a ready audience in the bureaucrats and military officers who could see the disaster that the economic follies of Abdülaziz was producing.

Lest it be thought that the Young Ottomans were solely idealists: the typical Young Ottoman was a son of a fairly highly placed family and had attended the new secular schools. Many, if not most, had been frustrated in attempts to advance to the highest government circles, so their opposition may have been more than philosophical. In European exile, they were mainly supported by personal or family money, and their parties and newspapers received funds from an Egyptian prince, Mustafa Fazıl, who acted partly from conviction, partly from a desire to discreetly blackmail the Ottoman government to make him next in line to be khedive (independent governor) of Egypt or grant him similar powers. Nevertheless, the writings of the Young Ottomans had great effect on those who wished change. They appealed especially to two groups, by no means always the same supporters – those who wanted faster, more liberal reforms and those who wanted a reformed Islam to take a part in government denied Islam by the Tanzimat.

The Young Ottoman reformers cannot be considered to have been in touch with the spirit of the common man in the Empire. Like the Men of the Tanzimat, they advocated European ways and were willing to impose them from the top. Unlike the Men of the Tanzimat, they believed some form of democracy was necessary if the Empire was to advance. Their ideas were often utopian in one area – nationalism. They believed that if the diverse ethnic groups of the Ottoman Empire were just allowed to vote for representatives they would submerge their nationalistic feelings and come together in a new Ottoman nationality, forgetting the *millet* system and the new nationalist ideas imported from Europe. As later events were to prove, this was wishful thinking at its worst. Many of them also believed that Islam was essentially democratic and fitted easily into a constitutional system. While this may have been true in theory, conservative Muslims did not agree with the analysis.

The difficulty with the Young Ottoman thought was its neglect of the real feeling of the people of the Empire. European nationalism was a popular phenomenon – the *people* of France and England felt loyalty, even love, for their motherland. Loyalty in the Ottoman Empire was to the Ottoman dynasty or, even more, to one's religion and local region. 'Ottoman nationality' would have to be imposed from the top, unless the people saw the need of such feeling. The reformers had no plan for instilling their brand of nationalism in the people. This exemplifies the fact that they were democrats in theory, but not necessarily men who understood the people for whom they avowedly spoke.

The Young Ottomans were political philosophers, not practical men of affairs. Many of them might wish for revolutionary change, but they were utterly incapable of bringing it about. For action, those who wanted change had to look to those who knew the uses of power. Their ideas were ultimately carried out by high-level bureaucrats, under the leadership of Midhat Paşa.

Ahmed Şefik Midhat Paşa was a Tanzimat bureaucrat who had served with distinction as a governor in Bulgaria and Iraq (governor of Niş in 1861–64, of the Danube province in 1864–68, and of the province of Baghdad in 1869–72), as well as in positions in Istanbul. His reforms in the provinces had made him an exemplar of Tanzimat reformers. He served briefly as Grand Vezir in 1872, was ousted by political enemies, but remained at the centre of the Ottoman government in other ministerial positions. Somewhere in their careers, Midhat and other high officials had been converted to the idea of constitutional government. The conversion was surely helped by what could only be viewed as the sad state of the Empire under Abdülaziz. After Ali died the sultan had named a number of Grand Vezirs in quick succession, intending to keep the bureaucracy off balance and retain power for himself. Such a policy also kept work from getting done. Affairs of state were taking a dangerous turn, with revolts looming in Bosnia, Crete, and Bulgaria and Great Power intervention in the affairs of the Empire increasing. Worst of all, the Empire was bankrupt. Poor government meant inefficient tax collection. The deficit was made up by borrowing at high rates of interest. One-third of government income was going to pay off debts. Salaries of soldiers and bureaucrats were perpetually in arrears. Therefore, there was good reason for Midhat and his companions to believe that a change in the system was needed. A self-serving motive for the bureaucrats' constitutionalism must also be considered: Abdülaziz was draining power from the bureaucracy and putting it into his own hands; perhaps a constitutional government might reverse the trend.

Midhat was serving as Minister Without Portfolio when Abdülaziz's financial and political mistakes finally drove the bureaucrats to depose him (1875). He was replaced by a son of Abdülmecid, who reigned briefly as Murat V. However, Murat, an alcoholic and a paranoid, proved to be mentally unstable. After a brief reign, in 1876 he was deposed in favour of his brother, Abdülhamit II. Midhat and his supporters took advantage of a confused political state to press for a constitutional government. The Young Ottomans returned home from European exile to put their ideas into practice. They joined their ideas with the practical abilities of Midhat and his supporters to produce a constitution. Midhat was chosen Grand Vezir on December 19, 1876 and the first Ottoman constitution promulgated on December 23.

The constitution and first parliament

The Ottoman constitution had the trappings of European representative government. It called for a two-chamber parliament, an independent judiciary, a system of cabinet ministers overseeing the bureaucracy, freedom of religion, and taxes graduated by income of the tax-payer. Subjects were granted considerable personal freedoms. However, all was not as it seemed.

Midhat had been forced to compromise with conservatives and with the sultan to pass the constitution. The rights allowed the sultan in the document were considerable: he could declare war, make treaties, coin money, and make binding laws by decree – all without any parliamentary approval. In fact, all laws passed by parliament had to be acceptable to him or he could simply not publish them and they would not take effect. Unlike, for example, the British parliamentary system, ministers of state were chosen by the sultan, not the parliament, and were responsible to him. He was under no obligation to choose the Grand Vezir (Prime Minister) from the largest party in parliament. Finally, the sultan could declare a state of emergency, dissolve parliament, and only recall it when he wished. The actual democratic principles of the constitution were more than a little flawed. The Muslims of the Empire might also have felt that democracy was not served by the division of the vote, which was done by religions.

Largely because Europeans had to be placated, Christian subjects were given more electoral power than their numbers merited. Christians were allowed 44 deputies, Muslims 71, not in any way representing the true proportions in the population. A Christian male's vote was worth up to twice as much as a Muslim male's vote. As in Europe and America at the time, women were not allowed to vote.

The reign of Abdülhamit II

It is probably accurate to say that few of the subjects of the Ottoman sultan knew or cared about democracy. Like most members of economically underdeveloped societies, they cared first about ensuring full stomachs for themselves and their families, then about the values that were closest to them, such as religion and the culture bequeathed to them by their ancestors. For them to develop an interest in democracy they would first have to know what it was, then be convinced that it could bring benefits to them. The vast majority of the Ottoman people had no concept of democracy. There had never been a democracy in the Middle East, and it must have been difficult, even for those who favoured democracy in theory, to abandon the old ways for an untried new path.

The democracy of the Ottoman constitution was a thing of intellectuals, bureaucrats, and politicians. It had not taken root among the people of the Empire, most of whom were agricultural workers far removed from the capital and parliament in both distance and understanding. Had they known the details of the constitution, they might actually have resisted it. It made little provision for problems of taxation and agriculture that were important to them.

Abdülhamit was not the sort to give credence to the abstract benefits of democracy, especially when democracy threatened his own power. The constitution left much power in the sultan's hands, but it left the parliament the right to complain. In particular, and to the sultan's consternation, members of parliament complained of the sultan's handling of the 1877–78 war with Russia (see below). The war was indeed a disaster, with massive Muslim civilian and military mortality and whole regions lost to the Empire. As the parliament's complaints increased, the sultan may have seen danger when a state spoke internationally with many voices and was internally divided while it was beset by enemies. Or he may have seen the complaints as the first step toward increased parliamentary powers or perhaps parliamentary control of the military. Whatever his reasoning, Abdülhamit decided that the parliament was not working as he wished, so he simply ended it. Under the constitution the sultan had extensive emergency powers. He made use of his powers to dissolve the parliament on February 14,

1878. There was protest from reformers and the intellectuals who had been the Young Ottomans, but no reaction from the people as a whole. The constitution had not been theirs. Even the reformist bureaucrats who might have disputed the sultan's action were more occupied with the loss in the Russian war of 1877–78 than with democratic issues. The existence of the Empire was at stake in 1878. In times of grave danger, humans often concern themselves with survival and rally behind authority. So it was in the Ottoman Empire. Abdülhamit successfully advanced his own authority at a time of national disaster. He then proceeded to rule according to the traditional Ottoman ideal of government – a powerful sultan in absolute control.

Government, diplomacy, and reform

In many ways Abdülhamit's government followed in the paths of the Tanzimat reformers. He was a true heir of the Tanzimat. The bureaucrats and sultans who had led past reforms were reformers, but not democrats. They had created a government structure that centralized control in Istanbul, and that control could as easily be exercised by a sultan as by a bureaucracy. The Men of the Tanzimat had been concerned with the economic, military, and administrative reorganization of the Empire, as was Abdülhamit II. Like them, he built roads and railways, improved and increased the number of schools, and centralized the administration of the Empire. Like them he reformed the government: new government ministries, such as the ministries of police and of post and telegraph, were created. The population registration system was made more complete. A new accounting council oversaw expenditures. For the provinces, Abdülhamit promulgated centralizing regulations for governors and civil servants, while improvements in communications allowed the sultan to watch civil servants ever more closely. The sultan was fulfilling the intentions of the Tanzimat – improving the scope and efficiency of the government and centralizing power in Istanbul. Thus, in its most basic interests, Abdülhamit's rule can be considered an extension of the Tanzimat.

International affairs in Abdülhamit's reign can be summarized easily – he held off disaster for thirty years. Soon after Abdülhamit II took the throne the Empire was defeated in the Russo–Turkish War of 1877–78. Russia had advanced to easy striking distance of Istanbul when it dictated terms. The Ottomans were forced to accept. Under the terms of the treaty of San Stephano (March 3, 1878), Russia seized a large section of northeastern Anatolia (the Kars, Ardahan, and Batum districts) and Bessarabia. A Great Bulgaria was to be created, stretching from the Black Sea to Albania and from the Danube to the Aegean. Russia expected that the new state would be dependent on Russia and would open a path for Russian control of the Balkans. It was not to be. Britain and Austria, with the support of Bismarck's Germany, opposed the treaty. A European congress called by

Bismarck at Berlin forced the Russians to accept less. Bulgaria was reduced to a smaller tributary kingdom along the Danube. Southern Bulgaria was made a largely autonomous province of the Ottoman Empire, under the name Eastern Rumelia. The Ottomans retained the central and southern Balkans (Macedonia) and Albania. Austria took Bosnia, nominally governing it as an autonomous part of the Ottoman Empire. In the East, Russian conquests were slightly limited. In return for Britain's support in the Congress of Berlin, the Ottomans were forced to accept British occupation of the island of Cyprus, making the British 'friends' of the Ottomans major beneficiaries of the congress. The treaty of Berlin was signed on July 13, 1878.

Abdülhamit was forced to accept the loss of Cyprus, northeast Anatolia, and much of Ottoman Europe, integral parts of the Empire, early in his reign. The other losses of territory during his reign were losses in name only, although they caused great indignation in the Empire: the French occupied Tunisia in 1881 and the British occupied Egypt in 1882. An Eastern Rumelian revolt in 1885 resulted in unification with Bulgaria in 1886. These countries had only nominally been part of the Ottoman Empire, so the real Ottoman loss was minor, although public opinion in the Empire was inflamed by the European imperialism. In the only war of his reign, Abdülhamit's forces defeated Greek invaders on the Ottoman southern Macedonian border in 1899, but the European powers intervened and the Ottomans gained nothing.

It might be thought that the record of Abdülhamit's losses after the Congress of Berlin, which cannot reasonably be blamed on him, were surely blows to imperial prestige, even if they were not losses of territories that were actually ruled by the Ottomans. But the losses must be compared to the realities of Ottoman power – or lack of it. The Ottomans could not defeat any of the European powers, and Abdülhamit knew it. He managed to forestall disastrous war. Potential occasions of war were not lacking: Armenian rebellions in the 1890s could easily have led to intervention by Russia or even Britain. When Austria seized Bosnia-Herzegovina and the Bulgarians took Eastern Rumelia, strong voices calling for war had to be resisted. The sultan's conservatism in foreign affairs and the skill of his diplomats contributed to Ottoman survival at those times. They were not the only, or even the main factor that kept the empire from disaster. The balance of power and the Europeans' fear of each other were more responsible. Nevertheless, Abdülhamit II must be accounted successful in international affairs. Few who saw the defeat of the Ottomans in 1878 could have expected that the empire would survive for decades thereafter.

The economy

Abdülhamit was a builder-sultan, but not only in the old way of building great palaces and mosques. His construction was of railways and telegraph lines. Railway track in the Empire increased more than threefold during his reign, improved roads almost sixfold. Most areas of government-sponsored enterprises thrived – mining, agricultural exports, etc. Local industry developed, as well, although European manufactures and the effect of the capitulations slowed growth considerably. In short, when Abdülhamit II left the sultanate the physical state of the Ottoman Empire was much better than when he took the throne.

In the area of finance Abdülhamit II proved to be much more able than his predecessors, although given their failings this was perhaps not remarkable. The excessive borrowing of his predecessors and the need to pay war reparations to Russia had nearly brought the Empire to financial ruin. Abdülhamit's government put the case to European banks and governments that if the Empire became bankrupt, no one would benefit. Rescheduling of the debt was needed. The Europeans would not accept rescheduling unless they were guaranteed steady repayment. Between them, the sultan, the European governments, and the bankers struck a deal. In 1881, Abdülhamit promulgated the Decree of Muharrem (the Muslim month in which it was declared).

Ottoman borrowing and the Public Debt Administration

Abdülhamit II had little choice but to make a deal with the European financiers and governments who held the Empire's debts. The alternative would probably have been much more onerous European control of the Ottoman Empire. That is what happened in Egypt: the khedive of Egypt, having defaulted on his loans, was forced to accept virtual European control of his government in 1876, with European officials in charge of finance and public works ministries. The khedive, Ismail, was himself forced by England and France to abdicate in 1879. An army revolt briefly ejected the Europeans, but a British invasion in 1882 ended Egyptian independence. The lesson – better to make a bad deal than to lose everything. The Europeans felt they had to take a hard line on default, regardless of the problems of states or the possible justice of their complaints against the usury of European banks. If the Europeans had accepted Ottoman default on their debts, the international repercussions would have grievously damaged European finance. Put another way, if the Ottomans had got away with it, everyone would have wanted to do so. So Abdülhamit had no choice but to proclaim the Decree of Muharrem of 1881.

The arrangement the sultan made with European banks created the Ottoman Public Debt Administration. In exchange for turning over state revenues to the Public Debt Administration, the Ottoman debt was renegotiated to a manageable level, almost 50 per cent was forgiven. (European bankers also knew when they had to yield.) The Public Debt Administration was empowered to collect taxes, exploit state revenues, and pay Ottoman

Revenues of the Public Debt Administration, five year averages by fiscal year, 1882/3 to 1906/7 (£T thousands)

	1882/3– 1886/7	1887/8– 1891/2	1892/3– 1896/7	1897/8– 1901/2	1902/3– 1906/7
Basic Revenues*	1867	1956	2117	2197	2576
Other Revenues	402	372	387	341	385
Expenses	−388	−392	−346	−419	−523
Net Revenue	1952	1936	2157	2120	2538

* tobacco, salt, official stamps, spirits, fisheries, silk (some averaging and rounding errors)

creditors from the proceeds. A seven-member council of representatives of bondholders governed the Administration – one each from Britain, France, Germany, Holland, Italy, Austria-Hungary, and a member from the Ottoman Bank (a private enterprise). The Ottoman government had a non-voting representative on the council.

Much of the income that would normally have gone to the Ottoman state went to the Public Debt Administration. Taxes on silk, fishing, alcoholic spirits, official stamps needed for all legal documents, and tobacco, as well as the tribute from Eastern Rumelia, Cyprus, Greece, Bulgaria, and Montenegro went to the Public Debt Administration. (A separate European-controlled entity, the Tobacco Régie, was later created to exploit tobacco profits.) As European economic interest in the Ottoman Empire grew, the scope of the Public Debt Administration expanded, overseeing, for example, tax farms and customs collections, the proceeds of which had been pledged to European debt holders. The Europeans who controlled the Public Debt Administration proved to be very efficient tax-collectors. The figures in the table[2] indicate high rates of return, as well as a significant amount spent on administrators' salaries and other expenses. The total amount collected from 1897/8–1901/2, £T 2,538,000 for example, was equivalent to 29 per cent of all the Ottoman government collected in revenues in those years. Effectively none of this money went to the government, although after 1903, a small share was remitted.

(Tables in this chapter list two types of Ottoman money – the silver kuruş and the gold lira, which was sometimes abbreviated '£T' by contemporary English speakers. Conversion values varied, but one lira was officially equal to 100 kuruş. In the late nineteenth and early twentieth centuries, one gold lira was worth approximately 0.91 British pounds sterling, 4.4 U.S. dollars, or 22.8 French francs.)

[2] Abbreviated from Roger Owen, *The Middle East in the World Economy,* London and New York, 1981, p. 193.

The Public Debt enterprise was enormous. By World War I, the Public Debt Administration had expanded to a staff of more than 5,000. Europeans held the higher administrative positions. For comparison, there were 8,000 teachers in all the Ottoman state schools in 1913. Virtually every Ottoman city and many large towns had Public Debt collection offices. In Istanbul, the Public Debt Administration building sat high on a hill in the Old City of Stambul, where it was a constant reminder of the relative positions of the Ottoman Empire and Europe. Resentment naturally followed, not least among those tax-farmers and bureaucrats who had lost their positions to the Europeans.

The Ottoman Empire did not stop borrowing after the Decree of Muharrem. Instead, borrowing from Europeans became easier. European banks and investors now readily loaned to the Ottomans, because they could arrange that the Public Debt Administration would oversee the resources that the Ottomans had pledged for collection and collateral. Public Debt Administration management was a condition of loans. This was true of borrowing for public works, such as railways. The tax on sheep from certain regions, for example, was assigned as a 'guarantee' that the investors would make a certain, agreed profit from the railways they built. If they did not make enough from the railway, they took the taxes – investment without risk. To make sure that the revenues were available to repay the investors, the Public Debt Administration was assigned to collect the sheep taxes, backed when necessary by Ottoman troops to make sure the peasants paid.

Collection of taxes had always been the mark of real power in the Middle East and the Balkans. Traditionally, the sultan collected and provided security in return. Who was now in charge?

Despite the loss of economic sovereignty, it must be said that the presence of the Public Debt Administration did hold benefits for the Ottomans. Prior to the Decree of Muharrem, the Ottomans had only been receiving approximately half of the amounts contracted for their most recent loans. In other words, the Ottoman government took out a loan, received only half the agreed upon sum, but was expected to repay the original sum (i.e., twice what it had received) and to pay interest on the original sum. This was called the 'discount', or 'the difference between nominal and issue price'. It was justified by the supposed danger of lending money to the Ottomans. Since all might be lost if the Ottomans went bankrupt, investors had to be promised incredible gain for their investments. This was, in fact, fiscal hypocrisy, because the European governments were not about to allow their bankers to go broke. Some way would be found to make the Ottomans pay, as events proved. (The high discount explains how the Europeans could agree to the provisions of the Decree of Muharrem that halved what was owed them – high rates of interest that had accrued and the initial discount meant that even losing half of what they were owed 'on paper' still left them with a tidy income.) After the Decree of Muharrem, the rates paid by the Ottomans did lower. The discount dropped to between 10 and 15 per cent. The benefit from this was somewhat limited, however, by the need to repay so many old loans with newly borrowed money.

In some ways, the Ottoman Empire was at war with European investors. The investors won. The interests of the two 'sides' were inherently at odds. The Ottomans wished to invest to develop industry; the Europeans wished to maximize profits from agriculture, from which came their main profits. The Ottomans wished to become economically and militarily strong; the Europeans only wished them to survive at a level that would allow them to pay their bills – to get as much as possible without, quite, killing the golden goose. Unfortunately for the Ottomans, there was nowhere else for them to turn for investments for development or to repay old loans. They were presented with what was in effect a cartel that opposed the interests of creditors. More often than not, the Europeans collaborated so that there would be no competition in the granting of loans. Competition would have driven down the price. The Public Debt Administration was particularly guilty of what would be labelled questionable business practices today. It arranged and facilitated loans to the financial enrichment of its principals, who were the same investors who offered new loans. The principals then made money from their Public Debt Administration investment, from the loan itself, and from the financial services offered by the banks, both in Europe and Istanbul, which they also controlled. The Ottoman Bank, for example, which had a seat on the Public Debt Administration Council, was owned by European investors and distributed £T 30 million to its investors between 1863 and 1909.

The effect of borrowing on the state

The table below gives the yearly deficit of the Ottoman government. To understand the fiscal situation of the Ottoman government, the exact percentages in the table are not important. As numbers often do, they conceal all sorts of tactics for economic survival, such as sometimes not paying officials who received their actual pay in a somewhat illegal manner. In many of the years in the table, much was owed in taxes, but had not been yet collected. So the picture was not quite as bad as it looked, but it was bad enough. The solution arrived at was to borrow more.

The Ottoman government had no choice but to continue borrowing. Railways might be expensive, and the conditions of their construction fiscally absurd, but railways were needed if the Empire was ever to advance. Lack of funds did not mean the Russians were no longer a threat; guns were needed and soldiers had to be paid. The Ottoman situation was an impossible one. Through the Public Debt Administration, major assets were paying off old loans, and therefore much of the money needed to run

Excess of expenditures over revenues

Fiscal year	Per cent* overspent	Fiscal year	Per cent* overspent
1887–88	23	1898–99	16
1888–89	17	1899–00	3
1889–90	5	1900–01	8
1890–91	11	1901–02	7
1891–92	3	1902–03	10
1892–93	5	1903–04	16
1893–94	7	1904–09	n.a.
1894–95	9	1909–10	3
1895–96	7	1910–11	17
1896–97	10	1911–12	29
1897–98	21		

* percentage of actual revenues

the government had already been spent. Yet the costs of running the Empire did not diminish. The Ottomans could try to increase efficiency in both income production and tax collection, and they did both. Recorded treasury revenues increased by 73 per cent from 1888 to 1910. It was not enough. The fact that the Ottoman Empire was basically an agricultural state with little industrialization necessarily held down tax collections. Farm production could simply never be as lucrative a source of tax revenue as was business. In the last half century of the Ottoman Empire, the main taxes on land, agricultural production, and animals brought in an average of more than twenty times the tax income brought by the business profits tax.

Most damaging of all, little of the money borrowed went to constructive purposes. Like a creditor who opens new credit card accounts to pay the interest on his old credit cards, the Ottomans were forced to take out new loans to pay for old ones:

> Over the whole period 1854–1914, the gross amount borrowed has been put at £T 399.5 million. Of this £T 135.5 million, or 34 per cent, represents commissions and the difference between nominal and issue price; £T 178.9 million, or 45 per cent, was used to liquidate previous debts; £T 22.3 million, or 6 per cent, for military expenditure; £T 20 million, or 5 per cent, to cover budget deficits; £T 18.1 million, or 5 per cent, was invested productively; and the balance was paid to the treasury or put to other uses. Clearly Turkey showed little benefit from its huge debt.[3]

[3] Charles Issawi (paraphrasing K. Fişek), *An Economic History of the Middle East and North Africa*, New York, 1982, p. 65.

Abdülhamit II had saved the fiscal integrity of the Ottoman Empire, but at a price. The sums used to pay Ottoman debts could not be used to pay school teachers' salaries or to buy weapons to defend the Empire. And the Ottomans had lost a significant amount of sovereignty when they allowed Europeans to collect their taxes. Throughout his administration, Abdülhamit dealt with European bankers, matching concessions from them with increased government revenues to pay off loans, and engaging in a complicated balancing act, never falling into bankruptcy. He did not fall into the financial disasters that had claimed earlier sultans. Despite this, Abdülhamit did not change the fundamental nature of the Ottoman's fiscal problems. The Empire still lived by borrowing, and needed to borrow to survive. What he did was hold off the reckoning.

A changed economy?

After years of reform, a casual observer in the early twentieth century might have felt the economic situation in the Ottoman Empire to be better than it was. Surely there were many more good highways and more large government and private buildings than ever before. Railways connected ports to the interior over routes that had been only dirt tracks thirty years before. Ships crowded the harbours of Istanbul, İzmir, Beirut, and Salonica. But all was not as it seemed.

The bright star of the Ottoman economy was agriculture. Fruits, tobacco, and other cash crops were strong exports, gaining much-needed hard currency. The foreign exchange was much-needed, because the Ottoman industrial sector was minuscule. Two hundred times as many machines were imported as exported, 40 times as many rubber products, 20 times as many arms. Almost twice as many textiles came into the Ottoman Empire as left. Ottoman manufacturing was in fact a 'niche market'. High-quality manufactured goods were primarily imports, but Ottoman entrepreneurs had found ways to insert themselves into the market. For example, Ottoman government statistics listed large numbers of

Foreign Trade, 1880–1913

	Imports	Exports
1880–84	19.58	11.19
1885–89	20.26	12.96
1890–94	24.01	14.16
1895–99	23.30	14.95
1900–04	24.75	16.08
1905–09	32.89	18.84
1910–13	43.03	26.68

'clock factories' in major cities, but these were occupied with putting Ottoman faces on European works.

There was, of course, much manufacturing carried on in the Empire, as there always had been. Most of this was traditional. Leather goods, wagons, tiles, basic wooden goods, and the like could all be produced much more cheaply close to the consumer than they could be imported. Some materials were easy enough to produce or expensive enough to import for local production to hold the market. For example, paper making was relatively easy and could be done in Ottoman cities. Making chemicals, on the other hand, needed advanced techniques, and so chemicals were imported. Thus the Ottomans employed ten times as many workers producing paper as chemicals.

The reasons for the bleak Ottoman economy have been analysed above. Most of them were internal problems – lack of capital, lack of skilled manpower, lack of capital goods. Some were simply the workings of the world market. Modern methods of transport made it possible for European countries with advanced production capabilities to send goods quickly and cheaply to underdeveloped lands, which craved goods they could not produce themselves. A major problem was the effect of the capitulations, which forced the Ottomans to accept disadvantageous terms of trade. Whatever the reasons, it does not take much economic training to look at the table and realize that the Ottomans were in financial trouble. The numbers in the tables are imperfect (Ottoman customs collectors were imperfect statisticians), but their story is accurate.

The question of autocracy

The question about Abdülhamit II's reign was whether his improvements were worth the price. Increased central authority necessarily meant less local autonomy, which upset many segments of the population who would rather control their own lands. Those who hoped for liberalization and democratization found no friend in Abdülhamit. A system of inspectors and spies watched over all, partly to detect corruption and mismanagement, partly to root out disloyalty to sultan and system. Physical reform and development were priorities of the government; freedom and political liberty were not.

As they were in many other areas, the Ottomans under Abdülhamit were first to confront dilemmas that would come to other countries later. While it would be comforting to believe that development and freedom are never in conflict, such was almost certainly not the case in the Ottoman Empire. In such a diverse society and large geographic area, beset by tremendous foreign pressures against economic development, the danger of fragmentation was great. Government by consensus and compromise, the hallmark of democracies, would have meant many factions attempting to run the state. The Christian minorities, the religious conservatives, the reformers, the merchants, and other groups all had conflicting aims. Nor did the foreigners, who had great power over the Empire, have common goals – England, France, and Russia each had different aims. None, including the Europeans, would accept the give-and-take of democracy. England might be a democracy at home, but it had no desire to see a strong and unified popular will triumph in the Ottoman Empire.

One alternative was a relatively benevolent autocracy, which was what Abdülhamit provided. Central authority forced disparate forces to work together. A strong sultan could stand, insofar as was possible, against European incursions. The proof was in the success of Abdülhamit's rule. After the 1877–78 war with Russia, throughout Abdülhamit's rule, the Empire lost no land. As stated above, the economic and administrative infrastructure of the Empire improved dramatically.

Does this mean that Abdülhamit II's reign was an unqualified success? No. As will be seen below, he did not pay sufficient attention to the important area of military preparedness. More fundamentally, he failed to prepare his people for the future. Democracy and personal freedom are good in themselves. Once people have enough to eat and can think beyond survival they begin to think of their freedom. A wise ruler can begin to prepare them for it, supporting the institutions of democracy – local self-rule, popular assemblies, an increasingly independent judiciary, bureaucratic initiative, a relatively free press, and the like – long before they become a complete reality. This Abdülhamit never did. Correctly fearing that openings to democracy would eventually lead to the demise of the sultan's authority, he opposed gradual change toward democracy. The press was censored, an efficient secret police watched bureaucrats, intellectuals and each other, opponents were exiled, the schools were forbidden to teach 'radical' ideas. A great proponent of economic progress, he tried to stand in the way of the political progress that should have followed it. The result was years lost in the progress to democracy. The ultimate result was revolution.

The Young Turk revolution

Abdülhamit bred his own opposition. The schools he built and supported necessarily opened European ideas to Ottoman students. Some naturally questioned his autocratic rule. Like their predecessors, the Young Ottomans, a new group of constitutionalists, the Young Turks, believed that a turn to democracy was essential for the survival of the Empire. They also resented European interference with the Empire and looked to even faster reform of the Ottoman system and economy. They were convinced that the Turks had been neglected in favour of the Christian minorities and the

Western powers by Abdülhamit's government. Unlike the Young Ottomans, the Young Turks advocated differing degrees of *Turkish* nationalism. The Young Ottoman constitutionalists had intended to create an *Ottoman* nationality that encompassed many ethnic groups.

The ultimate success of revolt against Abdülhamit depended on the Ottoman military. The army had the power to change the government, and it was disaffected with Abdülhamit II. In fact, it was students in the military medical school who began to set up revolutionary cells. They organized the Committee of Union and Progress (*İttihat ve Terakki Cemiyeti*, CUP, first begun as the Ottoman Unity Society in 1889). Its cells soon spread to all advanced schools and in the civil bureaucracy. Many of the most promising young military officers during their schooling became confirmed members of the Committee.

Military conditions in the Ottoman Empire exacerbated the resentments of the military. In the first decade of the twentieth century they were involved in a bloody guerilla war in Macedonia. Bulgarian and Greek guerilla bands were fighting the Ottoman forces and each other to take control of Macedonia. The Greek and Bulgarian governments supported the guerillas, giving them supplies and support as well as staging areas for their raids. Many Greeks and Bulgarians in Macedonia also supported them, either because of nationalism or coercion. The Ottoman army could neither eradicate the threat nor properly protect the civilians who were the targets of the guerillas. Ottoman officers felt that they were poorly supported from Istanbul, and there was more than the usual military demand for more of everything behind their complaints. At its available strength in Macedonia the army could not win, and the European powers were beginning to intervene in Macedonia 'to prevent the bloodshed'. Austria and Russia had demanded that the gendarmerie and finances of Macedonia be put under European control and, in 1905, had forced the sultan to accept European officers and controllers in Macedonia. Experience had taught the Ottoman officers that such intervention would end in the loss of Ottoman territories. They felt, with some justification, that Abdülhamit was withholding men and supplies from the army because he was afraid of their power, and thus risking the Empire's survival.

The revolution

The immediate cause of revolt in the Macedonian army was a practical one – the soldiers had not been paid. Abdülhamit had the bad luck of military problems emerging at the same time as a low in government finances. 1907 had been a year of crop failures; tax collections were below the needs of the government, and foreign banks had to be paid before bureaucrats or soldiers. Many soldiers who otherwise might not have revolted listened more closely to rebel ideas when their pay was in arrears. Revolts had already taken place in 1906 and 1907. Units of the Third Army in Macedonia openly called for return of the constitution in 1908. Some of Abdülhamit's agents, including the commander sent by the sultan to calm the rebellion, were assassinated. Ottoman soldiers took to the hills in guerilla bands. Uprisings began in Macedonian cities. A genuine revolution had begun and was likely to spread. However, on July 23, 1908, Abdülhamit II surprised the rebels by giving in, restoring the constitution, and calling for elections.

In 1908, after a pause of thirty years, Ottoman democratic political life began once again, although 'democratic' is perhaps too definite a word to describe political life in 1908. Most of the population took no part in the organization of the political forces that vied for control. These included the sultan, who by nature of respect for his office was a political force, and two main political groups – the Committee of Union and Progress and the Liberal Union. The Committee of Union and Progress, caught unawares by Abdülhamit's declaration, did not create a political party. The military, which had brought on the revolution, was divided into a group that believed in intervention in politics and one that felt politics should be left to politicians, as long as politicians treated the military properly. Instead, the CUP backed nationalist-oriented reform candidates in the election. The opposition was the Liberal Union (only one of many names adopted by the party over a decade), more organized than the CUP-backed candidates, but still not what is ordinarily called a political party. Its ideology was more favourable to the Christian minorities and less inclined to the CUP aims of ridding the Empire of European interference. Political exiles returned home, wrote political tracts, and campaigned. Many of them joined the side of the Liberal Union. Highly-placed bureaucrats, men who were committed to the Tanzimat system of authoritarian, centralized reform and distrustful of the CUP's 'new men', also gravitated to the Liberal side. Before the election, Abdülhamit chose as Grand Vezir a bureaucrat from the latter group, Mehmet Kâmil Paşa, who had already been Grand Vezir twice in the 1890s.

The election took place in November and December, 1908. (Distance made it impossible to carry out all balloting at the same time.) Candidates who supported the CUP won a bare majority, but the parliament was very divided among conflicting interests. All the major *millet*s were represented, as well as political views ranging from Islamic conservative to extreme nationalist. On December 17, 1908 the sultan opened the parliament. By February, 1909, delegates who sided with the CUP had removed Mehmet Kâmil from power and replaced him with Hüseyin Hilmi Paşa, a bureaucrat sympathetic to the CUP.

The Turkish nationalist reformers had seemingly triumphed. They immediately set upon reform. Recognizing that finance was the major obstacle to reform, they began to lower government expenses by cutting thousands of government jobs. Bureaucrats not amenable to CUP ideas of reform were sacked or transferred. However, these measures had little effect on overwhelming financial problems. International affairs were also threatening. As part of the settlement of the 1877–78 Russo–Turkish War, Bosnia had been put under Austrian control and Bulgaria had become two autonomous provinces, Bulgaria and Eastern Rumelia. Bulgaria was unified in 1885, but both Bulgaria and Bosnia remained legally a part of the Ottoman Empire. In the chaos that followed the revolution, Bulgaria declared itself independent (October 5, 1908) and Austria annexed Bosnia (October 6, 1908). Crete, which had been autonomous since 1878, united with Greece (October 7, 1908). Presented with *faits accomplis*, the new government had to make political accommodations with a very unpopular situation about which it could do nothing.

In late winter and early spring of 1909, many people in Istanbul were unhappy with the new government – political conservatives who detested the diminution of the sultan's power, religious reactionaries who feared advancing westernization, bureaucrats out of a job, empire loyalists who keenly felt the loss of Bulgaria and, especially, Bosnia, and anyone who had lost power when the old order changed. Not even the army was satisfied. The officers who had led the CUP revolt were 'new men', often from bureaucratic or lower-middle-class families, educated in the military schools. The older form of officers – local soldiers who had risen through the ranks or owed their appointments to their families' position, viewed the new men as opponents and, one suspects, *déclassé* specimens of why their world was going to hell. All these were enemies of the revolution.

The counter-revolution

Abdülhamit II had acted with political acumen. Faced with a revolt, he had become a democrat overnight, or at least had saved his throne by acting like one. Other elements in Ottoman society had not accepted the changes so easily. Of these, reactionary Muslims (by no means Muslims as a whole) and traditional army officers were the greatest threat. The former could mobilize religious students to riot in the streets. The latter had troops under their command. On April 12, 1909, they staged their own revolution in the capital. Religious students and soldiers marched on the parliament, pro-CUP officers and two parliamentary deputies were killed, and the remaining CUP deputies fled the city.

It was here that Abdülhamit made a mistake. Overestimating the power of the conservatives, he accepted their actions which, after all, could mean a return of some of his own authority. The sultan did not so much promote the counter-revolution as agree to it, but he accepted the forced resignation of the CUP-backed cabinet. Liberal Union politicians, demonstrating their lack of commitment to the new democracy, supported the rebels. A new cabinet, supported only by a minority of the parliament, was installed.

The rebels, the Liberal Union, and Abdülhamit had erred. When news of the revolt reached Macedonia the general in charge of the Macedonian army, Mahmud Şevket Paşa, immediately commandeered trains and his troops 'marched' on Istanbul by train. They were greeted along the way by CUP politicians. Encountering only minor opposition, they took the city on April 24. On April 27 the parliament deposed Abdülhamit II. His younger brother, Mehmet V, was named sultan, but real power was obviously in the hands of the officers of the Macedonian army and the CUP.

The government of the Committee of Union and Progress

The intervention of the army in politics has been a factor in Middle Eastern politics throughout the twentieth century. Modern Middle Eastern army officers usually have been reformers, but have frequently been as impatient with the slow pace of democracy as they have been with the authority of kings. Democracy by nature entails compromise among various factions, each with its own political agenda. This often means that reforms advance slowly, because opposing groups have to be placated. The temptation of military reformers has been to seize power and advance reforms rapidly, ignoring or suppressing those who oppose change. The question, as with any autocracy, is whether it is worth it. Does the acceleration of economic and administrative reform justify ending democracy or even suspending democracy for a while? Whatever is philosophically correct, Middle Easterners have often felt that the answer is 'yes'. Modern Turks, for example, have accepted limited military intervention in politics, and in each case the military has soon returned authority to a democratic system. The answer may be the same as it should have been for Abdülhamit II—authoritarian government may be necessary, but only if the authority works to reform the system, develop the underpinnings of democracy, and return the government to elected officials.

As in other areas of reform, the Ottomans were the first to experiment with reform led by the military. The Ottoman military was in a unique position to direct reform: the armed forces had held a special place in the Ottoman Empire since its earliest days, when the state *was* the army. In the nineteenth century the state had begun to identify itself more as did Western European governments, primarily as a provider of needed services for its subjects. Nevertheless, the armed forces retained a special position. Beset by enemies, the people looked to it for survival. The army was also at the forefront of westernization. The first Western-style schools were army schools, officer-training academies and military medical schools. Out of necessity, army and navy officers were immersed in Western methods. If they were to defend the Empire, officers had to know Western military techniques. To learn these, they had to know Western languages and read Western texts. In the process, they also imbibed Western political ideas. The new officers were reformers. It is also true that in any country the military has the potential to lead because it has the respect of the people, who believe it can 'get things done'. (Americans who doubt this might consider the presidential elections of Washington, Jackson, Harrison, Taylor, Grant, and Eisenhower.) However, the most important reason for military control of politics is that the army has the guns. In the Ottoman Empire, despite infighting in the military and the opposition of many officers, the Committee of Union and Progress leaders ultimately had the backing of the army. In the end this was more important than their popular mandate from the elections of 1908, and so they ruled.

The committee and the military

Even though the leaders of the CUP were primarily military officers, they were not necessarily loved by those who led the army. Mahmud Şevket Paşa, who led the defeat of the counter-revolution, took control of the army in 1909, serving as Inspector-General of the Ottoman European armies and *de facto* head soldier. His view was that the army's purpose was to defend the state, not to advance the cause of the Committee of Union and Progress. As with many soldiers, he equated the defence of the state with the defence of the army, which led to numerous battles with the civilian leadership and the CUP over military budgets and authority. Other, younger military officers also opposed the CUP 'politicians'. Nevertheless, the army and the Committee were at first forced to coexist, each supporting the other, for fear that their opponents would do away with the leaders of both the CUP and the army, given the chance. After the events of 1909, the army took a hand in many areas of government, including tax collection and public order in the provinces. Martial law remained in force.

The CUP and the military were closely tied by mutual membership. The Committee had begun its life as a secret revolutionary society and never really lost that character. Its membership always remained secret, but much of it was drawn from the military. Officers in all ranks might be announced or unannounced members of the CUP structure. They had a dual loyalty, which infuriated those who wished the army to be independent of politics just as much as it angered those who wished the army itself to be in charge. The military was divided between pro-CUP and anti-CUP officers.

Politics and war

The parliamentary government of 1910 was essentially democratic, if disorganized and confused. The CUP, stung by claims that its initial refusal to take a direct part in politics had contributed to the counter-revolution, organized a political party. Nominally, CUP-backers held a firm majority, but in fact they divided into several small 'parties' within the party, each following its own leaders. Like the other parties in the parliament, they were much affected by the traditional idea of parties in the Ottoman Empire, which were more dependent on ties to individuals than to ideologies. Opposition was furnished by parties of religious conservatives and the old Liberal Unionists, who had been outlawed after the counter-revolution but appeared with a new name. The Ottoman parliament did not prove to be a particularly effective body. It was successful in passing administrative reforms and, of necessity, in increasing the military budget and improving the forces, which had seriously declined under Abdülhamit, but it did not initiate much reform. Argument between parties too often took the place of action.

The parliament's failings were highlighted by the Tripolitanian war (1911–12). The Italians invaded the last Ottoman possession in Africa, Libya, on October 5, 1911. Hampered by distance and disorganization, the Ottomans quickly lost coastal Libya to the Italians. Only a small force of Ottoman soldiers, volunteers led by Colonel Enver of the CUP (see below) kept up active resistance. Alongside Libyan tribesmen, they fought what was essentially a guerilla war against the Italians. The Liberals and even CUP deputies questioned CUP war policies in the parliament, and the CUP party began to break up. To forestall disaster, Grand Vezir Sait Halim Paşa called a snap election. The CUP party won a resounding victory in the election of 1912, but used press censorship and threats of violence to soundly defeat its enemies. This was surely a mistake, as they would very likely have won, although admittedly a less overwhelming victory, without such methods. The CUP tactics played into the hands of the opposition. The Liberals by themselves could have done nothing, but they were joined by disaffected junior officers with a following in the military, which was increasingly divided along the pro- and anti-CUP axis. When the cabinet put forth bills to amend the constitution to give itself more power, a group calling itself the 'Saviour Officers' threatened revolution. Şevket Paşa resigned in disgust at the turn of events. The government feared to stand up to the rebels. Sait Halim's cabinet resigned and the parliament was dissolved (August 5, 1912).

It was the turn of the Liberals to rule once again, and they presided over disaster. The Balkan countries were preparing for war and the Ottomans cleared the decks. A brief caretaker government under Ahmet Muhtar Paşa made peace with the Italians in 1912, losing both Libya and the Dodecanese islands. Kâmil Paşa then returned to power as Grand Vezir, once more leading an unelected government brought into being by an anti-democratic rebellion. (The CUP may have, in effect, stuffed the ballot boxes, but Kâmil and his Liberal friends had no recourse to ballots whatsoever.) Meanwhile, the First Balkan War (see the next chapter) had begun. The Ottomans lost quickly, in part because the new government had not followed the strategic plans written during the CUP government's rule. With defeat came hundreds of thousands of refugees in Istanbul and western Anatolia, food shortages in the capital, and financial loss that meant that soldiers and bureaucrats went unpaid.

The Empire's existence was threatened, and the CUP and the military made common cause. On January 23, 1913, a CUP-led group burst into a meeting of the cabinet, shot the Minister of War, Nâzim Paşa, and forced Grand Vezir Kâmil to resign. The CUP had seized power from those who had committed the first illegality – the rebellion of the 'Saviour Officers' that had closed the elected parliament in 1912. The Liberals were driven from power, but they had not given up. On July 15 Liberals attempted a new coup, killing Mahmud Şevket but failing to take control. The Liberal Union was not formally outlawed, but had no further chance to seize power. The CUP took complete charge of the government. New elections that were held at the end of 1913 returned a Unionist majority.

Although parliament continued to meet, from 1913 actual authority in the Ottoman Empire was in the hands of the Committee of Union and Progress. Sait Halim Paşa was once again named Grand Vezir, but three leading members of the Committee of Union and Progress were the strongest forces in the government. They were known as the Triumvirate. Two of the members of the Triumvirate were military men, Cemal Paşa and Enver Paşa. The third, Talat Paşa, was a bureaucrat turned politician. Talat served as Minister of the Interior, in charge, among other things, of the police. Enver was Minister of War. Cemal became Minister of the Navy and later Governor of Syria during World War I. The three had risen from relatively humble backgrounds, very different from the traditional Ottoman upper-class leaders of government. Talat's family had been poor, and he had originally risen through the bureaucracy of the Ottoman postal service. Enver's father had been a low-level bureaucrat, Cemal's a professional soldier. It was a mark of the success of earlier reforms that the middle class could assume rule.

The CUP government that ruled from 1913 to 1918 has been called a dictatorship of the Triumvirate, but this is less than accurate. It would be more true to say that it was the party that ruled, and the three were the strongest, but by no means the only, voices in the party. The CUP was rapidly evolving into something resembling a real political party, with offices all over the empire tied into local power structures. There was certainly no commitment to multi-party democracy. Rather, the system can be considered the first of the one-party governing systems that were later to be seen all over the developing world.

The reforms of the Committee of Union and Progress

The reforms of the CUP must be judged more by their intentions than their successes. Ottoman defeat in the First World War ensured that many reforms

Expenditures of Certain Ottoman Ministries, 1910–11 (millions of kuruş)

Interior	Police and Gendarmery	Finance	Army and Navy	Public Works	Education	External Debt
126,958	140,860	358,596	1,223,560	83,552	78,283	1,128,797

Loans Contracted	700,000	
– Discount	120,244	
Loans received	579,756	

Revenues	2,878,303
Expenditures	3,378,328
Shortfall	500,025

had only begun when the Empire ended. Despite that, the CUP reforms were impressive: Istanbul was modernized. Streets and sewers were built. Telephone, trams, and gas, electric, and water lines were all extended throughout the city. The city government was completely reorganized, with a city council and public advisory boards. Insofar as was possible in a city whose skyline was dominated by great mosques, Istanbul began to resemble a European metropolis. The Ottoman military was completely reorganized. In the ultimate triumph of westernization, the armed forces were sometimes actually placed under the *control* of European advisors. As will be seen in Chapter 11, the reforms were remarkably successful. An army that had been defeated in 1912 by Bulgaria and Greece was able to stand up to Russia and Great Britain by 1914.

The CUP government did not have time to build many businesses, railways, or highways, except military enterprises. The World War intervened and took all the state's effort and capital. Infrastructure improvements were primarily extensions of those begun by Abdülhamit II. They were beset by the eternal Ottoman problem of finance. The table indicates the nature of the problem. Note the low levels of expenditure on education and public works. These were the very areas that were most in need of support – training, production, and commerce. Yet it was the military and the debt (including the costs of processing it) that took the lion's share. Was this wrong? Probably not, for it would do no good to develop an economy that would be destroyed by the next Russian invasion. Nevertheless, the figures do indicate the nature of the problem. The list of income and expenditures is also telling. How could a government with such a balance sheet long escape bankruptcy and collapse? Note that the shortfall is less than half one-half the amount of the military expenditure, but six times the expenditure on education.

Perhaps the greatest reforms of the CUP were those that fundamentally changed the Ottoman system and Ottoman relations with the outside world. The reforms of the Tanzimat and after had always been hampered by the need to compromise with Islamic tradition. New law courts had been established, but they coexisted with the old Islamic courts. Vast economic resources controlled by Islamic foundations (*vakıf*s) were virtually untaxable at a time when the Empire was often bankrupt. The CUP government took a major step against this duality by asserting the dominance of state over religion. Religious foundations were placed under a government ministry's control. Religious judges were placed under the authority of the Ministry of Justice, and Islamic judges were made paid officials of the state, their decisions subject to appeal to secular courts. The state oversaw the training and examined the competence of the members of the religious courts. A secular family law was tentatively put in place. Educational opportunities for women, including higher schools, were expanded. Islam was still accepted as the state religion, but it was under the administrative control of the state.

The CUP also acted to regularize the place of the Ottoman Empire in the world, as an independent state like other modern states. Ironically, this self-assertion came only at the end of the Empire. The World War allowed the Ottoman government to abolish the capitulations. During the war, for the first time in centuries, the Ottoman economy was under Ottoman control. Foreign post offices were closed. All foreigners were made subject to the same laws as applied to Ottoman citizens. In short, the Empire began to claim the same rights and duties that European countries expected for themselves.

Success or failure?

It is tempting to think that Ottoman reforms were a failure After all, they ultimately failed in their main purpose – to save the Empire. That is true. Despite the efforts of reformers, in World War I the Ottomans were defeated by the Europeans, who divided much of the Ottoman Empire among themselves. The reformers were not able to stop the European conquerors. On the other hand, as will be seen below, the Turks were able to save their homeland, modern Turkey, for themselves. They could not have done so if the Ottoman reformers had not modernized their army, built railways, roads, and telegraph lines, and trained officers and civil officials in modern ways. In that way, at least, the Ottoman reforms were a success.

It is also important to appreciate how much the Ottomans accomplished in a short time. From 1826, when the reforms actually began, to 1914, when the First World War changed everything, is a short historical span of time. In 1826, power was decentralized among provincial governors, local autonomous rulers, and chieftains. The army was almost nonexistent. There were no Ottoman newspapers, few printed books. Roads were mud. Messages took weeks to travel short distances, carried by horse. Ottoman officials and most of the populace were ignorant of the world around them.

By 1914, there had been great changes – modern schools, railways, tele-graph lines. The government at least approximated to a European form of organization. Orders given in Istanbul were followed in Damascus and Baghdad. The army was able to stand against England, France, and Russia during almost four years of World War I. All this was achieved in spite of overwhelming economic pressures from Europe and repeated batterings from first the Russians, then the Balkan countries, as will be described in the next chapter. The Ottoman reforms were more successful than could have ever been imagined in 1826.

In many ways the Ottomans were the first to experiment with the reforms attempted later in what we now call developing nations. Many of the problems are exactly the same. Cou tries in today's Asia, Africa, and Latin America, for example, have experienced the same credit problems as those experienced by the Ottomans. They have borrowed to buy the machines, goods, and trained advisors needed to bring them into the mod-ern world, confident that their economic progress would bring the wealth that would pay off the loans. Like the Ottomans, they have found that they were overconfident. They have found that breaking into world markets and competing with economically advanced nations has been no easy task. They have also found that believing in democracy is not enough if the people are not convinced that it will bring real benefits. Like the Ottomans, today's developing countries have depended on elites to advance reform and often on the army to foster it. Real democracy, when it has been achieved at all, has taken time to develop.

Chapter 10 ....

The Human Disaster

The Human Disaster

Wars, especially wars fought away from Western Europe or America, are most often taught as if they were board games. Forces of soldiers are moved across the historical board, winning or losing, and territory is exchanged. After the game has gone on long enough, one side admits it has lost and the board is put away until the next game. Those who die in the game are soldiers, game pieces, whose nature is to battle and die. Awkward factors such as civilian casualties are seldom mentioned.

To illustrate this vision of war one can remember the Crimea. History textbooks always mention the Crimean War (1853–56). The war was undoubtedly important to Europe for its effect on diplomacy, the balance of power, and Western economic penetration of the Middle East. Moreover, it was a war that caught the popular imagination of Europe. The heroism captured in Tennyson's 'Charge of the Light Brigade' is still taught to schoolchildren. There is even a film, which features Errol Flynn in the famous charge. Despite this, the Crimean War was far from a purely European affair. From the film, the poem, or most history books one would never know that many more Turkish soldiers fought in the war than French or English. However, as reported the story is a simple one: Russia wanted to control the Holy Places in Jerusalem, demanding special privileges from the Ottomans and wishing to exclude traditional Catholic and Protestant rights, among other diplomatic demands. France and Britain opposed the Russian wishes and war began. After the Light Brigade died and Russia lost the Crimean city of Sebastopol the war ended. A peace treaty was signed. End of story.

In fact, where the loss of human beings is concerned, the most important fact of the war was not the charge of the Light Brigade, nor the Russian battle loss in the Crimea. The most important human outcome of the war was the expulsion from the Crimea of hundreds of thousands of Crimean Turks and the deaths of many of them. Because the Russians had conquered the Crimea in 1774 and retained it after the Crimean War, an entire population was displaced or destroyed. It was one of the great human disasters of modern times, but it is not mentioned when the battles of the Crimean War are described. Massive civilian losses do not fit into the presentation of war as board game.

The Crimean War was only one, and not the worst, of the great losses of civilian life that occurred in the Ottoman Empire and surrounding territories in the nineteenth and early twentieth centuries. Even though they are relatively unknown in the West, the great massacres and forced migration of Turks and other Muslim peoples in those times were some of the greatest disasters in human history. Millions died, and millions more were exiled from their homes. The two factors that caused this loss were nationalism and Russian imperialism.

The demographic imperative

The Ottoman Empire was a state of many peoples. It contained Turks, Greeks, Arabs, Armenians, Bulgarians, Serbs, Albanians, and many others. They were not always separated into individual groups that lived apart from each other. The Empire's cities contained Christian and Muslim populations speaking many different languages. In the countryside, Christian villages often were within sight of Muslim villages. Sometimes one village contained peasants of two or more religions. As the nineteenth century began the peoples were thoroughly mixed. In Thrace (north and west of Istanbul), for example, there were Greek, Bulgarian, and Turkish villages and Greeks, Bulgarians, Turks, Jews, and others lived in the cities. To the east, in eastern Anatolia and the southern Caucasus region, the populations were also mixed. Muslims (Turks, Kurds, and other ethnic groups) were a majority in all areas of Anatolia and the Caucasus except Georgia, but they lived intermixed with Christians. Armenian Christians were scattered throughout the villages and cities of the east. In western and northern Anatolia, Greeks made a significant minority in a Turkish majority. In Greece, Greeks were the majority, with a significant Turkish minority. Turks were a large minority in Bulgaria. Other regions were similarly mixed.

In the regions that are today in Ukraine, southern European Russia, Georgia, Armenia, and Azerbaijan the population was less mixed, but it was not what it is today. Muslims, Turks and others, were the overwhelmingly majority in the Crimea and lands to the north of it and in the western and eastern Caucasus. In the late 1700s the Christian groups that today make up the main population of the Crimea and the western Caucasus had not yet become dominant.

The mixed nature of the populations of the region was a problem for those who planned political change. The Russian Empire, intent on the conquest of southern lands, saw the Muslim populations of those lands as a threat. Once conquered, they would be a restive population, never loyal to the Russians, always willing to support invaders who might free them. In short, they could not be trusted. The Russian solution was whenever possible to remove them. Muslims were to be forced out and replaced by Russians. If sufficient numbers of Russians were not available, other Slavs, particularly Ukrainians, were to be brought in. Lacking Slavs, non-Slavic Christians were the next choice; in the southern Caucasus and eastern Anatolia, Armenians in particular were imported. These populations would be much more likely to be loyal to the Tsar.

A similar problem existed for the nationalists who carved new states from the Ottoman Empire. A Greece, Bulgaria, Serbia, or Armenia with a large Turkish population would be in danger of revolt by its Muslim subjects. Because the revolutionaries had not been loyal to the Ottoman Empire, they assumed that Turks and other Muslims would not be loyal to the new, non-Muslim states – a reasonable assumption. Muslims, it was felt, would remain loyal to the Ottomans and would try to return their lands to the Empire. Moreover, the Christians did not wish to live side-by-side with those who had been seen as their masters. As with the Russians, the solution was to force the Turks from the new states. The cry of 'Bulgaria for the Bulgarians' or 'Greece for the Greeks' meant that the Turks whose families had lived there for more than 400 years were to be evicted.

The Crimean Tatars

The Crimea was a vassal state of the Ottoman Empire, ruled by its own leaders, *han*s. The *Tatars* were Muslim Turks who were linguistically and culturally almost the same as the Turks of the Ottoman Empire, but with a sense of a separate identity. Nevertheless, their troops had been a loyal mainstay of the Ottoman Empire for centuries. By the late 1700s they had lived in the Crimean Peninsula and surrounding territories for more than 500 years.

The Russians under Catherine the Great conquered the Crimea in 1774 and formally annexed it in 1783. They began a policy of populating their new territory with Christians, some from Russia, some from other lands, including the Ottoman Empire. Before the Russian conquest few non-Turks lived in the Crimea, but that situation changed. The Russian government began to seize Tatar lands. The lands were distributed to Russian nobles. Christians were drawn to the Crimea with promises of free land and low taxes. Fearing the Russians, who had previously evicted or killed the Muslims of southern Russia and the southern Ukraine, perhaps

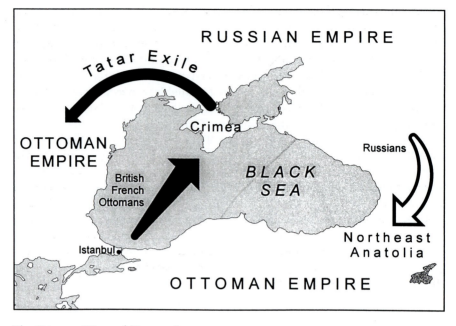

The Crimean War and Tatar exile.

100,000 Tatars fled their country in the late 1700s. Those who stayed were still a majority, but they were exposed to persecution and discrimination designed to force their departure.

The final days of the Tatars in the Crimea came during and immediately after the Crimean War. The Russians had accused them of collaborating with the Ottomans against the Russians. Undoubtedly the Tatars would have done so, had they been able, but they had been completely disarmed by the Russians, and had been so for decades. During the war Tatar villages were raided continuously by Cossack troops of the Tsar. The Cossacks were Christian tribesmen, loyal to the Russian government, who had fought the Tatars for generations. Mutual raiding between the Cossacks and Tatars had created hatred that readily came to the fore, but now the Cossacks were the only side with guns. How much of their persecution of the disarmed Tatars resulted from official orders and how much from ancestral hatreds is unknown. The result was the same. Surviving Tatar villagers were forced to pay 'protection money' so that the Cossacks would leave them alone. At the end of the war the seizure of lands increased. Tatars were forced to work as servants on their old lands. Russian administrators collected high illegal taxes for their own pockets, in addition to already high 'legal' taxes. Raids on Tatar villages continued.

The Tatars found themselves without any legal protection. Courts and police were Russian and did not hear Tatar complaints. The government seized religious property and Muslim schools. Schools, courts, and all organs of government were Russian and Christian. Tatars were unable to live on their old lands, unable to appeal to the protection of the law, and, worst of all to them, were unable to live a communal life as Muslims. Soon after the Crimean War they emigrated *en masse* from the Crimea. (Descendants of the small number who remained were eventually deported to Central Asia by Stalin in the 1940s, from which they began to return only in the 1980s.)

The Tatars fled on foot and by sea to their brother Turks in the Ottoman Empire, who took them in. Everything had been left behind. There was little to give them. More than 300,000 fled to an Ottoman Empire that was unprepared for great numbers of refugees. They lived in camps until lands could be distributed to them. But the Ottoman Empire was poor, too poor to provide the medicines and even the food necessary for their survival. Thousands died in the camps before they could be settled in the Empire. Aid from other countries was almost nonexistent. Nevertheless, the Tatars were finally settled, straining tremendously the already meagre resources of the Ottomans.

Exile in the East

The Caucasian lands were a far frontier of the Ottoman Empire. At the end of the eighteenth century the Ottomans controlled the southwestern Caucasian lands, including the city of Batum. The Persian Empire extended north to Derbent and reigned over the south central and southeastern Caucasus. The Caucasian holdings of both empires were heavily Muslim in population, with Turks the largest ethnic group. Independent Muslim tribes populated and controlled the northern Caucasian lands. Only Georgia (capital Tiflis) was a Christian kingdom, a vassal of the Persians. Numerous Armenian enclaves were scattered through the south Caucasus.

The Russians had fought border wars with the north Caucasian tribes for generations. In the 1790s they began to extend their military power southward. Their intentions at first may have been to secure their own lands from raids and increase the commercial presence of Russian merchants, but the vassalage of Christian Georgia to Muslim Persia provided them with their first pretext for wider conquests. In the late 1700s the Georgian king threw in his lot with the Russians against the Persians, hoping to preserve Georgian autonomy. Instead, a Russian army took Georgia, which was incorporated into the Russian Empire, giving the Russians a far outpost in the south. Beginning in 1796, the Russians conquered the west Caucasian khanates from the Persian Empire. These khanates were nominally vassals of the Persians, but were in fact autonomous Turkish principalities, occupying

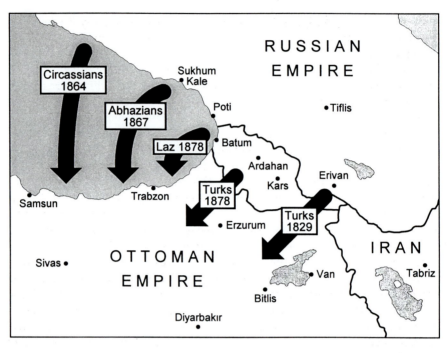

RUSSIAN EMPIRE

Circassians 1864

Sukhum Kale

Abhazians 1867

Poti

• Tiflis

Laz 1878

Batum

Ardahan

Erivan

Turks 1878

Kars

Trabzon

Samsun

Turks 1829

• Erzurum

IRAN

Sivas •

OTTOMAN EMPIRE

• Van

Tabriz

Bitlis

Diyarbakır

Expulsions of Caucasian Muslims.

approximately the combined areas of today's Republic of Azerbaijan and Republic of Armenia. Aided by local Armenian contingents and spies, the Russian seized the khanates one by one, leaving only the khanate of Erivan in Persian hands. The details of the conquest and its effects on the local Turkish population are little known. Massacre of Turks in Ganja (called by the Russians Elizavetpol) and other areas and suppression of Islamic institutions have been documented, but with little detail.

The conquest of Erivan and the great exchange of population

Today the Russian province of Erivan is the main part of the Armenian Republic, but in the 1820s Turkish Muslims made up the majority of its population. The Armenian population whose descendants would live in the Armenian Republic were in the 1820s scattered over the Caucasus and eastern Anatolia. In 1826 the Russians began a great forced exchange of population that was to create an Armenia in Erivan and cause great suffering to both the Turks and the Armenians.

The Russians defeated the Persians in the war of 1826–28 and the Ottomans in the war of 1828–29. Their victory left them in secure control of the southern Caucasus lands (called by the Russians Trans-Caucasia).

They forced approximately one-third of the Muslims, mainly Turks, from the province of Erivan and replaced them with Armenian migrants from the Ottoman Empire and Persia.

The forced migration of the Turks of Erivan was the beginning of a great population exchange that was to continue for almost a hundred years. Armenians came from the Ottoman Empire and Persia to take the place of Muslims who were forced to flee south.

In the years that followed the 1826–29 wars the migration of both Armenians and Turks continued. Some left their homes for better living conditions. This was especially true of the Armenians from Anatolia and Persia, who were drawn to the Russian Empire by economic incentives such as employment and low taxes as much as by nationalistic sentiment. Others left out of fear. In the 1877–78 Russo–Ottoman War more than 60,000 Turks fled the Kars-Ardahan region of Anatolia which had been conquered by the Russians. Their places were taken by Armenians who left the Ottoman East. Armenians had welcomed the Russian invaders who seemed likely to keep extensive lands in eastern Anatolia. When the other European powers forced the Russians to leave most of their conquests perhaps 25,000 Armenians left with the Russian armies, fearful of Muslim reprisals. Forty thousand Muslim Laz people were also forced out by the Russians, as will be described below. The exchanges continued until just after the end of World War I. By the time they were over, previously Muslim regions of the Caucasus were almost completely Christian in population and previously Armenian areas of eastern Anatolia were Muslim.

The ongoing exchange of population changed the demographic picture of the East and caused great hardship and hatred on both sides. If blame were to be assigned to anyone it would be to the Russian imperialists, but the hatred that developed was between the Muslims and the Armenians. By the end of the nineteenth century sides had been drawn. It mattered little that the peasants of the East, whether Armenian or Muslim, originally could only have wanted peace and the chance to get on with planting and harvesting. As the Russians advanced both Turks and Armenians were gradually drawn into the conflict that had its bloody conclusion in the First World War.

The Caucasian exiles

The Muslims who suffered the worst collective fate at the hands of the Russians were not ethnic Turks. Today their descendants are Turks, as citizens of the Turkish Republic, but until Russian conquest they were independent tribesmen living in the western Caucasus. The Circassians, the Abhazians, and the Laz lived on the Black Sea coast and coastal plains,

335

regions that were coveted by the Russians. Much of their land was fertile. More important, it lay on the important coastal communication routes on the Black Sea.

Due to the military prowess of the Caucasians, especially the Circassians, the Russians left real conquest of their lands until they had already taken the central and southern Caucasian regions. From the 1830s until the end of the Crimean War the Russians were occupied with the hard-fought but hopeless war of independence fought by the Muslims of the Caucasian mountains under a great leader, Shayh Shamil. Once the mountaineers were defeated, the Russians turned their attention at last to the Circassians and Abhazians.

From the start of the Russian campaign against the Circassians the plan was to dispossess them. Russian troops went from village to village, burning homes, forcing out the inhabitants, and killing those who remained. The methods used were what would later be categorized as State Terror. The Russians knew that the Circassian men would be difficult to defeat, because they took to the mountains and forests and fought guerilla war, so the Russians attacked the women, children and aged who were left in the villages. Once a few villages in a district had been levelled and their inhabitants killed, the other villagers of the district fled. The Circassian men who would have fought on were unwilling to do so when fighting meant the deaths of their families.

By 1864 the Russians had herded the Circassians to Black Sea ports and forced them onto ships. The ships had been sent by the Ottomans. Despite the recent financial calamity of settling the Crimean refugees, the Ottomans had no choice but to try to save their brother Muslims. They did so, but as with the Crimeans there was little they could offer the refugees. The Russians had seized all the refugees' possessions and sent them off without supplies. When they reached Ottoman refugee camps in Black Sea ports the Ottomans could only provide them with basic food and shelter, and not always that. Hundreds of thousands died of disease and starvation.

In 1867, the Russians attacked south and the Abhazian Muslims suffered the same fate as the Circassians. They, too, were driven to the ships and sent off to the Ottoman Empire. The Ottomans accepted them. After the 1877–78 war the last of the Muslim coastal peoples, the Laz, were also exiled by the Russians. The coast of the Caucasus was now free for Russian settlement. Although it remained a largely depopulated wasteland for many years after the Circassian migration, the north coast was ultimately populated by Slavs. The south coast was mainly taken over by Georgians, and remains today with Georgia. The descendants of the small proportion of the Circassians, Abhazians, and Laz who were able to remain in the Caucasus are a small minority in their homelands.

The sufferings of the Caucasian migrants was immense. Of the 1.2 million Circassians and Abhazians who departed their lands, only two-thirds survived. The rest were killed by the Russians or died of disease or starvation. Very few peoples in history have suffered such a loss.

The loss of the Circassians and Abhazians was also a political and economic loss for the Ottomans, a gain for the Russians. By driving out the Caucasian Muslims, the Russians had managed to increase their land and improve their commercial and military position on the Black Sea. At the same time, they had grievously wounded their enemy, the Ottoman Empire. It was the Ottomans, without any real assistance, who were forced to feed and care for the refugees and to find them land and livelihood. The refugees from the Crimea and the Caucasus were equal to almost 10 per cent of the population of Ottoman Anatolia. Any modern state would find it very difficult to support such an influx of refugees, even with international support and aid. Imagine the cost to the Ottomans, who had neither support nor aid and were themselves poor. Along with the costs of the wars with Russia, the costs of the refugees tremendously weakened the Ottoman Empire and were a major contribution to its ultimate destruction.

Greek independence

As explained in the previous chapter, the nineteenth century was a time of nationalism. European nationalism was rapidly infecting the Ottoman Empire. However, the nationalist revolutionaries in the Ottoman Empire had a demographic problem. One of the cardinal principles of nationalism can be summarized as 'The Land for the Nation'. Such a sentiment always works against those who are not defined as members of the nation. In American history, the slogan 'America for the Americans' meant trouble for recent immigrants. (The slogan could have been used against the ancestors of the bigots, but they did not notice such problems.) Among the Balkan Christian peoples, and later among the Armenians, it was assumed that a new national state demanded what nineteenth-century writers called 'racial unity' or even 'racial purity'. (Nineteenth-century nationalists used the concept of 'race' differently from the manner in which it is used today. They spoke of the 'English Race', the German Race', and even the 'American Race'.) Those who were not members of the nation were to be excluded, and primary among those to be banned from the state were Turks.

Turks were a sizeable minority in many of the Balkan territories of the Ottoman Empire. As national states successfully revolted, the presence of Turks, seen as part of the old system of Ottoman dominance, was intolerable to many. Furthermore, the nationalists saw the same potential problem as seen by the Russian imperialists – if Turks were left behind after a revolution, might they not support an Ottoman re-conquest? The solution

337

was obvious. A mixture of ethnic and religious hatred and practical politics sealed the fate of the Turks.

The first of the major national revolutions in the Balkans began in Greece in 1821. Whether at that early date what we call nationalism or an older religious separatism was at work in the Greek revolution is a matter of speculation. However, the revolution's effect on the Turks of Greece is better known. When the call to revolt was heeded in the Morea (today southern Greece), the first act of the rebels was the slaughter of all the Turks who fell into their hands. Peasants interested in appropriating the lands of the Turks joined in the massacres. As the most famous historian of the Greek revolution, a man with vast sympathy for Greek independence, wrote:

> In the meantime the Christian population had attacked and murdered the Mussulman population in every part of the peninsula. The towers and country homes of the Mussulmans were burned down, and their property was destroyed, in order to render the return of those who had escaped into the fortresses hopeless. From the 26th of March until Easter Sunday, which fell, in the year 1821, on the 22nd of April, it is supposed that fifteen thousand [Muslim] souls perished in cold blood and that about three thousand farmhouses or Turkish dwellings were laid waste.[1]

The only Turks to escape were those who were able to flee quickly to the relative safety of fortress cities held by the Ottoman army, such as Athens. Even the cities were not always refuges:

> For three days the miserable [Turkish] inhabitants were given over to the lust and cruelty of a mob of savages. Neither sex nor age was spared. Women and children were tortured before being put to death. So great was the slaughter that [Greek guerilla leader] Kolokotrones himself says that, when he entered the town, from the gate of the citadel his horse's hoofs never touched the ground. His path of triumph was carpeted with corpses. At the end of two days, the wretched remnant of the Mussulmans were deliberately collected, to the number of some two thousand souls, of every age and sex, but principally women and children, were led out to a ravine in the neighboring mountains, and there butchered like cattle.[2]

By the end of the rebellion and creation of the new Greek kingdom, the Turks whose ancestors had lived in southern Greece for centuries, were

---

[1] George Finlay, *History of the Greek Revolution*, London, 1861, p. 187.
[2] W. Alison Phillips, *The War of Greek Independence, 1821 to 1833*, New York, 1897, pp. 60–61.

dead or exiled. The governments of Europe were anxious to set up an independent Greek state, so anxious that through military action they forced the Ottoman government to capitulate. What they did not force was the repatriation of the surviving Turkish refugees. Their lands were forfeit. The Turks of southern Greece had thus been violently removed. The strategy of 'removing' Turks to create a homogenous national state was an obvious success. It was to be repeated.

Serbia and Bulgaria, 1875–78

By the middle of the nineteenth century nationalism had grown strong among the Serbs of two autonomous states within the Ottoman Empire – Serbia and Montenegro. Although the Ottomans claimed Montenegro as an integral part of the Empire, it was in fact independent. Russia supported Montenegran independence financially and diplomatically. Few Muslims had ever lived in Montenegro's mountainous, barren, and dangerous territory, though Serbia had a Muslim community until 1830. The country had become largely autonomous in 1817, but an Ottoman governor still resided in Belgrade, the capital, and Ottoman garrisons were in major fortresses. In 1830, Serbia was declared fully autonomous. This was a result of the Russo–Turkish War of 1828–29. Under the treaty of Edirne, which ended the war, and through further concessions forced by the Russians, the Ottomans gave up all real control of the country. As part of the agreement, Muslims were evicted from most of the country. Between 15,000 and 20,000 Muslims left Serbia either after the treaty or during an anti-Ottoman rebellion in the 1820s.

Russian support for Serbian and Montenegran independence and expulsion of Muslim populations was to be a central component of the history of the two countries throughout the nineteenth century.

Serbia and Montenegro both coveted the territory of Ottoman Bosnia-Herzogovina. The Ottoman province of Bosnia, which included Bosnia in the north and Herzegovina in the south, was almost 50 per cent Muslim in population, but had large Orthodox (Serbian) and Catholic (Croatian) minorities. In 1875, Serbs in Bosnia began a rebellion, intending to join the province to Serbia and Montenegro, with the active support of those two states. The rebellion was particularly bloody. Ottoman officials and Muslim civilians were targeted for murder in order to drive both government and Muslim civilians from the province. However, the Ottoman army was able to put down the revolt. Serbia, thwarted by the Ottoman success, declared war, but it, too, was defeated by the Ottomans in 1876. Then events in Bulgaria took the stage.

Bulgarian nationalists began a revolt in 1876. The Ottoman army was busy with the revolt in Bosnia and the Serbian War. The course of the

Bulgarian revolt was similar to what had occurred fifty years earlier in Greece – in the first days of the revolt 1,000 Turkish peasants were killed in cold blood. The difference between Bulgaria and Greece was the presence of many more Turks in the former. Because the army was fighting elsewhere, the Ottoman government armed local Turks, as well as Circassian and Tatar refugees who had been settled in Bulgaria, and allowed them to put down the rebels. They did so with the same ferocity the rebels had used in killing Turks. Between 3,000 and 12,000 Bulgarian Christians died before the revolt was crushed.

Russia declared war on the Ottoman Empire in 1877. Serbia had attacked the Ottomans in 1876 and had been defeated. To protect Serbia and advance her own cause, Russia had demanded that the Ottomans divide their European possessions into small, autonomous Christian states. The Ottomans had refused. After initially holding a defensive position the Ottomans were defeated and forced to retreat. The Ottoman defeat was a signal for the slaughter of the Turks of Bulgaria.

In 1877 and 1878 the Russians made use in Bulgaria of all the tactics they had perfected in the Caucasus. Their official agents were the Cossacks and sometimes other army units. To these were joined Bulgarian revolutionaries and Bulgarian peasants eager to seize the lands, crops, and cattle of the Turks. The tactics were once again those of State Terror. In a typical Turkish village, Cossacks would disarm the villagers, then surround the village and shoot all but a few who tried to escape. Hemmed in, the Turks were attacked by Bulgarians, who murdered the inhabitants. The variants on the system included Russian use of artillery that levelled villages, villagers driven into slavery, and slow, rather than quick death for the villagers, especially women. The scenes recorded by European diplomats equal any pictures of inhumanity and horror in history. They fill many volumes, but are too gruesome to present here.

The plan to drive Turks out of Bulgaria was facilitated by the few who were allowed to flee destroyed villages. They spread the word to others, and soon the refugees filled the roads. Hundreds of thousands of Turks fled into enclaves where they were protected by Ottoman troops – over 200,000 in the Şumla-Varna region, 100,000 in the Rhodope Mountains, etc. More than 200,000 others fled into Istanbul and Anatolia. Many of the refugees were Crimean Tatars and Circassians whose families had already endured one exile. The conditions in the refugee camps were abysmal, the only alleviation being a little aid from British charitable organizations and whatever the Ottomans could provide. Disease and starvation were once again the main killers. Of 45,000 refugees in the city of Edirne, 16,000 had typhus and 100 to 120 died each day. Refugees were sheltered in mosques, public buildings, and whatever other quarters could be found. The great Ayasofya mosque in Istanbul housed 4,000, of whom 25 to 30 died each day, to be replaced by other refugees.

When peace came in 1878, European powers intervened and called the Congress of Berlin to set the terms of the Russian victory. The Russians were forced by the British, Germans, and others who dominated the Congress to agree to let the Turkish refugees return to their homes, but they seldom did so. Many of those who tried to return were murdered or enslaved, and many refused to leave their refugee enclaves until the Ottomans, once again, took them into settlements in Anatolia. As had happened in the Caucasus and the Crimea, it was up to the Ottoman Empire to try to save the lives of the refugees.

Of the 1.5 million Muslims, mainly Turks, along with Circassians and some Slavic-speaking Muslims, in pre-war Bulgaria, less than 700,000 remained after the wars and subsequent emigration. 216,000, one-third, of the Muslims of Bulgaria had been murdered or died of disease and starvation as refugees. The rest were permanent exiles from their lands. Although their numbers are not known as precisely, Jews suffered exile and death, as well, both because they remained loyal to the Ottomans and because of anti-semitism. A common cry in Bulgaria was 'Turks and Jews out'.

When Russia triumphed, Serbia and Montenegro were also given pieces of Ottoman land. In the Serbian-occupied territories, only 17 per cent of the Muslims remained ten years after the war. The Montenegrans killed or expelled all the Muslims in the territories they occupied. Bosnia was seized by the Austrians, who had been promised the territory by the Russians as a condition for remaining neutral in war. Many Muslims fled the province rather than live under Austrian domination. Many others had died in the 1875 rebellion. Between 1875 and 1879 approximately one-third of the Muslims of Bosnia-Herzogovina either emigrated or died.

Commenting on the Russian actions against the Turkish refugees in Bulgaria, a British official government investigator remarked, 'I can come to no other conclusion but that the Russians are carrying out a fixed policy of exterminating the Moslem race'. In a report to the Foreign Office the British Ambassador to the Ottoman Empire, Sir Henry Layard, accurately summarized Russian intentions:

> Those who have watched the proceedings of the Russians can scarcely doubt that their deliberate object has been to drive the Turkish race out of the provinces they have occupied and replace it with the Slav. Such has been the policy of Russia in other countries she has conquered.

The Balkan Wars

After Bulgaria had been detached from the Ottoman Empire and Austria had seized Bosnia and Herzegovina in 1878, the region left to the Ottoman

Ottoman Adversaries in the
First Balkan War, 1912-13

0   100

miles

The Balkan Wars.

Empire in Europe was predominantly Muslim. A little more than 50 per cent of the population were Muslims (primarily Turks, in the east and north, and secondarily Albanians, in the west). The Balkan Wars reduced this majority Muslim population to a distinct minority.

As will be seen in the next chapter, the Balkan Wars were a rapid defeat for the Ottoman Empire. In 1912, Greece, Bulgaria, Serbia, and Montenegro all declared war on the Ottoman Empire with the intention of seizing Ottoman lands. Ottoman armies were unable to defend the Muslim population or give them time to escape. The experience of the Bulgarians in cementing their national state through forced migration was a lesson well learned by the Balkan states. Their actions ensured that the majority Muslim population would not remain after their conquest.

The type of devastation visited upon the Turks was what has already been described for other areas and other times. Turkish villages were pillaged then burned to the ground. European observers spoke of inhabitants driven into barns or coffee houses, which were then burned down, and of piles of bodies. In many villages the men were killed quickly, the women more slowly. City dwellers did not escape similar treatment. Most of the horrors inflicted on the population are too horrible to be described here.

Ottoman soldiers came in for particular harm. Recognized standards of treatment of prisoners of war were not adhered to. For example, when the Bulgarians took the city of Edirne after a long siege the defenders were gathered and interned on an island in the river and deliberately starved until more than half had died. Many of the survivors were led off and never heard from again. Edirne, though, was one of the few places were the tables were turned. When the Ottomans retook the city in the second Balkan War they exacted their vengeance against the Bulgarians.

The shock troops of the Balkan nations were the guerilla bands (called *komitajis*) supported by Bulgaria, Serbia, and Greece. They operated in advance of the armies, attacking Turkish villages and forcing the villagers onto the roads. In Albania, Montenegran soldiers devastated the region from their borders to the sea. In many ways, the sufferings of the Muslims in the Balkan Wars were worse than in 1877–78. This was partly due to the difference between the Cossacks and the Balkan guerilla bands. The Cossacks were in military units, under military orders which they carried out. The guerrillas were only loosely under any orders. Hatred and desire for plunder were driving forces for them, not orders. This resulted in a high Muslim mortality. Also, in the Bulgarian War of 1877–78 the Russians had effectively organized the removal of Turks. The situation in the Balkan Wars was much more confused and thus more dangerous to the Turks and other Muslims. Refugees were often driven from lands conquered by one army into lands soon conquered by another. For example, the Turks of Thrace might be driven eastward by the Greeks, then attacked once again by Bulgarians marching south. Some were pushed back and forth between armies, with a resultant death rate greater than that in 1877–78.

Among the invading armies there was obviously a deliberate intention to ensure that the Turks would never return. Muslim houses, villages, and quarters of cities were destroyed so that the refugees would have nothing to which they could return. A British vice-consul who observed the war wrote the Foreign Office that, 'The track of the invading [Bulgarian] army is marked by 80 miles of ruined villages'.

Refugees

Muslim refugees fled on foot to the mountains, the sea coast and, if they could make it, to Istanbul and Anatolia. They were joined by Jews, equally persecuted by the invaders. Great numbers died on the journey; European observers estimated that half the refugees from many areas never reached sanctuary. Those who gathered in Salonica and other ports were taken to

Anatolia by ship or left in caravans after the wars' end. A detailed Ottoman count of the refugees who were settled in the Empire after the wars showed 413,000 survivors. Many had first passed through refugee camps where disease took a terrible toll. In the great camp outside Istanbul, for example, cholera broke out. In other camps, typhus and typhoid were widespread.

Once again, it fell to the Ottoman Empire to settle and care for the refugees, with limited resources. They were mainly settled in western Anatolia and eastern Thrace. It should be remembered that many of the migrants were the descendants of families that had already come from the Crimea or Circassia, been settled in Bulgaria, forced to flee once again in 1877–78, and now in flight once again, this time to western Anatolia. They were to be uprooted again in 1918.

The effects of imperialism and nationalism

As the Ottoman Empire came to the period of the First World War it had already suffered greater blows than any other combatants were to suffer in the Great War. Beginning at the end of the eighteenth century, the Ottoman Empire was forced to absorb millions of refugees. The refugees arrived with nothing. All their property and belongings had been taken from them. They came to an Empire that was ill-prepared to receive them. If they were to survive, food, shelter, and ultimately land would have to be provided for them. It was provided, but at great cost.

The refugees came just as the Ottomans were attempting to reform. It was a time at which all resources should have been given over to new schools, new industries, and all the needs of modernization. Instead, government resources went to settling refugees. Worse, even greater resources went into defending the Empire in losing battles with the Russians and others. Taken together, losses in war and the cost of settling the refugees were perhaps the main reason Ottoman reform was only a limited success.

The lost territories

Much of the Ottoman investment in modernization had been spent in Ottoman Europe. From the Ottoman viewpoint it was all wasted. When the Russians invaded, public buildings, schools, and businesses were all either destroyed or given to other masters. The infrastructure built by the Ottomans was given over to those who would use it against them in the Balkan Wars. Government investment and borrowing had not only been useless, it ultimately worked against the Empire.

The Ottomans worked against a timetable of destruction. They fever-ishly strove to develop a region so that it could survive economically and militarily, only to see it fall to enemies. Refugees fled into the remaining regions, which the Ottomans also tried to develop. These too were lost. The Ottomans tried to keep one step ahead of disaster. They failed. Given the forces arrayed against them, it is hard to see how they could have succeeded.

Political effects

One of the worst effects of Russian imperialism, nationalism, and the migration of Muslim refugees was the destruction of the system of religious toleration that had been one of the highest achievements of the Empire. The *millet* system had never been perfect. In modern terms, non-Muslims had been 'second-class citizens', excluded from most governing. However, the Ottoman system had allowed Muslims, Jews, and many different sects of Christianity to coexist for centuries. No great empire since ancient times had tolerated such religious pluralism. One need only compare the survival of many religions to the intolerance of Europe to see what a feat was Ottoman tolerance.

Now the *millet* system was slowly collapsing. In the east, Armenians saw Muslims as those who stood in the way of their national aspirations. Muslims saw Armenians as the allies of the Russians who had so persecuted Muslims. In Greece, Bulgaria, and elsewhere Christian subjects of the sultan had risen to help invaders or to slaughter Turks. In revenge, Turks had retaliated. This naturally affected the relations of the Christians and Muslims who remained in the Empire. Most Muslims and most Christians could not have wanted war, and religious or ethnic hatred originally may have been limited to a minority of ardent nationalists, but who could tell how Greeks, Armenians, or Muslims might feel or act in the inevitable war? Hatred and suspicion replaced tolerance on all sides.

It was the loss of ethnic tolerance and division of the peoples of the empire into national groups that more than anything else doomed the people of the Ottoman Empire. They were to culminate in the disaster of World War I.

Chapter 11

The Great War, 1912–18

Overleaf

The end of the Gallipoli campaign: British evacuation at Suvla Bay. Ottoman victories at Gallipoli and in Iraq in 1916 showed their military skill and determination, unfortunately not matched by their resources. (*Illustrated London News*. February 12, 1916, p. 201.)

The Great War, 1912–18

Until an even greater war arrived, the First World War was always known to Europeans and Americans as the Great War. For the Middle East the term still applies. Nothing that has happened since the First World War has had such a great effect on the Middle East or on the lives of its people. At the end of the war, national boundaries, rulers, and allegiances had irrevocably changed. Much of the population, especially that of Ottoman Europe and Anatolia, had died or been displaced. During the war no other region (including Russia after the Revolution) had seen such death and devastation. In terms of human misery the Great War in the Middle East was one of the worst ever fought.

With the possible exception of the Crusades, no period of Middle Eastern history is more misunderstood in the West than the period of World War I. Few realize the extent of the destruction wreaked on the Ottoman Empire in the war. The only facet of the war that is widely known is the suffering of Christian minority groups in the Empire – the corresponding suffering of Turks and other Muslims is virtually unrecognized. During the war, the Ottoman Empire was allied with the Germans against the British, on whose side America eventually came into the war. Britain, Canada, and the United States were all filled with wartime propaganda against the Turks. The propaganda fed on religious and racial prejudices that were already there. Of course, there also was much propaganda directed against the Germans. However, once the war had ended, the libels spread about the Germans were disavowed. Books were even written by propagandists explaining how they had lied about the Germans. There were many Americans of German extraction, who fought for the truth about their people. However, because no sizeable body of Turks lived in either Western Europe or America, there were no lobbying groups to defend the good name of the Turks. After the war, no one in the West spoke up for the Turks, nor were the wartime lies about the Turks studied or disowned. For their own part,

The Ottoman Empire in 1914.

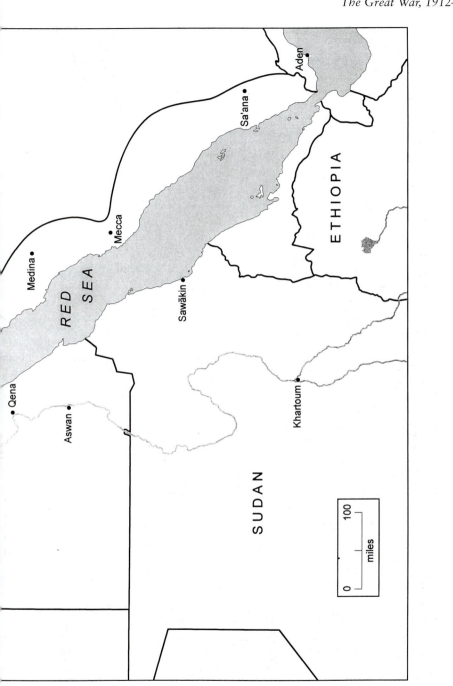

RED SEA

Medina •

Mecca •

Sa'ana •

Aden •

ETHIOPIA

Sawākin •

Qena •

Aswan •

Khartoum •

SUDAN

100

miles

0

the Turks were too busy with reconstruction of a war-torn land to be concerned with their image overseas. The result was a history that ignored or distorted many of the events and results of World War I. Only recently has this changed, as historians have begun to consider the First World War from all sides.

The military situation before the First World War

At the beginning of the twentieth century the European powers had already for some time been preparing themselves for war. Armaments had increased to unprecedented levels as the powers divided themselves into blocs of allies. The Ottomans, although allied to no one, could be expected to be drawn into war. They were unprepared. When the Committee of Union and Progress had taken control in Istanbul Ottoman military might was at a low ebb. Rightly fearful of revolutionary feeling among the military, sultan Abdülhamit II had not maintained military strength as he might have. The officer corps was particularly in need of support, better education, and pay increases. When the new Ottoman government took control in 1908 they were forced to look immediately to defences that had been neglected. They set to the task, but it took time.

Obviously, the relative poverty and lack of economic infrastructure of the Ottoman Empire was a military disadvantage. As World War I approached the Ottoman Empire was dependent on European factories for ships of war, heavy artillery, and other means of warfare. Although the nineteenth century reforms had vastly improved Ottoman communications and transport, roads and railways were still deficient. In 1912 there was still no railway that connected Istanbul with the Arab provinces. Shipments from the Arab world had to be taken off trains near Adana, transhipped by road over mountain passes, then put on northern railways. Many potential areas of battle were unserved by modern transport systems, particularly in northeast Anatolia. Militarily, the worst part of this was that troops and supplies took long to get to battle fronts. For example, in the Balkan Wars troops from the Arab provinces did not arrive in Europe until the First Balkan War was over.

The one positive factor for the Ottomans was the quality of their fighting men. The Turkish soldiers were capable of enduring immense hardships and followed their commanders into seemingly impossible battles. Contemporary and modern analysts used words such as 'magnificent bravery' to describe them, and it was to them that the long survival of the Empire against much stronger enemies was primarily due. Unfortunately, their bravery also resulted in extreme mortality.

The biggest difficulty for the Ottoman army was the impossible geographic situation of the Empire in Europe and Anatolia at the turn of the century. The Russian conquests of 1878 had robbed the Ottomans of strategic borders and lands necessary for defence. Defending a far-flung Empire had always been a daunting task. The enemies of the Ottomans were richer, more technologically mature, and often had far larger populations. To this was now added a great geographic disadvantage. In the east, the fortress cities of Kars and Batum had passed into Russian hands in 1878. Other fortified cities, such as Ardahan, were lost as well. The Russians had taken mountain chains and very high and easily-defended ground in northeastern Anatolia. Cities and defensive passes were joined to Russia by new railways and roads. Thus the best sites for a defence of Anatolia had been lost. Ottoman Europe was a defensive nightmare of very long borders, numerous enemies, and terrain that was difficult to defend. The borders of Bulgaria had been extended so far south that only a narrow bottleneck in Thrace connected the mass of Ottoman Europe with the rest of the Empire. If troops were concentrated there to keep lines of communication open, the long borders in Europe would be undefended. Without control of the sea, which the Ottomans did not have, the Empire's European possessions and army in Europe could be cut off by one Bulgarian thrust. The capital could readily come under the guns of an enemy. This in fact was what happened in the Balkan Wars.

The Balkan Wars

In October of 1912, Greece, Bulgaria, Serbia, and Montenegro all declared war on the Ottoman Empire. Each nation intended to satisfy its desire for territory at the Empire's expense. Each had long felt that most of the Ottoman land in Europe was its by right. The claims overlapped, but the claimants agreed to cooperate, at least until the Ottomans were defeated. They attacked Ottoman Europe on all sides.

The Ottomans found themselves in an impossible position from the start. Troops divided along the long borders were defeated quickly by the Balkan nations or forced into fortress towns. The Bulgarians struck south and cut off Europe from the rest of the Empire, ending any possibility of retreat. Bulgarians almost reached Istanbul itself before they were stopped by the Turks at defensive lines north of the city at the end of the year. By April, 1913, the major cities of Scutari, Yanina, and Edirne, filled with Ottoman soldiers and refugee Muslims, had fallen. Under the terms of the treaty of London (May 30, 1913), all of Ottoman Europe, with the exception of a small area north of Istanbul, had been lost.

The only salvation for the Ottomans, partial though it was, came when the Balkan allies fell out. In preparation for war, they had agreed in spring, 1912 to drive the Ottomans from Europe first, then divide the conquered lands. Once the Ottomans were defeated ancient rivalries among the allies appeared. Serbia, Greece, and Bulgaria all claimed Macedonia. The Bulgarians had born the brunt of the fighting, yet had taken what they considered to be far less than their share. Bulgaria attacked its erstwhile allies and the Second Balkan War ensued, Romania now joining the others against Bulgaria. The Ottoman army, finally reinforced by troops from Asia, also attacked Bulgarian positions and retook eastern Thrace, including Edirne. With small alterations, the resulting Ottoman European boundaries were the same as those of present-day Turkey in Thrace.

Lessons of the Balkan Wars

The military lesson of the Balkan Wars was an obvious one – the Empire had to build up its military might quickly if it were to survive. Revenues from the Balkans had been lost, as had much of the Ottoman army, yet what remained had to be built into a stronger force than before. Help was needed, wherever it was offered. As it transpired, the help came from Germany.

The political lesson was an even harder one. The Ottomans had been taught that for them military defeat was not simply a loss of territory, treasure, and prestige. In the Balkan Wars, military loss meant the extermination of vast numbers of Turks and the exile of many more. Twenty-seven per cent of the Turks and other Muslims of the Ottoman Balkans had died, 35 per cent had become refugees. If the Ottomans failed in the next war, even more would be driven from their homes. Judging by the history of the past century, the history of the expulsions from Greece, the Crimea, the Caucasus, and now the Balkans, it was not too much to expect that the next war might not just be the end of the Ottomans, but the end of the Turks in their homeland.

The sides are drawn

The First World War began, in part, because of the Balkan Wars. Serbia had greatly increased its territory in the Balkan Wars, and Austria-Hungary feared Serbian influence on the Serbs in the Austro-Hungarian Empire. With the assassination of Archduke Francis Ferdinand by a Serbian nationalist (June 28, 1914) as an excuse, Austria attempted to crush Serbian independence, declaring war with Serbia on July 28, 1914. Russia mobilized to assist Serbia and, when Russia refused to stop its mobilization, Germany declared war on Russia (August 1), then on Russia's ally, France (August 3). England declared war on Germany on August 4. Other war declarations followed.

The Ottoman Empire initially stayed out of the war. Opinions in the ruling circles of the Committee of Union and Progress were divided. England, by allying itself with the Ottomans' ancestral enemy, Russia, had turned its back on the Ottomans, but sentiment for England and France was still high. Commercial, political, and cultural ties with England and France were strong. Those who wished for greater democracy in the Empire naturally looked to the two great democracies as models. Moreover, the 'Western' education of members of the Ottoman bureaucracy and intellectuals had usually in reality been French education, or at least education in French, which had opened to the Ottomans French literature, French political philosophy, and affection for things French. On the other hand, the Germans had greatly aided the Ottomans after the Balkan Wars. German military advisors had rebuilt the Ottoman army. The effects of British advisors on the Ottoman navy and French advisors on the Ottoman gendarmery were far less. Germans were also building a great trunk line, the 'Berlin to Baghdad railway' that would unite the Ottoman Empire. Therefore, Ottoman leaders felt a pull toward both sides in the war. In the end, it was only the dictates of survival that brought the Ottomans into the war on the side of the Germans.

Why ally with the Germans?

After the war Britain, France, and the United States damned the Ottoman Empire for having taken the side of the Germans. They portrayed the Germans as evil and, as naturally followed, anyone who sided with evil was also evil. Today's historians have taken a more even-handed approach to World War I, recognizing that neither side had a patent on good or evil. Unlike the second war, when Hitler's malevolence overshadowed all, dispassionate studies have called into question the traditional view of the first war as 'good guys versus bad guys'. The question nevertheless remains – Why did the Ottomans join the Germans?

In fact, the Ottomans had no choice.

For a hundred years before the First World War the British had usually been the Ottomans' only allies. They were strange allies, demanding the island of Cyprus as their price for helping the Ottomans in 1878, seizing Egypt, which was at least nominally Ottoman soil, and exploiting the Ottomans economically. However, they did oppose the dismemberment of the Ottoman Empire. They also supported the Ottomans diplomatically on many occasions and were generally supportive of Ottoman political reform. This was in their own interest. British policy was always to maintain the balance of power. They traditionally opposed the most dominant land power on the European continent. Fear of Russian dominance in Europe meant supporting Russia's enemy, the Ottoman Empire. A stronger Russia, occupying Istanbul and thus having naval access to the Mediterranean, would have been a threat to Great Britain and its colonies. Moreover, the British were economically well-placed in the Ottoman Empire. For them, the Ottoman Empire was 'a nice little earner'. Only the perception of grave danger to Great Britain itself could cause the British to jeopardize such a source of income.

The rise of German power necessitated a change in British policy. After German unification (1871) the power the British feared in Europe became Germany, not Russia. German military might was formidable on land and Germany was building a first-class navy. German industry at first equalled, then overtook Britain's. German trade with the rest of the world was greater than British trade. Germany wanted colonies, and Britain and France had all the good ones. A shift in British policy, in opposition to Germany, was called for. In 1907 Britain and Russia agreed to the Anglo-Russian Entente, which divided spheres of influence in Persia, agreed to British predominance in Afghanistan, and erased other difficulties between the two empires. Ominously for the Ottomans, the British also agreed that they would look favourably on a change in the Russian position in the Straits (the Bosphorus and the Dardanelles), which were sovereign Ottoman territory long coveted by Russia. Other than Germany, the only other European power to whom the Ottomans could look was France, and it too became allied with the Russians.

From 1907 to 1914 there was much of the maddening diplomacy that was common to that time; allegiances changed and politicians squabbled, but in the end the Anglo-French-Russian Alliance, known as the Triple Entente, held steady. Support for the Ottomans was a casualty of the change in British policy.

To understand why the Ottomans were forced to side with the Germans, one should consider what would have happened to the Ottomans had the Russians won the war. Russian intentions toward Ottoman territory had long been obvious. The British, because of the dictates of the European balance of power, had helped to prevent Russia from seizing Istanbul, eastern Anatolia, and perhaps more. Now the Ottoman Empire needed Germany to take the place of Britain in defending its integrity. A victorious Russia could be expected to take what it wanted from the Ottomans without European opposition. Therefore, joining the Germans was the only reasonable choice. German victory would by no means be ideal for the Ottomans – a victorious Germany would exercise too much economic and political power over the Empire – but it was far preferable to Russian victory. Ironically, had the Ottomans remained neutral, the Russian Revolution might have removed the threat to the Ottoman Empire, but there was no way to know that in 1914.

First steps to war

No one took opinion polls, but it is likely that most of the Turks had little desire to enter the war. The Ottoman experience in the Balkan Wars had

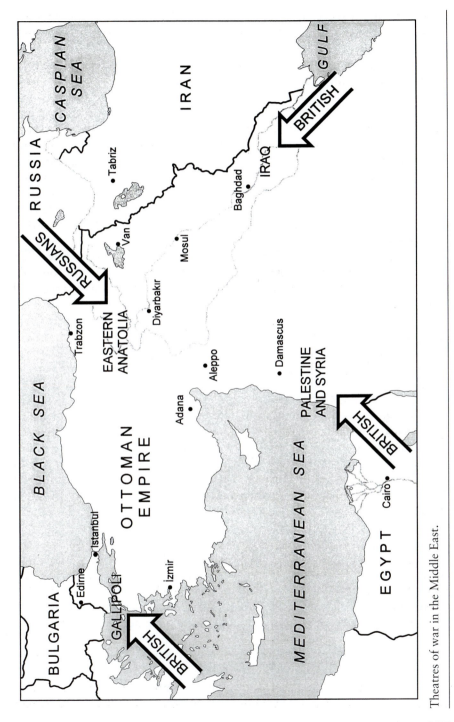

Theatres of war in the Middle East.

not made the prospect of another war appealing. The Ottoman cabinet was divided into those who wanted neutrality, or even alliance with Britain and France, and those who favoured Germany. The latter acted. Enver Paşa, the War Minister, and Sait Halim Paşa, who held the offices of Foreign Minister and Prime Minister, met with German representatives and signed a secret treaty on August 2, 1914. The rest of the cabinet reluctantly went along with this, but opponents of the alliance used their considerable political skills to forestall any belligerent actions. The treaty was still secret and might not have come into force, but fate intervened.

The British had shown that they had little desire to draw the Ottomans to their side, perhaps because their Russian allies would not have approved. Approaches by pro-British cabinet members such as Cemal Paşa, the Minister of the Navy, were repulsed. Worse came when the British infuriated the Ottomans by confiscating (August 3, 1914) two battleships which had been constructed for the Ottomans in British naval yards and paid for – ships that were to be the backbone of a new Ottoman fleet. At that juncture, two German battle cruisers, the Goeben and the Breslau, were chased across the Mediterranean to Ottoman neutral waters by a British fleet. By the laws of war, the Ottomans should have either interned them for the duration of the war or sent them out to meet the British. Instead, the Germans 'sold' the ships to the Ottoman navy. The Germans also forwarded two million kuruş in gold to the Ottomans for their war effort. The German sailors, in new Ottoman uniforms, proceeded into the Black Sea and bombarded Russian ports. On November 2, Russia declared war on the Ottomans. Britain and France followed on November 5.

The Ottomans aimed an economic blow at the Allies, cancelling payments on foreign debt owed to them and unilaterally ending the capitulations. Mobilization was declared. German advisors took up positions in key ministries, in fact taking control of much of the Ministry of War. Enver Paşa took over control of Ottoman armies in eastern Anatolia, planning a rapid attack on what he thought were weak Russian defences. War had begun.

The war

So soon after its defeat in the Balkan Wars, the Ottoman army was not ready to attack. Ottoman forces should have taken a defensive position and stuck to it. Defence was called for, because the main Ottoman enemies, Russia and Britain, were militarily superior. Russia had more soldiers, Britain had vastly superior military technology and naval forces. On the defensive, the weaker could still triumph; it takes more men and force to charge up a hill toward a defended position than it does to sit in a bunker and shoot the men as they charge. Enver Paşa took the offensive. Enver was convinced he was a strategic genius, but really he was a cowboy.

Under Enver's guidance, the Ottoman army bravely stepped into one of the worst disasters of the war. In early November of 1914, the Russians had crossed the Ottoman border in northeastern Anatolia, but had been beaten back. Instead of fortifying his positions, Enver attacked. The enormity of his decision can only be appreciated if one considers the winter weather and geography of the northeast. Snow covers everything, sometimes to a height of ten to twenty feet. Roads are impassable, and wise peasants bring their animals and themselves indoors and remain there for months. The mountain passes to be crossed can be over 2,000 metres (6,500 feet) high.

Enver found that the commanders in the east would not cooperate with his plans, which they thought were impossible. They resigned or were sacked and he took personal control. His plans called for the Turkish soldiers to surprise the enemy by crossing a mountain pass thought unusable. The soldiers had few winter uniforms or warm coats, no winter boots. They set out on December 22, 1914. The pass was too high for trees, so they had no fires to warm themselves, and there was a blizzard. Incredibly, the soldiers marched to their destination, although the initial 95,000 was now 70,000. Enver threw the exhausted, frozen survivors into battle against 65,000 Russians. The Russians were the ones in defensive position, and the Turks lost. Of the original 95,000 Turkish soldiers, 75,000 had died by the time the campaign ended in early January. Their passing and the loss of almost all their machine guns and artillery left the path to eastern Anatolia open to the Russians.

Although fewer died, the first Ottoman actions against the British were also a triumph of courage over sense. The war in the Arab world began with an Ottoman assault on the British-run Suez Canal. Knowing that the British occupation of Egypt was unpopular, the Ottomans hoped for a popular uprising that would aid their cause. It never materialized. In January of 1915, the Ottoman attack on the canal was defeated. The British, fearful of the possible success of other attacks, began to divert men and war materials to Egypt, marshalling their forces until they could attack and end the threat forever. Here, as in northeastern Anatolia, the Ottomans should have taken the defensive from the start. The desert was their ally. Destroying a few wells could hold up an invading army for months. Guerilla attacks were enough to keep the British off balance. It is also possible that the British would not have mounted a major campaign in coastal Syria if the Suez Canal had not been threatened.

The losses in Egypt and, especially, in the northeast dealt a serious blow to the Ottomans. They were thrown on the defensive, where they fought successfully. But they should have been on the defensive with a force strengthened by the 75,000 men who died in the mountains of northeastern

Anatolia. There was one benefit from it all – Enver Paşa returned to Istanbul and left the war in more capable hands.

Victories

Once Enver retired from active involvement on the battlefield, things improved. The Ottomans fought on four major fronts – the east (Transcaucasia and eastern Anatolia), Iraq, Palestine/Syria, and Gallipoli – as well as in other regions such as Galicia and Arabia. Considering the low state of the Ottoman armed forces after the Balkan Wars and the losses in Egypt and Anatolia, it is remarkable that they did so well.

The Gallipoli campaign began as a British plan to drive the Ottomans out of the war quickly through an audacious 'master stroke' that proved that not only the Ottomans could waste lives on dreams of glory. According to the plan, British warships would force the Dardanelles, then Allied forces, mainly soldiers from Australia and New Zealand would land on the European side of the Straits, on the Gallipoli Peninsula, and march on to Istanbul. The Allied attack would put the Turks out of the war by capturing the capital while most Turkish armed forces were fighting elsewhere. The Allies would have a clear sea road to bring materials of war to Russia, which desperately needed them. Such was the plan, put into action in February, 1915. It was defeated at sea by artillery and mines, which sunk three British battleships and kept the rest of the navy at bay. On land, the Allies were only able to take the beaches, exposing them to fire from well-organized Turkish troops on the high ground. Eventually, with more than 200,000 casualties, the Allies were forced to retreat. They had completely evacuated the Gallipoli Peninsula by January 9, 1916.

The British landed in southern Iraq on November 16, 1914. Their intention was to move up the River Tigris, take Baghdad, and control southern Iraq, thus securing British oil wells in Iran from Ottoman attack. As they slowly moved up the river, the Ottoman forces fell back, organizing and waiting until the British supply lines were stretched and easily cut by guerilla action. Finally, the Ottoman army made a stand at Selman Pak, near Baghdad, and utterly defeated the British, who retreated to Kut ul-Amara. There the British were put under a long siege, surrendering on April 29, 1916.

The British defeats at Gallipoli and in Iraq had a significant effect on the outcome of the war. Had the British taken the Straits, their plan to force the Ottomans out of the war and to open supply lines to Russia would have succeeded, with great effect on future events in Russia. As the map indicates, victory in Iraq in 1916 would have joined Russian and British forces. As it was, the Russians arrived in 1916, but the British only in 1917, after the Russian army had disintegrated. A 1916 victory would have turned the Ottoman flank in the Arab lands, caused the loss of Syria, and opened

Great Britain and Russia in the Ottoman East.

Mediterranean ports and the Tigris–Euphrates river system to supply the Russians.

Some of the credit for the initial Ottoman successes must be given to the Germans. They supplied considerable amounts of gold to finance the Ottoman state and the war effort. German advisors provided the organization and tactical expertise that the Ottoman army had lacked until they arrived. Their influence was especially seen behind the scenes in the efficient transport of military supplies and establishing military communications. Most important, they provided a model for the Ottoman officer corps. German advice was resented, but usually taken. At the highest level, German generals actually took command of Ottoman armies in Europe, Palestine, and Iraq. However, it would be a mistake to ascribe Ottoman success to Germans alone. Without the solid defence of Turkish officers under Mustafa Kemal, the British would have won at Gallipoli.

At the end of the war, it was Turkish generals who repulsed the invasion of Anatolia. In Iraq, it was the Ottoman field commander who forced the British surrender in 1916. (This commander, Halil Paşa, wanted strong forces to remain in Iraq. Had he been listened to, the Ottoman victory might have been longer-lasting, but German wishes were followed instead, and most of the Ottoman soldiers were withdrawn.) Yet the most important fighters were the foot soldiers. The Turkish soldier fought for ten years, from 1912 to 1922 (the first Balkan War through to the Turkish War of Independence), often without basic supplies or clothing. To modern readers, stories of soldiers marching over mountains with rags wound around their feet rather than shoes appear melodramatic and unlikely. In the Ottoman wars, the stories were true. German generals in their memoirs remark again and again on the barefoot, hungry soldiers who fought so well.

Defeats

Despite its original victories, the Ottoman Empire was overstretched by war on many fronts. By 1916 the British had begun invasions of the Ottoman Arab provinces that were to be ultimately successful. From bases in southern Iraq British troops began very cautiously to move forward in 1916. Slowed by Ottoman defences, but aided by the fact that Ottoman troops had been withdrawn to fight elsewhere, they took Baghdad on March 11, 1917.

British forces moved from Egypt in 1917, taking Jerusalem on December 9 of that year. Rather than attempt any quick victories, the British generals advanced slowly. The Ottomans, who had neither the men nor the resources to win a protracted war, were forced to retreat slowly. Though the Ottomans under German and Turkish leadership fought well and greatly slowed the British advance, they lost. It was a war of attrition that used British capabilities to their best advantage. For example, while the Ottoman army was dependent on desert wells in the Palestine campaign, the British army built a pipeline that carried fresh water from Egypt. Most of Syria had fallen by October, 1918.

The Ottoman campaign in eastern Anatolia was hampered by the need to deal with a massive Armenian revolt as well as with the Russian army. Beset by internal revolt and the loss of men in Enver's Paşa's debacle, when the Russians attacked the Turks could only fall back and wait for new troops to arrive. In 1916 the Russians took most of eastern Anatolia, including the cities of Van, Erzurum, and Trabzon. The Ottomans, under Mustafa Kemal and others, won small engagements and held their line, but a new offensive was expected in 1917.

The map on the previous page indicates the extent of the Ottoman defeat. In 1917, the Ottoman army was being driven out of Palestine and most of Iraq (Baghdad fell in March). The east was in Russian hands, and it was expected that the Russians in Anatolia would soon join up with the British in Iraq. All that would be left to the Ottomans was a small part of Europe and western and central Anatolia, territories which would also soon be lost. The Germans had troubles of their own. The entrance of the United States into the war ended the chance for assistance from the Germans. Their efforts were needed on their own western front. The situation in what remained of the Ottoman Empire reflected battlefield disasters. Ottoman soldiers were in rags. The internal transport system was breaking down, so peasants could not get their crops to hungry cities. More than a million Muslim refugees had crowded into regions still held by the Ottomans. The government's credit was gone and supplies were low.

Just when things were darkest, the Russian Revolution offered the Ottomans a respite in the east. With the coming of the Revolution, Russian soldiers in eastern Anatolia, like their compatriots on the European front, began to abandon their posts and walk home. By the end of 1917 all that was left in the east were Russian officers, Armenian troops who had fought in the Russian army, and Armenian irregulars. The Ottoman army attacked to regain its territory. Troops loyal to the new Armenian Republic were defeated, and the Ottomans marched all the way to Batum and Baku, securing the east until the end of the war.

The Armenian question

The Ottomans fought two wars in eastern Anatolia – the war with the Russian Empire and a civil war with Armenian rebels. While they were confronting the Russians on the Caucasian front the Ottomans were also forced to put down a revolution behind the lines. From the start, the internal war in the east became a war of peoples, Armenians against Muslims, in which all the inhabitants of the east were forced to become combatants if they were to have a chance to survive.

The disaster of the 1890s rebellions seem to have taught the Armenian nationalists that such revolts could not work without guaranteed outside assistance. The last great flare-up of nationalist rebellion, in Adana in 1909, did not spread. The intention of the 1890s rebellions had been to bring European countries into the conflict, as had happened in Bulgaria. It was assumed that out of sympathy for the Armenians the Europeans would force the Ottomans to allow the creation of an Armenian state. This had not happened. Russia had not invaded and Britain, at that time, was still interested in keeping the Ottoman Empire intact. These earlier rebellions had been failures, so the revolutionaries changed tactics. Instead of open rebellion, they spent the first decade of the twentieth century developing their revolutionary infrastructure, smuggling weapons into the Ottoman Empire, and planning for future opportunities.

The First World War presented the opportunity for a new Armenian rebellion. Supporters of the revolution would not be lacking. Russia could be expected to attempt an invasion of the east and Britain was an enemy of the Ottoman Empire. Both would be glad to support any rebellion that would sap Ottoman strength. In view of the Russian war aims of conquering eastern Anatolia for themselves, it is doubtful if they would have ever accepted a separate Armenian state, especially given that they had never allowed a measure of autonomy to Russian Armenia. But for the revolutionaries Russian rule was preferable to Ottoman rule. The sides were thus drawn – Russians and Armenian nationalists against the Ottomans and the local Muslims.

Armenian rebellion in the east actually began before the Russians and Ottomans traded fire. In the late summer of 1914, before war was declared, arms and supplies began to be taken from hidden depots. (One cache discovered by the Ottomans even included Russian army uniforms.) By the time war began, Armenian bands were active all across the east. They quickly became a major military threat. The Ottoman army and much of the rural police force (gendarmes) had been sent to the Russian front, leaving scant forces to oppose the rebellion. Attempts were made by the Armenians to seize cities, including Urfa, Muş, Zeytun, and Kara Hisar-ı Şarkı.

Much of the Armenian rebellion took the form of classic guerilla operations behind Ottoman lines. Communications lines and roads were particular targets, as were army recruiting offices, gendarmerie posts, and other agencies of government. The Ottomans were forced to withdraw whole divisions from the front to combat the rebels. Cities and mountain redoubts were retaken by the army. Therefore, in terms of taking and holding land, the rebellion was initially not a success. It was, however, a success in 'softening-up' the Ottoman forces for Russian invasion. The best example of this lay in the most successful of the Armenian actions, the taking of the city of Van.

Van was the chief city of southeastern Anatolia. It had a large Armenian population, members of which had secreted arms in great numbers. Because of the war, only small detachments of security forces were in the city. In April of 1915, Armenian rebels infiltrated the city and began to attack the police force. By the beginning of May the Ottoman forces had been compelled to leave the city to the rebels. The government rushed soldiers to the city, but the rebels held out against the army for a month. This allowed the Russian army, spearheaded by Armenian units from Russian Armenia, to move south and relieve the Armenians. The city had been held until the Russians could take it. One month after the Russian invasion the Ottomans were able to counter-attack and regain the city, but it was lost again a few months later to a new Russian attack.

The events in Van were typical of the beginning of civil war all over the east. In the beginning of the revolt Armenian bands attacked Muslim villages, most of them ethnically Kurdish, and slaughtered the inhabitants. After the Armenians seized Van few Muslims were left alive in the city or surrounding villages. Those who could not escape were killed. Kurdish tribesmen responded by killing any Armenians who fell into their hands. The Armenian rebellion quickly became a war of extermination. If you were caught by the other side, you were killed. Neither side spared women or children. In such a war everyone was forced to take sides; the alternative would have been to die without the chance to defend yourself. Most of those who killed must have felt they had no choice.

Perhaps the worst mortality came among refugees on all sides. Muslim refugees, fleeing from Van and from the path of the Russian army, had no food or shelter. They were attacked on the roads by Armenian guerilla bands. When the Ottomans counter-attacked it was the turn of the Armenians to suffer. Then, on the second Russian invasion, the Muslims who had returned to their homes had to flee once again. At the end of the war, the Armenians finally were forced out, leaving Anatolia forever. Had they won the war, it would have been the Muslims who were the exiles. Refugees on both sides died more from starvation, cholera, typhus, and typhoid than from bullets. To a lesser or greater degree this was true all over the east.

Both Armenians and Muslims were exiled or deported from their homes throughout the war, with great loss of life. Following the rebellion in the east and the successful taking of Van, the Ottoman government ordered the deportation of the Armenians of Anatolia to Syria. They reasoned that the Armenians were in many places a real threat to lives and government in the Empire and in other places a potential threat, and that they had to be removed to the south, far from invading Russian or Allied troops. On the ensuing forced marches great numbers of Armenians died from hunger and attacks, many of them killed by the tribesmen who were involved in a war to the death with the Armenians. There is no question but that the convoys were not well protected by the Ottomans. However, more than 200,000 Armenian deportees arrived safely in Greater Syria. Muslims, both Turks and Kurds, were also forcibly exiled by Armenians. All over eastern Anatolia more than a million Muslims were forced from their homes by Armenian nationalists and Russian soldiers.

The Armenian–Muslim civil war carried on past the end of the First World War. As stated above, the Russian Revolution ended the Russian occupation of Anatolia. With the Russian collapse the Armenian nationalist dream of ruling eastern Anatolia ended for a short time. Armenian hopes revived when the Ottomans were defeated. In 1918, Russian rule over Russian Armenia seemed to be gone forever, and the Ottomans were defeated. The Allies were extremely sympathetic to Armenian nationalist desires for a state. An Armenian Republic had risen in Erivan (Russian Armenia). It claimed and occupied much of eastern Anatolia. Once again the Armenian refugees returned and the Muslim refugees fled. The final episode would come with the rise of the Turkish nationalists and final possession of the east by the Turks, to be seen in the next chapter.

The defeat of the Empire

The end came for the Ottoman Empire on October 27, 1918. The British, representing the Allies, accepted Ottoman surrender in an armistice signed at Mudros. Ottoman armies were still intact in eastern and southern Anatolia, but they could not hold out, especially since their wartime allies, the Germans and the Austrians, were finished. The British, assuming the Turks were broken, enforced a harsh armistice. All Ottoman soldiers were to be demobilized, all ports, forts, and communications surrendered. Allied officers were to supervise the collection and destruction of Ottoman weapons. The Turks were to be left with only a small police force for security.

Nothing was written in the armistice agreement of the Allies' real intentions, which was to dismember the Empire. According to the terms, the Allies were to be allowed to occupy certain strategic areas such as ports and their ships were allowed free access to the Straits. The only region specifically allocated to Allied occupation was a small area of southern Anatolia near Antep and the right to move into eastern Anatolia 'in case of disorder'. They violated the spirit of the agreement by occupying part of the Black Sea coast in March, 1919 and by occupying Istanbul itself in November of that year. The most damaging occupation was the invasion of İzmir by the Greek army, aided and supported by the Allies, in May, 1919. In the east, efforts of the local Muslim majority in Kars to establish a majority government were broken by force by the British and authority given over to the Armenians. Anatolia was being divided among the victors and their friends.

The Allied activities were the culmination of plans that had begun early in the war. Various European countries, especially Russia, had planned and worked for years for the division of the Ottoman Empire. Possession of the Straits and an open route to the Mediterranean had long been a Russian goal, as had possession of eastern Anatolia. The European politics of balance of power had worked against this. Now the British, who had always been the main proponents of the balance of power, decided that their interests were better served by carving a part of the Ottoman Empire for themselves. They had, in fact, begun to stake their claim in 1878 by claiming Cyprus and in 1882 by seizing Egypt. The Gulf had become a 'British Lake' through stationing British 'advisors' to Gulf tribal leaders and bases and troops in the Arabian Peninsula and Iran. Once oil was discovered in Iran and Ottoman Iraq, the region became even more tempting to the

British. It was primarily British companies that exploited the oil finds and Britain looked to the oil as necessary to their fleet, which ran on Middle Eastern oil. The French had cultural and economic ties to coastal Syria (today Lebanon and Syria). They, too, wished to extend their control there. All the European powers had the impetus of making sure that another power did not take more than they did. In addition, popular sentiment in Europe wanted the Holy Land to be in Christian hands.

During the war the Allies had discussed the dismemberment of the Ottoman Empire. They had divided the prospective spoils of war in two agreements, the Sykes-Picot Agreement and the so-called Constantinople Agreement of 1916. Russia was to be given Eastern Anatolia, the Straits, and Istanbul, France Syria and Cicicia, Britain Iraq, and Italy southern Anatolia. Other accords and promises were entered into, as well. As part of the price for revolting against the Ottomans, Sharif Hussein of Mecca was promised extensive lands, some of the same lands the British and French had agreed to divide among themselves. Britain had also promised in the Balfour Declaration to foster a national home for the Jews in some of the same lands. British and French actions after the war indicated that of the conflicting promises the ones they meant to keep were those they had made to themselves.

The actions of the Allies immediately after the war were in concordance with the plans previously set. The one exception was in eastern Anatolia and the Straits, regions which had been given to the Russians. The Russian Empire was in civil war and soon would be in the hands of the Bolsheviks, so the promises to Russia were withdrawn. Instead, the Straits were taken by the British and French, their final disposition uncertain. The area of eastern Anatolia which was to have been taken by Russia was given over to the new Armenian Republic.

Many Turks in Istanbul were dumbfounded by the Allied moves. Led by those who had opposed the war, they had pleaded for implementation of Woodrow Wilson's 'Fourteen Points' in the Ottoman Empire. The Fourteen Points had called for self-determination of peoples, and Turks were an absolute majority in Anatolia, as were other Muslims in the rest of the Empire. An active Turkish Wilsonian League had even been formed in Istanbul. Nevertheless, the Fourteen Points were ignored and the wishes of the Turkish majority disregarded. The sultan's government, under the thumb of the Allied occupation, was impotent, but the Turks in the villages and cities of Anatolia were neither dumbfounded nor impotent. They organized resistance.

Chapter 12

Revival, 1918–23

Overleaf

The Turkish War of Independence: Mustafa Kemal and İsmet Paşas. Photograph taken during the Greek advance through Western Anatolia, when it appeared that the resistance organized by Mustafa Kemal would be futile. (*Illustrated London News*. August 7, 1920, p. 204.)

Revival, 1918–23

For the Turks, battle did not end when the First World War came to a close. Three years of bloody conflicts in eastern and western Anatolia followed the armistice that ended the Great War. Out of those conflicts, which have become known as the Turkish War of Independence, came the demise of the Ottoman Empire and the creation of the Turkish Republic. The War of Independence marked a fundamental change in the Turks themselves and in their government.

It is difficult not to cast the War of Independence in heroic, even melodramatic terms, because the cause of the Turks at first looked so impossible. For more than a century, Turks and other Muslims had been forced from their homes in the Caucasus region, the Crimea, and the Balkans. One generation might have been forced from the Crimea or the Caucasus into Ottoman Bulgaria, the next generation forced from Bulgaria into Ottoman Macedonia, the next generation forced into Anatolia. Now the Ottoman Empire had been finally defeated; its provinces in Europe and the Arab world were lost. Anatolia, the last refuge, was certainly all that remained to the Turks, but Anatolia too was threatened. Invaders came into both the east and the west, driving the Turkish population before them. Politically, there was nowhere the Turks could turn. The Germans and Austrians had shared in their defeat. The British and French were decided on a vengeful peace. What was left to the Turks was a devastated nation of refugees, awaiting its own destruction.

Any bookie giving odds on Turkish survival would have listed them at ten to one against. Nevertheless, the Turks did manage to overcome both their enemies and the odds. They saved the Turkish heartland of the old Empire and guaranteed a home for the Turks in Anatolia and eastern Thrace.

Like the accounts of the Balkan Wars, World War I, and the earlier wars, the story of the War of Independence is one of human suffering, as well as military action. Exile and mortality were the rule, as they had been in the earlier wars. The difference was that the Turks won this war. At the end of the war, the invaders had been repulsed. The enemies of the Turks were forced, however grudgingly, to accept a Turkish state. This time, the refugees were able to return to their homes.

The situation

The Allies had demanded, and received, an unconditional surrender from the Ottomans at the armistice of Mudros (October 30, 1918). All the Ottomans had received in return were Allied promises that were almost immediately broken. It quickly became obvious that the Ottomans were to pay a great price for losing the war.

The Arab lands of the Empire had been taken by the British by the end of the war. A modification of the wartime agreements between the Allies was put into effect. The British took the southern Syrian provinces (today's Israel and Jordan) and Iraq. The French, who had not been active in the Middle Eastern war, were nevertheless given the northern Syrian provinces (today's Syria and Lebanon). In addition, the British agreed to the French claim to the region of southern Anatolia that adjoined Syria (Cilicia and its hinterlands). European control over the Middle East and other areas was in the form of 'mandates' of the League of Nations. The *Covenant* that created the League of Nations stated that the mandates were systems whereby 'advanced nations' would care for 'peoples not yet able to stand by themselves under the strenuous conditions of the modern world'. No one in the League bothered to ask those peoples if they wanted help.

By the end of 1918 the occupation of Anatolia and Thrace had begun. In the east, Ottoman troops had been evacuated from the area they had regained at the end of the war. The new Armenian Republic claimed almost all of eastern Anatolia and held much of it. In the south, Ottoman troops had withdrawn from Cilicia before French troops, led by an Armenian legion, took over the territory. In the west, with the blessing of the Allies, Greek troops landed at İzmir in May of 1919 and began to advance inland. Italian forces seized the southern Anatolian coast in January, 1919. The Ottoman capital had been seized by the Allies. All over Anatolia, Allied 'Control Officers' were collecting weapons and overseeing the demobilization of Turkish troops. In Paris at the Peace Conference, the Allies were deliberating the final disposition of the Ottoman Empire.

The government of the sultan, seemingly with no other course available to it, tried appeasement. A new Prime Minister, Damad Ferit Paşa, was appointed. His government was drawn from political enemies of the Committee of Union and Progress government that had fought the war. To appease the British, especially, 'special' courts were created to try members of the wartime government on spurious evidence. Ottoman generals all over Anatolia were ordered to cooperate fully with the Allies, even when the Allies acted in violation of the armistice principles. Damad Ferit Paşa himself travelled to Paris to the Peace Conference to plead that all troubles had been caused by the old administration. His approach was to give in to the Allies on every issue, in the hope that the conquerors would be merciful. It was a forlorn hope. The new Istanbul government had misread both the Allies' good will and their own people's will to resist.

The Prime Minister and his cabinet undoubtedly felt that appeasement was the only way for the Turks to survive. They put their trust in the 'Fourteen Points' of American President Woodrow Wilson, which guaranteed self-determination of peoples. The Allied conquest of the Arab provinces was not opposed by the Ottoman government, but Turks were an overwhelming majority in their own ethnic homeland, and it was believed that the philosophy avowed by the Allies should have guaranteed them sovereignty, at least sovereignty over Thrace, Istanbul, and Anatolia. (The table[1] lists Muslims rather than Turkish-speakers, because the Ottomans kept population records by religion, not language group.) However, such trust assumed that the Allies were willing to abide by their principles. The Allies were in fact not willing to allow self-determination to the Turks. Instead, they planned to divide Anatolia and Thrace among the Greeks, Italians, French, and Armenians. The fate of Istanbul was uncertain. The Turks were to be left with only the north and centre of Anatolia, and even this would probably be under the control of a European power or America. The United States was under great internal and external pressure to accept the League of Nations mandate for Anatolia, but ultimately refused. The U.S. Congress foresaw much trouble and little profit in control over Anatolia.

The symbolic and political core of Allied control of the Ottoman Empire was the occupation of Istanbul. On November 13, 1918, Allied troops landed in Istanbul and took control of the capital city. From that point on the Ottoman government was free to exercise its authority only in areas allowed to it by the British, who maintained the chief Allied military

The population of Ottoman Anatolia in 1912 by religion group

Muslim	14,536,000
Greek Orthodox	1,254,000
Armenian*	1,493,000
Jewish	77,000
Other	176,000
Total	17,536,000

* Armenian Gregorian and Protestant.

[1] Justin McCarthy, *Muslims and Minorities*, New York, 1983, p. 110.

force in the city. British 'advisors' were assigned to government ministries to ensure compliance with Allied orders. While local administration, such as the police force, was nominally in the hands of the government, the government was in fact obliged to use its forces as the occupiers wished. Decisions were made by a High Commission with British, Italian, and French members. The British Admiral Calthorpe was made High Commissioner, with the understanding that he, not the sultan, was to be the final authority in the empire.

The Peace Conference and treaty of Sèvres

The forces that had opposed the Ottomans during the past century, with the exception of temporarily suspended Russian imperialism, gathered at the Paris Peace Conference. On the agenda was the dismemberment of the Ottoman Empire. After some debate among the powers, the Sykes-Picot agreement and other wartime plans were modified to leave Britain in possession of Palestine and Iraq (present day Iraq, Israel, Gaza, the West Bank, and Jordan) and to give France northern Syria and Cilicia (today's Syria, Lebanon, and south central Turkey). Greece and Armenia were given extensive tracts in eastern and western Anatolia. British promises of Arab sovereignty over Arab lands, made during the war to the Sharif of Mecca to convince him to revolt against the Ottomans, were largely forgotten.

Throughout the Conference the Allies acted as if the Turks were so thoroughly defeated that they would accept any Allied demand. Indeed, the government of Ferit Paşa had given no indication otherwise. The final treaty that was imposed on the Ottomans, the treaty of Sèvres, contained Allied wishes first, the wishes of Greece and Armenia second. Neither the needs of Turks nor the political and demographic realities of Turkey were considered. On August 10, 1920, the Ottoman government signed.

In some ways the treaty of Sèvres can be compared to the Versailles treaty with Germany that had such disastrous results for European history. Both were punitive treaties, imposed by victors who adopted a high moral tone to hide self-interest. Both treaties contained economic clauses intended to ensure that the vanquished would never rise again. Both limited the military strength and territory of the loser. However, the Sèvres treaty was the harsher.

The treaty of Sèvres detached all but a small part of what remained in Ottoman Europe after the Balkan Wars and gave it to Greece. Greece also received the city of İzmir and the province surrounding it. The Armenian Republic, after a decision delegated to President Wilson by the Allies, received all of northeastern Anatolia. Italy and France took lands in southern Anatolia. Istanbul and the Marmara region were left under nominal Ottoman sovereignty, but with actual Allied control. Even the small territory left to the Ottoman Empire could not be effectively controlled or defended

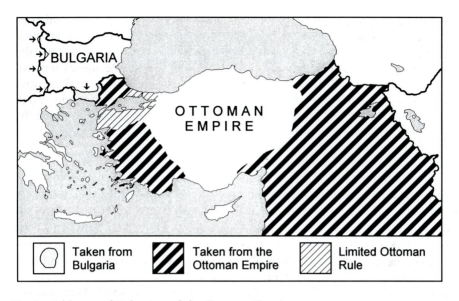

| | Taken from Bulgaria | | Taken from the Ottoman Empire | | Limited Ottoman Rule |

Territorial losses of Bulgaria and the Ottoman Empire.

---

by an army restricted by the treaty to 50,000 men. All Ottoman finances were to be under the regulation of an Allied commission. The capitulations were restored, ending the right of the state to set its own customs dues or control its own courts. In short, economic policy was to be completely decided by the Allies. With so many of the productive regions of the Empire detached, there would not be many assets left to supervise.

Bulgaria and Turkey: a comparison of loss

Whatever standard of comparison is used, the Ottoman Empire was to have suffered at the hands of the Allies more than any of the other defeated nations. The territorial exactions and (relative) economic payments demanded of the Turks were considerably worse than those demanded of the Germans. Like the Austrian Empire, the Ottoman Empire was to be dismembered. However, the Austrians were left with a compact state in most of the regions of their Empire that were predominantly German-speaking. No such grace was given to the Turks. All of the non-Turkish and most of the Turkish regions were to be excised.

A comparison to the post-war fate of Bulgaria shows the extent of the disaster planned for the Turks. Bulgaria, too, had been an ally of Germany in the First World War. Like the Ottomans, it had been defeated. Yet the difference in proposed territorial losses of the two is dramatic. Even neglecting the loss of the entire Arab Middle East and comparing only the Turkish sections of the Ottoman Empire with Bulgaria, the Turks were

375

obviously treated much more harshly. Bulgaria was to lose four very small defensive regions on its western border and the region that joined it to the Aegean Sea, which it had only first taken in 1913. The Ottoman Empire in Anatolia and eastern Thrace, on the other hand, was to lose control of half of its land. Although Bulgaria did lose minor port facilities on the Aegean Sea, no major Bulgarian cities were taken. The Turks were to lose their major city in Europe, Edirne, the main city on the Aegean, İzmir, the main city in the south, Adana, and the north, Trabzon, and all the large cities of the east – Erzurum, Kars, Van, etc. Of the largest and most important Turkish cities, only Istanbul was nominally to remain to the Turks, and that was to be under actual Allied control. Other comparisons could be made: the most fertile lands of Bulgaria remained; the most fertile lands of Turkey were taken. Bulgarians were left in effective control of their economy; the Turks were not. In each category, the Turks fared worse. (The map actually understates the loss to the Turks. It assumes that the Italians, French, and Greeks might have been forced by the others to take less than they originally planned.)

Of two wartime enemies of the Allies, why should the fate of one be so much more harsh? Contrary to what might be thought, the difference could not have been due to the presence of minorities in Turkey, which might cause exceptional measures to be applied. Bulgaria actually had a larger minority percentage in its population. There was a greater percentage of Muslims in Bulgaria than Christians in Anatolia, but the Allies cared considerably more about the fate of Christian minorities than Muslim minorities.

The real reason for the severe treatment of the Turks in the Sèvres treaty was Allied prejudice and self-interest. Italy, France, and Britain all wanted parts of the Ottoman Empire, so it was easy to neglect ethical matters such as self-determination and the Fourteen Points. Prejudice against Turks and Muslims ensured that no one in Europe or America complained about such selective political ethics.

Those who had relied on the good will and moral sense of the Allies had been mistaken. The Allies had no intention of abiding by the Fourteen Points. There were Turks who had seen this long before the Sèvres treaty was signed. They organized a national resistance.

The Turkish national resistance

The national resistance of the Turks drew upon all elements of society. The spark came from the invasion of İzmir and subsequent attacks on the Turks of Anatolia. The invasion galvanized a prostrate people. At first, resistance was local and relatively ineffective. Villagers organized into self-defence units.

Driven into the mountains by the invaders, they made guerilla raids on Greek troops and civilians. As the movement grew, it became more organized. Officials of the old Committee of Union and Progress, their political opponents, and a new group of local leaders who had never seen national power all cooperated to create what were called Societies for the Defence of the Rights of Turks. They were joined by units of the Ottoman army and gendarmerie. Large amounts of munitions and supplies were smuggled into Anatolia by sympathetic bureaucrats and officers of the Istanbul government. But the resistance units were still without any centralized structure. Acting independently, they could do little.

The organization of the disparate units of the resistance finally came under the control of senior officers of the old Ottoman army, led by a hero of the Great War, Mustafa Kemal. Trained in the Ottoman military schools, Kemal had become one of the revolutionary officers who overthrew Abdülhamit II. However, he had not taken political office; he had remained in the officer corps. Mustafa Kemal had emerged from the war as a recognized hero for the Turks. He had saved the defence at Gallipoli and held the Russians off in brilliant campaigns in the east. When the war ended he was in charge of the still intact Ottoman army in the south. Even though that army was in retreat, with almost no supplies, Kemal had managed to keep it together. The sultan's government summoned him to Istanbul, perhaps with the aim of using his prestige to smooth the disarming of the Ottoman forces.

Mustafa Kemal was appointed as Inspector General of Ottoman Forces in north and northeastern Anatolia. His authority encompassed both civil and military affairs. His orders were to disarm the remaining Ottoman soldiers, hinder any resistance, and generally pacify the region. His plan was the opposite. Like other Ottoman officers sent out with similar orders, such as Kâzim Karabekir on the Armenian border, his real intention was resistance. It is hard to believe that the Ottoman officials who assigned such officers could not have known the officers' intentions.

Mustafa Kemal landed at the Black Sea port of Samsun on May 19, 1919. His job was at first more political than military. Local officials and military units had to be convinced, first, that successful resistance was possible and, second, that they should cooperate and accept a central authority. The latter was most difficult. Generals and officials, who were used to command, naturally each saw themselves as the proper commanders of the movement. Muslim religious leaders opposed the Greeks and Armenians, but also disliked 'Europeanized', secular, reforming politicians and military officers. Local leaders feared any centralized control. Ottoman governors were torn between duty to the sultan and to their people. Kemal met with all of them, travelled to their cities, camps, and strongholds, and somehow convinced them to unite on a common goal.

On June 23, the Istanbul government revoked Mustafa Kemal's authority. It was too late. He and other military authorities had already agreed on a national course of action, based on the interests of the Turkish nation, not the interests of the Istanbul government. They called for a national congress of representatives from all provinces to lead the Turks, because the Istanbul government was under foreign domination. A preliminary regional congress at Erzurum met in July and August of 1919, with Mustafa Kemal and Kâzim Karabekir in attendance. It declared that the Armenian and Greek occupations of Anatolia were intolerable, called for national unity, and demanded that the central government allow the election of a national assembly to represent the will of the nation. The congress stated that it was decided upon a course of defending its national rights. A second congress in Sivas drew delegates from all over Anatolia and Thrace. It too demanded territorial integrity and called upon the Istanbul government to make no agreements with the Allies that would compromise the rights of the Muslim majority. A political organization had been forged, hereafter called the Turkish Nationalists.

Some members of the Ottoman government recognized the power of the Nationalist cause and for a time seemed to sympathize with it. For a brief time, the Ottoman government let the Turks decide their own future. The conciliatory Damad Ferit Paşa was replaced as Grand Vezir and elections to the Ottoman Parliament were called. Amazingly, the British occupiers, who were the real masters in Istanbul, did not realize what was afoot and accepted the election. The new Ottoman parliament met on January 12, 1920. It was soon apparent that it represented anti-Allied, anti-occupation, pro-Turkish Nationalist sentiments. On February 17, the parliament passed the National Pact, the basic declaration of Turkish nationalism and independence, which included the demands of the Sivas congress. In retrospect, it can be seen that the Pact called for nothing more than the application of Wilson's Fourteen Points to Anatolia and Thrace. It demanded that plebiscites be held to decide the will of the people, guaranteed minority rights, and stated that national sovereignty and independence were essential. These were not radical demands, but they infuriated the British, who had no intention of putting the philosophy of the Fourteen Points into practice.

The British brought pressure to bear on the Ottoman government to act against Mustafa Kemal and the new power of the Nationalists. When Ottoman actions were judged insufficient the British took matters into their own hands. In March they forced the deposition of the Grand Vezir, then the arrest of officials and officers favourable to the Nationalists. One hundred and fifty of these were taken by the British to internment on the island of Malta. Istanbul was placed under Allied martial law, members of parliament were arrested, and parliament dissolved. Damad Ferit Paşa was brought back as Grand Vezir and the new government condemned Mustafa

Kemal and his followers to death. In every real sense, this was the end of the Ottoman Empire.

The Grand National Assembly

The British assault on the democratically elected Ottoman parliament actually benefited the Nationalist cause. It removed the moral and political authority of the Istanbul government, which all could now see was solely an agent of the Allies. Prior to the Allied actions in Istanbul, Mustafa Kemal and the Nationalists had been respected, perhaps even seen as national saviours, but loyalty to the sultanate had kept back much potential support. Turks had been ruled by the sultan's government for six hundred years; it was difficult to change such a long allegiance. Now there was no other choice. Many members of the dissolved parliament escaped to Kemal's headquarters in Ankara. There, on April 23, 1920 a new parliament, the Grand National Assembly, was founded, with Mustafa Kemal as its president. Its members were the members of the Ottoman parliament who had escaped capture by the British and representatives of regional resistance movements.

The Assembly broke decisively with the Istanbul government. One of its first declarations was that, since the sultan was under foreign control, all authority was in the hands of the Assembly. Normal government in the provinces not under foreign control was speedily brought under the Assembly's control. Of greatest importance, a unified and centralized army and military command were created, with one of Mustafa Kemal's chief allies, İsmet Paşa, as Chief of the General Staff. The Grand National Assembly organized the Turks for war. As he had earlier, Mustafa Kemal used his political skills to keep disparate elements in the parliament from fighting with each other, rather than uniting to defeat their true enemies. Led by him, the Assembly drew together Turkish forces from all parts of Anatolia to fight the invaders.

The war in the east

The end of World War I had left eastern Anatolia and the Caucasus in confusion. During the war most of the land had changed hands many times. Refugees had moved in and out of the region along with their armies. The Ottoman Army had won in the end and had occupied eastern Anatolia and the section of the east that had been taken by the Russians in 1878 (the Kars-Ardahan region, still more than 50 per cent Muslim under Russian rule, even after mass Muslim emigration). Armenian forces held the province of Erivan, which they reconstituted as the new Armenian Republic.

The situation changed with the Armistice. The Ottoman Army of the East, still intact, withdrew to the 1878 boundaries. In the Kars-Ardahan region local Turks established an independent state. However, the Armenian Republic also claimed the region, as well as extensive territories within Anatolia. The British supported the Armenian claims. In April of 1919 the British Army occupied the region, disarmed the Turks, and gave control to the Armenian Republic. They then withdrew, leaving civil war behind them. Armenian soldiers destroyed lowland Turkish villages, killed their inhabitants, and forced survivors into exile. Kurdish tribes and Turkish refugees drove out Armenians from the highlands, but the Armenian Republic was in control of the cities and main roads.

The war between the Turks and Armenians was continuing in the Armenian Republic and Azerbaijan, also a new republic. Supported by the Allies and thus much better armed than the local Muslims, the Armenians were able to drive the Turks and Kurds from the Armenian Republic, 'exchanged' with Armenians driven from Azerbaijan. By the end of the civil war, 180,000 Muslims, two-thirds of the Muslim population of the province of Erivan Province, had either been killed or had fled.

The Armenian Republic was undeniably a threat to the Turks in eastern Anatolia. It claimed all the land that Russia had held in World War I and more as part of a new Greater Armenia. On their own, the Armenians could never have taken the land, because they were a small minority of the population of the region, but they were not on their own. At the Peace Conference, the Allies had assigned President Wilson the task of setting the boundaries of Greater Armenia. His award included all of eastern Anatolia and nearby regions. No consideration was given to the fact that the Turks and other Muslims were the overwhelming majority in eastern Anatolia (see the figure given earlier). The Allies were intent on seeing that Armenia gained that territory, and the Turks could not know if the Allies were willing to shed their own blood to bring it about. The refugees and great mortality of the First World War in the east had taught the Turks what they could expect from such a state.

The Ottoman Army in northeastern Anatolia had never completely disbanded. British control officers who had been sent out to collect their weapons had little success. The officer in charge of the troops, Kâzim Karabekir, had been a hero of the Ottoman–Armenian War in 1918. He had seen the fate of the Turks at that time. Now he refused the orders of both the British and the sultan. Rather he mobilized his own troops and the local Turkish forces to resist the Armenians. Despite the need of troops to repulse the Greek invasion in the west, the Grand National Assembly made him commander in the east and allowed the Turkish troops to remain in the east.

Spring of 1920 saw continuous border skirmishes between Turks and Armenians. The Turks fleeing from Kars-Ardahan and Erivan reported massacres. In October, Karabekir advanced. His forces took Kars on October 30 and advanced to the pre-1878 border. The Armenian Republic sued for peace. In the treaty of Alexandropol (December 3, 1920), the Turkish–Armenian border was set at the pre-1878 boundary. Kars and Ardahan were returned to the Turks. The Armenian Republic was soon after taken by the Bolsheviks, but the border was accepted by them also. The war in the east was over.

The war in the south

Many claimed the region called Cilicia (main city, Adana), in southern Anatolia. By numbers the region was more than three-quarters Turkish, but there had been an Armenian kingdom in Cilicia in the Middle Ages and the French had demanded the region as one of their post-war acquisitions. As might be expected, the Allies made the decision, and the French claim was accepted.

The French had relatively few troops in the Middle East, and those they had were busy in subduing Syria and Lebanon. At the end of 1918, they therefore sent some French officers, troops from the French colonies, and members of the Armenian Legion to take Cilicia. The Armenian Legion had been formed of Armenian volunteers whose avowed purpose was to take southern and eastern Anatolia for a new Armenia. At first, the Legionnaires had an easy time. Ottoman troops had been withdrawn to the west and local Turks were unorganized. The main cities were easily taken.

Troubles began in Cilicia almost immediately upon the French invasion. The Legion was joined by tens of thousands of Armenian refugees who had been in Syria and Egypt. Together, they began to persecute local Turks, forcing some to flee, others to organize resistance. The cities were in French hands, but the Turks controlled the mountains. The French soon realized that they had created a situation that threatened their rule. They disbanded the Armenian Legion in Cilicia, but the Legionnaires stayed, organized into partisan bands. Attacks on Turks increased, as did Turkish resistance.

By winter of 1919 Armenian and Turkish bands warred throughout Cilicia. French soldiers moved up from Syria and controlled the cities. Turkish nationalist forces, including units of the old Ottoman army, also began to operate in the countryside. The Turks finally met the French and Armenians at the city of Maraş. Turkish forces took the city, forcing the French and Armenians to retreat. On the retreat, the Armenians destroyed every Turkish village in their path. As the Turks advanced, Armenians in turn fled or died.

The French expected a continuation of the Turkish attack that would drive them out of Cilicia, and perhaps extend to Syria itself. They cut their losses. On October 20, 1921, the French signed a treaty with the Turkish Nationalists in which they agreed to leave Cilicia. More important, the French disavowed the treaty of Sèvres and at least implicitly accepted the Nationalists as the new Turkish government. From that point on, even though they avowed their solidarity with their allies, the French did not support the dismemberment of Anatolia.

The war in the west

The Turkish War of Independence can be said to have actually begun on May 15, 1919. On that date, with the support of a fleet of Allied ships, Greek troops landed at the city of İzmir. The Ottoman garrison of the city, under orders of the sultan's government not to resist, remained in its barracks. Under the terms of the Allied award of İzmir, called by its Greek name, Smyrna, by the Allies, the Greeks were to occupy the small area around the city for five years, after which a plebiscite would be taken to decide if the Greeks should remain. Greek forces did not abide by those terms and quickly spread beyond the Allied award. Greek troops advanced quickly into the rest of the province of Aydın (of which İzmir was the capital), with only feeble objections from their British mentors.

From the first day of the occupation the Greeks put into practice the techniques long applied to the Turks of the Balkans. Beginning in İzmir on the day of the invasion, Turks were attacked by Greek soldiers and civilians. As reported by European observers, Turkish neighbourhoods of the city were ransacked, Turkish stores looted, and 700–800 Turks killed immediately. Violence spread to the villages of the province as the Greek army advanced.

Elements of the Ottoman army and Turkish guerilla forces in the province of Aydın resisted the Greek advance. Acting without authority from the sultan, they managed to halt the Greeks by temporarily retaking the city of Aydın and stopping the Greek advance at Pergama. However, the Turks were hampered by lack of manpower and war matériel. In Istanbul, the government gave no support to the resistance. Local peasants needed time if they were to organize into fighting units. Therefore, the Turks could not hold. By the end of July the Greeks had taken the province.

As the Greeks moved through the province of Aydın they acted in accordance with a deliberate plan in each city and village. First, local policeman (gendarmes) were disarmed. Their weapons were distributed to local Greeks. Ottoman officials were often imprisoned or killed. Turkish houses in the towns and villages were then pillaged. In the city of Menemen,

300–400 Turks were killed and the Turkish quarter emptied of Turks, then pillaged. The governor of Aydın and other Turkish officials in the city of Aydın were killed, then the Turkish quarter burned and the inhabitants killed by Greek machine guns mounted on the roofs. The Turks of other cities shared the same fate. Untold numbers of villages were robbed and destroyed. Even British officials, well-disposed toward the Greeks, reported their horror at the Greek actions. The result was flight of the Turkish population. More than one million Turks ultimately became refugees from the regions taken by the Greeks. The pattern of forced population change seen so many times in the Balkans was being re-enacted in western Anatolia.

The Allies and the Greeks

Obviously, the Greeks could not have taken control in western Anatolia without the aid of the Allies, particularly the British. The British were from 1919 to 1922 the main support of the Greek invasion. The British Prime Minister, David Lloyd George, felt a special affinity for the Greek Prime Minister, Eleutherios Venizelos, and a special disdain for non-Christians. He thus did all he could to aid the Greek cause, short of committing British troops. The British navy supervised the Greek invasion while the British plenipotentiary in Istanbul forced the Ottoman government not to issue orders to the army to resist. The Greek army was originally only authorized by the Allies at the peace conference to take the city of İzmir and its hinterland district. When they broke this restriction the British convinced the conference to excuse them. The Greeks advanced farther.

After their occupation of Istanbul, the British had extended their control from Istanbul into the region of İzmit, to the west (July, 1920). While the British remained in charge the Turks were physically safe. However, as they had given Kars in the east over to the Armenian Republic, so they gave İzmit to the Greeks (November, 1920). Then the pattern seen in other provinces was repeated – pillage and massacre of the Turks. Turks once again fled in great numbers. The British and other Allies also allowed the Greeks to march into eastern Thrace in July of 1920. Separated from Anatolia by the Allied forces in Istanbul and the Straits region (the region of the Dardanelles and Bosphorus), the Turks of Thrace could not put up a strong resistance.

Why did the British offer such support? At home, a combination of wartime propaganda and religious feeling had put the British public behind actions against the Turks, and Lloyd George was above all a politician who alternately shaped and followed the popular will. But British politicians saw benefit to the British Empire in their actions. Greece was viewed as a friend that would secure the Aegean, the Straits, and the eastern Mediterranean in friendly hands. The Turks could not be expected to support British aims. It was a strange variation of the traditional British strategy in

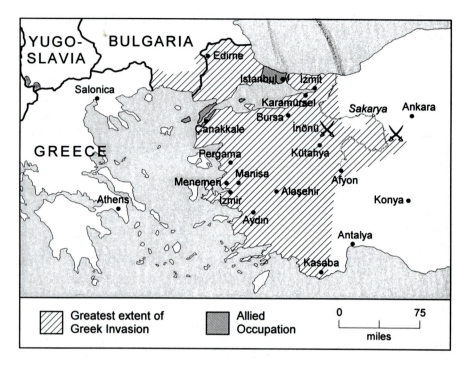

The Turkish War of Independence.

the region which until a decade before had relied on the Ottomans to secure the balance of power.

The Greek advance

The Greek Army had taken southwestern Anatolia, the province of Aydın, and had consolidated their position by spring of 1920. In summer they advanced north as far as Bursa, encountering only light resistance. They then struck east, toward the Turkish Nationalist capital of Ankara, to remove the threat of the Turkish Resistance.

In Ankara, Mustafa Kemal had been fighting political battles to keep his coalition together while the Turkish troops trained. The army had to be reformed from disparate units into a cohesive structure. Moreover, many of the Turkish forces had to be turned from peasants into trained fighters. The training was still incomplete in January, 1921, as the Greek army moved east. Under the command of İsmet Paşa, the Turks made their stand at the River İnönü. They held the Greeks, who retreated. A new Greek offensive was halted in April, 1921, once again at the İnönü. However, the Turks could not follow up their victory. Neither their military strength nor their finances were yet up to an advance.

Two events helped turn the tide for the Turks. At the end of 1920 Kâzim Karabekir's forces defeated the Armenians in the east, which meant that troops and supplies could now be sent westward for the fight against the Greeks. On March 16, 1921 the Turkish Nationalists signed a treaty of friendship with the Soviets, an agreement which was to bring arms and money to the Turks.

The final Greek advance began in the summer of 1921. The Turks were forced to retreat to the River Sakarya, near Ankara. Many felt the capital would be lost, and with it perhaps the war. The Grand National Assembly named Mustafa Kemal Commander-in-Chief with total civil and military authority.

The battle of the Sakarya began on August 13. Both sides fought absolute war, without quarter. Both also ran short of supplies, the Greeks because of long supply lines. Finally, on September 13 the Greek army fled. Again, the Turks were unable to pursue their victory, but for the first time the Europeans began to see the possibility of Turkish victory. The French, realists as always, signed a treaty in Ankara (October 20, 1921) in which they recognized the Turkish Nationalist government and agreed to leave Cilicia, freeing more Turkish troops. Italy, too, had realized that any hope of holding land in Anatolia was impossible.

The Nationalists were prepared to advance in August of 1922. The Greek army was defeated by the end of the month. Survivors fled to İzmir, where Allied ships took them to Greece. İzmir itself, along with the other major cities of western Anatolia, fell within two weeks. On September 18, Mustafa Kemal announced to the Grand National Assembly that all Greek opposition in Anatolia was over. Only the British forces in the Straits Zone and the Greeks in eastern Thrace remained. War between Britain and Turkey was only narrowly averted, largely because the British military commander, General Harrington, and Mustafa Kemal kept cool heads. (The British government had asked the French in the Straits Zone to stand with them against the Nationalists. The French had refused.) At the end of September the British prevailed upon the Greeks to evacuate eastern Thrace. Armistice talks between the British and the Turks began. The Independence War had been won.

The treaty of Lausanne

The treaty of Sèvres was dead in all but the hearts of the British. They still hoped to salvage at least some of the treaty provisions as a new peace conference met at Lausanne, Switzerland on November 20, 1922. There was little chance that the British might succeed. Their ultimate threat – to fight the Turks in the Straits Zone – had already been proved to be hollow. If they were going to fight, they would have done so already. The British people had been sick of war in 1918; they were all the less likely to support war in 1922, long after demobilization at home. Time also worked for the

Turks. The British wished to be done with their great mistake in Anatolia. Politicians never wish their mistakes to be mentioned daily in the press. A drawn-out peace conference could not help but remind the British people that their officials had backed the losing side.

The Turks, on the other hand, could not demand everything they might want. The Arab lands were gone forever. Some accommodation would have to be made with the European bankers who had financed the Ottoman debt. Accommodation would also have to be made with the European powers on other questions, such as freedom of navigation in the Straits. If the Turks were to deal economically and politically with the Europeans in the future, they would have to build some good will. In addition, the Turks too wanted an end to war. As will be seen below, Anatolia had been largely destroyed by the wars. Peace was needed to build up the land once again.

The Lausanne Conference dragged on for months. Whenever the Allies brought up points such as the capitulations or the division of Anatolia the Turkish side, led by İsmet Paşa, simply refused to listen. The objectionable matters came up again and again, until the Allied side was worn down and the Turks won most major points. The Turks did relinquish their claim to Mosul (today northern Iraq) in favour of a later decision by the Council of the League of Nations (which gave it to Iraq) and Hatay (main city, Antakya), which was held by the French until 1938, when it was first declared independent, then became part of the Turkish Republic in 1939. The Straits were neutralized (control returned to the Turks in 1936). The legal status of the Christian minorities and foreigners in Turkey, one of the great problems of Ottoman times, was settled clearly – they were to be allowed the same rights as others in the new Republic. Social and religious institutions of Christians, such as schools, were specifically allowed.

The Greeks and Turks settled their war differences. There were to be no reparations. In Thrace a demilitarized zone was established between the two recent combatants. Both sides recognized that it would be difficult for Greeks and Turks to live together after their recent history. The two therefore arranged an exchange of populations. Greeks in eastern Thrace and Anatolia were exchanged for Turks in Greece. Only the two areas where the two were very sizeable minorities were excepted: Greeks in Istanbul remained, as did Turks in western Thrace.

On October 1, 1923, in accordance with the terms of the Treaty, the last British troops left Istanbul.

The price of war

The Turkish Nationalists had won their wars, but they had inherited desolation. The most productive region of Anatolia, the southwest, was largely destroyed. The worst damage had come during the Greek retreat. As they fled, Greek soldiers and civilians destroyed whatever they were forced to leave behind. The devastation was planned. Greek military officers set fire bombs to destroy cities and villages and ordered the cutting down of olive trees and the killing of farm animals. A post-war census counted 1.7 million sheep lost during the Independence War, 134,000 horses, 64,000 goats and mules, and hundreds of thousands of other farm animals. More than 140,000 buildings had been destroyed in the occupied areas of western Anatolia. The cities had fared worst: 13,633 of the 14,773 buildings in Manisa had been destroyed, 4,350 of the 4,500 in Alaşehir, 830 of the 847 in Karamürsel, etc. The destruction, as well as the loss of Christian business-men and entrepreneurs, shattered the economy. Civil order had been broken because Ottoman officials and policemen had been among the first to die in the invasion. Worst of all, the Muslim population of the area invaded by Greece was 1.2 million smaller than in 1913, before the wars. Incredible numbers had died.

Similar devastation was seen in the east. Much of the southeast had been destroyed in World War I. The Old City of Van, for example, was completely gone. Before the war, the city of Bitlis had 7,500 houses; only 1,000 remained after the war. Many rural districts had lost more than half their houses, both Muslim and Armenian. The northeast had fared better during the Great War, largely because the Russians had planned to remain in occupation and so protected their assets. In the Turco–Armenian War that followed, however, the situation changed. As in the Greek retreat in the west, the worst destruction came during the Armenian retreat. The Ottoman general who entered Erzincan after the Armenian retreat from the city estimated that 1,000 houses had been destroyed. Four hundred build-ings in Bayburt were burned down. Few of the Turkish villages on the line of retreat survived. The death rates were among the most appalling in modern warfare. Of the Muslims who had lived in the province of Van in 1912, 62 per cent had been lost by 1922, as had 42 per cent in the province of Bitlis, and 31 per cent in the province of Erzurum.

Of course, Turks were by no means the only ones to suffer. The Christian communities of Anatolia were largely gone. Turkish suffering has naturally been stressed in this book, a history of Turks, but Jews, Greeks, Armenians and members of other communities had felt the universal horror of the war. Like the Turks, they had suffered fearsome mortality. During World War I and the Anatolian War that followed, 10 per cent of the Anatolian population had permanently emigrated, 20 per cent had died – a much worse mortality than that of any other country in the First World War. Slightly more than 300,000 Anatolian Greeks had died, slightly less than 600,000 Armenians, and almost 3 million Muslims.

Much of the new Turkish Republic was a wasteland. It would take generations for the people and the land to recover.

The Turks and the Turkish Republic

The political changes that created the modern Turkish Republic came mainly after the period considered in this book. Mustafa Kemal (later Atatürk) emerged from the Independence War with great prestige. He had truly been the saviour of his nation. After the war he used his prestige to shape the new nation politically, socially, and economically. Already in 1922 the Grand National Assembly had abolished the sultanate in favour of a Republic, which was formally declared on October 29, 1923. The new capital was in Ankara, not the Ottoman city, Istanbul. A radical break with the tradition of centuries was underway.

The Turks themselves had changed in the wars. They now identified themselves as Turks. Through the Ottoman centuries the Turks had been the mainstay of a great empire. The Ottoman Empire long had been called 'Turkey' in the West, and the sultans were indeed proud of their Turkish nomadic ancestors, but the Ottomans never identified themselves as a Turkish Empire. They were an Islamic Empire, the last in a succession of great Muslim empires that had begun with the Prophet Muhammad's successors. The Ottoman court, administrative, and military language was Turkish. High culture in the Empire, although eclectic, and popular culture in Anatolia and Thrace can only be called Turkish. However, the Turks were not a political group. There was little recognition of 'nationhood' in the modern European sense. In the final Ottoman years, philosophers, historians, writers, and sociologists had declared that common culture and language dictated that there was a Turkish nation, just as there was a French or German nation. The belief does not seem to have spread far among the Turks of Anatolia and Thrace.

World War I and, especially, the Turkish War of Independence changed the popular will. Turks were forced to stand together as Turks against invaders, without assistance. Their brother Muslims could only offer sympathy. The Arabs, for three hundred years subjects of the Ottoman Empire, had their own troubles with European domination. Standing on their own, the Turks found that they were Turks – attacked because they were Turks, driven from their homes because they were Turks, forced to defend themselves as Turks, able to rely on no one but other Turks. It was the genius of Mustafa Kemal that he was able to draw on new national identity, strengthen it, and use it in the Independence War. He was to draw on national feeling once again after the wars to create a new system of government, radically reforming the old political culture of the Ottomans and creating the Turkish Republic.

handwritten annotation: Sinam Pasha: Renewed struggle with Habsburgs this to Seige of Viena

Glossary

handwritten annotation: 1634 - Cara mustafa Pasha - Christian hater.

Ahi	a member of an urban defence fraternity tied to guilds and mystic brotherhoods
akıncı	a raider
askeri	military, Ottoman 'ruling class'
avarız	extraordinary tax
ayan	a notable, autonomous local leader, especially in the Ottoman Balkans
azab	a marine
bahşiş	a tip, payment for a judicial or bureaucratic service rendered
bedestan	a covered market
bey	honorific title, prince or ruler in Anatolia in pre-Ottoman and early Ottoman times
beylerbeyi	governor-general in early Ottoman times
beylerbeyilik	greater province governed by a *beylerbeyi* and overseeing constituent *sancak*s
beylik	principality, region of Anatolia ruled by a *bey*
capitulations	agreements with European states that afforded privileges such as reduction in customs duties
caravansaray	hostel/fortress to protect merchant caravans
çarşı	a market
Catholicos	supreme bishop of the Armenian Gregorian Church
child levy	forced recruitment of Christian children for the *devşirme*
cizye	tax collected from non-Muslims
defterdar	Keeper of the Register, Chief Defterdar – head of the Ottoman financial administration/bureaucracy
Der Saadet	Istanbul
derbend	mountain pass, stronghold
derebey	autonomous local leader, especially in Ottoman Anatolia

dervish	member of a mystic fraternity
devşirme	slaves of the sultans, recruited through the child levy, Ottoman administrators and slave soldiers
dhimmi	Christians and Jews
divan	council of state
Divan-ı Hümayun	Imperial Council, chief deliberative body of government
emanet	revenue source whose officials were salaried
fetva	decision by a *mufti* declaring the legality of an action under Islamic Law
gazi	fighter of the Faith of Islam
han	ruler, especially among the early Turks, also a large commercial building
Hatt-ı Hümayun	decree of the sultan
ikta	land held in exchange for military service under Seljuks
iltizam	tax farm
imam	in Shia Islam a leader descended from Ali who should rule Islam by right
imaret	a soup kitchen for the poor
jihad	holy war to defend or expand the rule of Islam
kadı	Muslim judge
kadıasker	a chief military Islamic judge
kafes	area of the imperial harem in which princes were secluded
kalemiye	Ottoman scribal institution/bureaucracy
kanun	adminsitrative secular law
kanunname	code of laws
kapalı çarşı	covered market, especially the Grand Bazaar in Istanbul
kapı kulları	slaves of the sultan, slave soldiers and administrators
kapudan	admiral
kethüda	leader of a guild
kızılbaş	Shia Muslim Turks, especially those who supported the Safavis
komitaji	guerilla or partisan group member
kul	slave
madhhab	one of the legal systems/schools in Islam
mamluk	military slave, especially in Egypt
medrese	Islamic school
mehr	bride price
mescid	a small mosque or place of worship
millet	a state-recognized community defined by religion
miri	lands owned by the sultan, state lands

mufti	jurisconsult, a Muslim theologian who gave legal decisions
muhtar	elder or head man of a village
muhtesib	Inspector of Markets
mülk	private property
müsellem	a salaried cavalryman
Nizam-i Cedid	European-style army of Selim II
öşür	tithe, tax on agricultural produce
raya	flock, the sultan's tax-paying subjects
reis	chief, naval captain
Rum	Roman (i.e., Byzantine), Greek
rüşdiye	middle school
salname	yearbook
sancak	province in early Ottoman times, later a sub-province
sancakbeyi	governor of a *sancak*
sekban	salaried soldier in service of an Ottoman governor
shaman	holy man of pre-Islamic Turks
Sharia	Islamic Law
Shia	Muslims who believe in following the guidance of a divinely-chosen *imam*; the minority in Islam
sipahi	cavalryman
sufı	mystic
sultan	ruler, emperor
Sunnah	the behaviour of the Prophet Muhammad, taken as a religious and legal model
Sunni	Muslims who believe in following the consensus (*ijma*) of the community of believers as expressed by the *ulema*; the majority in Islam
şeyh	elder, leader and spiritual guide of a mystic fraternity
Şeyhülislam	Chief Mufti of the Ottoman Empire, head of the religious establishment
Tanzimatçılar	Men of the Tanzimat, officials and bureaucrats who carried out the Tanzimat reforms
Tatars	Turks of what today is southern Ukraine and southern European Russia
tekke	a dervish lodge
Tercüme Odası	The Translation Office of the Ottoman foreign ministry
timar	*miri* land held in exchange for miliary service
timarlı sipahi	a cavalryman holding a *timar*
ulema	group of Muslim theologians/jurists
vakıf	a tax-exempt pious foundation
vezir	minister of state
vilâyet	a province in later Ottoman times

The Ottoman Turks

yalı	a large waterside residence
yaya	a salaried foot soldier
yeni çeri	janissary
yörük	a two-pasture nomad

Index